The Making of T. S. Eliot's Plays

THE MAKING OF
T.S. ELIOT'S PLAYS

E. MARTIN BROWNE

CAMBRIDGE
AT THE UNIVERSITY PRESS
1969

Published by the Syndics of the Cambridge University Press
Bentley House, 200 Euston Road, London N.W.1
American Branch: 32 East 57th Street, New York, N.Y.10022

Standard Book Number: 521 07372 3

Library of Congress Catalogue Card Number: 69–19371

Printed by offset in Great Britain
by Alden & Mowbray Ltd
at the Alden Press, Oxford

to

HENZIE

perhaps she is my *guardian*

Contents

Preface

This book is a record of the way in which T. S. Eliot's plays came to be written and of their first appearances on the stage. Much of its contents are from Eliot's pen. I have been generously given leave to peruse drafts, notes and letters in a number of collections apart from my own, and to publish those passages which seemed to further the understanding of the growth of each play. The unique advantage which I enjoy in doing this is that I worked with Eliot from 1933 to 1958, directing the first productions of all the plays written during that time, and acting as consultant in their making.

The book is intended for those who wish to study Eliot's drama. How many, many times has the wish been expressed that we had available to us, from the great writers of the past, material which would show their work in progress and allow us to see how it grew in their minds! Here, for students in the future, is such material.

Those of them who wish to concentrate on a particular play, especially on the later ones of which John Hayward preserved the working drafts in his collection at King's College, Cambridge, will be able to produce more detailed accounts of its evolution than I have attempted here. Similarly, those who wish to follow some particular line of thought, or trace some particular image, from play to play, will find a fruitful field of study. It seemed to me that what I could most usefully do was to plot the course of Eliot's development as a dramatist and of his relationship with the theatre. For this purpose, I have drawn upon my memory, as well as from written material of all kinds, with which I have tried to document the story as fully as possible.

In doing so, I have included many letters, not all relevant only to the matter in hand. For the book is also the record of a friendship extending over thirty-five years, which, though it found its expression mainly in relation to the making and staging of the plays, grew constantly closer.

I have not included *Sweeney Agonistes*. This is not because I value it less highly than the subsequent plays, but because I have no first-hand knowledge about it. It was written in 1926–7, having apparently been in Eliot's mind since 1924.[1] Its first production was made in 1934 by the Group Theatre.[2] I do not think, therefore, that I can add anything useful to the many studies of *Sweeney* and its influence on the poet's subsequent writings. The opportunities that followed from our meeting in 1930 called forth from Eliot quite another kind of drama, and though I believe that some of the experiments made in the *Sweeney* fragments would have enriched his playwriting had they been followed up, the change in his thinking, as well as the nature of the circumstances for which he wrote, precluded this, and only traces of them can be discerned in the later plays.

I have quoted only a very few passages from the published plays. It seemed wrong to bulk out the book by placing long passages of the published work beside the drafts from which I have drawn. I have therefore given references throughout to the volume of *Collected Plays* (Faber and Faber, 1962). This does not include *The Rock*, which its author allowed to go out of print, as an occasional piece, when the original printings were exhausted; this can however be found in libraries, and the choruses are preserved in the *Collected Poems*. I am indebted to Faber and Faber Ltd, and in particular to Mr Peter du Sautoy, for permission to make the quotations I have taken both from the plays and from the critical works, and for assistance and encouragement throughout. My greatest debt is to Valerie Eliot, the loving guardian of her husband's work, who has allowed me to use so large an amount of his letters and the material from his workshop, and also has personally put some of this at my disposal. She has warmly encouraged me in this enterprise, which would have been quite impossible without her generosity.

Dr A. N. L. Munby, Librarian of King's College, Cambridge, has done everything he could to facilitate my use of the John Hayward collection which is in his care. The staffs of the T. S. Eliot collection in the Houghton Library of Harvard University, and of the Bodleian Library, Oxford, where the author's script of *The Rock* is housed, have also shown me much kindness. From all these, I acknowledge with gratitude the permission to reproduce material in their collections.

[1] See David E. Jones, *The Plays of T. S. Eliot* (Routledge and Kegan Paul, London, 1960), p. 27.　　　　　　　　　　　　　　　　[2] See below p. 38.

Preface

I am grateful to the following who have most kindly allowed me to use unpublished material, and in some instances have provided it: Mr Robert Medley for biographical notes on Rupert Doone and letters from Eliot to him; Mrs Martin Shaw for letters from her husband; Mrs Stella Mary Newton for a letter from her husband Eric Newton; Miss Gwynneth Thurburn for notes specially prepared for me; Dame Marie Rambert for a letter from her husband Ashley Dukes; Mr Frank Morley for his 'Memo' on *The Family Reunion*; Sir John Gielgud for two letters; Professor Hugh Hunt for a letter; Mrs Henry Sherek for notes and letters from her husband.

Among published works, I acknowledge with thanks the permission kindly given to make short quotations from the following: *T. S. Eliot, the Man and his Work* (Chatto and Windus); *Fogie* by Marion Cole (Peter Davies Ltd); *Tobias and the Angel* by James Bridie (Constable and Co.); *The Plays of T. S. Eliot* by David E. Jones (Routledge and Kegan Paul); *The Christian Tradition in the Modern British Verse Drama* by William V. Spanos (Rutgers University Press).

The chapter on *The Cocktail Party* is a recension and expansion of the Judith Wilson Lecture which I delivered at Cambridge in 1966 and which was published by the Cambridge University Press. It was from this that the present book came to be projected; and I am deeply indebted to members of the Press who have helped it forward.

London.   E. M. B.
November 1968

List of Manuscripts,

Typescripts and Printed Copies of the Plays
consulted in the preparation of this book

List of Manuscripts

THE COCKTAIL PARTY

'One-Eyed Riley', three Acts out of a projected four, carbon copy	E. Martin Browne	*CP*/1
First Act, revise of what became Act One, scenes 1 and 2, carbon copy	E. Martin Browne	*CP*/2
First Act, same contents but a different typing, carbon copy	John Hayward collection	*CP*/3
Edinburgh Festival typescript of whole play, with extensive revisions	E. Martin Browne	*CP*/Edin.

THE CONFIDENTIAL CLERK

Ur-Clerk, with descriptive cast list and full synopsis	John Hayward collection	*Ur-Clerk*
First draft	John Hayward collection	*CC*/1D
Second rough	John Hayward collection	*CC*/2R
Second draft	John Hayward collection	*CC*/2D
Third rough	John Hayward collection	*CC*/3R
Third draft	John Hayward collection	*CC*/3D
Edinburgh Festival typescript with revisions	E. Martin Browne and John Hayward collection 'D 11'	*CC*/Edin.

THE ELDER STATESMAN

SYNOPSES

Green Synopsis of Acts One and Two	John Hayward collection	
White Synopsis of Acts One and Two	John Hayward collection	
Act Three, (a), (b), (c)	Mrs T. S. Eliot	

ACT ONE

First rough, no carbon	John Hayward collection	*ES*/1R
First carbon'd rough	Mrs Eliot	*ES*/1CR
Pages 1–15, and 1–7 of intermediate typings	Mrs Eliot	
Second draft TSE ('Call butler Lambert' in author's hand on front)	Mrs Eliot	*ES*/2D
'9.ii.58'—copy with this date in author's hand	Mrs Eliot	*ES*/9.ii.58

ACT TWO

First rough, no carbon	John Hayward collection	*ES*/1R
Carbon of first carbon'd rough	Mrs Eliot	*ES*/1CR
Pages 18a, 35ff, and two sets of roughs of the five-handed scene at end	Mrs Eliot	*ES*/II MS

List of Manuscripts

'20.2.58'—copy dated thus in Mrs Eliot's hand	Mrs Eliot	*ES*/20 2.58
ACT THREE		
Manuscript	Mrs Eliot	*ES*/III MS
First rough typescripts, also various other typescripts	Mrs Eliot	*ES*/III/R
WHOLE PLAY		
Edinburgh Festival typescript	Mrs Eliot, also EMB	*ES*/Edin.

Note. In the quotations from drafts of the plays, textual emendations by T. S. Eliot, not shown typographically, are given in footnotes. These are indicated by symbols (†, ‡, §). Other footnotes are indicated by numerals.

1

The Rock

For some time before 1930, T. S. Eliot had been drawn towards writing for the theatre. Though the two fragments of *Sweeney Agonistes* were the only dramatic pieces to have come from his pen, and though no one had yet had the temerity to produce anything so unusual, the signs were evident both in his poetry and his criticism that he had the gifts of a playwright. Many of the characters portrayed in his poems remain more real than many of those created by his contemporaries for the stage; and his critical essays on drama show an understanding not only literary but also theatrical. So it was natural that, at a moment when he felt the need, both personally and professionally, for a new line of creative work, his mind should turn to the drama.

But opportunities for a poet were not easy to find in the theatre at that time. Prose naturalism was in the ascendant, and managers regarded verse with the gravest suspicion. Even the Shakespearian companies which had flourished earlier in the century had fallen on evil days; and those poets who did write plays contented themselves with the hope of production at one of the small specialist theatres such as John Masefield's at Boars Hill, Oxford, or by amateurs. This meant that, though some of them were making valuable experiments in poetic form, they could not test these against the reaction of a general audience. Eliot's influence in the renovation of poetry had by this time begun to affect a wide circle of readers; but it could not do the same for theatregoers unless he was given a stage for which to write.

This was brought about in a quite unexpected way, but the man to whose intervention it was first of all due was one whose influence in these matters was unique and lasting. George Bell became Bishop of Chichester in 1929. He had been Dean of Canterbury, where his pioneer work will be noted in a later chapter. At Chichester, he had at once taken a practical step towards the re-establishment of drama as an ally of the Church by appointing me as Director of Religious Drama for the diocese, a post created by him for the first time in the Church's history. I had taken it up in September 1930.

Bell's main objective was to persuade artists of the first rank that the Church wanted to offer them the opportunity to use their creative gifts. He knew that Eliot was interested in writing plays. So he planned a weekend at the Palace, Chichester, at which Eliot, my wife and I would be among the guests. This took place in December 1930.

It did not seem to promise quick results. Mr Eliot did not join much in the conversation among the ten people who made up the party. On the Sunday evening, the bishop asked him to read *Ash Wednesday*, which had been published in that year. At the end, there was a long silence; our hesitating attempts to talk about the poem were not at all assisted by the author, who always believed that a work of art must speak for itself. I was made acutely aware of what, in the plays also, I have always found true, that his writing must be absorbed before it can be understood.

More must have happened in that weekend, however, than we suspected. Mrs Bell preserved Eliot's 'bread-and-butter' letter:

> 68 Clarence Gate Gardens
> Regents Park, N.W.1
> 18.xii.30

Dear Mrs Bell,

Enough time has passed for me to be able to say with conviction that I did not return with a cold. Even had this happened, I should have had no reason to repine, after such a very delightful happy weekend. (I was about to add the adjective 'profitable', but that it sounds cold, calculating or designing)—Anyway, I shall not forget your hospitality: and I look forward to the possibility of another invitation at a more clement time of year, when my wife would be able to come too.

> Yours very sincerely,
> *T. S. Eliot*

Eliot and I saw little of each other for eighteen months; then I received a letter from him about a play by someone else on which he wanted my opinion. In answering fully about the play, I said how 'truly delighted' I was to hear from him again; and ended:

I do seriously want to see you on a definite matter as soon as you can spare time for me.

The time did not come until some months later, since he was just leaving to take up residence at Harvard for the academic year 1932–3. But the delay proved advantageous, since it enabled me to work my way through the preliminaries which made possible a clear-cut approach to him on the 'definite matter'.

For nearly forty years, my wife and I have tried to keep in note form a diary of events day by day, and it is from this that I can trace the beginnings of what eventually became Eliot's first full-length work for the stage. Under the date 16 March 1933 I find the entry:

Rev. R. Webb-Odell to lunch about Church-Building Pageant.

He had come down to our Sussex home for a day of detailed discussion.

Webb-Odell was a great, jolly polar-bear of a man, with the bear's habit of shifting from foot to foot. He was an able organiser, and had been appointed by the anglican diocese of London to direct the Forty-Five Churches Fund.

He was to attempt the colossal task of raising, principally from the existing churches of London, the money to build and endow forty-five new churches, to meet the needs of the rapidly growing suburbs to the north of the Thames. (South of the river is another diocese, Southwark, and each has responsibility for its own expansion.) This was the period of fastest growth in the Greater London area, and even though the diocese was trying to transfer resources from the centre, whence the residential population was disappearing, to the periphery where most of it went to live, there were (and are) plenty of traditional, legal and aesthetic barriers against such action. In any case, the demands were outstripping the old resources, and the new needs were very different from the old. It was a challenge not only to redeployment but to rethinking on a fundamental level—a challenge which remains, in a far more drastic form, today.

Webb-Odell had convinced his committee that some major demonstration of the need and purpose of the appeal was called for. He believed that this could be done by recalling the great history of the Church in London, and commending to the people the task of carrying on the tradition which it enshrined. He remembered with particular satisfaction a very successful pageant of the London Church given in the garden of the bishop's palace at Fulham in 1909; and wished for an up-to-date revision of this.

I never saw a script of it, but am familiar with the *genre*. The open-air pageant was in its heyday before the First World War, though it continued to flourish until the Second. Its purpose is to celebrate the history either of a place or of an institution, and it does so by showing a chronological series of scenes, each led up to by a processional entry. It gives a great multitude of amateurs, concerned with the subject of the pageant, an opportunity of taking part without any severe strain on their ability (the leading actors are usually chosen rather for their lineage or other connection with the affair in hand than for skill in acting) except, for some of them, that of riding a horse. The total effect can hardly be called dramatic; it is a display of panoply, a more relaxed and less disciplined version of a great parade.

I was at that time preparing a 'pageant' called *The Acts of Saint Richard* for performance in the garden of the bishop's palace at Chichester. The sainted thirteenth-century Bishop of Chichester had a shrine behind the high altar of the cathedral; and a presentation of his life, ending with a procession to the place of his shrine, seemed an appropriate celebration of the centenary of the Oxford Movement which occurred that year. This show was on a more intimate scale than the pageants proper, and it had spoken scenes, the work of E. Werge-Oram. It was devised so that each could be prepared by a different parish in the diocese, with only Richard, the principal character, obliged to attend all rehearsals, and myself as a peripatetic director who would finally bring the whole together on the site during the last couple of days.

It was doubtless because he had heard of this, as well as of the post I held in the diocese, that Webb-Odell had asked me to undertake the London venture. In this too it would be essential that a different parish should undertake each of the main scenes; and, indeed, he himself had already decided what some of the required scenes must be, and approached several of the larger parishes about performing these.

He had, however, made one drastic change in the conditions. The new version was to be for performance in a theatre; he was determined to take a large house in central London for a period of two weeks. This, to my mind, invalidated the idea of a pageant, since processions on any considerable scale became impossible, and the effect would rather be that of a series of tableaux. It would certainly need the addition of a speech commentary, through which in fact the ideas behind the show would have to be conveyed. I felt very doubtful about the success of such a venture, which could hardly avoid being a bore in comparison to the entertainment normally provided in a theatre.

However, I faithfully attempted to provide a scenario according to his requirements. The result is dated 27 May 1933, and since visits to Webb-Odell in London are recorded on 29 May and 1 June, it was obviously discussed in some detail.

It is interesting to look at this in relation to the pattern that eventually emerged. It is titled

A Provisional Scheme

for SPECTACLE OF LONDON CHURCH BUILDING, in a theatre
May 1934

Permanent Set: An Arch (Gothic) not quite completed, as false proscenium; in the base and columns, spaces for figures to stand. Draw-curtains in the arch. On main stage, at back, a platform about 8–10 feet high, with space underneath: moveable steps to approach this. Neutral surround curtains. Plain sky-cloth behind.

Chorus of speakers dressed to match the stone of the arch, and forming part of its base and columns, more or less (in number) according to the progress of events.

Scenes played in *dumb-show*, except for use of actual historical sermons where necessary and available.

The scenes are arranged in historical order, beginning from the command of Christ: 'Go ye into all the world and preach the Gospel . . .', and proceeding through Roman and Saxon Britain to the consecration of Westminster Abbey at the end of Part I. Part II runs through the Middle Ages to the Reformation, with a scene of iconoclasm as climax; Part III runs from the consecration of Wren's St Paul's, the cathedral of London diocese on the site of the British and Saxon churches, through the church-building drive initiated by Bishop Blomfield in the nineteenth century to a symbolic finale including the actors from previous scenes and representatives of the contemporary Church.

The Chorus is given the role of narrator-cum-commentator, but is totally uninvolved in the progress of the story.

This attempt served to stimulate the planning of a few of the scenes and to bring out a few ideas that proved useful afterwards. But its chief value was as a proof, both to me and to Webb-Odell, that the pageant plan would not give us what we wanted. It was unexciting in itself; and it gave no opportunity of confronting the situation of 1934. Some way must be found to focus attention on present needs and hopes, and to see the past in a perspective view from the present. We needed a framework of dramatic action in a contemporary setting. And, to lift the imagination of the audience to a height from which it could see the immediate business of church-building as part of the continuing work of the Church, we needed a poet. Spectacle there should be, but as an imaginative stimulus to action.

Webb-Odell saw the point, and what was more he made his committee see it. They accepted the idea; but they were dubious of my assertion that the man to carry it out was T. S. Eliot. 'Too modern: too difficult.' During the summer, I find three more meetings with Webb-Odell in the record; and I remember that other names were canvassed. All the time, I felt sure that only Eliot could sound the notes which would evoke a strong response.

He was, first of all, the major poet of his time: and in a sense in which that description can rarely be applied. He had re-formed the language of poetry, and every creative mind among English writers was under his influence, every young person awakening to the value of words found a special value in *his* words. His was the distinctive voice of the age.

And it was at the same time the voice of a prophet. It revealed the age to itself, whether by means of an ironic picture of its life or of a plain statement of its shortcomings. The voice could remind one of Amos in its sharpness, of Job in its despair. But equally, it could echo both in their ultimate hope.

For it was the voice of one who had very lately, after a long and agonising struggle, found rest in the faith of the English Church. This faith, therefore, meant passionately more to him than to most of those who had always had it. He was also a highly skilled craftsman, willing, in order to learn at first hand a new part of his craft, to submit to the regimen imposed by a commission, and to work for a specific and limited purpose.

On 22 September, he and I lunched together, and no doubt this was when, having received a positive answer from the committee, I offered him the commission. On 6 October, the diary says 'lunched T. S. Eliot at Diner Francais[1] and visited Odell'. So it appears that by then the poet had accepted the invitation.

[1] A small and inexpensive restaurant in Old Compton Street.

The Rock

Meanwhile, the theatre had been secured. Webb-Odell had approached Lilian Baylis, one of the great characters of the English theatre. It was she who had built up the Old Vic, an old music-hall situated in one of the poorest districts on the south bank of the Thames, into the people's theatre for Shakespeare and opera. Combining absolute dedication with acute business sense, letting nothing stop her and expecting her company to do the same, she had raised a charitable enterprise into what was virtually a national theatre. In 1932, she had achieved a long-held ambition by reconstructing another famous old theatre, Sadler's Wells in Islington, and opening it to share a repertory with the Old Vic. (Later, the 'Vic' was to be devoted to plays and the 'Wells' to opera, but at this time the productions of both moved from one to the other.)

Lilian Baylis was a firm believer and a keen churchwoman. Webb-Odell asked her if she could let Sadler's Wells to him for two weeks after the conclusion of her season; and she welcomed the proposal with enthusiasm. On 16 October I was 'in London: T. S. Eliot and Lilian Baylis'. I wish I had a record of that meeting!

The commission which Eliot had accepted did not seem a particularly promising one for a dramatist. But he did not regard the task in that way. 'I cannot consider myself the author of the "play"', he wrote in the Prefatory Note to the published text, 'but only of the words which are printed here.' He did not feel either able or willing to be responsible for the scenario of a kind of show of which he had no experience; but he was willing to provide the words for one which I should create, so long as he felt himself in sympathy with it.

The request came at a moment when he felt he had exhausted, for a time at least, his lyric vein:

To be, at such a moment, commissioned to write something which, good or bad, must be delivered by a certain date, may have the effect that vigorous cranking sometimes has upon a motor car when the battery is run down. The task was clearly laid out: I had only to write the words of prose dialogue for scenes of the usual historical pageant pattern, for which I had been given a scenario.[1]

Let me pause there, leaving the rest of his description while I recall the labour through which the scenario was born. I have a vivid memory of lunches with Eliot—I can trace three in those weeks and there may have been more—at which we sat opposite to each other

[1] T. S. Eliot, 'The Three Voices of Poetry', *On Poetry and Poets* (Faber and Faber, London, 1957), p. 91.

hoping to see light on how the play about building could be built. How could we get away from the toils of chronology? What pattern of contemporary action would allow us to include the prescribed historical scenes without their appearing as excrescences? It was my responsibility, not his; but he shared with his characteristic patience in my struggle, which I wanted to share with him in order that whatever came out of it should be the right framework for his words.

The evening before we were to face the coming of the deadline— it looks from the diary as if that must have been 30 November—I had at last an inspiration on which I worked far into the night. At that time, producers like Charles Cochran and André Charlot were making a great success with a type of revue which, instead of being a collection of separate 'numbers', had a thread of plot. Might it not be possible to weave a thread out of the building of a contemporary church—one of those which the Fund was created to assist—and to use the scenes from the past as illustrations to the builders of the way in which the Church had tackled, and therefore could still tackle, its problems?

I managed to rough out a first half in which this worked quite well. The second half was less firmly planned, but at least I had something hopeful to take to our last luncheon of the series. Eliot greeted it with relief and a reasonable amount of hope.[1]

The setting is conceived roughly in the same way as that in the first scenario; a 'hill' at the back and a neutral surround, though the Gothic arch has gone. The building is to be constructed around the hill, stage by stage, as the play goes on. It opens with a new figure, the Rock; and the principal characters of the story are the group of workmen who do the building. They are concerned enough to discuss the nature of what they are putting up; and it is out of their thoughts and the problems they meet that the historical scenes are made to arise. The builders are made free of time, so that the characters from the past can speak to them, and can give them the kind of help that is represented by the idea of the Communion of Saints:

> Thus your fathers were made
> Fellow-citizens of the saints, of the household of God, being built upon the
> foundation
> Of apostles and prophets, Christ Jesus Himself the chief corner-stone.
> *(The Rock, p. 19)*

---

[1] Typescript entitled 'London Church-Building Pageant-Play', pencil-marked in Eliot's hand 'Browne's Scenario', in the Bodleian Library.

The Rock

The scenes are introduced on the basis of Dunne's theory of time, which was used a good deal by J. B. Priestley during the 'thirties and so was familiar in the theatre. One of the workmen explains it:

> the past, wot's be'ind you, is wot's goin' to 'appen in the future, bein' as the future 'as already 'appened.

> *(The Rock,* pp. 15–16)

Accordingly the scenes are not introduced in chronological order but rather as they are called up by the experiences of 1934.

The plan of the action follows the building of the sanctuary, from the foundations to the finished and decorated structure. In the first half, the preparing of the foundations is paralleled by the conversion of Saxon London through the preaching of Mellitus, and the difficulties of bad ground by the story of the Norman Rahere who built St Bartholomew's, Smithfield. Thereafter, the conflicts are not with natural forces but with men. The builders are assailed by an Agitator, and their defiant watchfulness is set beside that of Nehemiah and his men as they rebuilt the walls of Jerusalem. The Agitator, having failed to persuade them that they should not be working on a building 'which is only for the purpose of dopin' the workers', goes on to incite the crowd to destroy the half-built church; and this is matched with the pillage and martyrdom in the Danish invasions of the tenth and eleventh centuries.

To end this first half, the action must clearly return to the twentieth century. In my scenario, I had a scene during an air-raid in the recent war. But there were misgivings about this. On 8 January, Eliot wrote to me that we must meet the next week:

> the matter we must consider is the finale of Part I. You will remember perhaps that I had certain qualms about any suggestion of the late war. Recently I have had a letter from the Master of the Temple[1] and one from Pat McCormick[2] on this point, and they both feel very strongly about the undesirability of any such allusion. I think that we ought to defer in any case to such opinion, which probably represents what many other people would feel. The difficulty is to think of some other appropriate catastrophe to end off this part of the play.

The First World War was then still vivid in people's minds; and in retrospect I am sure that just for this reason—that it was past and yet too present to be seen in perspective—the instinct which forbade its use in the play was a right one.

[1] Dr Carpenter, whose people were doing the Crusade scene.
[2] Of St Anne's, Soho.

The Rock

It was Eliot himself who conceived the scene we finally used. In the detailed abstract which I later made for him of the various scenes, this appears exactly as he used it, and I think it was entirely his invention. It was certainly a most effective one. The abstract has three headings:

1. Jesus the Saviour of Man
2. Man the Saviour of Man
3. Man the Destroyer of Man

and he has used these lines in one of the speeches. But the line of thought is applied to the current expressions of false values. Using 'free' verse with great effect, he satirises the two totalitarian ideologies, Communism and Fascism, which at the time were competing ever more vociferously for men's minds, and sets against these groups the figure of the Plutocrat, suavely introducing the Golden Calf as the alternative god.

This is therefore the only one of the acted scenes of which, as he phrases it in the Prefatory Note, Eliot himself is 'literally the author'. Though he had not felt able to plan the whole play, this scene proves how acute his dramatic sense already was. It makes use of the methods of the German Expressionists of the 'twenties, reminding one of some of the earlier plays of W. H. Auden and Christopher Isherwood who were influenced by them. It calls for precise and disciplined movement to match the suggestion of the mechanisation of thought inherent in the mass movements of the Red and the Black Shirts. The Plutocrat, high priest of private enterprise, was played by the Rev. Clarence May, a popular preacher in the West End who habitually used current plays as the texts for his sermons and had the gifts of an actor. The scene was wholeheartedly enjoyed by the Sadler's Wells audiences.

But I remember how difficult it was to get from most of the amateur cast, even of this most vigorous of the scenes, the necessary precision and verve. It sometimes seemed impossible that a show which made such demands on mostly inexperienced amateurs could come to success. Only a few days before the first night Eliot wrote to Rupert Doone:

The pageant at the moment, except for a few bright performances, seems to me to be in a limp and chaotic state. I don't know whether it is a peculiarity of amateurs belonging to parochial congregations, or whether it is found in all very amateur collections, but most of the players seem to me dismally lacking in vitality.

Having seen very little of previous rehearsals, Eliot no doubt got a shock when he witnessed the trials of putting together so huge a show with an untrained cast; and at that stage it looked a superhuman task to make an entertainment out of it. This was another part of the experience which Eliot had come into it to get: to see at first hand at least the final throes of making a production.

He was a very silent witness. This was not only due to his strong sense of theatre-decorum. He was never one to offer comment on things with which he was not fully acquainted; he confined himself to the plea of every author: 'I wish they would speak my lines exactly as I wrote them', and to points on the reading of the verse. It was not till several years and several plays later that he would discuss points of production with me during rehearsal.

But to return to the scenario. Part II, as I have said, was less firmly planned than Part I. But the original plan is more compact than the one which is revealed in the published text. Various additions, to meet demands for prescribed scenes and to take advantage of bright ideas, crept in, to make the Part a good deal longer than was desirable. And basically, it suffers from the fact that as the church nears completion the scope for dramatic conflict necessarily decreases, and is replaced by the less exciting display of achievement.

It began with Bishop Blomfield, a favourite of Webb-Odell, 'an uninspiring man who did a wonderful work' in the nineteenth century. His remarks, already drafted by Eliot in December 1933, were invigorating; but the Crusade scenes which followed from them had not sufficient motivation; and from this point on the Part tended to become diffuse. Returning to the modern church, the east end is shown 'nearly finished'; and now comes the question of what to put in it. The conflict becomes one rather of taste than of good and evil. The rather frivolous discussion between visitors who take differing views of church decoration leads to a scene telescoping the two orgies of iconoclasm in Stuart and in Tudor times. Then, to contrast with these, craftsmen are seen—painters, stone and wood carvers, metal workers, etc.—employing their skills to beautify the church; and this leads to the final dedication of the building, paralleled by a series of sympathetic processions recalling the great consecrations of the past—Westminster Abbey, Dick Whittington's church of St

Michael, Paternoster Royal, St Paul's, and churches of the nine-teenth century; the climax is reached when the Rock himself comes to bless the new church.

This synopsis will make it clear that there is less energy and cohesion here than in Part I; and the relative success of the result in performance depended upon incidental accretions of beauty or humour. One such, though a total irrelevance, was particularly dear to Eliot and certainly repaid inclusion. He had always had a great partiality for the English music-hall; and he took delight in writing a ditty for the foreman and his wife, an attractive variation on the old song 'At Trinity Church I met my doom'.

In order to break up the flow of processions which threatened to carry the last section downhill into mere pageantry, I suggested a short scene of action to introduce and humanise each of them. Eliot dutifully wrote for me the legend of St Peter and the Fisherman at Westminster, and the dinner-table talk of Wren, Pepys and Evelyn. As it turned out, the Part grew too long and towards the middle of rehearsals I found myself wanting to tighten the show up by cutting at whatever point seemed possible. But with an amateur cast, the director cannot be as ruthless as with professionals. To cut out, or even to shorten, a scene on which time and labour have voluntarily been spent is likely to cause extreme disappointment and may spread dismay, or at least uncertainty, among the rest of the cast. Diplomatic considerations forbade me to reduce some of my own excesses, and obliged me to mix caution with firmness in resisting the actors' desire to add to the 'fat' of their parts. One had to consider too those who had made costumes and properties which might be sacrificed. A great machine had been set in motion, whose wheels only continued to turn because of the goodwill of those hundreds of people who were voluntarily manning it; and one had thus to meet the cost of maintaining the happy spirit which prevailed throughout the show.

Most of the sacrifices I demanded therefore fell to the lot of the professional artists: and by this time the second principal contributor was hard at work with us. The spectacular scenes, especially those in dumb show, demanded music; and the whole piece was conceived in terms of music as well as of words. We were ideally fortunate in securing the collaboration of Martin Shaw.

He was a composer of immense fertility and resource, who had spent much of his life in the revivification of English Church music, notably by going back, beyond the more esoteric cathedral tradition, to the springs of folk music in song, dance and carol. *Songs of Praise* and the *Oxford Book of Carols* bear his stamp. He had also made music for the theatre, both for musical shows and for 'straight' plays. He knew how to make people sing and play, and what they were capable of: and he was accustomed to working with amateurs, while making professional demands in respect of standard.

With us, he would be short of money to pay an orchestra which must therefore be partly amateur; he would be short of time in which to fit the music to the performance. But this sort of difficulty was well within his experience, and he brought to the work the same sort of dedicated understanding as Eliot himself. They were happy collaborators. Eliot wrote to Shaw about the time of the first night (the letter, like many others, has no date):

As I have not seen you since Saturday—when I was too much worried about my own part of the show to attend, I must write to tell you how much I like your music throughout.

One thing that impresses me, and that has been most valuable for the success of the play, is your versatility and adaptability. I have myself been irked by having to write bits and snippets, seeing how I should have liked to develop them dramatically if I had had the scope; and I imagine that you have had to curb yourself, and subdue your inspiration, still more than I. It is the music that justifies, for instance, the ballet, or the scene ... of the Craftsmen I am quite unqualified to criticise or praise, technically, but I write as a collaborator, to express my satisfaction.

I hope that this effort will not be the end either of our acquaintance as human beings, or of our collaboration as workmen.

Eliot's reference to the frustrations inherent in such a show—and they are as familiar in professional revue as they became here—was of course justified. I had to ask Eliot sometimes to remodel passages, not to meet his own wishes but to get me out of some production problem, often caused by the players' inexperience or lack of talent. I remember how distressed Martin Shaw was when I had to cut a repeat in the scene of the Red and Black Shirts, spoiling the musical pattern, because the actors simply could not hold the scene up for long enough. In such a show, one has to use many who have offered for the cause rather than from the compulsion which drives the born actor.

But of this also one can have too much. For 'Bert', the foreman who led the little band of workmen building the contemporary church, I was offered the services of Vincent Howson, the vicar of an East End parish who had formerly been a member of Sir Frank Benson's famous Shakespearian Company. Since moving from stage to church, he had formed The East End Amateurs, with whom he had regularly produced pantomime and variety shows, taking advantage of the local cockney talent. He was very keen both to offer his own professional skill and to bring in a group of his amateurs to play these scenes with him. But he was faced with 'a grave difficulty', as he pointed out to me in a long letter dated 29 March 1934 (only two months before the opening). He felt that Mr Eliot's dialogue was 'not true cockney . . . there are words introduced alien to the language, not only long words, but slang words'. He went on to give instances and expound his view of how the cockney thinks; and also to urge that the 'pointing' of lines sometimes needed adjustment to make sure of their effect.

This was an honest difference of opinion with one whose acting skill, albeit of a somewhat old-fashioned kind, was indispensable to us. I did not in the end recruit the other workmen from his group but from the University College, London, Dramatic Society. They found Eliot's cockneys, who were clearly products of Workers' Educational Association evening classes, with a Bert who enjoyed reading history and political economy, quite playable; but we had to allow Mr Howson to adjust his part—and with it, to some extent, the others—to suit himself. Eliot explains in the Prefatory Note:

The Rev. Vincent Howson has so completely rewritten, amplified and condensed the dialogue between himself ('Bert') and his mates, that he deserves the title of joint author.

This reconstruction was made as rehearsals were beginning. The original material was being written before Christmas; on 7 December I have a letter from Eliot which says

I also add a couple of pages of the workmen's dialogue for your consideration. There is a gap to be filled in with a few bricklayers' terms, which I shall obtain from an expert. [As the Prefatory Note shows, this was Frank Morley.]

It seems desirable to print these pages, so that those who care to do so may compare them with the published version. They show, I think, that Eliot's ear was as quick, and his dramatic sense as sure, in writing for the cockney workmen as for the people in the very different social *milieu* of *Sweeney*. He has the pleasant conceit of giving

The Rock

Anglo-Saxon names to the modern labourers, who will first meet, across the gulf of time, their fellows from Saxon England:

(ETHELBERT, ALFRED and EDWIN, *Anglo-Saxon labourers*)
ETHELBERT (*singing*)   A pick-axe and a spade, a spade,
                    For and a winding-sheet.
   I 'eard that at the Old Vic once. That's Shakespeare, that is. He wrote some good songs, Shakespeare.
ALFRED   Time to knock off, Bert.
ETHELBERT   Now look here, my lad, it's high time I had a word with you about you bein' so sharp on knockin' off. I tell you this is a church we're buildin'; yet you want to knock off on the dot same as if it was a bank. I tell you, you put in an extra ten minutes or so every night and it'll be for the good of your soul.
ALFRED   Well, I can't see as it makes any difference to you or me whether it's a church or a bank. You don't get paid any more for buildin' a church nor a bank, do you? I get my money just the same, and that's all the same to me.
EDWIN   And the landlord of the Bunch of Grapes gets *your* money, Fred, so it's all the same to *him.*
ALFRED   None of your bloody half larks. I say once they're built, what's the good of a church or a bank to you or me?
ETHELBERT   Ah, you're lucky to have a man of experience like me about, to tell you what, you wandering in the mazes of your own conceit, if you take my meaning. You've got to look at it this way. You build a bank, we'll say, and you take a proper kind of pride in your work; some day you think you'll stop in and admire your handiwork, in a manner of speaking. Well, you step in and look about, and what's the first thing you see? A blooming old commissionaire in uniform, like as not your own drill sergeant when you was recruited. 'What d'you want here?' he says in all probability, looking as if he thought you was come to crack the safe. 'I helped to build this place', you says proud enough, 'and I'm just having a look round.' 'You have a look round the way you come', he says, 'and if you helped to build this place, you ought to know your way out of it', he says; 'this bank is for them as has business here, and we don't want no sightseers and tourists', he says. I'm just giving you a bit of an imaginary conversation, as you might say. Well, you build a church, and you step into it with the same intentions, and as like as not you won't find a soul in the place, leastwise not as far as molesting you goes. You can stop there all day if you like, except in winter for it not being very well heated, which is because the folks that runs churches mostly hasn't money enough to keep 'em warm, and for similar reasons the upholstery is not always of the most downy, as you might say. And maybe the parson's there, and sees you pokin' about. That 'appened to me once. And we fell into conversation, and I discovered that he didn't know nothing more than an infant about brickwork, so I explained to him how we ... and he was most interested. 'Well', he says, 'that's most

15

interesting. It's funny, isn't it', he says, 'I serve this place and I didn't know how it was made, and you made it and you don't know how to use it.' Come to think it over, there was some reason in his words. A church is for you and me just as much as for anybody else; and this is the point I was trying to bring home to you, it's another difference between building a church and building a bank.

ALFRED Well, where does the money come from to build 'em, that's what I'm curious to know. Same old hidden hand, I guess, same as with the banks.

EDWIN No, come to think about it, that's where you're wrong. I saw a piece about this in the paper. This church is being built half on subscriptions and half on hope, from the look of things. And the people what subscribe don't all own racing stables, neither. And there's a question I'd like to put for your consideration, Fred: did you ever hear of any rich bloke got a peerage through building churches? No, there's some reason in what Bert says; and I'm willing to do a bit more than a day's work here, 'cause when I come to think seriously about taking a wife, I'm coming to this church to get tied up.

It may seem extraordinary that a man who had set himself such supremely high standards in the use of language, who had re-created English poetry to so large an extent, should have been able to endure the kind of compromise which was inherent in such a task as this, and to devote his precious time to so ephemeral a product. But as I watched him confronting these situations, I realised that he was taking a professional view of it all. This was the job to be done: and by doing it, even the drudgery of it, he was learning something about the theatre from the inside. He wanted to write for the stage; well then, he would do what the stage asked of him, and do it as well as he could. And he would find out by experience how far the writer has to give in to the dictates of the others who are in the job with him, and will give his work the only true life it can have, by putting it on the stage.

This is a quality which I came to respect more and more deeply as I directed for Eliot over the next twenty-four years. In his letter to Martin Shaw he described himself as a 'workman'; and it is a just description. He was no romantic about the writer's craft: he saw it as a hard, continuous struggle,

> the intolerable wrestle
> With words and meanings,

as he calls it in *East Coker* where he has much to say about his experience of it. And he learned that the playwright has to endure also the wrestle, sometimes equally intolerable, with his colleagues in the most diversified of all the arts. I do not know whether, when he wrote the two *Sweeney* fragments, he consciously desired to see them on the stage, but I do know that one of his main reasons for accepting the Forty-Five Churches Fund commission was that it had a guaranteed audience for its two weeks' run in a large theatre. He would thus be assured of witnessing the response of audiences, even though he feared, as he says in a letter to Bonamy Dobrée (10 May 1934), 'a dull and lethargic audience for that sort of affair'. But as Dobrée testifies,

He need not have feared. The audience (which included my wife and myself) seemed far from lethargic.[1]

The chief attraction, however, of this commission was the opportunity afforded by that part of my plan which I have not so far mentioned, but which to me also was the most important. In the revue on which the show was modelled, there would be a Chorus of girls displaying their charms. In this one, the Chorus would instead use their voices to win response to the poet's thought. This was a sphere in which he could enjoy a freedom limited only by the need to introduce, in more or less detail, the scene which followed.

It is interesting to trace the way in which the eventual composition and character of the Chorus was evolved. In my first scenario, I had had a 'chorus of speakers dressed to match the stone of the arch'. In the second, there is a Chorus 'dressed in the colours of the spectrum', representing the universal Church, and also one of 'Apostles and Prophets'. The cast list accompanying this shows

Chorus of the Church (2 semi-choruses, women)
Chorus of Apostles and Prophets (men)

There also appears, for the first time, the Rock; and he is identified with St Peter.

Eliot clearly felt that he would prefer this figure to be more abstract in character; and the Chorus which was to attend him thus reverted to the original conception of stone-like figures, growing out of the rock on which they stood, surrounding the Rock as symbolising the foundation of the Church. They acquired the function of the Prophets also, and so it was feasible to use speakers of both sexes in

---

[1] Bonamy Dobrée in *T. S. Eliot, the Man and his Work*, ed. Allen Tate (Chatto and Windus, London, 1967), p. 83.

the one group, which gave a far greater range and richness to the vocal quality.

The shape of each Part for them was roughly similar; an opening ode leading into dialogue with the Rock, and three major choral odes, besides the shorter passages needed to link scene with scene. The total stage time involved was roughly forty minutes, which allowed for great variety. We worked out a schedule of duration for each chorus, and the time-sheet which came back to the author from the group during preparation shows how nearly accurate he was in his fulfilment of my estimate. Again the workman! Yet this did not inhibit him from filling the odes with many felicities, ranging from the grandeur of prophetic utterances comparable with (and sometimes based on) those of the Old Testament to satire of contemporary ways of living which proved barbed enough to raise general laughter from an audience of 1500 each night.

And this despite the fact that the Chorus was conceived as a group of impersonal, abstract figures. Wearing half-masks and stiff robes which allied them to the rock-foundation on which the church was being built and to the Rock himself, they spoke with the voice of the poet. If we return to 'The Three Voices of Poetry', from which I quoted earlier, we can find out how he himself regarded them:

I had also to provide a number of choral passages in verse, the content of which was left to my own devices: except for the reasonable stipulation that all the choruses were expected to have some relevance to the purpose of the pageant, and each chorus was to occupy a precise number of minutes of stage time. But in carrying out this second part of my task, there was nothing to call my attention to the third, or dramatic voice: it was the second voice, that of myself addressing—indeed haranguing—an audience, that was most distinctly audible . . . This chorus of *The Rock* was not a dramatic voice; though many lines were distributed, the personages were unindividuated. Its members were speaking *for me*, not uttering words that really represented any supposed character of their own.[1]

The distinction which Eliot drew in this lecture is of particular relevance in relation to the Chorus, which had in the period after the First World War become almost an essential part of the poets' equipment in writing plays. His 'second voice' is that of 'the poet addressing the audience', while the third 'is the voice of the poet when he attempts to create a dramatic character'. His description of

---

[1] *On Poetry and Poets*, p. 91.

The Rock

The Rock Chorus as exclusively speaking with the second voice may be accepted without qualification, for of course he was not here writing the chorus as part of a play—rather of a piece designed to force upon the audience's attention certain facts and a way to deal with them. But in view of Eliot's development of the chorus in his next play it may be useful here to speak of the use of the chorus at that time, especially since it has now disappeared once more, almost entirely, from the stage.

I suppose that the revival of the chorus began with the translation of Greek plays, most popularly by Gilbert Murray, in the early days of this century. His *Trojan Women* and *Electra* were published in 1905, *Medea* and *Iphigenia in Tauris* in 1910. Eliot made a violent attack on Murray as a disciple of Swinburne who tried to adapt his style to the Greek classics for which it was utterly unsuited. But the Murray translations, thanks largely to the direction of Harley Granville-Barker and later to the acting of Sybil Thorndike, held the stage for a good many years, and their success encouraged contemporary poets to use the chorus in their own plays.

They felt the need of it, I suspect, as they came to realise that the impetus of the Shakespearian tradition in poetic drama was at last exhausted. The great poets of the nineteenth century had not turned out any really convincing plays, and though one may adduce the clumsiness of their construction as one reason, I think that Eliot has pinpointed the chief cause in 'The Music of Poetry':

It is not primarily lack of plot, or lack of action and suspense, or imperfect realisation of character, or lack of anything of what is called 'theatre', that makes these plays so lifeless; it is primarily that their rhythm of speech is something that we cannot associate with any human being except a poetry reciter.[1]

The chorus, at this moment, provided for the poets a form distinctively their own. Choral speaking was already being practised, on lyric poetry, by the teachers who were advancing the new study of speech in education, so that there were bodies of trained people who were overjoyed to find a new outlet for their talents in the drama.

But on a deeper level than this, the poets, who were outsiders in the current theatre of naturalism, felt the need to go back to the springs of the drama in ritual form and communal expression.

[1] *On Poetry and Poets*, p. 34.

The Rock

The dramatic revival of choral speech, both in translation from the Greek and in new poets' plays, coincides with the beginning of the revival of the medieval plays which sprang, most scholars still believe, from the ritual root of the *Quem Quaeritis* and its successors in liturgical drama. Parallel with this again is the study of the Japanese *Noh* by Yeats and some of his followers, and the results in such plays as Yeats's *Calvary* and *Resurrection*, or Gordon Bottomley's plays of Scottish legend patterned on the *Noh*.

Bottomley did some most valuable pioneer work in shaping the chorus for use on the stage. His choruses are usually much less involved in the action than even the Greek ones; often they consist of abstract figures—Snow, Winds, Trees, Mountain Mist. If human, they are as powerless to intervene in the tragic crisis as the Chorus in *Medea* are to open the doors to stop Medea murdering her children. They give to the individual story its distance (as in the *Noh*) and its poetic, universal dimension. And when, in 1933, Bottomley wrote a play for a Christian church, *The Acts of Saint Peter* for the octocentenary of Exeter Cathedral, he used the chorus of worshippers as a human curtain between scenes, following the curtain-folding ritual of Yeats which he had adopted in earlier plays.

Bottomley, for us, is on the far side of the watershed that is Eliot's lyric verse; and his choral writing, clean and speakable though it is, belongs to a past age. In *The Rock* choruses Eliot once more ushers in the new one. They may be uneven, tentative experiments written against the clock; but these choruses are the most dramatically vital part of the play. They combine prophetic thunder with colloquial speech; and they use the orchestra of varied voices, male and female, to create continual dramatic contrast. The verse-rhythms are equally varied, from the rolling periods of the Old Testament in the King James version to the crisp phrases of contemporary satire; and at times, the two are combined:

III

Much is your reading, but not the Word of God,
Much is your building, but not the House of God.
Will you build me a house of plaster, with corrugated roofing,
To be filled with a litter of Sunday newspapers?

The demands made on the speakers are severe. Some passages are very complex, such as this on the Incarnation:

The Rock

VII

Then came, at a predetermined moment, a moment in time and of time,
A moment not out of time, but in time, in what we call history; transecting,
    bisecting the world of time, a moment in time but not like a moment of
    time,
A moment in time but time was made through that moment: for without
    the meaning there is no time, and that moment of time gave the meaning.

Unless this is delivered in the exact phrasing shown, with its punctuation faithfully observed, it cannot be understood. With the passages of social criticism it is easier to make an impact. But their barbs, however amusingly sharp, are pointed in order to call the attention back and back again to the main theme: the purpose of God with the Church. At the beginning of Part II, there stands a great chorus for which this is the author's draft synopsis:

History of world from Creation. Gradual struggle and striving together towards true faith. Rise and fall of Religions, each carrying a race to a certain point of development and then arrest and decay. Xtianity alone seemed capable of leading men to greater and greater heights. But is man now failing Xtianity? Decay of the whole world.
(Stichomythia of 2 chorus leaders, M and F.)
Rock on time and Eternity.

Following this in the manuscript notes are the first two paragraphs of the chorus (pp. 49, 50) almost in their final form. The new hope given by the Incarnation, in the passage quoted above, is developed until it is negatived by the new desertion of today:

But it seems that something has happened that has never happened before:
    though we know not just when, or why or how, or where.
Men have left GOD not for other gods, they say, but for no god; and this
    has never happened before
That men both deny gods and worship gods, professing first Reason,
And then Money, and Power, and what they call Life, or Race, or Dialectic.
The Church disowned, the towers overthrown, the bells upturned, what
    have we to do
But stand with empty hands and palms turned upwards
In an age which advances progressively backwards?

(*The Rock*, pp. 50–1)

More than one reviewer used about such passages as these the word 'Jeremiad'; and found the dominant note to be a pessimism which was to be expected from the author of *The Waste Land*. But the play contains in equal measure the other half of the prophet's insight; the Chorus are immediately rebuked by the Rock:

21

The Rock

O faint-hearted, and easily unsettled, and easily lost
In the blinding movement of time, sinking and borne away;
Remember, all you who are numbered for GOD,
In every moment of time you live where two worlds cross,
In every moment you live at a point of intersection,
Remember, living in time, you must live also now in Eternity.

(*The Rock*, p. 52)

The values of Eternity are continually recalled to our minds, and the eternal significance of the Church which 'must be forever building, and always decaying, and always being restored'.[1]

Neither of the two worlds is to be forgotten; because the play lays stress on eternal values it is all the less escapist:

'Our citizenship is in Heaven': yes, but that is the model and type for your citizenship upon earth.

(*The Rock*, p. 20)

The author's concern with the present state of society is passionate and compassionate. Though he may castigate the materialist indifference of the affluent, he is moved with profound pity for those who suffer from society's misgovernment, and most of all for the unemployed. The play was written at a time when unemployment was a spectre that had haunted for many years some parts of Britain, and when it had eroded not only the material condition of the workers and their families but their self-respect, leaving them with a sense of uselessness that sapped the very will to live. I do not remember any work of the time in which this plight is portrayed more poignantly than in *The Rock*. In the opening section, the Workmen, looking forward hopefully to their task of building, are answered from the dimness beyond by the Unemployed:

No man has hired us
With pocketed hands
And lowered faces
We stand about in open places
And shiver in unlit rooms.
Only the wind moves
Over empty fields, untilled
Where the plough rests, at an angle
To the furrow. In this land
There shall be one cigarette to two men,

[1] *The Rock*, p. 20.

22

The Rock

To two women one half pint of bitter
Ale. In this land
No man had hired us.

(The Rock, p. 10)

The last lines of this chant are heard again in the first chorus of Part II. And later in Part I, in the prophetic chorus which begins with the Old Testament cry

The Word of the Lord came unto me, saying ...

one of the prophets returns to the plight of the people of London's East End:

A Cry from the East:
What shall be done to the shore of smoky ships?
Will you leave my people forgetful and forgotten
To idleness, labour, and delirious stupor?
There shall be left the broken chimney,
The peeled hull, a pile of rusty iron,
In a street of scattered brick where the goat climbs,
Where My Word is unspoken.

(The Rock, p. 29)

The vivid picture of industrial waste and squalor is to remain in the eyes of those who live in 'the land of lobelias and tennis flannels':

Shall we lift up our feet among perpetual ruins?

(The Rock, p. 30)

The other social theme which recurs most strongly is the lack of community:

What life have you if you have not life together?
There is no life that is not in community ...

And now you live dispersed on ribbon roads,
And no man knows or cares who is his neighbour
Unless his neighbour makes too much disturbance ...

(The Rock, p. 21)

The instability of modern society increases the indifference of people to each other. Febrile enthusiasms for 'nation or race or what you call humanity' cloak the real fact of the increasing depersonalisation of our life.

But to the Chorus who bemoan these things, the Rock comes with one positive command.

The Rock

Take no thought of the harvest,
But only of proper sowing.

(The Rock, p. 9)

For the Christian, who lives at the point of intersection, 'where two worlds cross', is called to pay attention to the life he is in now, leaving the eternal outcome to God. The play is very much concerned, then, with the bettering of this life, especially in terms of personal relationships and the building of a common way of living. But at the same time, the building whose construction forms the plot of the play is a symbol of the everlasting; and the final passages of the Chorus are devoted to the offering of human gifts in the service of God and the praise of Him to whom they are dedicated.

In the last chorus but one, the summary of the artistic gifts to be offered ends with one of Eliot's most pregnant definitions of the 'intolerable wrestle with words and meanings':

> Out of the slimy mud of words, out of the sleet and hail of verbal
> imprecisions,
> Approximate thoughts and feelings, words that have taken the place of
> thoughts and feelings,
> There spring the perfect order of speech, and the beauty of incantation.

(The Rock, p. 75)

This is intensely personal to him; and he was always conscious of his own failure to measure up to the standard he set himself with words (see *East Coker* again). In meeting his deadlines, the workman had had to give less care than he would have wished to this particular 'raid on the inarticulate'; and as he had kept faithfully up to schedule, he asked me whether he could have an extra few weeks to work on the final chorus, while the rest were rehearsed.

An author's manuscript draft of this chorus has been preserved. It is a fascinating document, for it shows how, as the whole chorus takes form, the poet is allowing images to suggest themselves to his mind and noting them in their half-shaped state. Some of the passages remain, at this stage, in prose: most of these will emerge as long-flowing lines reminiscent of Paul Claudel. This poet certainly had a considerable influence on Eliot at the time; and one can detect occasional echoes of his style, such as

> the Spirit who moved on the face of the waters like a lantern set on the
> back of a tortoise

(The Rock, p. 19)

The Rock

In its final form, the ode passes from these loosely flowing lines to more regular ones, reflecting the passage from the danger of satanic chaos to divine order. It reverts for a moment to the looser form in speaking of the frailty of fragmented human nature, rising through aspiration to the final note of praise.

Here then is the draft:[1]

STROPHE   The church built, adorned, dedicated, wedded to Christ. One light burns in the darkness. What of the future? Shall the Church vis[ible] and invis[ible] go forth to conquer the world?

ANTISTROPHE   The great snake lies ever sleeping at the bottom of the pit of the world, curled round the Tree. From time to time awakens, famished, and reaches his neck to devour. Let us not look into the pit and seek to plumb the Mystery of Iniquity. What fellowship hath righteousness with unrighteousness, and light with darkness?

Wherefore come out from among them and be ye separate.

STROPHE   Let us therefore in the light meditate on the Light.

O Light Invisible
Too bright for mortal sight
We thank thee for the little light the light of altar and sanctuary
Light of the solitary in midnight meditation
Light through the window
Sun lighting west front of English church at evening—crossing the furrow.
Moon and
Starlight faint light where the   glowworm showing the
   bat fluttering over the pool   reach and spread of
        squeaks   a dozen blades of
Light through water showing the   grass
   sea gods the passing shadow of Argo
      and scattered
      returned precious
Light from stones. Light from colour
   mosaic, fresco, silk curtains.

In the rhythm of earthly life we are glad when the day ends,
When the play ends, we tire of worship and we sleep and are glad to sleep,
Controlled by the blood and the day and night and seasons.
And the candle must be extinguished the candle must be relighted
We forever here light and quench the flame
   children who are quickly tired and fall asleep in the middle of play
We are tired children watching the fireworks
   late in the night, and can endure only a little light
Therefore we thank thee for the little light
   that Thou hast not made the light too great for us.

[1] This, like all the unpublished draft material in this chapter, is from the Bodleian Library collection.

We thank Thee who hast inspired us to build, finding life
    through our fingers, and that when we have built an altar
    to the Invisible Light we may set thereon
    the little visible lights, suitable to our vision.
And we thank Thee for darkness to remind us of light.

To compare this draft with the final form of this chorus, the most
carefully wrought piece in the play, is to learn a great deal about how
inspiration came to Eliot and how his mind shaped it.

The chief instrument used for that purpose was the *Gloria in
Excelsis*; the final version is patterned on the phrases of that hymn
from the Mass, which has provided a framework into which the
imagery already present in the poet's mind can be fitted. This use of a
liturgical hymn was, as we shall see, repeated in *Murder in the
Cathedral*; and, like the story-lines he took for later plays from the
Greek classics, it gave him a sense of security. It is a characteristic
manifestation of the combination in his temperament of adventurous-
ness and caution, and of his need to feel himself launching his flights
from a pad of classic structure.

The Rock himself ends the play. In the published version, his last
speech is headed

THE ROCK, now ST PETER

As I have said, Eliot wanted to keep his identity undefined for as
long as possible, and it was in keeping with the conception of the
Chorus that he should also be regarded rather as a symbolic than a
historical figure. On 6 December, I wrote to Eliot about him:

Of whom is the Rock symbolical? I originally conceived him as St. Peter—'on
this Rock will I build my Church . . .' But some have thought of 1 Cor. 10.4:
'And that Rock was Christ.' If you've got definite views, I shall be really glad
of them. But you may not yet have considered the point.

I find that Eliot tried a final speech for him, summing up the purpose
of the action and introducing the real bishop, who was to take over
and give audience and players his episcopal benediction. There are
several drafts of which the following is one:

Now I must leave you, but remember this:
Whenever you set spade to ground, trowel to brick,
Put roof to wall and raise therein the altar,
There shall I be with you, and shall be with you
The Xtian builders of old times and other lands.
You have seen one church built here in players' show

The Rock

Within [the compass of] our [evening's] entertainment.
When you go out and look again on London
Give then a thought to what you ought to build
Seeing so much there that you should destroy.
(The sheep are many and ill-cared-for, the sheepfolds poor and few.)
A blessing now on you and on your work.
My blessing you shall have, but not from me
But as is right a shepherd of your flock
And one in my succession. London to London.

The points are well taken: but by that time, after the exaltation of the final chorus, such preaching was dramatically inappropriate: so the Rock merely echoed the Chorus's mood as he revealed the bishop. His part turned out to be rather a small one.

But he gave the title to the play. I find that this was not agreed to without a good deal of cogitation. On 6 December I am already asking 'have you thought of a title yet?'; and by 11 January I am saying 'we need a title terribly badly' and making a crop of suggestions, none of which appealed either to myself or to Eliot. Webb-Odell writes on 5 February that I have suggested 'Many Mansions', which Eliot thinks 'not bad'; but Webb-Odell also points out that Lady Keeble (Lillah McCarthy) dubbed the show (in the *Observer* of 4 February) *The Rock*; and he asks what is wrong with this.

Eliot's reply (8 February) is characteristic both of him and of the tensions of that period:

My only objection to *The Rock* is that the Rock himself, if he gives the title to the production, will be identified by most people as St. Peter pure and simple, which does directly conjure up to my mind the Petrine Claims—which are hardly appropriate. Do you think this is a considerable objection or not? If not, then perhaps this is the best title.

It was, I am sure; and in the event we were able to maintain the symbolic nature of the character. This was thanks to Eliot's handling of the matter in the writing, but even more, perhaps, to the designer.

I had met Stella Mary Pearce at a Scottish drama school in the summer of 1932, when she and my wife and I were all on the staff. She had been both an actress and a designer for the stage, and also had a *salon de haute couture* in Bond Street in which she showed designs combining ideas in advance of the current vogue with an acute sense of history in fashion. I wanted for *The Rock* a designer who could lift the play completely out of Wardour Street and make the visual appearance of the characters correspond with the vitality which Eliot was injecting into their words. It was a colossal task, for there were 330 characters in the scenes, and at the end there were added representatives of each decade of the nineteenth century to bring the assembled members of the English Church up to date. And practically all of these costumes had to be made by amateur, often by unskilled, labour.

I had seen Miss Pearce teaching amateurs at the St Andrews School and realised that she could get surprising, almost miraculous results from them; but even so, I feared that she would be daunted by the task of directing thirty groups all over London in the making of costumes, some of which were of considerable complexity and none of which conformed to the stereotypes of 'historical costume'. But she accepted; and began the creation of a visual scheme to cover the whole great canvas we were to show. Each scene had its own colour-scheme, and all these related to an overall plan building up to the use of the full range of the spectrum. Most striking effects were produced by the introduction of a new colour-note at certain points; the most memorable was the white for the craftsmen miming the decoration of the sanctuary of the new church, under Doreen Woodcock's inventive direction.

Stella had one consultation with representatives of each group who met her early in the proceedings in central London. When they were well under way, she paid one visit to the group in its own workroom to inspect progress and give further instructions. Otherwise, they managed the whole job themselves. This was one of the most surprising and satisfying things about the production. It proved that, given first-class instruction on a task clearly defined, with the methods of execution clearly laid down, groups of amateurs could make costumes that met the standards of a theatre where professional decor was expected.

The requirements were stringent. Not only did the groups make costumes; they also made wigs, out of various materials, from hair to paper, and shoes which would last for three weeks of hard work. Many scenes had formalised make-up, to tone with the colour-scheme of their scene and to match costumes which often had a symbolic quality. All this also was in the hands of the group.

By the time we came to production, Stella had married Eric Newton, then a painter and mosaic artist, and becoming known as

one of the leading art critics and historians of our time. He undertook
to do the setting, and these two thus created the visual presentation
of the symbols of the Church

forever building, and always decaying, and always being restored

to match Eliot's conception.

Eric Newton writes to him on 10 March 1934:

Dear Mr. Eliot,

Martin Browne tells me this morning that you would like to see a rough
sketch of what the stage will look like for *The Rock*. Here is an indication of
what (at the moment) I am thinking of doing. The Rock itself and the columns
at the sides will be permanent, though curtains can be drawn across in front of
the rock and some of the columns. The semicircular apse behind is only seen
in completeness at the end—as also the altar and crucifix. In earlier scenes the
apse will be non-existent or half-built—showing sky behind—and the rock will
have no altar.

I think the proportions are roughly correct but I shall be making a model
soon, which will show exactly the disposition and relative positions of each
portion of the set.

Yours very truly,
Eric Newton

P.S. At the end the apse will be decorated with huge archangels. The rest will
be quite plain.

The 'huge archangels', done in an elongated style which had the
monumental effect of early Byzantine work, and the crucifix over the
altar which went with them, were first shown being executed by
the craftsmen, who were also working on the stone carving of the
Lamb for the altar-front and the furnishings. At the beginning, the
unadorned hill of rock was occupied by the Rock himself and his
Chorus of sixteen.

These figures combined with the setting to establish the concept of
the eternal Church, founded upon a Rock. Stella boldly dressed them
in stiff robes of hessian draped in statuesque folds, and gave them
half-masks. The first appearance was formidable: and those who saw
the actors off-stage regretted that such a handsome group of young
people were so disguised! But of course this was the proper expression
of the grandeur of Eliot's conception, and strongly stressed the
prophetic aspect of the writing. What gave us all much pleasure was
that the severity of the dressing did not at all inhibit the audience
from enjoying the sallies of wit which issued from these impassive
faces. Indeed, I think the costuming had the effect of concentrating

attention on the words, and so allowed them to provoke laughter as hearty as I can remember at the description of the departed commuters:

> And the wind shall say: 'Here were decent godless people:
> Their only monument the asphalt road
> And a thousand lost golf balls'
>
> (*The Rock*, p. 30)

As we have seen, Eliot was deeply concerned that *The Rock* should express the social as well as the spiritual impulse of the community. It had been planned from the first that the revue should have a theme-song, to be introduced at various points during the show and, it was hoped, to be widely sung afterwards in London. The refrain, which Eliot devised first, shows how much his mind was filled with the needs of the workless, the homeless, those who felt themselves excluded:

> A Church for us all and work for us all and God's world for us all even unto this last.

There are several pages of drafts for verses, all of which show the same domination:

> Dwellings for all men,
> Churches for all.
> Shall the fruit fall, then,
> By the waste wall?
> Shall the fruit fall, then,
> The harvest be waste,
> When the Saviour of all men
> Our sowing has graced?
>
> Father and mother,
> Daughter and son,
> Sister and brother,
> All shall be one
> When we raise the towers
> And at the new shrine
> In this London of ours
> Take the Bread and the Wine.

The latter verse was evidently a response (though not the one finally adopted) to a point made by Martin Shaw in a characteristically shorthand note written at the beginning of April:

30

The Rock

My dear Eliot,

A Happy Easter . . . Version first class. v. 3 one awkward musical place—last line really wants another syllable at beginning:

In this London of ours
Oh of yours and of mine

Without that syllable there is a musical hiatus . . . Could this be done? Otherwise it won't sing well. 'Ours' can't be sung like 'towers' unfortunately. So sorry.

Best wishes:

M. S.

Shall we print three verses and say 'go back to 1st. verse to end with if you want to?' I think 3 enough for singing.

The reference to printing is concerned with the publication of the song as a separate song-sheet; in the published version of *The Rock* there are altogether four verses.[1]

The first verse, as Martin Shaw suggested, was repeated not only in the song-sheet but at the end of the show, and quite a good proportion of the audience picked up his tune well enough to join the cast and singers:

Ill done and undone
London so fair
We will build London
Bright in dark air,
With new bricks and mortar
Beside the Thames bord
Queen of Island and Water,
A House of Our Lord

A Church for us all and work for us all and God's world for us all even unto this last.

The period of final rehearsals, in the theatre itself, was naturally a hectic one. With a cast of this size, the theatre dressing rooms could not possibly accommodate more than those engaged in the principal scenes. Even so, each room was used in succession by two or even three groups of players. To add to this, we had to accept the best accommodation available for the people who came into the large ensembles, a church hall about a mile away. A shuttle service of buses operated between this hall and the stage door. All this was under the control of John Trustram, a young solicitor whom Webb-Odell had introduced to me; and he made the huge machine run without a hitch.

[1] *The Rock*, pp. 19, 28, 64.

The Rock

Backstage, Judith Furse as stage manager had twenty-two scene-changes and an elaborate lighting plot. In the pit, Martin Shaw and his conductor, Dr G. F. Brockless, had Lloyds Light Orchestra augmented to about forty players, and a small choir of picked singers.

We started work in the theatre on Thursday evening, with a dress rehearsal of Part I; Part II on Friday, and a complete rehearsal on Saturday afternoon and evening. Some detailed polishing was done on Sunday (then a practice much frowned upon), and on the afternoon of the opening day I attended a matinée at another theatre.

The Rock opened its two weeks' run on 28 May 1934. A large part of its audiences had been secured, and to some extent indoctrinated, in advance; but they were substantially increased as the run progressed by the general public who read the notices. It may not be amiss to quote from some of these in order to show how much impact the play made.

The Times began its review as follows:

The theatre, that long-lost child of the English Church, made a notable reunion with its parent at Sadler's Wells last night. Mr. Eliot's pageant play looked first to liturgy for its dramatic form, though wisely imitating also the ready and popular stage modes, such as music-hall, ballet and mime . . .

The players were uneven and certain scenes overlong, but the points, aided by the music, were always made. The chorus would come between, and by their beauty of speech and variations of pace impart a new impetus . . .

Mr. Eliot . . . has created a new thing in the theatre and made smoother the path towards a contemporary poetic drama.

(29 May 1934)

The *Morning Post* agrees that 'we have had nothing quite like' this 'stupendous effort'. 'In its frank jumble of Church history' the *Daily Telegraph* finds Mr Eliot's pageant play, 'unlike his earlier poetry, pellucidly clear, but it is no less startling than *The Waste Land* in its poetry, its imaginative brilliance and its satirical force'.

In the *Spectator* Derek Verschoyle takes Mr Eliot to task because in the conflict between the Church and the World, which is the main theme, 'the case for neither of these opposed causes is conclusively stated', and requires that the poet should be dealing with the reasons for dissatisfaction with the Church, which lie 'in, for example, despair of the Church's attitude to such questions as Housing and Population'. The author replied to this critique, but of course the critic based his view on assumptions so different from Eliot's own that each hit wide of the other's real point of attack.

32

The Rock

The *New Statesman*, however, carried a notice by Francis Birrell in which the merits of the work as a contribution to the theatre are appreciated:

The magnificent verse, the crashing Hebraic choruses which Mr. Eliot has written for *The Rock* had best be studied in the book (Faber and Faber, 2s. 6d.) and obviously cannot be fully appreciated after a single hearing, admirable in every way as is the elocution at Sadler's Wells. But it is clear that these choruses, the most prolonged effort the poet has given us since *The Waste Land*, are admirably suited for dramatic delivery, and, unlike most modern poetic drama, really written to be spoken as well as read. In fact all the way through, both in the prose and verse passages, and in what the film writers would call the continuation, Mr. Eliot shows himself a greater master of theatrical technique than all our professional dramatists put together.

(2 June 1934)

This notice is excessively laudatory, as Eliot himself would have been the first to aver; but it does recognise the advent of a new and original dramatic talent. L. A. G. Strong in the *Observer* ventures to 'think that *The Rock* will be a landmark in dramatic literature'. If that is true, the mark's significance is as the first of a series of posts delimiting a territory which still remains in the unique possession of T. S. Eliot; and this territory it will be my task in following chapters to explore.

2

Murder in the Cathedral

Among the audience attending *The Rock* during the second week was George Bell. He had come to see what had evolved from the contacts made at that weekend in 1930, and to judge for himself whether he had been right in urging Eliot, when they met then and subsequently, to write for the stage. Clearly, the performance convinced him that he had been a good prophet; and soon afterwards he approached Eliot about writing a play for the Canterbury Festival of the following year, 1935.

Although he had left Canterbury in 1929, and was not to return until he retired from Chichester in 1958, the year of his death, Bell kept very closely in touch with the Friends of Canterbury Cathedral. He had founded this organisation while he was dean. Its primary purpose was to bring together those all over the world who were prepared to take an active part in assisting the Chapter to preserve the fabric of the cathedral for posterity. But from the first it was encouraged to make offerings towards the beautifying of the cathedral by presenting objects of use and decoration, and also to sponsor a festival of the performing arts within the precincts. George Bell himself had begun this work with his historic presentation of Masefield's *The Coming of Christ* in the cathedral in 1928, and this was followed by visiting productions in the two following years. He took a great part behind the scenes in building the pattern of a regular annual Festival of the Arts, held during the month of June. The first play to be specially produced for this was Tennyson's *Becket*, which was given in 1932 and 1933. For the next year, a play by Laurence Binyon called *The Young King* was already available. This also dealt with the Henry II–Becket story, but concentrating attention on the king's eldest son who was crowned to succeed Henry but died before doing so.

George Bell had set aside the proceeds of *The Coming of Christ* as a fund for the commissioning of new plays for the Festival. This, he felt, was the purpose towards which it must move if it were to play any effective part in supplying the greatest need in the collaboration of drama and the Church, the need for creative writing. The supply of existing plays of merit was very small, and not only was it necessary to extend them but to encourage each new generation of writers to see anew for itself the relationship between the life of man and his faith. So it was to this purpose that the funds available were to be dedicated; and it was the first of these commissions that Bell offered to the author of *The Rock*.

Closely associated with Bell in all this had been Laurence Irving, grandson of the great Sir Henry and a distinguished theatrical designer. He lived at Whitstable, five miles from Canterbury, and had been one of the cast of *The Coming of Christ* as well as giving much help in the task of carrying out Charles Ricketts's magnificent costume-designs which was undertaken by the Ladies of Canterbury in the deanery drawing room. Bell relied greatly on Irving's advice in the building up of the Festival, and he was the chief spokesman for it on the Council of the Friends. When the process of commissioning plays began, Laurence Irving carried out most of the negotiations, and was responsible for securing Charles Williams, Dorothy Sayers, Christopher Hassall, Christopher Fry and the others who produced the series of plays which made the Canterbury Festivals of the 1930s and 1940s unique in the world.

Eliot accepted Bell's invitation, so Irving says, on the condition that I should produce the play. He seems never to have hesitated about his choice of subject. Thomas Becket had been, as we have seen, a leading character on the Canterbury stage for the last three years, and most writers would have looked for fresh material. The commission required that the subject should relate to Canterbury, and there is no lack of interesting characters in her history. Thomas Becket, however, stands apart from all the rest. He is Canterbury's saint, and was the most popular saint of Western Europe throughout the later Middle Ages. Such a devotion as he inspired does not happen without reason; and it leaves behind it, despite the historian's clinical analysis or the unbeliever's derisive misunderstanding, a kind of aura which does not fade away. The name of Thomas of Canterbury still has power over the hearts of men. This is not only because the controversy about his motives still fascinates them, but because the centuries of devotion

35

have left a legacy, a residue of conviction that the values for which he gave his life are in essence permanent, and therefore relevant to our time as to his own:

> It is not in time that my death shall be known;
> It is out of time that my decision is taken
> If you call that decision
> To which my whole being gives entire consent.
> I give my life
> To the Law of God above the Law of Man.[1]

Thomas was Eliot's own first name; and Thomas Becket's gift of his life to 'the Law of God above the Law of Man' had been consciously and specifically made by Thomas Eliot a few years before. He had a share of the absolutism, the intransigence, of his namesake when ultimate values were concerned. Neither in belief nor in poetry would he compromise those things which he held timelessly certain; and at the moment when he was called upon to write his play, he found that the basic conflict of the twentieth century came very near to repeating that of the twelfth. *Murder in the Cathedral* shows only one of the protagonists in the historical struggle; the other is shadowy, and his shadow may suggest the fascist parallels, especially when the Knights are given colloquial twentieth-century prose in which to address the audience after the murder.

Eliot was of course acutely sensitive to the fact that his play would be staged only about fifty yards from the spot where Becket died. The martyrdom took place in the chapel of St Benedict, at the foot of the flight of stairs which leads from the north nave-aisle to the ambulatory round the choir. Becket came down these stairs to meet the Knights, and turned off into the little chapel, where he was slain before the altar. Beside the chapel is the door into the cloisters, and half-way along the eastern walk is the entrance to the chapter house, where the Festival plays were given. This sense of proximity to the actual event affected the author at least as much as the audience.

Beyond the chapel of the martyrdom stretches the huge building, most of it erected in its present form with money given by the thousands of pilgrims who had sought the shrine of the 'holy blessed martyr' Thomas. Though the shrine in which his body was housed after 1220, with its incrustation of gold and jewels, was razed to the

---

[1] Becket in *Murder in the Cathedral, Collected Plays*, p. 46.

ground by Henry VIII in 1538, the cathedral itself remains as a remembrance of the devotion to him, a mighty monument indeed. And this fact undoubtedly strengthened the author's inclination, already present, to write in a style closely allied with those of the dramas which sprang, both in Greece and in medieval Europe, from liturgy. The purpose of the play was to be the same as that of most Greek tragedies—to celebrate the cult associated with a sacred spot by displaying the story of its origin. Eliot's play about Beckct, in the precincts of Canterbury Cathedral, would not concentrate on the political conflict, still less on the personal quarrel, which led to his death; it would seek to show how and why he became 'another Saint in Canterbury'.

But this does not mean that Eliot was writing in a political vacuum, as we have seen; nor was he writing in a theatrical one. He was fully conscious of the eclectic nature of the occasion:

my play was to be produced for a rather special kind of audience—an audience of those serious people who go to 'festivals' and expect to have to put up with poetry—though perhaps on this occasion some of them were not quite prepared for what they got. And finally, it was a religious play, and people who go deliberately to a religious play expect to be patiently bored and to satisfy themselves with the feeling that they have done something meritorious.[1]

And while he had accepted George Bell's invitation—because he really wanted to see the Church and the Arts return to a closer alliance, and because this subject in that place appealed to him so much—he was also discussing with Ashley Dukes and Rupert Doone a plan for quite another kind of alliance.

Ashley Dukes was a critic and playwright of a finely civilised mind, who had much experience in the theatre as a translator of plays and had recently made his biggest success with an original comedy, *The Man with a Load of Mischief*. He had put most of the proceeds of his work, a few years before, into the purchase of a Sunday School building no longer needed by a church in Notting Hill Gate. His wife, Marie Rambert (now Dame Marie), was one of the two pioneers of the present great age of British ballet; and the building was to serve as headquarters and training school for Ballet Rambert. But it was also to house a small theatre, in which not only studio ballet performances but plays could be given. The Mercury Theatre was

[1] T S. Eliot, 'Poetry and Drama' in *On Poetry and Poets* (Faber and Faber, London, 1957), p. 79.

opened in 1932; and Dukes was immediately in pursuit of his principal objective for it—the production of poetic plays.

In 1934, *Sweeney Agonistes* had its first production, but not on the Mercury stage. The man responsible for this was Rupert Doone, one of the most intriguing personalities of the theatre of the 'thirties. He came from a Worcestershire family in humble circumstances but with a background which included a link with the Shakespeares and which accounts for his range of intellectual and artistic interests. Leaving home at sixteen he became, through many struggles and privations, a ballet dancer, and finally rose to the most coveted position in that profession—*premier danseur* in the Diaghileff company. But only for a few weeks: the great impresario died in the same year, 1929.

Doone left the ballet to enter a new field: he went to the Festival Theatre, Cambridge, where Tyrone Guthrie was working with Anmer Hall, to learn acting and production. This was typical of his endlessly questing mind; and there, as before in the ballet, he found natural friendship with the most imaginative artists of the day. From a play-reading circle at Cambridge there developed the Group Theatre.

Within a year the Group had its own rooms on the top floor of a building in Great Newport Street, between Leicester Square underground station and where the Arts Theatre now stands. Its purpose was the synthesis of all the elements of theatre—movement, mime, rhythm, speech and design—the 'total theatre' of which we have heard so much since then. Doone associated with himself such artists (then hardly known to fame) as Benjamin Britten, Brian Easdaile, John Piper, Henry Moore. The reputation of his seasons rests on the series of original plays he produced between 1934 and 1939, by such writers as W. H. Auden and Christopher Isherwood, Louis MacNeice, Stephen Spender and, to begin with, T. S. Eliot.

Sweeney Agonistes was the first play by Eliot to be produced on any stage. It was given in the Group Theatre rooms early in 1934. The production was repeated the next year when the Group had an extended season at the Westminster Theatre. Meanwhile, discussions were begun by Doone with Ashley Dukes about a season of plays by Yeats and Eliot at the Mercury. Robert Medley, Doone's designer and close friend, from whose memoir most of the above material is gratefully derived, tells me that there were many conferences during the period of *The Rock* and afterwards, and the producer and

38

manager naturally hoped that Eliot's new play, which he was already set on writing, would be part of their season. Eliot, however, was cautious, as was his wont:

25 July, 1934

Dear Mr. Doone,

I am glad to hear from you further about your plans, and sympathise with you on the point of theatrical construction. I don't see how I can definitely promise a play at any particular time. With the amount of time I have to give, there might be a full year's work in writing one play, and one can never anticipate what distractions and interruptions might not appear during that time. In any case it is extremely unlikely that I could even think of finishing it until next summer.

If I write the play I have in mind, it would require a chorus, and my recent experience warns me that choruses need long and arduous training . . .

Yours very sincerely,
T. S. Eliot

This letter was written about the time of George Bell's invitation, and 'the play I have in mind' was presumably *Murder in the Cathedral*. We all tried to accommodate each other, so that if possible both projects could be fulfilled. There was a notion that at Canterbury, where the Festival itself could only supply amateur players, the Group Theatre production might be created under my direction and afterwards be re-cast and brought to the Mercury. Doone got a first draft of portions of the play in prose, and Medley says that Doone urged Eliot to use verse: as we shall see, he exercised an important influence on another aspect of the play's development.

The scheme, in its first form, came to nothing. Yeats was inaccessible and difficult; there was not sufficient assurance of support (no Arts Council to turn to in those days!); and Doone became involved in the Group's season at the Westminster:

20 March, 1935

My dear Doone,

I am very sorry to get your letter of the 18th, and to know that after you have taken so much time and trouble over this business, you feel obliged to retire. Obviously it is impossible for any one man to produce five plays in the time at your disposal. I am afraid that the whole thing has been badly muddled. Whether the issue would have been more successful had Yeats been able to be in London I do not know. And also, unless there was someone behind such a scheme with the time and the influence to get adequate support it would come to nothing. This end of it was obviously not your business and I don't consider that it was mine.

39

I'm sorriest on account of Auden, and I hope that you will be able to make arrangements with the Westminster Theatre to give him a show in the autumn. As for myself, I want to assure you that I have found your criticisms very valuable, and but for this abortive undertaking I should not have had the benefit of them.

Yours ever,

T. S. Eliot

Doone did in fact put on two plays of Auden at the Westminster; and Eliot's play did find its way, by a different route, to the Mercury.

I have no copy of the first draft which reached me: it is seldom, unfortunately, that one is not obliged to return such a document with one's observations on it, and Eliot often did not make a carbon copy of his first typescript. But the Houghton Library, Harvard, contains a number of pages of manuscript notes which, though they are not dated, serve to show something of the way in which Eliot's mind moved towards the form of the play.

'It would require a chorus': and the notes begin with a draft of the opening ode. What follows confirms the impression left by this, that the play is to be cast in a formal mould like that of Greek tragedy. The notes begin with the second paragraph of the ode as we know it; they represent the working out of thematic material, leaving the means of getting the actresses on to the stage to be provided later:

> When golden October declines into darkened November
> The apples are gathered, the fields are stripped, and the New Year waits in darkness
> When the labourer scrapes off a muddy boot and stretch[1] out his hand to the fire
> And the New Year waits, destiny waits for the coming
> Who shall stretch out his hand to the fire of All Hallows
> And remember the Saints who wait, and who shall
> Stretch out his hand to the fire, and deny his master?
>
> Seven years and summer is over
> Seven years and the cord stretched tight
> Kings rule and barons rule
> Why should the spring bring consolation
> For autumn fires and winter fogs
> What shall we do in the heat of summer
> But wait at the gate for another October.

[1] *Sic.*

What shall the slain gain
   Between the temple and the altar
   Ghosts wait
      without the gate
   The people wait
      The sheep unfed
   Rumours are bred. Shadows delate
   Those who move between the missal and the psalter.
Come happy December, who shall observe you who shall observe you
Who shall declare you. Shall
The son of man be born again in the litter of scorn
While the poor wait
           outside the gate
And the lord lies drunk in the hall
And the king confers with advisers of State

This draft sets the pattern for the use throughout the play of the cycle of seasons, and for the relation of the Church's year to the natural year. The verse form for the longer, flowing lines, too, has established itself in the poet's ear; but that for the shorter lines is to undergo alteration.

The next page is the Priest's speech which leads to the entrance of the Herald:

I see nothing quite conclusive / no abiding over in the art of temporal government
Kings rule and barons rule
The strong man strongly and the weak man by caprice.
They have but one law, to seize the power and keep it
And the strong can manipulate the greed and passions of others
And the weak are devoured by their own.

Servant (Herald) announces arrival of Thomas to Priest.
Priest expresses jubilation. Servant recounts forebodings of Thomas.

    Chorus of women 'here is no continuing city'.

S. Thos. arrives. Discourses with Priest.

    Discusses Church and State with Chorus.

     Chorus: Christ conquers.
    Becket: never conquest, only unending battle.
       Talk with Herbert and John

This is all the material which represents Part I of the play in these first notes.

It will be noticed that there appear two historical characters,

41

Herbert of Bosham and John, Dean of Salisbury. In the finished play, the latter is referred to in Thomas's speech directly after his arrival, but Herbert has not even a mention. They were Thomas's closest friends and advisers; and it would be natural for Eliot to seize upon them as the interlocutors whom he would need to make dramatic dialogue. They have clearly been sacrificed to the formal pattern. In the printed cast list, no characters are given names: even the Knights who kill Becket and whose names are well known are listed as First, Second, Third and Fourth. This is the terminus of the process by which history, though its sources are treated with the most careful respect, is subjected to theme; the human action is subordinated to the divine, the action in time to the timeless movement of God's will.

But within this movement, within this formality, there is room for acute characterisation of the unnamed individuals. The three Priests are clearly differentiated: the First is shrewd and worldly-wise but a coward and a child in spiritual things; the Second is strong, positive, managing, but without the spiritual perception of the Third, who being detached from worldly things can be open to the wind of prophecy. The Herald, a 'know-all' who delights in telling a story or still more a confidential 'spicy bit', is a clearly-cut cameo; and the Knights are highly individual once they relax their military formation.

In the notes, practically none of the background history is told or provided for. When the Priests' scene came to be written up, some was worked in there; but there remained a very large problem, as I remember from the time when a draft (which was in verse) reached me. It was complete, practically as printed, up to the end of the scene of Thomas's arrival on 2 December 1170. But since the rest of the play (already planned, as we shall see) concerns Christmas Day and the day of the murder (29 December), how is it to show Thomas achieving the state of mind indicated by the sermon on Christmas Day, and how in the process is the necessary historical detail to be introduced?

This was the author's question to me: and my answer was in terms of the same kind of historical writing which would have been involved in the use of Herbert of Bosham and John of Salisbury. Between 2 December and Christmas Day, I suggested, it was possible, even likely, that persons who wished to influence his behaviour in various directions should have visited Thomas.

42

Among these could have been a crony of his gay youth, a fellow-politician bent on persuading him back into the chancellorship as Henry's ally, and a baron who, seeing that he had quarrelled with the king, always the principal enemy of the baronage, hoped to talk him into throwing in his lot with them. These visitors would have enough with which to work on Becket's mind, while in the process conveying to the audience the history of the conflict between Church and State.

Eliot liked this idea well enough to draft the series of scenes. I cannot now trace a copy of this draft: but I know that he and I agreed when we read it over that however effective it might be in itself, it did not suit the style of the play. At this point, Rupert Doone, who also saw the draft, provided the solution. Let the visitors appear, not as figments of the author's imagination but of Thomas's: as Tempters embodying the conflicts in his own mind.

This accorded both with the formal pattern and with the need to focus the action on Thomas's spiritual struggle. Eliot rewrote the scenes in this way; and gained from it the chance to create the Fourth Tempter, in whose scene the play advances into a new territory. This is by far the most dramatic of the temptations, since the battle here is not, like the others, already in the past but is raging in Becket's soul as the death he has foreseen draws nearer: it is the conflict of motive. He has no doubt that he must stand firm for his beliefs even unto death: but why does he run upon that death? Is it for post-humous glory in the eyes of men? Is it for the eternal glory of heaven? Is it for the humiliation of his enemies on earth? Or for their condemnation to hell?

This scene enables Eliot to bring into his drama the whole future of Becket's cult, and to cast an ironic glance upon subsequent treatments of the history in which his motives were accorded scant respect. Becket is tempted to follow the path which these historians affirm that he took: to 'do the right deed for the wrong reason'. Thus the scene gives a forward perspective to the play.

It also provides the climax of Becket's personal agony. The Tempter in his final thrust turns back upon Becket the very words he himself has used on his arrival, transmuting the idea of human action as a revolution round the still centre where God dwells into the treadmill of a meaningless existence. After this, Becket is silent for some five minutes; Chorus, Tempters and Priests from their several points of view combine to present images of despair; at last it is the earnest, impassioned plea of the Women:

Thomas Archbishop, save us, save us, save yourself that we may be saved

that penetrates his heart and enables him to gain freedom.

What does Eliot mean by this moment? There are no words in Becket's mouth as the Tempters retire. On the stage, he has in some way to banish them; but the author, when I asked him how complete was the victory over the Fourth Tempter, reminded me that none of us can attain final victory while we live. Becket is still saying, on the day of his death:

I have only to make perfect my will.

So the banishment of the Tempters, however dramatically final it appears at the moment, is only *for* the moment; and the speech in which he recapitulates the experiences of his life in the light of the crisis through which he has just passed, finishes with a prayer for protection. The notes in the Houghton Library, as we have seen, end this part of the play with the words:

never conquest, only unending battle.

At this point we can turn to some later pages in the notes wherein the Tempters' scenes are sketched, presumably for the first time. They begin with a few lines which reflect the mood of the First Tempter, but which Eliot's brother, Henry, who began the Houghton Library collection of his work, observes 'are not in any edition of *Murder in the Cathedral*, but are partly identical with lines of the unfinished MS, *Bellegarde*':

Leaping pleasures pass tunefully
Follow futility greedily/easily grasped
Held in the hand matchless a moment
Fade fast impaired by impotence
Slip from fingers slip
When fingered.

The gaiety suggested in the first three lines may have set the mood for the First Tempter's scene, of which there is yet no trace, but which Eliot worked up into vivid nostalgia for 'the springtime fancy'. Without break, however, the MS passes on to some lines which

44

remain in the final text for the Second Tempter, who tries to attract
Thomas back to secular preeminence:

Power possessed grows to glory
lasting\a life a permanent possession
Rule over men reckon no madness
To the man of God what gladness?
　　　　　　Sadness
Only to those giving love to God alone
Fare forward between two files of shadows[1]
Mirth and merrymaking, strength & sweetness[1]
Fiddling to feebleness, doomed to disdain[1]
And Godlovers' longings, lost in God[1]
Shall he who held the solid substance
Wander waking
Sleep supinely　　in shallow shadows.
Power is present. Holiness hereafter.

Who then?

　　　The Chancellor.
　　　　　　King and Chancellor
King commands, Chancellor rules.
This is a sentence not taught in the Schools
To set down the great, protect the poor
Beneath the throne of God can man do more
Disarm the ruffian, strengthen the laws
Rule for the good of the better cause
Dispense justice, make all even
Is thrive on earth, and perhaps in heaven.

What means?

　　　Real power
Is purchased at price of certain submission
Your spiritual power is earthly perdition.

No!

　　Yes. Bravery will be broken
Cabined in Canterbury, realmless ruler
Self bound servant of a powerless pope

[1] These four lines were printed in the first edition but subsequently cut, since the author
agreed with me in finding them over-obscure. The rest of the material, with very slight
modifications, still stands.

No!

Men must manoeuvre. Monarchs also,
Waging wars abroad, need fast friends at home.
Private policy is public profit
Dignity may always be saved.

You forget the bishops
Whom I have laid under excommunication

That shall be saved. For public pardon

Obviously the quarrel with Henry was one of the matters which it was most essential to treat, and no doubt Eliot bent his mind to this before other aspects of the history. Indeed, the Third Tempter's scene about the barons does not appear in the notes at all. But there is a synopsis of the Fourth:

1. Deceitfulness of previous offers.
    King and barons will always hate him and betray him.
2. Glory of spiritual power on earth.
3. (a) Glory on earth after death.
    (b) Other side—shrine desecrated and looted.
                        Historians. Poets.
4. Glory in heaven. Sainthood.
                Thomas turns on him
                    who are you?
NO! Will not resign one pride to cherish another.
                What is to be done?
                Conformity to will of God.

Reverting to the headings quoted on page 41, we next find the words:

Xmas eve. Preaches.

The sermon was an integral part of the original plan of the play, as it was of the historical story. It had been conceived as happening at the Midnight Mass, and the words 'It was in this same night' were to stand without the addition of 'which has just passed'. But the record shows that Becket in fact preached at the morning Mass on Christmas Day, and Eliot acceded to this. The last few sentences were reproduced from the eyewitness accounts, but the rest was the author's own; he took the opportunity of allowing Thomas to expound in this way the nature of the peace to which he had attained through the temptations, and his surrender to the will of God in respect of the

46

martyrdom which he believed to be near. This sermon has always been the best-remembered scene of the play, the one which comes instantly to the mind of almost everyone who thinks of it. Partly perhaps this is because the diction of its straightforward and beautifully cadenced prose is simpler than any of the verse; but mainly because the author was exactly right in calculating that when the hero reveals his heart in saying farewell to his people he will win the maximum response.

After the indication of the sermon, the notes go on as follows:

Dismisses Herbert of Bosham
Warnings of end
Chorus
    Goes out
Enter 4 Knights

The next page gives a timetable. This is something which Eliot always found helpful, however far he decided later to depart from it. He remodelled this play so much that the timetable became obsolete, but certain points in it are still of interest. It begins after the opening chorus, which had already been sketched in some detail:

Priests talk	5 min.
Servant and Priests	10
Chorus	5
S.T. Priests & Chorus	15
Sermon	5
Dismisses Herbert	10
Warnings	15
Chorus	10
Knights	10
Chorus	5

The calculation was probably made at a very early stage. When he undertook to write 'the words' (as he says) for *The Rock*, Eliot asked me at once for as exact a timetable as I could give him. Here he is presumably working to the limit of one and a half hours for the play which was laid down at Canterbury. These figures add up to ninety minutes, with only the first chorus omitted.

They do not allow for the Visitors, whether men or tempters, in Part I; but they give a lot of time to two scenes which have disappeared from the final text. Ten minutes for the dismissal of Herbert of Bosham means that that friend was to play a crucial role in the play; and fifteen minutes for 'Warnings' ('of end', we remember from the previous page) indicates an extended passage of whose character we have no evidence. It does not correspond to the scene of the Priests with the banners which appears in the first edition; this was worked out later, as we shall see. Indeed, the fact that there is a total of twenty-five minutes of playing time between the end of the sermon and the entrance of the Knights may mean that Visitors of some kind were to appear at this point. During the three and a half weeks between Becket's return to Canterbury and his assassination the air was, according to eyewitnesses, full of prophecies of doom, to which only Becket himself paid no attention. Some of these may well have been included in the first conception. And they were to be followed by a chorus to lead up to the Knights' entry.

This chorus was drafted at an early stage. Then I was faced with the demand that there should be no interval in the Canterbury performance, and was doubtful whether the chorus would stand well immediately after the sermon or would make the passage of time sufficiently clear. I therefore suggested the alternative, that a scene should be created for the Priests, using the liturgical days of the calendar which fall between Christmas and 29 December:

26th: Saint Stephen, the first martyr
27th: Saint John the Evangelist and supposed author of the Revelation
28th: The Holy Innocents massacred at Bethlehem by Herod's order

This could provide a clear indication of the passage of time, and also an opportunity, by indicating the aspect of sainthood illustrated by each feast, to place Thomas in the calendar of saints. The Introit, the scriptural passage which begins the Mass for each of the days, would provide the springboard for its scene.

Eliot adopted the plan, but added a brilliant stroke. He brought the ritual succession of days suddenly to immediate life by making the Priests begin, for the 29th (a 'ferial' day with no saint to celebrate), the Introit *Gaudeamus*. This is the Proper of a Saint. They sing the opening phrase without premeditation, and then question each other as if to say 'What made us do that?' It is the Third Priest, the one with prophetic insight, who reminds his fellows that

> Every day is the day we should fear from or hope from . . .
>   The critical moment
> That is always now and here.

And indeed, it is so much 'now and here' that his speech signals the entrance of the murderers.

This sequence was used at Canterbury; but when the play was to move to a theatre, where there would be an interval, I felt that it would be better to open Part II with a chorus as originally planned. I wrote to the author in early October 1935, asking if it were possible that the chorus which he had drafted earlier could be finished for use at the Mercury Theatre. He replied (9 October):

> I am afraid that you are right about the opening of Act II. I will send you a copy of the chorus which I wrote and suppressed, but I am not sure that you will think it suitable. I am perfectly ready to write a new one, but the time is very short for rehearsals anyway.

There was certainly no need for a new one: that chorus

> Does the bird sing in the south?

is one of the most beautiful lyric passages in the play, and admirably fulfils its dramatic function, providing a parallel both to the nature-cycle and to the waiting tension of the opening.

'Enter 4 Knights' reads the next note; and under it '(Have Knights in twice?)'.

Following this question up, Eliot made a careful study of the voluminous contemporary records of Thomas's confrontations with the Knights, and followed the eyewitness accounts in making the Knights leave after the first acrimonious scene to fetch their arms. None of the material he finally used is indicated in these notes; there is only a page containing a series of thoughts which finally came to be used in several different parts of the play:

> p. 2. Th. declares that any State which puts
> law of man before law of God is
> working its own ruin.
> I am no traitor to the King, or enemy of the State,
> The King is his own enemy, the State the State's.
> The Kingdom of God is greater than the Kingdom of Man
> The Law of God above the law of Man.
> And those who put their faith only in worldly order
> Are stabilising chaos, perpetuate disorder
> ~~Degrading the country which they~~
> Degrading what they serve ~~say they serve.~~

These passages show that the idea developed in the Second Tempter was from the first allied to that expressed in the scene before the murder beginning 'Bar the door'. In the final text, the lines

Those who put their faith in worldly order etc.

appear in Thomas's reflective speech after he has rejected the Second Tempter.[1] 'The Law of God above the law of Man' is that to which he 'gives his life' by ordering the Priests to 'open the door'.[2] The words 'No traitor to the King' occur in the last defiance of the Knights before the altar of his martyrdom.[3] So these may be regarded as seminal thoughts, which ran through the author's mind as he elaborated from his sketch.

The next page contains, in their final form, two of the three verses of the Knights' drunken song as they enter the cathedral.

Are you washed in the Blood of the Lamb?
Are you marked with the mark of the Beast?
Come down Daniel to the lions den
Come down Daniel and join in the feast.

Where is Becket the Cheapside brat
Where is Becket the faithless priest
Come down Daniel to the lions den
Come down Daniel and join in the feast.

This is obviously related to Vachel Lindsay's 'Daniel Jazz', which was widely current in the 'twenties and perhaps may be reckoned the precursor of a movement towards religious jazz-poetry which has flourished since the Second World War. *Sweeney Agonistes* shows that Eliot was attracted by this medium and it is surprising that he did not develop it further.

There is next a snatch from the final dialogue with Reginald FitzUrse:

Traitor to me as my faithless vassal,
Traitor to me as your spiritual lord,
Traitor to God in desecrating His Church.
        Kn.   renegade
No faith do I owe to a ~~traitor to the King~~
And what I owe shall now be paid.
        Th.
Now
    To Almighty God, to the blessed Mary ever Virgin,

[1] *Collected Plays*, p. 22.   [2] *Ibid.*, pp. 45–6.   [3] *Ibid.*, p. 46.

to the blessed John the Bptist to the holy apos.
P & P to the blessed martyr Denis and to all the
saints I commend my cause and that of the Church.

This final prayer is conflated from the original authorities.
There follows the first sketch for one of the most powerful passages given to the Chorus:[1]

Clear the air! clear the sky! wash the wind! take stone from stone and wash them
The land is foul, the water is foul, our beasts and ourselves are defiled.

Can I ever return—
Can I again look at the day & its common things, shall I
see them all smeared in blood, through a curtain of falling blood—

I cling to these things, these common habits—
Nothing remains substantial—

The terror by day that ends in sleep
The terror by night that ends in daily action
But the talk in the marketplace, the hand on the broom,
The nighttime heaping of the ashes,
        new log
The ~~morning~~ for the fire at dawn,
Every horror had its definition
Every sorrow had its end
In life there is not time to grieve long.

These things made limit to our suffering† . . .

But this, this is out of life, this is out of time
An instant eternity of evil and wrong.

The process of revision and expansion can be seen here in a very interesting way. There are the flashes of inspiration such as '*clean*' for 'clear' the sky. There is the development backwards into the preceding passage of an image which has suggested itself at a later point; the *blood* which stands here only in the frighteningly visual metaphor of the 'curtain of falling blood', is later introduced repeatedly during the preceding lines.

[1] For the final version, see *Collected Plays*, pp. 47–8.
† An arrow in manuscript indicates that this line should be transferred to stand after
        The new log for the fire at dawn

Another development has been suggested by the phrase (itself afterwards omitted):

> These common habits

Some of these 'habits' were established in our minds during the second chorus of Part I. Now they are repeated as counterpoint to the tragic climax. The sense that of these common things 'nothing remains substantial' is given in the final version by the simple repetition of the opening line. Before Thomas's return it was

> We do not wish anything to happen.[1]

Now, after his death, it is:

> We did not wish anything to happen.[1]

The final section of this chorus has not yet been thought of; but the fact that the Knights' *apologia* is to follow has already been established; for on the next page we have its synopsis:

1st Chairman: We wish to put our case to you. Not a speaker myself. Introduces.
2d. Your prejudices have been in favour of Archbp. King's aims. Good Erastian views.
     What would *you* say to an Achbp.
     Try to put yourselves in our place.
3d. The young one. Apologises for being tipsy on entrance, & noisy. Unpleasant business. We get nothing out of this.
4th. Who killed the Achbp.

In the event, no. 3 was put before no. 2; this was an improvement, since his lighter touch and ingratiating manner, with his collection of English-country-gentleman's clichés, served to accustom the audience to the transition from the high and dignified emotion of the ritual murder to the direct attack and conversational tone of the apology. It was necessary, when the audience had received the sharp shock of this change, to allow it to re-adjust its mind before the Second Knight could have a fair chance of convincing it by his carefully reasoned argument for the Erastian view. For, as David Jones[2] has cogently said, this scene is 'the temptation of the audience', through which it must pass before it can share the final celebration of the martyrdom;

---

[1] *Collected Plays*, pp. 15, 47.
[2] *The Plays of T. S. Eliot* (Routledge and Kegan Paul, London, 1960), p. 61.

and to make of this a true testing, the arguments of the tempters must be allowed their proper opportunity.

The Third Knight is described as 'the young one'; and this idea of him is perpetuated in the earlier editions of the play in the Chairman's words:

> I shall call upon our youngest member to speak first

and was carried out in the Canterbury production. But when I cast the play for London later in 1935, I came upon an older actor, Norman Chidgey, who seemed to have exactly the right qualities for the part, and who particularly could give to the Third Tempter (doubled, as we shall see later, with the Knight) the kind of rough authority which he needs. Eliot allowed the line to be revised: 'our eldest member'; and incorporated this alteration in the later editions. But it is still open to producers, if they have the right young actor, to revert to Eliot's original picture of the young squire who cannot take his liquor.

There have been critics, and members of many audiences, who have found this scene an excrescence upon the play. The notes show that it was an integral part of the original plan; and it clearly parallels the Temptations in matter and the Sermon as a prose passage of direct address. Eliot himself says that it 'is a kind of trick . . . I may, for aught I know, have been slightly under the influence of *Saint Joan*'.[1] But this does not make it an excrescence, any more than is Shaw's Epilogue (which was also criticised as such). Its immediate purpose, as Eliot says, was 'to shock the audience out of their complacency'; but once that has been achieved, it has the effect of a real temptation; many are the spectators who have found themselves agreeing with the Knights' propositions, since they accord far more with the presuppositions on which our society is based than do those to which the Chorus assent in the last scene.

The Chairman's exit-speech is not suggested in the notes, nor the Priests' prophetic apostrophe to the departing Knights, embodying the legends of their future. The last page is a summary of the final chorus:

1. Adoration of God.
2. Thanksgiving for his mercies. The blood of the saints shall enrich the earth. The creation of holy places.

[1] T. S. Eliot, 'Poetry and Drama', in *On Poetry and Poets*, p. 81.

3. We acknowledge our transgressions our responsibility for all the evil in
                                       martyrs
the world . . . for the blood of ~~saints~~ shed.
4. Lord have mercy upon us, & Thomas pray for us.

In the development of the first heading, Eliot rounded off the
pattern begun in the opening chorus, the pattern in which the cycle of
the natural year was seen as integrated with that of the spiritual.
There, the Chorus feared its interruption by cataclysmic happenings; here, the natural order is re-established as the spiritual purpose
of the action has been achieved, and 'the voices of seasons' can offer
praise to their Maker through the 'scrubbers and sweepers of Canterbury' who are their mouthpieces.

Then the Chorus turn to the specific grounds for thankfulness
deriving from the action itself; it has enriched the earth by adding to
the holy places where 'the intersection of the timeless with time' can be
celebrated, where the earth is for ever renewed by the blessing of God.

But that very blessing is the thing which, in their inmost hearts, men
fear most. The final paragraph of the chorus seems originally to have
been an acknowledgement of 'responsibility for all the evil in the
world'; but as the play developed this aspect of common responsibility
was already made clear in the earlier choruses where the women
accept not only responsibility for but identification with the evil that
has brought about the murder:

> I have consented, Lord Archbishop, have consented . . .
> We are soiled by a filth that we cannot clean, united to supernatural
>   vermin . . .

So the final paragraph eventually takes the thought further: speaking
not only for themselves who have been involved in this particular
crime but, clearly, for the audience as well, they acknowledge
themselves as

>   type of the common man,
> Of the men and women who shut the door and sit by the fire;
> Who fear the blessing of God

and would rather face the worst that men can do than the terrible
challenge of the love of God. It is on this account that we all need the
mercy of God, and especially the prayers of those who have met the
challenge, as has the new saint, Thomas of Canterbury.

At the time when these notes were written, the play was provi-

54

sionally titled *Fear in the Way*. I realised that this phrase, taken from the same chapter of Ecclesiastes which supplied the images used by the Third Priest in the opening scene, was relevant both to Becket's temptations and to the experience through which the Chorus had to pass; but as a play-title I did not feel it to be attractive. If the play were to have any future beyond its week at Canterbury, this title would not bring the public in. Eliot himself did not feel at all certain about it and was open to other suggestions.

Just before Christmas 1934, he came for a weekend to our home at Rottingdean, Sussex. This visit had been postponed several times, but the final moment was fortunate, since it coincided with two productions in the neighbourhood. On the Saturday afternoon we went to Eastbourne to see a play by Mona Swann, one of the principal exponents of the art of Choral Speech, who at her school, Moira House, had evolved a method of making plays from the words of the King James version of the Bible, using the Psalms as a medium of community expression. On the Sunday evening we ourselves staged a 'triple bill' in the village church, two of the items being the Annunciation from the Lincoln Cycle of Mystery Plays and Richard Aldington's translation of the Liège Nativity.

All this was a help to a young couple entertaining a very silent guest. Eliot was never a talkative man, and he was at that time passing through one of the most painful periods of his personal life. Of such things he hardly spoke to his most intimate friends, and no indication of his distress reached us. But conversation did not flow easily, and we were aware of his weariness. I remember that during our dress rehearsal in the afternoon of Sunday I asked my wife to go with another member of the cast to fetch a property which had been left behind in a cupboard in our living room. She opened the door, and saw in an armchair our guest, fast asleep. They took off their shoes, crept past on their hands and knees, recovered the missing object, and crept out again without waking him.

The performance over, we sat down to supper during which conversation moved freely from the plays he had seen at the weekend (the medieval ones, he thought, were the best) to the play he was working on. My wife (Henzie Raeburn) had by now become a friend whose theatrical knowledge and intuition Eliot valued; and it may well have been at this time that she offered the title, *Murder in the Cathedral*. He had always wanted the ritual aspect of the play to be balanced by the homicidal; he was a devotee of Sherlock Holmes; and this title, with its sardonic implications, had a contemporary quality which would induce in an audience an attitude favourable to the acceptance of the ironies, particularly in the Knights' apology, as a natural part of the play. After that due consideration which was always given to any suggestion, this one was gratefully accepted. The title was a 'selling' one; and if it proved deceptive to some who came to see, as they expected, a thriller, the great reputation which the play gained soon made its true nature known. I am sure that its author never regretted the choice.

Early in the New Year my wife and I went to York, where I was to direct the first season of repertory under the new civic management at the Theatre Royal. It is not until after we left York that the diary of that year records, on 24 March, 'read Eliot's play Part One'. From then on, there were frequent meetings until rehearsals started at Canterbury on 7 May.

The Festival plays were produced in the chapter house. Bell's experiment with *The Coming of Christ* had proved that spoken drama in the cathedral nave was acoustically impossible; Masefield and Holst had relied on musical items for their main effects, and those passages which were spoken had not been effective. So, after a couple of productions in the open outside the West Front, the plays had been moved into the chapter house.

This is a rectangular building of the early fourteenth century, with arcading round the walls to provide a range of raised stalls for the monks and, on the east wall, more imposing ones, raised higher, for the prior and other officers. At the end of the century, the walls were heightened and the roof given a barrel vault of Irish bog oak. The resulting building is a fine one, but the height makes it over-resonant, and it was of course not planned for dramatic performances.

The simplest possible provision had been made for such events by installing a platform the full width of the building (thirty-six feet) at the east end. But to increase seating space it had been made only nine feet deep. These are not good dimensions for a stage; not only is there very little scope for movement from front to back, but it is difficult for actors to pass each other when many are on stage and they need to move from side to side.

The only door to the building was at the back of the auditorium, ninety feet from the stage. This meant that all entrances and exits must be made through the narrow central aisle between the seats, unless any actors were concealed on stage before the door was opened for the arrival of the spectators. (In the following year, the headmaster of the King's School, who was also a canon, persuaded the chapter to cut a doorway through the north wall on to the stage so that he could use the building for school performances, and the Festival thereafter benefited from this.)

Laurence Irving had designed a permanent stage setting consisting of screens seven feet high, matched with the arcading in construction and painted to reproduce the Victorian colours on the old stone. These screens provided small 'wings' where actors could wait between scenes. I added, for this play, a double flight of steps in front and two platforms at the side front of the stage, slightly higher than the main area, in the shape of quarter circles. On these, the Chorus had to spend the entire play save for the few moments when they could intrude upon the action in the centre.

I remember complaining to the author that, since I had no egress for any of them, the number of persons on stage during the Temptations was an embarrassment. Beginning with a Chorus of eleven, he had added three Priests, Becket and four Tempters, and for twenty minutes, while the latter's duologues went on, all the other characters had to 'freeze' in full view. It was indeed a strain for the actors; but for the ritual pattern of the play it was justified. I had the Tempters enter in a body through the audience and stand at the foot of the steps, each going up in turn to confront Becket, then retiring into one of the niches of the arcading backstage and holding his menacing position until at the end of the act all four together advanced from behind upon Becket. When he banished them, they had to make as swiftly as possible the long exit through the audience.

I had an additional reason for this exit. I wanted to 'double' the parts of the Tempters with those of the four Knights. I had to find amateur actors in Canterbury to play most of these parts, and to use a few good ones was much more satisfactory than to dilute the quality by increasing the number. Later, when I was looking for a professional cast, the same thing held true: it is easier to get a good actor to play a part which appears in both acts than a part which is confined to one.

But there was a reason more important than this of convenience. I believed, and still believe, that this doubling helps the audience to grasp one of the main theses of the play by showing a parallel between the force that Becket is fighting within himself and the antagonists from without. If the Knights' apology is 'the temptation of the audience', the point that emerges from this doubling is that the false values offered to Becket and to the audience, in the twelfth century and in the twentieth, are the same. I retained this practice when I did the play with a professional cast, and the author concurred. It was only much later that he became doubtful about it. The matter has been much discussed, and so it may be of interest to set against one another his two statements on it. In the prefatory notes to the edition of 1937:

When, as was originally intended, the parts of the Tempters are doubled with those of the Knights . . .

and in a letter to me on 20 September 1956:

I am by no means now sure that it is not better to have the knights played by different actors from the tempters. I like to leave questions for the audience to resolve for themselves, and one question which is left for them if the knights and tempters are different actors, is whether the fourth tempter is an evil angel or possibly a good angel. After all, the fourth tempter is gradually leading Becket on to his sudden resolution and simplification of his difficulties.

By this time, he had himself played the voice of the Fourth Tempter in the film; and perhaps this had influenced his thinking. But it was in any case always true that he liked 'to leave questions for the audience to resolve for themselves'.

The Friends of the Cathedral were governed by a council of people eminent in the district or in the various fields which their activities covered from time to time; but the real work and the real power lay in the hands of Margaret Babington. This remarkable woman had been chosen by George Bell as steward and treasurer of the Friends when he founded them. She was the daughter of a retired clergyman living in the Precincts, and had had a long experience of upholding her eccentric widower-father in the care of a large country-town parish. She was tall, trim and dignified, with a tremendous dynamic energy, but also with a keen sense of humour and the voice of a young girl. Throwing herself with unsparing dedication into the service of the cathedral, she had gathered 1430 Friends within a year, and 4000 by the time of *Murder in the Cathedral*.

George Bell had enjoined upon her and upon his successor, when he was called to the see of Chichester in 1929, that the Friends should adopt as part of their responsibility the Festival of Music and Drama. Miss Babington had gone about this with as much vigour as she showed in the running of the Friends, and had built it up into a very full week's programme of first-class events, with the 'Friends' Day' on the final Saturday as its climax. There were orchestral and choral concerts with the collaboration of Sir Adrian Boult and the B.B.C. Orchestra, serenades in the cloisters, lectures in the chapter house by distinguished speakers, and a day for Youth. On each day, the play, which was the centrepiece, received one or two performances.

All this work was done as an offering to the cathedral in the spirit of the Friends. Much of it was purely voluntary, and where fees were paid they were nominal. Canterbury residents offered hospitality to the artists; and many friendships were formed in these years which survived into times when such generosity was no longer possible. The Festival of the 'thirties was perhaps a product of its decade which could not survive the war; but its effect on the theatre, especially in its relationship with the Church, has outlasted its time.

The amateurs of the cast were to be selected by me from those who were willing to give the evenings to rehearsal during the weeks of April, May and early June. Some were members of local societies, some were in various ways connected with the cathedral or the King's and St Edmund's Schools. Before making my selection, I read the play to all who had applied.

This was in a hotel room, early in April. It is an occasion which I remember very well. Miss Babington introduced me to the company, and I talked a little about the author's approach to the subject, then read them the passages which would concern them, giving enough cue to convey an impression of the mood when they entered the action. I came to the end of the tremendous chorus which accompanies the murder:

> Clear the air! clean the sky! wash the wind! take the stone
> from the stone, take the skin from the arm, take the muscle
> from the bone, and wash them. Wash the stone, wash the bone,
> wash the brain, wash the soul, wash them, wash them!

FIRST KNIGHT We beg you to give us your attention for a few moments . . .

A gasp went round the room. The shock had worked as the author intended, this first time, as it was to work on so many audiences thereafter. It is always difficult to recollect, when an effect has become familiar, how startling it was at first impact; so I am glad to be able to look back to that evening in Canterbury—as well as the early performances—and realise how powerful it was. The shock is greater than that of the Epilogue in *St Joan*: for one thing, Shaw had accustomed us to expect such tactics from him, and for another, *Murder in the Cathedral* is up to this point written in a vein of high religious poetry and for production in circumstances approximating to those of a church service. No curtain falls between the moment of tragic climax and the colloquial argument, so that the sudden descent makes the maximum impact.

A parenthesis may be in order here, to record what Eliot told me years later. He had given the scene a strongly comic effect by the use of cliché, and we had reinforced this, as I have said, by putting the Third Knight's speech at the beginning. When the play was given in Paris, Henri Fluchère naturally gave a faithful rendering in his translation of the English expressions, which to the French audience had no comic overtones. The scene became entirely serious, and, Eliot found, very frightening. Perhaps the shadow from across the eastward border of France fell more menacingly than it had in England. At any rate, this made a strong impression on the author; and I think that however much English audiences laugh at the scene, it is well that this kind of menace should underlie its performance.

I gave seven weeks altogether to rehearsals. At that time, I had no other work, and we had to live carefully. We rented a tiny bungalow from a school-teacher who was on leave. It was called 'Geralda', and was situated in a dreary seaside town called Tankerton, some five miles from Canterbury. Rehearsals with the amateurs started on 8 May and pursued a slow and not very exhilarating course, until on 30 May Robert Speaight arrived.

He has himself written more than once about the part of Becket and his experience in playing it, and his performance won such fame that there is no need for me to enlarge upon it. We had known each other since 1917, and although he could hardly have been more unsuited physically to the role—he was 31 and Becket was 56, he was of middle height and Becket was six feet four—I knew that he had those things which matter so much more than the physical; a deep sympathy with Eliot's writing and point of view, an understanding of the nature of Becket's experience, and an outstanding ability to speak dramatic verse. When we began to rehearse the part, the process was an exploration, shared also with my wife who took a number of rehearsals for me when I fell ill, of a character whose reactions we had to discover. For, as Speaight has written, 'I asked myself... how the positive character of Becket could be reconciled with so passive a protagonist?' We had to find out together that 'the initiatives were the initiatives of grace'.[1]

This approach to a chief character was to repeat itself in Eliot's work. We have seen that there is a problem for the actor in the climax of the temptation scene, and how little Becket has to say in the whole first Part. The sermon gives him the opportunity to reveal himself. We worked hard to achieve the balance between the many sides of the picture. Becket is no parish priest. He has been a great man of and in the world, the most successful of administrators and politicians, the most brilliant of ambassadors. As archbishop, he has transferred this power of personality to the service of the Church, and he has not lost it, but has added a new dimension to it, in the six years of exile, under the discipline of hard living and hard praying in an austere monastery. And during the first part of the play, since his return to Canterbury, he has been through a spiritual crisis, and been saved from its dangers by grace. The peace thus gained is to be described to his beloved people in simple words, but not by a simple man. The discoveries we made here were the foundation for the whole performance.

Frank Napier, a professional actor who was to become a leading figure in the Canterbury Festivals, came to play the Second Tempter and Knight, and I myself played the Fourth Tempter. The final addition to the cast was the Chorus, which only arrived the day before the first night. This was a huge risk, but I had to take it in order to get a Chorus under the direction of Elsie Fogerty, who had created that in *The Rock*. To this process I shall devote a separate chapter.

Meanwhile, the Ladies of Canterbury had been busy on the costumes designed by Stella Mary Pearce. After her success with *The Rock*, it was natural, almost inevitable, to turn to her for the new play. Much of her treatment of it was dictated by the walls of the arcading. They were painted in elaborate patterns and in cold colours which, under the glare from the west window, took the eye to a disturbing extent. The costumes must somehow transfer attention from

[1] *T. S. Eliot: the Man and his Work*, ed. Allen Tate (Chatto and Windus, London, 1967), p. 183.

the walls to the characters. To do this, she adopted some bold methods. The dominant colour in the Tempters' dresses was bright yellow. The Chorus, who had to remain in sight throughout the play, were given garments which provided for as much variety of appearance as possible. They had unshaped robes divided vertically into two shades of green and decorated with strong patterns in deep red and blue, giving the effect of figures of early stained glass, and allowing of constant change of colours as the figures moved from grouping to grouping. The women wore plain headcloths slightly green in tint.

The Knights had, over chain mail, tunics and cloaks of heraldic colours derived from Professor Tristram's reconstruction on the Black Prince's tomb of the heraldry of the four murderers. The Priests of course had Benedictine habits; and Becket wore, as was his custom, a habit with a cloak for travelling. We considered putting him in full mass vestments for the sermon, but the practical difficulties ruled this out. When these were later removed by transfer to a theatre, we tried it, but came to the conclusion that the actor had a better chance of establishing the right contact with his audience in this speech if he remained in his accustomed garb.

Miss Pearce took up a suggestion of mine, once more directed at simplifying the audience's difficulties. Very few of them would know enough of the history to be able to appreciate from the allusions in the text the exact significance of each Tempter. And since the play was given a contemporary relevance by the speeches of the Knights (played by the same actors), it would, I felt, help towards understanding if the Tempters had in their costume a suggestion of the parallel type in our own day. Miss Pearce carried this out with great skill and wit. Each of the first three was given a divided skirt, correct for the period but able to suggest, by its decoration, modern male trousers. The First Tempter's indicated striped trousers, and we went so far as to give him, within a coronet, the top hat of the gay 'man about town' to whom he corresponded. The Second, the politician, had a suggestion of medals on his breast. The Third, the 'country lord', borrowed from the Crecy memorial window in Gloucester Cathedral a stick which looked like a rough-hewn golf-club, and wore diamond checks (heraldic in origin) to give the effect of a 'plus-four' suit. The Fourth, habited like Becket whose mind he inhabited, bore on his costume the palms and crowns of the martyrdom to which he tempted Becket 'for the wrong reason'.

Now that the play, and hence the history behind it, are so much more familiar, this kind of treatment would no doubt be unnecessary and might even be distracting; but I have no doubt that it had the desired effect of making the play clearer and sharper to its first audiences. When we moved it to a theatre, the Tempters' clothes were re-designed with a dark background; but the Chorus costumes remained the same. This was a limiting factor in that it restricted the Chorus to their liturgical function in the play, and prevented the development of that other aspect, 'the poor, the poor women of Canterbury'.

The author saw no rehearsals but the final dress rehearsal at which the whole cast was at long last gathered together for the first time. We had suffered from illness, from the other distractions that beset amateur actors, from the periodic absence of the leading man who had to fulfil other commitments from time to time in order to afford the luxury of doing a great part for practically no money, and from the separate training of the Chorus at their drama school in London. At this rehearsal I had also to add the music, consisting only of the liturgical numbers appropriate to the scenes—the opening of vespers, the introits for the banner-scene, the *Dies Irae* and the *Te Deum* which were the musical bases of two of the choruses. These were performed by the warden and students of St Augustine's College, in a small gallery rigged up above the entrance door. Lighting was minimal. At the last moment we decided that the sunshine from the west window was flattening the stage effect so seriously that we must improvise a cover for it. With such tasks the last hours were occupied before the first performance on the evening of 15 June 1935.

This is already recognised as a significant date in the history of twentieth-century drama; and looking at the notices one can see that most of the critics who attended were aware that something new had come into the theatre. One of the most acute was the writer of the London Letter in the *New Yorker* magazine (3 July 1935), Samuel Jeake, Jr. He begins 'We ought of course to have gone to Ascot': but they went to Canterbury instead:

Thus, without any preliminary fuss or fanfare, without advertisements in the newspapers, or any advance announcements except through Church channels, a poetic play was staged in the Chapter House which may well mark a turning point in English drama . . .

Murder in the Cathedral

One hadn't listened five minutes before one felt that one was witnessing a play which had the quality of greatness . . . It transcends the particular beliefs on which it has been built—or rather, it creates its own beliefs out of its own sheer livingness—exactly as *Everyman* does, or *Œdipus Rex*, and incidentally with striking technical resemblances to both.

One's feeling was that here at last was the English language literally being *used*, itself becoming the stuff of drama, turning alive with its own natural poetry. And Eliot's formalisation wasn't at all the sort of thing one has grown accustomed to expect of poetic drama—no trace of sham antique or artiness about it; nothing in the 'dead' sense, 'poetic'. No, the thing was direct and terribly real, the poetry of the choruses was as simple and immediate in its meaning as our own daily lives, and the transition into satirical modern prose at the end, when the four knights turned and addressed the audience, came without shock. It is a triumph of poetic genius that out of such actionless material—the mere conflict of a mind with itself—a play so deeply moving, and so exciting, should have been written; and so rich, moreover, in the various language of *humanity*. That is perhaps the greatest surprise about it—in the play Eliot has become human, and tender, with a tenderness and a humanity which have nowhere else in our time found such beauty of form.

I have quoted Mr Jeake at such length because this is the kind of reaction which was typical of those who came to the play without preconceptions. The professional critics were of course more circumspect in assessing the first play of so controversial a writer. Charles Morgan, in *The Times*, found that 'Mr. Eliot's writing and Mr. Martin Browne's production are continuously keen and clear' and he welcomes the fact that Mr Eliot 'has written in a way that may be generally understood'—in contrast, he implies, to his earlier poetry of 'private symbols'. He is worried by the rhymes and the 'limping jingle that reminds the hearer of nothing so much as the "book" of a pantomime'. But he recognises in the language, particularly of the chorus, 'a fresh vigour that fully justifies his departure from the customary forms of dramatic verse'.

W. A. Darlington, in the *Daily Telegraph*, comments on the recurring difficulty involved in bringing the man of letters into the theatre, and says

How good it is, then, to be able to salute in T. S. Eliot a distinguished man of letters who can use the stage for his purpose while not depriving it of its own quality.

John Pudney in the *New Statesman* begins

Mr. Eliot is to be thanked for having broken away from the naturalistic tradition of historical drama . . . It is a production which breaks through the façade of pageant to provide another dimension. The difficulty of writing poetry in a contemporary idiom to interpret specific actions has foiled many writers who have not the long wind or the integrity. This play . . . demonstrates that the medium is a vital one.

He goes on to analyse the 'use of open running rhythm with sharp strokes of repetition and invocation'. Darlington speaks of the 'system of stresses, alliteration and assonance which has been present in our language since Anglo-Saxon times'; and notes how 'It rises to great beauty at moments. At others it serves, by a certain deliberate ordinariness of phrase, to point the recurrent suggestion that ancient and modern are one.'

The play, then, had made the designed impact; but would it survive transference from the very special place in and for which it had been created? Would it attract audiences of a more generalised character than Canterbury's 'rather special kind of audience—an audience of those serious people who go to "festivals" and expect to have to put up with poetry'?[1]

Ashley Dukes came to see the play, and at once decided that he would like to put these questions to the test at the Mercury. While I was engaged on another production outside London, I went up to meet Eliot and discuss the plan before we met Dukes. Evidently we reached quick agreement about a production in the autumn, though the casting and other matters were postponed till late September by previous engagements of my own.

I was of course to get an entirely professional cast; but as the Mercury held only 136 persons and had no subsidy, the salaries available for so large a body of players were exceedingly small. We began the season at the following rates: ten pounds a week for Speaight as Becket, three for the rest of us men, and thirty shillings for the Chorus. These latter were to be students who had just left the Central School and were to have their first job with us; and of course to be free to leave when they found more lucrative work, being replaced through the School. Miss Fogerty and Miss Gwynneth Thurburn undertook to train, and keep in training, this group of their graduates. It was only through the supply thus assured of 'an efficient as well as comely bevy' (as one reviewer called them) that the production was enabled to enter on its run.

It proved to be a long one. The opening date was 1 November,

[1] T. S. Eliot, 'Poetry and Drama', in *On Poetry and Poets*, p. 79.

which seemed peculiarly appropriate as being All Saints' Day. Next morning we found that we had a stroke of luck. Charles Morgan was on holiday, and in his stead *The Times* (which did not in those days publish the names of its reviewers) had sent Dermot Morrah. He had none of the inhibitions felt by his principal about writing 'quotable' notices; and he ended his review with the words 'this is the one great play by a contemporary dramatist now to be seen in England'. This was enough, with the appreciative recapitulations published in other papers, to assure us of a firm success.

Apart from this uncovenanted mercy, the review seems to me to be worth preserving in full:

MERCURY THEATRE

'MURDER IN THE CATHEDRAL'
by T. S. Eliot

Thomas Becket	Robert Speaight
First Priest	Alfred Clark
Second Priest	Charles Petry
Third Priest	Frank Napier
First Tempter and Knight	Guy Spaull
Second Tempter and Knight	G. R. Schjelderup
Third Tempter and Knight	Norman Chidgey
Fourth Tempter and Knight	E. Martin Browne
Chorus of Women of Canterbury	Mary Christian, Cecilia Colley, Dorothy Gall, Lettice Haffenden, Elizabeth Latham, Katherine Stenhouse, Phoebe Waterfield, Geraldine White

Mr. Eliot's drama of Thomas Becket was first presented in the Chapter House at Canterbury, and was fully reviewed in *The Times* of June 17. Transferred to the public stage it takes rank at once as a tragedy of the first distinction.

Its mode is the original dramatic mode of ritual; its theme is the theme out of which drama itself, and some would say even religion, first grew—the story of the priest-king who is slain for his people. But, although there is much in the treatment to recall the earlier Greek drama, and particularly the chorus of Aeschylus in the *Supplices*, there is also not a little that belongs to Becket's own age. Not only are the underlying ideas singularly true to Becket's own (which is dramatically of little relevance); but there is something entirely medieval in the hard, keen drive of thought towards its goal. The drama, however, is not confined by the temporal accidents of its setting; and does not actually need what is a none the less delightful scene of comic relief, in which the four murdering knights drive home the point that the conflict presented is eternal.

Some of the finest poetry in the play is given to the chorus of women of

Murder in the Cathedral

Canterbury, whose part is also vitally dramatic, for it links in the Greek manner the high ritual of the action with common life. It is handled with a finely free discipline by Miss Elsie Fogerty, who has found eight ladies able to deliver the lines, in antistrophe or in unison, with melodious, moving, and fluid elocution. One of them in particular can speak verse as purely as Mr. Robert Speaight himself; and Mr. Speaight shows once more that he has no superior in that art on the London stage. Mr. Eliot has given him an opportunity that any actor might envy, to portray mind and spirit together at war with the innermost temptations that can beset the heroic soul; and he plays the part with a fire repressed until it is transmuted into light. Mr. Norman Chidgey, as the plain Englishman who believes in his country and fair play, carries off the comic honours.

Criticism can, of course, find, if not obvious faults, at least points on which Mr. Eliot must expect controversy. Occasionally—as when Becket is confronted with the fourth tempter, who tempts him with his own aspiration to martyrdom, the argument becomes too subtle to be readily apprehended under the conditions of the stage. Mr. Eliot's revolt against 'poetic diction' in unpoetical circumstance is so extreme that his actors sometimes unconsciously criticise it by using their arts of elocution to smooth over his deliberate violences of rhythm and rhyme. These are trifles. It remains to say that this is the one great play by a contemporary dramatist now to be seen in England; and, while giving honour to Mr. Ashley Dukes for presenting it, to note the estimate of public taste implied by his choice of the smallest theatre in London.

(The Times, 2 November 1935)

It may be of interest to record the fortunes of the play from the time it reached London; for the course it took is in several ways unusual, and owed much to the understanding of the two managers involved. Ashley Dukes regarded it from the first not as a show which should be 'milked' for the longest possible run in the fashion common in the West End, but as a masterpiece which should be seen as widely as possible by those who would most appreciate it. During the seven months of its initial run at the Mercury, it established his policy of presenting poetic drama there, and was seen by some 20,000 people. He took it off when it was doing excellent business in order to show it in university cities during term. We visited the old Oxford Playhouse for three days and the Arts, Cambridge, for three days in May 1936, and then went to the Gate Theatre, Dublin, for a week. In September the run at the Mercury was resumed.

It seemed strange at the time that no West End manager had either come to Canterbury to see the play of this famous poet or taken any notice of its success at the Mercury. It still puzzles me that the vision of those who controlled the London theatre was so narrow. The exception, however, finally appeared. J. P. Mitchelhill was a real-estate agent who had a personal love for the theatre but had never dreamt of involving himself in it. A short while before, he had bought, as part of a large property deal, the Duchess Theatre in Catherine Street, almost opposite the old Lyceum which Irving made famous. It was only a few years old, was built on an awkward site, and had not a good record of success. Mitchelhill determined that, with the help of an experienced friend, he would manage it himself. After an initial failure, he was able, by a choice of play at once acute and adventurous, to make this small house one of the best patronised in London, as it has remained. It was he who, coming that autumn to see *Murder in the Cathedral* for the first time, decided that he must have this production for the Duchess; and we moved there two days before our anniversary, on 30 October 1936.

The problem of setting arose. At Canterbury, the chapter house had provided the background; at the Mercury, a surround of deep blue curtains had enclosed only the furniture required for the action—archiepiscopal throne, pulpit and altar designed by Stella Mary Pearce. This had proved entirely satisfactory, allowing the play free scope to fill the small stage and its apron. But the Duchess was a proscenium theatre, and its stage was rendered shallow by the restricted site; it seemed to demand scenery. Frank Napier designed an architectural setting, Norman in style and triangular in shape. It was unassuming and efficient; but I think it proved that such drama flourishes best when the poet is allowed to create his own imaginative pictures in the minds of the audience.

During the play's period at the Duchess, it was televised from Alexandra Palace under the direction of G. More O'Ferrall for the B.B.C. The performance on Monday, 21 December, at the Duchess was transformed into an At Home given by Mitchelhill, who invited some 300 people to view on four screens set up in the stalls the most significant scenes from the 'live' television show. The production marked the first experiment in super-imposition; each Tempter was superimposed on the image of Becket as he emerged into the arch-bishop's conscious mind. It may thus have been a landmark in the development of television; and certainly the company that watched it contained many of those who have added to their distinction in the theatre a share in the promotion of that medium.

Early in 1937, Mitchelhill came to see me in my dressing room one night. He wished that at the conclusion of the play's run at the Duchess the provincial theatres should receive it: but he had had a poor reaction from the managements of the chief theatre-chains, who thought that the audience for this play was so different from that which normally attended their houses that it could not be a success. He had the offer of one week from the Grand Theatre, Leeds, then under local management, and of two from the Princes Theatre, Manchester, on unfavourable terms. He believed that, if only the Leeds week could show a strong response, the other theatres (which in those days mostly booked their attractions at short notice) would quickly fall into line. But it was a gamble; and its success depended on the right work being done in advance to get the Leeds audience there on the first night.

A short while before, I had likewise been visited by Herbert J. Malden. He had been manager of the Ambassadors Theatre, to which he afterwards returned; but at this time had retired from the West End. He had been so deeply stirred by the play that he told me 'if I can ever do anything to help this great play, let me know'. I felt sure that this was no empty offer; and asking Mitchelhill to give me a day or two to think about it, I rang up 'Jack' Malden for advice. The response came: 'I'll do the advance myself; and I'm sure we can succeed.' This was a gallant offer, for advance work is, if properly done, one of the most gruelling jobs in the theatre; and this was a particularly difficult assignment. Mitchelhill accepted and booked Leeds and Manchester; and Malden, accompanied by his daughter who was one of Mr Charles Cochran's 'Young Ladies' at the moment out of work, set off for Leeds. His policy was to build up party bookings from schools and churches so that he would have a large attendance early in the week, and so enable the local management to spread the word that they had a success and get in the general public.

He had a full house for the opening on Monday night, and a handsome sum in advance booking for the week. On the Tuesday, by lunchtime, seven more weeks were booked with the leading provincial theatres. They included the King's, Edinburgh, during the General Assembly of the Church of Scotland. Malden preceded the company throughout, and business was excellent. He had tapped a new audience for the theatre, one which has to some extent been available ever since for work of this calibre.

In the summer, the production went for five weeks to the Old Vic. This was the year in which Lilian Baylis died. It is good to remember her as hostess to this play, which represented so much that she stood for in drama, poetry and religion, for the five weeks from 8 June. *The Times* reviewer wrote that the company 'should be sure of their welcome back to London in a theatre where poetry is always given its due'; and other critics made it clear that the play had 'already taken rank as a classic' (*Horse and Hound*) and wrote of it as 'the one classically great play by a contemporary dramatist' (*Evening News*).

After the Old Vic season, we went to the Tewkesbury Festival for the week 19–24 July. Tewkesbury, a small Gloucestershire town, possesses one of the finest Norman abbey churches in England, and for the past two years had staged a Festival under the management of John Moore before the west front of this magnificent building. No setting could be more suitable, and the final procession in which the archbishop's body was carried up to the high altar was a moving variation on the Canterbury original.

For this is one of the features of the first production which has remained in many memories. Becket's body was borne down the central aisle of the chapter house and out into the cloister. The Priests and Chorus carried candles, and sang the litany which calls the roll of the saints to which Thomas's name has just been added. The procession continued all the way round the great cloister, and the dispersing audience could see and hear it in the distance.

At Tewkesbury, the opposite effect was obtained. The abbey nave was dark as the procession entered it from the lighted stage outside, and the flickering points of candle-light became smaller and smaller as the archbishop was carried towards the high altar.

The autumn was filled by a second tour, while plans were on foot for the long-promised visit to America. This had been made more difficult by the fact that permission had been granted, owing to a misunderstanding, for a previous production. At that time, one of the agencies of the New Deal was the Federal Theatre of the Works Progress Administration, which staged large-scale productions in the big old theatres on the downtown streets, with casts composed of up to 90 per cent out-of-work actors. The aim was naturally to use, not as in the commercial theatre, as few, but as many actors as possible. Halsted Welles made a production in which movement and spectacle compensated, so I was told, for the inability of many of his actors to master Eliot's poetry. With a distinguished older actor, Harry Irvine, to uphold the central role, he succeeded in winning great acclaim for the play and production. The limited run should have left a large public ready for a revival; but its scale and type, when it came, was so different as to prejudice our chances very severely.

We opened in Boston, with all the advantages of the Eliot name in the family's home-town and no comparisons, since the W.P.A. production had been seen only in New York. The reception was exceedingly warm, and we did increasingly well during our two weeks. But the opening days' business had not been good enough for Gilbert Miller, who had invited Ashley Dukes to bring the production over; and he suddenly cancelled the plans they had made together for an extended tour of large cities before New York and brought us straight in to Broadway. The only theatre available was the Ritz, now long consigned to television; it had a stage too small to take our set and no prestige. The suggestions which we had offered, from our English experience, about advance approach to the audience most suited for the play were ignored, and we found ourselves playing on the first night to the same audience that had attended a Lonsdale comedy produced by the same management two days earlier.

The auspices were not good; and though the critical reception was interested and appreciative, it did not suggest that the box office would be besieged. Miller was in Florida and apparently uninterested in the whole affair. Speaight and I, with the assistance of American friends, worked hard by day to find the audience which we were sure existed for the play; and by the end of three weeks we had queues at the box office. But the theatre had been let for another show; Miller was not willing to look for an alternative; and we played to our last, full houses in New York with the sadness born of a missed opportunity. The play has never, so far as I know, been professionally played there since.

In London, we revived it immediately after the war, first for two matinées in the West End to raise a fund for the re-establishment of the Canterbury Festival, and then, because the demand was so great for a three months' run at the Mercury. During this, King George VI, with his Queen and Princess Margaret, came to a performance graciously accepting our cramped conditions. In the interval, they came into the ballet studio which we used as a green room, to meet the cast. Rationing was still in full force, and the King was concerned as to how many clothing coupons had had to be spent on the voluminous robes of the Chorus. We were able to assure him that all the costumes were pre-war.

The Old Vic produced the play in 1953, with Robert Donat as a gentle Becket—his last role, and a recording was made of this performance. All over the world, theatres, schools, colleges and churches continue to give countless presentations of *Murder in the Cathedral*.

None of the plays has undergone so many minor textual alterations in the course of successive editions. For Canterbury, the text had to be abbreviated to a set length, and I was obliged to make some mutilations. Meanwhile, Eliot, unable to attend rehearsals, was preparing the first edition for Faber and Faber to be published simultaneously with the Canterbury production. The first edition is thus his own guess at what he wanted in the text without benefit of production experience. The special Canterbury edition was printed locally to be sold at the Festival only and then went out of print. It showed the special cuts, and the re-arrangements necessitated by the varying skills of the actors. Apart from that, however, there are many variations in the Faber printings; and though this is not a book of textual scholarship, it may be valuable to note some of them and the reasons behind them.

One series concerns the division of speeches. When using a group of characters such as the Priests or Knights, an author naturally does not concern himself at first with assigning all his lines to specific individuals. This was mostly done by me in production and adopted into the text afterwards. Thus, in the scene with the Messenger (who, by the way, was originally called Herald in the Greek convention, a title which it would seem better to have retained), the eager questions of the Priests were in the first edition assigned to the First Priest only; in production it was clear that the rest could not stand round and wait speechless while one of their number fired a whole battery of queries, and the division was made as in the subsequent editions. Similarly with their final scene, after the Third Priest's apostrophe to the departed Knights, the others divide the appeal to the new Saint.

Murder in the Cathedral

The re-assignment of the Knights' lines was made for a different reason. There were a few places in which the author had simply written 'Knights', leaving me to split the lines up if I liked, or, as with the opening attack on Becket and the final 'Traitor!' cry, to have them spoken in unison. But another consideration arose out of the doubling of the Tempters with the Knights. The Fourth Tempter, as we have seen, is the most insidious and his influence on Becket's soul is most penetrating. In the temptation of the audience, the same is true of the Fourth Knight, who is employing in reverse the same argument as the Tempter. The Knight asks the audience to believe that Becket has in fact concurred with the Tempter's prompting to will martyrdom for himself to satisfy his own pride, and thus has committed 'suicide'.

In the original text, the Fourth Knight takes part with the rest in the violent bullying of Becket that precedes the murder. I soon felt that, with the above interpretation in mind, this was unsuitable. Further, Edward Grim, the eyewitness, tells that 'the fourth knight prevented any from interfering so that the others might freely perpetrate the murder'.[1] It seemed to me that, dramatically, this figure should throughout be a figure of mystery, who while not participating in the violence could be felt to be the influence behind it. So, in the preface to the third edition (1937) Eliot writes:

At the suggestion of Mr. E. Martin Browne, I have in Part II reassigned most of the lines formerly attributed to the Fourth Knight. When, as was originally intended, the parts of the Tempters are doubled with those of the Knights, the advantages of these alterations should be obvious.

The Knights' exit speech in their first scene was initially weak:

Priest! monk! and servant! take, hold, detain,
Restrain this man, in the King's name;
Or answer with your bodies, if he escape before we come,
We come for the King's justice, we come again.

As critics were fond of pointing out, the tension was lowered by dividing the confrontation with the Knights into two; but first, this was the historical truth—'then the knights left, vehemently threatening the archbishop and uttering warnings on behalf of the king that he

---

[1] *Materials for the History of Thomas Becket, Archbishop of Canterbury*, Rolls Series, ed. James Craigie Robertson (London, 1875), II, 31 ff. Grim's account is translated by W. H. Hutton in *The English Saints* (Wells, Gardner, Darton & Co., London, 1903), pp. 253–6.

was to be carefully guarded, lest he escape'.[1] Also, the dramatist had some very important things to say before the final onslaught; the two Chorus speeches here, and Becket's own exposition to the Priests, contain some of the most powerful matter, both emotional and intellectual, in the play. But the sheer business of contriving a 'good exit' always troubled Eliot. As late as 31 December 1937, when we were rehearsing for the American tour, he sent me a version which neither of us felt happy with; and in the end he allowed to stand that which, I think, Ashley Dukes had suggested some time earlier. It is variously assigned in different editions, but should read thus:

FIRST KNIGHT   Priest! monk! and servant! take, hold, detain,
    Restrain this man in the King's name,
    Or answer with your bodies.
SECOND KNIGHT   Enough of words.
THE THREE KNIGHTS   We come for the King's justice, we come with swords.
(*Exeunt*)

It was also Ashley Dukes who had the idea of allowing the First Knight, as chairman of the 'meeting' after the murder, to characterise each of the speakers by an introductory phrase. Eliot took this up, and in his letter of 31 December 1937 he adopts most of Dukes's suggestions:

As for the public meeting. 'My neighbour in the country' seems to me quite right. I cannot get anything so concise for Morville. I thought that if I could suggest that he was an ambitious young politician, it might both sound contemporary and make a good contrast to Traci:
    'I shall next call upon Hugh de Morville—a name to remember. He is one of our younger statesmen, whom rumour has marked for high office (in the next ministerial shuffle?): there is no one better qualified to expound the constitutional aspect.'
This is too long, I know.[2] I can't think of any improvement for Brito, except that I think 'coming as he does of a family distinguished for its *loyalty* to the Church' would be better than *fidelity*.

De Morville's speech underwent a great deal of alteration from the first version at Canterbury, through the first Faber edition which already incorporated considerable changes made before the text had been played, to the text which became established. The first edition has:

[1] *Materials*, IV, 73.
[2] It was finally compressed to the single phrase 'who has made a special study of statecraft and constitutional law'.

Murder in the Cathedral

The King's aim has been perfectly consistent. During the reign of the late Queen Matilda and the irruption of the unhappy usurper Stephen, the kingdom was very much divided. Our King saw that the one thing needful was to restore order: to curb the excessive powers of local government, which were usually exercised for selfish and often for seditious ends, and to systematise the judiciary. There was utter chaos: there were three kinds of justice and three kinds of court: that of the King, that of the Bishops, and that of the baronage. I must repeat one point that the last speaker has made. While the late archbishop was Chancellor, he wholeheartedly supported the King's designs: this is an important point, which, if necessary, I can substantiate. Now the King intended that Becket, who had proved himself an extremely able administrator—no-one denies that—should unite the offices of Chancellor and Archbishop. No-one would have grudged him that; no-one than he was better qualified to fill at once these two most important posts. Had Becket concurred with the King's wishes . . .

The Canterbury version was more concise, laying stress on the King's reasoning rather than describing the situation he sought to remedy; for instance:

With a view to assimilating the ecclesiastical jurisdiction to his own, the King designed that Becket should unite the offices . . .

No doubt Eliot learned from watching the scene played that the overgrowth printed in the first edition should be pruned; and the final text[1] is a tauter version of this edition, rather than a reversion to Canterbury.

The other differences I wish to note concern Becket himself, and some of them raise interesting questions about ideas in the play. The first occurs in his opening speech.

> They know and do not know, that acting is suffering
> And suffering is action. Neither does the actor suffer . . .

This was the original text; but in rehearsal it became clear that 'acting' and 'actor' in the mouth of a player bore a double meaning; and the lines were altered to:

> They know and do not know, that action is suffering
> And suffering is action. Neither does the agent suffer . . .

The question why a phrase in this speech is omitted by the Fourth Tempter when he throws it back to Thomas has often been asked; it is the kind of question the author never wished to answer, and I can only give my own view. The 'pattern' which is to subsist through

[1] *Collected Plays*, p. 50.

action and suffering, in Becket's thinking is the pattern of God's purpose, which is imaged by the wheel turning in symmetrical order around the still centre where God rests. But when the Tempter adopts Becket's words, he interprets the pattern as the mechanical revolution of a wheel which moves automatically, without purpose, round a dead centre; and the lines

for the pattern is the action
and the suffering

cannot apply to this; indeed, if the Tempter used them, he would be denying the interpretation he is putting on the speech.[1]

In the Third Tempter's scene, Becket has, in the first edition only, three lines which never appear again. They are, I believe, based on a recorded saying. The speech dismissing the Tempter runs:

If the Archbishop cannot trust the Throne,
He has good cause to trust none but God alone.
It is not better to be thrown
To a thousand hungry appetites than to one.
At a future time this may be shown.
I ruled once as Chancellor . . .

Among the differences between the Canterbury and the first Faber editions, which as we have seen were in the press at the same time, one of the most considerable is in the penultimate speech of Thomas to the Knights at the end of their first encounter. Here is the Canterbury version:

It is not I who insult the King
But those who would have him more than King.
For there is higher than I or the King.
I am no traitor, no enemy of the State;
The King is his own enemy, the State the State's.
The Law of God is above the law of man,
The Kingdom of God above the kingdom of man.
It is not I, Becket from Cheapside,
It is not against me, Becket, that you strive.
It is not Becket who pronounces doom,
But the Law of Christ's Church, the judgement of Rome.

This includes material which re-occurs in the later scene with the Priests; and also some which seems to take colour from the current

[1] See also Nevill Coghill's views on this in the introduction (p. 17) to the educational edition of the play (Faber Educational Books, London, 1965).

preoccupation with the danger of dictatorship and the almighty State. In the first Faber edition, this has disappeared, along (perhaps regrettably) with the second line. Here, on the other hand, four lines are added on the theme of Rome's power, which were quickly dropped as weakening the challenge.

> It is not I who insult the King,
> And there is higher than I or the King.
> It is not I, Becket from Cheapside,
> It is not against me, Becket, that you strive.
> It is not Becket who pronounces doom,
> But the Law of Christ's Church, the judgement of Rome.
> Go then to Rome, or let Rome come
> Here, to you, in the person of her most unworthy son.
> Petty politicians in your endless adventure!
> Rome alone can absolve those who break Christ's indenture.

The scene with the Priests which falls between the two great choruses, and in which Becket is taken to vespers, underwent a similar change. In the Canterbury edition, except for a few extra interjections of fear from the Priests, the order and text of the speeches are as they were finally established. But in the first Faber edition Thomas has an extra speech, and the Priests' replies, to which one has also to be added, are in a different order:

PRIESTS (*severally*)   My Lord, you must not stop here. To the minster. Through the cloister. No time to waste. They are coming back, armed. To the altar, to the altar. They are here already. To the sanctuary. They are breaking in. We can barricade the minster doors. You cannot stay here. Force him to come. Seize him.

THOMAS   All my life they have been coming, these feet. All my life
I have waited. Death will come only when I am worthy,
And if I am worthy, there is no danger.
I have therefore only to make perfect my will.

PRIESTS   My Lord, they are coming. They will break through presently,
You will be killed. Come to the altar.

THOMAS   Peace! be quiet! remember where you are, and what is happening;
No life here is sought for but mine,
And I am not in danger: only near to death.

PRIESTS   Make haste, my Lord. Don't stop here talking. It is not right.
What shall become of us, my Lord, if you are killed; what shall become of us?

THOMAS   That again is another theme
To be developed and resolved in the pattern of time.
It is not for me to run from city to city;

> To meet death gladly is only
> The only way in which I can defend
> The Law of God, the holy canons.
> PRIESTS My Lord, to vespers . . .

There is, I think, no doubt that the shorter version is better; the extra material probably owed its inclusion rather to being recorded utterances than to the dramatic necessities of the scene. It ends with what is always a crux in production, the hustling of Becket by force into the cathedral; this is vouched for by the eyewitnesses, but is difficult to act, especially with only three Priests, without diminishing Thomas's strength and dignity at a crucial time.

I have left until last the Christmas sermon. The biblical text (Luke 2:14) is given by William Fitzstephen from first-hand knowledge. Eliot originally used it as in the King James version; but afterwards, realising that Becket would have spoken the Vulgate text:

> Gloria in altissmis Deo, et in terra pax hominibus bonae voluntatis

he altered the final words from

> and on earth peace, goodwill towards men

to a translation of the Latin:

> and on earth peace to men of goodwill.

Except for some small differences in wording, the later editions of the play, which may be taken as final, follow closely the Canterbury text. This was worked over in rehearsal by myself and my wife with Speaight, and we consulted the author about many small points, most of which he agreed to and which are now incorporated. But meanwhile, the first Faber edition was in the press with a number of different readings and one considerable expansion. This passage occurs in the following paragraph:

Beloved, we do not think of a martyr simply as a good Christian who has been killed because he is a Christian: for that would be solely to mourn. We do not think of him simply as a good Christian who has been elevated to the company of the Saints: for that would be simply to rejoice: and neither our mourning nor our rejoicing is as the world's is. A Christian martyrdom is no accident. Saints are not made by accident. Still less is a Christian martyrdom the effect of a man's will to become a Saint, as a man by willing and contriving may become a ruler of men. Ambition fortifies the will of man to become ruler over other men: it operates with deception, cajolery and violence, it is the action of impurity upon impurity. Not so in Heaven. A martyr, a saint, is always made by the design of God, for His love of men, to warn them and to lead them, to bring them back to His ways. A martyrdom is never the design of man; for the true martyr is he who has become the instrument of God, who has lost his will in the will of God, not lost it but found it, for he has found freedom in submission to God. The martyr no longer desires anything for himself, not even the glory of martyrdom. So thus as on earth the Church mourns and rejoices at once, in a fashion that the world cannot understand; so in Heaven the Saints are most high, having made themselves most low, seeing themselves not as we see them, but in the light of the Godhead from which they draw their being.

Here, again, the shorter version is by far the stronger; and it has stood the test of many thousands of performances.

The final paragraph is based on Fitzstephen's account:

he said that they had one martyr-Archbishop, Saint Elphege; it was possible that they would have another in a short time.[1]

and gathers up the thought of the whole into the farewell of Thomas to his people. The eyewitness testimony is that he showed himself deeply moved at this moment; but in playing, so powerful is the emotional effect on the audience that it is better for the actor to make only a restrained suggestion of his feeling. The final line reads in Canterbury:

I would have you ponder no longer on these things now, but at a later time.

But the first Faber edition already contains the alternative which has, rightly I am sure, remained current:

I would have you keep in your hearts these things that I say, and think of them at another time.

[1] *Materials*, III, 130. For translations of extracts see Coghill's edition.

3

The Chorus in Performance

I first met Elsie Fogerty in a church schoolroom in Folkestone in April 1926. I was on the staff of an Amateur Drama School as Producer, though still pretty inexperienced myself. So, in the interval between the morning sessions, I walked in to enrol as a student in the class of the famous teacher of speech. I saw a big, lively woman in a brown coat-and-skirt and velour hat, eating from its skin a banana which she had taken from a paper bag. I was frightened and yet fascinated by her personality; this was the reaction, as I later came to know, of almost every one of her students. But the fascination soon overcame the fright, especially as she communicated in vivid teaching and conversation a great store of knowledge on those subjects which meant most to me.

Just at that time I got a job in an American university, to start the following autumn, where part of my duties would be to teach speech to Drama students— a task for which I had no proper qualification. I appealed to Miss Fogerty for help, and she found time to give me an intensive course of private lessons. No one else, I am sure, could have enabled me to acquit myself even as well as I did for the next three years in a strange land: she not only taught me speech-technique but, quite as important, gave me an insight into my own character, and illuminated the relationship of speech to personality. For Elsie Fogerty speech was never an end in itself, but the expression of the human mind and soul.

These two paragraphs are the first of a number which I contributed to Marion Cole's biographical appreciation of this remarkable woman.[1] The story she tells in *Fogie* became interwoven with that of the creation of Eliot's first two plays, and my own work as director of them was closely linked with hers. So what I have to say in this chapter should be taken in the context of Miss Fogerty's life and work.

After my return from America, three years later, to work for George Bell, I renewed contact with her, and soon became to some extent involved in the Central School of Speech and Drama. She had founded the school at the Royal Albert Hall in 1906, combining her own speech classes with those which Sir Frank Benson had been

---

[1] Marion Cole, *Fogie* (Peter Davies Ltd., London, 1967).

running as an adjunct to his famous Shakespearian company. Since that time it has been one of the principal schools for stage-training in London; but it has also trained students, on an equal footing, for the teaching of speech and for speech therapy. This triple role was designed for it by Miss Fogerty. Two of these functions are blended in choral speech.

She had devoted her studious enthusiasm to this branch of dramatic art as long ago as 1900, when she produced Swinburne's *Atalanta in Calydon* and began to work with Ruby Ginner to re-create both the speech and the movement of the Greek choruses. These were always in the syllabus of the school, and many Greek choruses on the professional stage were supplied with groups of players trained by her. Since the end of the First World War, several other teachers of eminence had specialised in choral speech, and their students were keenly competitive. The Oxford Verse-Speaking Festivals provided a focus for their efforts, but did not of course afford opportunity for stage performances.

When I worked out the scenario for *The Rock*, with the most important part of the poet's work assigned to a speech chorus, I had in mind the hope that Miss Fogerty would provide and direct it. She was delighted that her school should be offered such an opportunity, and agreed that somehow the time should be found for her senior students to undertake it.

As has been said, the *Rock* Chorus was to consist of masked figures, male and female, speaking without movement and in stiff, stylised robes. Thus the whole dramatic effect would depend on speech; and its production would need all the skill and all the sensibility of Miss Fogerty and her colleague.

Gwynneth Thurburn, who afterwards succeeded Miss Fogerty as principal of the school, was doing most of the voice work, and it was she who provided the group which Eliot was to hear at my request. In 1967 she put on paper for me her recollections of her work on the choruses, and I gratefully quote from them in the following pages. She begins:

Martin Shaw, who had composed the music, said that the choruses should be intoned, but you suggested that Eliot should hear some good choral speaking before coming to a decision. It so happened that we had a particularly good set of girl speakers who had that year done very well at the Oxford Verse-Speaking Festival with, among other poems, Manley Hopkins' *The Leaden and the Golden*

Echo. I hastily polished it up as the choir was a bit rusty after the lapse of time. They responded extremely well and I think Eliot was impressed; anyway he decided that that was what he wanted, and I embarked upon a spare-time occupation which was to take up a large part of my life for the next few years.

The success of this undertaking depended equally, I should say, upon design and execution. In a speech chorus, the poet does not, as the composer does, determine the sound, whether vocal or instrumental, to be heard at each moment. This falls to the director, who divides the lines among the speakers, and suggests the interpretation to be given to each passage. The object is not to impose a pattern upon the group but to lead it to discover for itself the significance of what it is doing and, in the process, to find an identity which will express itself in a common impulse operating without conscious thought to give expression to the movement of its spirit.

In establishing such an identity, a body of students working together day by day has a great advantage. They know one another intimately, and are accustomed to reacting as a group. Because hety are young, their experience both of life and of work in the theatre is limited; and this means that the director tends to use the single voice less than he would with more mature actors. But there will be greater scope for the use of small groupings of various sizes, giving a variety of vocal colour. With a Chorus of both sexes, the range is subtle and very wide, and the gradations in power, from the single voice through the smaller groupings of voices all male, all female, or blended in a combination appropriate to the style and mood, to the full Chorus, are almost infinite.

This process of design was carried out largely in rehearsal, for though Miss Fogerty and Miss Thurburn could come to a class with a pretty good idea of who could do what, the best result was obtained by listening to alternative combinations of voices. I attended many of the Chorus rehearsals and we worked out the design together. As Miss Thurburn recalls,

Eliot often came too, seemingly enjoying himself, but shy and difficult to draw out if one wanted to know anything.

She also recalls the difficulty of getting a united approach from men and girls. In those days, drama schools had not yet established themselves as the necessary training-ground for professional actors; it is only since the Second World War that the profession has recognised formal training, rather than apprenticeship, as the proper preparation for an acting career. Consequently, the schools, in order to get an adequate proportion of male students, had in those days to allow them to take a shortened course; and one usually found that some of the men were going through the school in a single year instead of the two required for the girls or the three now required for all aspirants. So Miss Thurburn says:

The girls had a longer and more secure background of training to rely upon, and they therefore constituted a better team. I think, in general, that it is easier to get good co-ordination from a group of girls than it is with a group of men. With mixed choirs it is rather different.

I think it would be true to say that *The Rock* made it particularly easy to take advantage of the mixed choir. There were passages in which the sexes could be sharply opposed:

Women Men! polish your teeth on rising and retiring!
Men Women! polish your fingernails!
Together You polish the tooth of the dog and the talon of the cat.

There were passages in which their differing colour of voice made essential contrast. But more broadly speaking, the prophetic type of utterance was best given to the men, the lyric to the women, with both sharing in the ironic according to the mood and colour of the particular line.

In the result, the young speakers found the arduous experience rewarding. Miss Thurburn says:

The assembling of *The Rock* was very exciting and I remember how the choruses suddenly came to life, and especially the electric atmosphere generated in the audience at Sadler's Wells.

The critic of the *Church Times* assesses the result:

The great achievement of *The Rock* is the chorus. Mr. Eliot is greater as a poet than he is experienced as a dramatist, and he has put the best of his writing into the poetry of the choric comments on religion and life. The chorus itself, men and women from the Central School of Speech and Drama, is magnificently trained. With stone-coloured masks and dresses, standing in a solid and motion-less block round about the central figure of the Rock, the chorus, with its clear enunciation, its variety of tone, its emphasis and its pointed hits, gives direction to the play. In spite of its physical immobility, it is the chorus that gives the pace to the action of the players. (1 June 1934)

When he conceived *Murder in the Cathedral*, Eliot thought of his chorus in a different way:

The Chorus in Performance

The chorus in *Murder in the Cathedral* does, I think, represent some advance in dramatic development: that is to say, I set myself the task of writing lines, not for an anonymous chorus, but for a chorus of women of Canterbury—one might almost say, charwomen of Canterbury. I had to make some effort to identify myself with these women, instead of merely identifying them with myself.[1]

Eliot had from the first expected that Miss Fogerty's students would speak this chorus, and had realised that in asking for an all-women group he was likely to get the best out of them. Miss Fogerty gives a very interesting account of how she worked with the proposed players while Eliot listened at the back of the room:

in ten minutes I had forgotten that Eliot was there, and the students never knew. The problem was to find the exact number of speakers needed for each phrase in the chorus, and very soon we realised that we were doing not strictly choral work—but orchestral work; each speaker had to be like an instrument, in harmony with the other voices during the ensemble passages, but repeating a recurring phrase in an individual tone—just as flute or horn would do in an orchestra: one such phrase I still remember is the 'Living—and partly living' of the first chorus; we tried four voices before finding the one that could give—quite naturally—the strange discouraged hopelessness of that line.[2]

Eliot was convinced by what he heard, and next time I came to the school I was able to report that he had written three more choruses. Of their preparation Miss Thurburn says:

The verse was far more difficult to handle [than that of *The Rock*]. Not only did it depend on greater depth of understanding but the structure posed great problems, problems which were to remain long after the production had been launched. It is relatively easy to integrate and co-ordinate a choir speaking verse that has a solid architectural basis to its form. The variations and rhythms which Eliot used were fascinating, but the structure seemed to be more formless than, in fact, it was (our ears were not attuned to it as they are now). To keep it exact in repetition would have needed a conductor.

I think, too, that today we understand better what use he made of punctuation, or absence of it. Then, I had a great difficulty in making the students appreciate that this mattered at all and that absence of punctuation was, in fact, a signal, so that the use of a comma or a full-stop had real significance. On one occasion he came up to me during rehearsal and murmured very confidentially 'That should be a colon, not a semi-colon'. I think this was the only spontaneous remark he ever made in rehearsals.

[1] T. S. Eliot, 'Poetry and Drama' in *On Poetry and Poets* (Faber and Faber, London, 1957), p. 91.
[2] Marion Cole, *Fogie*, p. 165; reference should be made to this whole chapter.

The Chorus in Performance

These comments, recorded thirty years later, take us back to the time when this type of verse was new. We have seen Eliot freeing himself from the limitations of post-Shakespearian verse-drama, and now realise that his interpreters had to go through the same process. That this was successfully achieved, testimony such as that of Charles Morgan in *The Times* goes to show:

The Chorus is never a group of women dully chanting. Taught by Miss Fogerty how to use Mr. Eliot's rhythms, it has at once dramatic and intellectual impact.
(17 June 1935)

The task of mastering the new style of verse, and of making audible the complex passages spoken in chorus, was a very arduous one. At Canterbury, it was made far harder by the acoustics of the chapter house, which are among the worst I have ever met. Miss Fogerty gives a vivid account of her struggle with them;[1] and Miss Thurburn tells her part of the story from her side of the 'wings':

The first performance in the Chapter House was something of a nightmare for me. In the first place the acoustics made unison speaking well-nigh impossible, and in the second place we had hardly met the rest of the company and had not rehearsed long enough with them to know the continuity. On the first night I sat behind one of the screens and gave the leader her cue by tapping on it.

When the play came to London and a run of some length was evidently in prospect, the teacher-students who had given the first performance had to be replaced by stage-students, and indeed a succession of these had to be trained as the seniors left for other work. Miss Thurburn comments on this period:

I had to keep an almost nightly check on *tempo*. I think one of the problems of speaking Eliot lies in finding and retaining his tempo. There were certain passages which nearly always 'ran away'. How much of this difficulty was due to choral speaking being inherently difficult to time, and how much to the fact that the students were young and inexperienced, I do not know. What I do know is that some of the problems were solved by their youth and inexperience, and by the fact that having worked together for two years they were able to think and act together with the greatest ease.

After two years in England, the production was to go to America; and Miss Thurburn was asked to work over the choruses:

There had necessarily been a great many changes in people, and although the newcomers had the advantage of more experience they had not been through

[1] Marion Cole, *Fogie*, pp. 165–6.

the processes of growth and development which the original group had shared in starting from scratch. Most of them were working without any real roots; they came into an existing pattern without knowing what made it so.

Miss Fogerty, backed up by Miss Thurburn, stresses the necessity of starting with a homogeneous group, who have had a common training. Only so, they affirm, can action and speech come from 'a marked united impulse on the part of the whole group' which 'will be harmonious—yet they remain individuals, not acting under a uniform command'.[1] And it is true in my experience that a group becomes either mechanical or ragged unless this impulse continues to exist in it.

The common impulse must be felt throughout by all; even when a single person, or only a small number, is speaking, the whole group must be involved in the feelings expressed. Thought and feeling must flow from one to another so that there is no break, nor differentiation, in the experience. Each performer must be willing to allow himself or herself to become thus integrated into the group; for a Chorus is more than the sum of its individuals. Its essential function is to convey an experience felt in unity by all. Historically, the chorus existed before the drama, which arose out of it; and a Chorus must still be what it originally was, the group chosen to speak for the community.

To do this clearly and effectively requires a high degree of technical accomplishment. Each of the voices, which has been chosen to fill a certain place in the scheme of sound, must be properly produced and under proper control. There can be less allowance for variation in performance than is possible in individual parts, since it will affect the whole group and alter the scheme. There has to be much more technical work in order to achieve not only unison but also balance and harmony, without drilling.

Eliot's choral writing, as Miss Fogerty says, is distinguished by 'the way individual threads of character run through the whole of the chorus'. While one cannot go so far as to say that there are individual characters within the group, there are certainly 'threads of character', expressed in recurring lines of a certain mood: a mood of bitterness, a mood of unquenchable optimism, a mood of practical common sense, a mood of fearfulness, or the 'discouraged hopelessness' which Miss Fogerty, with her buoyant faith, found so strange.

[1] Marion Cole, *Fogie*, p. 164.

The Chorus in Performance

Her analogy with the orchestra is to some extent true of all choral writing—and one is reminded that the word *orchestra* originally meant the place where the Chorus danced out its part. But it does particularly apply to Eliot, even more than to the Greek dramatists for whom the ritual past was more insistent. Eliot has succeeded in the 'effort to identify myself with these women' to such good purpose that each speaker has her distinctive tone of voice. This means also that when they are blended, each, by preserving her own pitch and timbre, can contribute a distinctive sound to a whole which is not an anonymous unison but the harmony of persons thinking together, expressed in a series of chords.

Elsie Fogerty was wise enough to understand the dangers of this medium in which she achieved such a triumph:

> the leadership given by the person training the chorus tends to become tyrannous with a risk of bringing about a mannerism in the speaking with exaggerated striving after harmony; a monotonous stress develops, and very few people have an ear keen enough to understand the difference between speaking in tune and chanting. The musical note must never be the dominant effect, and the group must work until they can *speak* with harmonious inflection—not chant.[1]

The art has almost disappeared from our stage; dramatists, led by Eliot himself, have ceased to write for it, and the whole attitude to acting has shifted towards an ensemble of action rather than of speech. As Ashley Dukes says, 'the original conception, which was that of the Central School and its Principal, will have a place of its own in dramatic history'.[2] But like all masterpieces, *Murder in the Cathedral* has been and will be given many and divers interpretations, in which its Chorus will be handled in many different ways.

I myself have worked upon the play several times in the last thirty years, and each time have discovered fresh possibilities for the Chorus. During the war, the Pilgrim Players toured the play for three years as a part of their repertory. This travelling company had only four women; they became a true Chorus with a deep mutual understanding, but having so small a number I assigned far more of the lines to single speakers. Using more mature actresses, this had advantages, both because one could be sure of clarity and because the quality of the individual had more chance to make itself felt. When I used much larger numbers after the war, even as many as sixteen in

[1] Marion Cole, *Fogie*, p. 168.   [2] *Ibid.*, p. 167.

87

Gloucester Cathedral, I still tried to make use of this individual quality among my speakers. And all the time I was moving towards what I should like to call choral *acting*. It was still necessary that the speech should be of the first grade: the technical demands were still as exacting. But, especially when the uniformity of dress was given up in favour of a blended group of individual costumes, each actress became freer in emotional expression and differences of age, experience and character within the Chorus added to the richness of the whole.

Movement, too, became much freer. This had begun during the original production, when it was released from the cramped quarters of Canterbury and even more when it moved to larger stages than the Mercury. But the young actresses, especially of those days before the vigorous acrobatic training of the post-war years was introduced into drama schools, did not command the power of movement that would fully correspond with the emotion of the lines; and it has been only when using a Chorus of varied ages that I have gone further to meet this challenge. At the Old Vic in 1953, Robert Helpmann showed the way with movement designed by his own balletic genius; but he showed also the dangers of allowing the movement to take precedence over the speech. Eliot must be served first.

With all these things in mind, I approached my most recent production at the Yvonne Arnaud Theatre, Guildford, in 1967. My Chorus of six was drawn from auditions, and had to discover its own entity. The process proved the measure of truth in the dictum that a Chorus, to be successful, must have had a common training; these actresses had not worked together before. It was an arduous task for us all, and blemishes were certainly left, particularly in the unison work. But a common instinct did develop: the work itself captured them, and they had the great advantage of a strong leader, in Henzie Raeburn, who knew the play deeply. What pleased me about this performance was that within the unity each individual was able to act with power, so that some moments of great theatrical excitement were developed. For the first time, the Chorus at the murder was so overwhelming in its horror that the Knights had to fight hard to get the audience to accept their apology. In sum, the Chorus now became a full partner in the drama, expressing the feelings of the Christian community through the mouths of the poor women who loved their lord and archbishop. They never become realistic 'charwomen'—

they are far too articulate for that, and that is not the intention; but they do represent the people, the ordinary folk of a city committed by faith and loyalty to Becket and his Master. The Chorus should, I believe, fulfil this function and hold this place in the drama.

Such a view is in consonance with what we have recently seen in the Greeks' presentation of their own classics. Karolos Koun's production of *The Persians* of Aeschylus, which was shown in London, had a Chorus of this kind. It was 'magnificently trained', like the original *Murder in the Cathedral* Chorus; its range of speech inflection was tremendous, and its movement, although strictly controlled, was powerful. At the climaxes, its individual members, without breaking the unity, were able to rise to great heights of individual passion. In this production, the Chorus was by far the most exciting feature. The same, I believe, should be true in *Murder in the Cathedral*.

4

The Family Reunion

What kind of play was to follow *Murder in the Cathedral*? Naturally, its success produced a number of invitations to write further religious or historical plays; but Eliot was quite determined to refuse them all. He had always been wary of repeating himself; but in this matter he was motivated by a positive conviction. If the poets of the twentieth century were to find once more a place in the theatre, it could only be by writing of contemporary life. Verse must not be confined to characters in costume; it must be spoken by people who were living the same life as their audience.

So, while *Murder in the Cathedral* was continuing its perambulations around Britain, a play set in modern times was taking shape in its author's brain. The seed from which it sprang had been sown long since; as one can see from the epigraph of *Sweeney Agonistes*, Orestes and the Furies' pursuit of him had already a contemporary relevance in Eliot's mind. How it came to be envisaged as happening in a north-country mansion I do not know; but our diary tells that already on 14 November 1937, Eliot 'came to supper and read new play'.

When he finished, there was a long pause. He looked up, disappointed at our slow reaction: and we caught a sudden glimpse of the young poet, sensitive and unsure of himself. Our minds were divided between fascination and doubt. We were at once fascinated by the authenticity of the family and of the verse-form created for it; we were doubtful whether the central scenes of the play, which seemed cloudy compared to those in the family atmosphere, could emerge into full drama with their characters clearly defined and their purpose comprehensible. And this proved to be the author's chief task in the revisions which went on for a year from that time.

Of all his plays, this one was, and is, the most difficult to apprehend. It is also the one which, to me at least, has over the years yielded the most in fresh insight at each repeated contact.

The Family Reunion

In the Houghton Library collection is a typewritten scenario, which probably represents what Eliot read to us on that November evening (of which no copy exists). Between the pages headed '*Part I*' and '*Part II*' is one whose heading reads 'Act I scene ii Revise'. This was very likely a result of our meeting; it gives names to the characters, whereas in the scenario they are represented by letters or descriptions.

THE FAMILY REUNION

Part I

48 pp. Just after tea. Present, in a conventional upper middle class drawing room: the MOTHER (widow) distinctly the head of the family (successful marriage, money, three sons) but beneath the surface of dignity due to accidents of fortune, a bewildered person dependent in any emergency upon her younger sister (spinster) who has had a hard life and sees things as they are. There are two other sisters, still younger, spinsters, who go to form the chorus. There are two younger brothers

* (also of her husband, bachelors, men about town, respectable clubmen.* It
chorus) is the Mother's Birthday, and her three sons are expected.

Conversation shows that the eldest son, A. has lost his wife (after a year or so of marriage) who was washed overboard from a liner in a storm, when she should not have been on deck. The marriage was not approved of by the family.

Enter A. who has been abroad for some time. He has not been home since the drowning of his wife. He appears somewhat distraught, and
* sees peeps out of the window or draws the curtains hurriedly* (complaint
them? from his mother at not leaving this to the maid). Subsequent conversation shows that he thinks he is being followed, but is vague about the cause. Family perturbed, suspect nervous breakdown due to loss of wife. Gradually elicited that he pushed her overboard, or thinks he did. Mother suggests that he should go up and dress for dinner, and will feel better after a hot bath.

This gives opportunity for family to discuss A. and his mental condition. Suggestion that they should invite the Doctor to dinner and tip him off to form an opinion of A.'s condition. Nobody believes A.'s story of having pushed his wife over. Anxiety expressed why other two sons are late. They also are arriving from a distance.

Family disperse to dress. Room empty, Mother's COMPANION enters, dressed for dinner. Young woman, knew A. before he went away. A. dressed for dinner, re-enters. Duet. Towards the end the EUMENIDES appear in the embrasure of a window: one man and two women, in evening dress. A. sees them. The Companion does not appear to see them, she continues to talk, and as A. turns to answer

91

her they fade away. Then the members of the family re-enter, dressed for dinner. The doctor arrives. Decided not to wait for B. & C. but go in to dinner. This provides the interval.

Act I sc. II   Revise.

Mary is the daughter of a deceased first cousin of Amy's. She has been brought up at Wishwood. If Harry is 29, say she is 22. She is now an undergraduate in her last year at Oxford, and is back for the Easter vacation. All this must come out in conversation. She was 15 when she last saw Harry, and he was 22.

> Mary has a little money of her own, she is not financially dependent upon Amy, who has merely taken the part of guardian, given her a home.

She enters and soliloquises, about 5 inches, arranging flowers. Enter Harry and soliloquises behind her. She turns and greets him. Asks if he recognises her. Conventional questions. Harry admits he had looked forward to returning, but that it is not what he had expected. They agree that childhood was not a happy time for them. How she thought of him and he of her then should be brought out. She tries to persuade him however that his depression is only the shadows that he has brought with him. He refers obscurely to Furies. She endeavours to reassure him about all that past gloom and horror clearing up now that he has returned, and has almost succeeded when the Furies appear.

Part II

44 pp.   A. and the Doctor re-enter drawing-room, for the conversation which is to be an examination without A. knowing it. Doctor is old family friend. Eventually A. tells his story more fully. Doctor evidently incredulous and believes him deranged. The Pursuit of A. had begun as he returned home, or a sense of pursuit, but he only SAW THEM for the first time before dinner. Doctor more and more convinced that the loss of A.'s wife has upset his mind, and brought out some latent sense of guilt from early years, which he has materialised in this way. Sympathetic. A. who first made the admission to the family as if it was torn out of him, becomes more and more explicit and emphatic about it as he finds that his story is not believed, and the horror of being thought insane grows upon him.

The family re-enter. The news is brought (perhaps by a policeman, giving A. the impression that *he* is being wanted) that the second son, B. has been killed in a motor accident while hurrying to the party. Doctor hurries off to B. A. makes speech pointing out how much better off B. is than himself. Then news comes (by telephone this time) that C. (third son) has been arrested for forged endorsement (or some similar offense). Family grief momentarily overwhelmed by family sense of humiliation. Speech by A. in defence of C. Stage must be

cleared so that ELDEST AUNT can talk to A. alone. She is recognised as the only one of the family who has any influence over him.
Her attitude gradually changes. The EUMENIDES appear again to
A. Aunt pulls the curtains again. She agrees that A. must go to seek
his purgation. He leaves. Companion enters. Aunt and Companion left
alone on stage. They discuss A. Finally Companion says to Aunt: 'So
you saw them too?'

In Part I there might be a man-servant of A. who has been with him
abroad: he could be interrogated separately by the family to find out
what happened on the boat.

The basic pattern of the play is the family relationships and the
irruption into them of the force represented by the Furies. This is in
accord with Aeschylus' central plot, though his Chorus is of a totally
different kind. There are no names in the scenario; Eliot is thinking
first in terms of the pattern, allowing individualities to emerge later.

The mother is 'distinctly the head of the family', but beneath the
surface is 'a bewildered person'. This bewilderment and her 'dependence' on a sister, afterwards disappear. The sister is the eldest of the
other three; it is only in the next stage of development that she
becomes the youngest, as the mother acquires increased power.

The idea of the Chorus composed of two sisters and two brothers-
in-law is already present: and it is remarkable that when Eliot starts
to write their lines are practically complete in the first draft. They have
of course no responsibility to advance the action, so that their role
remains static and unaffected by alterations made to that end. But
they must have been one of the clearest features in Eliot's first conception. There is no sign yet of their emergence into 'individual
character parts',[1] which posed some delicate problems of transition.

The hero himself is called 'A', and of him also we learn very little.
He 'appears somewhat distraught' on first entrance; and as soon as he
goes off the family naturally discuss his 'mental condition', having
suspected 'nervous breakdown due to loss of wife'. The doctor whom
they call in becomes more and more convinced that he is 'deranged',
and as 'A' senses this 'the horror of being thought insane grows
upon him'.

Eliot evidently conceived his condition as deriving partly at least
from a family background. In the first draft of the Chorus which
follows the scene of Harry's revelation, its members indicate this

[1] 'Poetry and Drama', in *On Poetry and Poets* (Faber and Faber, London, 1957), p. 82.

possibility, together with their shrinking from any extraordinary experience:

> Why should we stand here like guilty conspirators, waiting for some revelation
> When the hidden shall be revealed, and the newsboy shall shout in the street?
> When the private shall be made public? Why do we huddle together
> In a horrid amity of common misfortune, what are we destined to suffer?
> Why should we be implicated, brought in and brought together?
> Is it the madness of great uncle Harry that will not be parted from Wishwood?
>
> . . .
>
> We like to be thought well of by others
> That we think well of ourselves.
> But the mania or the vision of others
> Must be kept apart from ourselves.
> So that any explanation will satisfy:
>
> . . .

(FR/D5, cf. Collected Plays, pp. 73–4)

In the later scenario for the final section of the play[1] there is a side-note that

Great uncle Harry was cursed by a witch?

The curse is retained, particularly in Agatha's rune-like speeches, though I am not sure whether it quite fits in with Harry's intensely personal experience, which seems rooted in the Christian concept of original sin rather than in that of a Greek curse or fate. Harry does not express his despair, while he is gripped by it, in terms of madness; it is isolation, hopelessness, flight. Only when he has been delivered from it does he speak of having been insane:

> . . . when one has just recovered sanity,
> And not yet assured in possession, that is when
> One begins to seem the maddest to other people.

(Collected Plays, p. 110)

In his isolation, Harry must have someone to talk to: and the two characters who supply this need are the Companion and the Eldest Aunt. They undergo even more radical transformation than he. The extra page of scenario for Act I scene ii is the beginning of a process which continues until the text is finalised. The first section of script which I print here, from the draft 'D5' in the John Hayward collection

[1] See below, p. 100.

which is probably Part I of what we listened to in November 1937, shows what a long way there was to go.

After 'Exeunt Omnes' to dress for dinner[1] there is a stage direction written in the author's hand, as are all the ascriptions of speeches, the names being still tentative. There are also some corrections in his hand, which I have shown above the words replaced.

(*Pause. Enter* MARY)

MARY[2] The spring is very late in this northern country,
    Late and unconfident, clings to the south wall,
(*Enter* HARRY)
    Deprecating, with thin apologetic bloom,
                        eastern (??)
    While the sun fights with the ~~northern~~ sea.

        .   .   .   brief
HARRY I have seen the summer come too soon, where winter is a ~~mere~~ for-
    mality,
      sharp
    A ~~brief~~ disturbance of the restless heat
    And the merciless sun. Giving no habituation,
    No hibernation into patient misery.
    Where one does not suffer?

MARY   Each one's pain
    Has its own climate, every climate its own torment.
    No doubt. So we seek, in one place or another
    The kind of suffering that we can endure.

HARRY And in the north?

MARY   The late spring heals the premature summer
    Of other climates. Coming late
    Is more honest. Its late flowers are more substantial.
    A flower needs something more than form and colour.
                autumn
    I had rather have my ~~late~~ flowers pinched by the frost
    Than withered by the heat.

HARRY It would have been better to have come here then.
    I need the time to entertain a long winter.
    Wherever I have been, one went away in winter
    And the winter was too short. And I have been
    Where there were no seasons, but always together

---

[1] Cf. *Collected Plays*, p. 74.
[2] Ascriptions of speeches not in D5, inserted by EMB.

In barbarous light or superstitious darkness
Warm germination and warm decay.

MARY   Where would you go?

HARRY   From pole to pole, to seek the dark season.

MARY   Only a peculiar fancy of escape, surely,
From one death to another. Perpetual exile
Of conscious climate, is imposing our own spectres—
Is it not?—upon the world, not living as a part of it.

HARRY   Spectres? What spectres?

MARY?   I only mean
Living at the mercy of our own spirit—
Not soul, I do not mean—and in that way, who knows
What it may not do?

HARRY   What it may not do.

MARY   Surely it is necessary to stay in one place
To acquire the rhythm of recurrent seasons
Which strengthen both hope and resignation.
So, growing older, we shall feel a little young
In the transition from season to season—
No older than the year, and younger in the next one,
With a kind of contentment.

HARRY   Are you contented?

MARY   That is not a simple question.
                              the
On the surface there is always a perpetual struggle
With difficult circumstances, unrealised ambitions,
And waking in the morning, the reminder of the ceiling
Of something more for which it is too late.
Is that not the same for everybody? But it seems to me
That the surface does not matter. The stillness in the depths
The stillness and the clarity—
Don't you think that it might be attainable?

HARRY   I have spent many years in travel,
You have been in England, yet you seem
Like someone who comes from a very long distance
Or the distant waterfall in the forest

Inaccessible, half-heard. Can I ever hear
Or see clearly?

.   .   .

MARY   You confuse yourself
  Surely, with apprehension. Like the man
  Convinced that he is paralysed, or the other
  Who believes that he is blind.

.   .   .

HARRY   What I see
  Is one dream or another. But the most real
  Is always the one I fear. The bright colour fades
  Together with the uncapturable emotion,
  And the eye adjusts itself to a twilight
              is seen to be
  Where the dead stone ~~becomes a hideous~~ batrachian,
    aphyllous branch
  The ~~dry tree~~ ophidian.

.   .   .

MARY   You bring your own landscape
  No more real than the other. And in a way I think
  You take yourself too seriously, like many people
  Who are highly sensitive. You would like to forget,
  You would like to go back to the first turning,
  And because you cannot obliterate the past
  You create your own torment and prefer it. Oh I know it is real.
  Made very real—by misdirected energy. Can't you be more humble?
  Harry?

.   .   .

HARRY   I see. It may well be as you say.
  But is it not too late? Am I anything more
  At last, than a shadow among my shadows?

.   .   .

MARY   Is your fear not also pride? You have become the actor
  Of a single role, fearful of a new one. Because you fear
  You may not appear so well in another one.
  Yet the world in which ~~you ought~~ to live is so close to you, Harry!
  As close as the other! Such a simple turn
  And you are there! The opening of a door
  Just at your hand, and you are there—
  ~~And smell the new cut grass under sunlight.~~

.   .   .

HARRY   I need much help.

.   .   .

MARY   No, you do not!
  You only need straightforward simple honesty.

.   .   .

97

HARRY   I hear your voice as, in the silence
Between two storms, one hears the moderate usual noises
In the grass and the leaves, of quiet life persisting
Which ordinarily pass unnoticed.
I think you may be right, though you hardly know
To whom you are speaking, or why you say it . . .
Is the spring then not an evil time, stinging with close delusive voices?

.   .   .

MARY   It is a time to be humble, accepting the life of whatever is living.

.   .   .

HARRY   Is it not a time when the branches bleed, and the ground is exasperated
crawling
with subterranean ~~movement~~?

.   .   .

MARY   It is with the moving things, both under and over the soil,
Living things, moving things, that we must be reconciled.

.   .   .

HARRY   But to what end but another autumn, recurrence of issue of blood and
congealing?

.   .   .

MARY   We lose and we gain, or it would not be movement, our movement.

.   .   .

HARRY   But then do we move except in identical circles, between the dark and
the light of the moon?

.   .   .

MARY   We move so, but we must submit to it, being creatures of the sun and
the moon, subject to the movement of spheres,
and
But also in a spiral move, ~~so~~ tomorrow does not bring
What we wanted yesterday, but ~~better~~, a different desire,
have
So the gain and loss of tomorrow ~~has~~ another meaning
From the loss and the gain of today. For each stage of the journey
A different signification of sorrow and joy

.   .   .

HARRY   So one never passes through the same door
Or returns to open that one overlooked.
I have to study a new joy and sorrow.
Whether you know what you are saying, or to whom you are speaking
news
It does not matter. You have given me ~~a word~~
Of a new world, †in the deep, in the abyss of light, a *new* world, ~~Mary~~ . . .
Stop!
What was that? Did you feel it?

.   .   .

† 'in the deep, in the abyss of light,' inserted in the author's hand'.

98

The Family Reunion

MARY   Feel what?

                    .   .   .

HARRY   That apprehension deeper than any sense,
      Deeper than the sense of smell, but like a smell
      In that it is indescribable, a sweet and bitter smell
      From another world. I know it, I know it!
      More potent than ever before, a kind of odour, a vapour dissolving
      All other worlds into its own reality. O Mary!
      Stop, stop. Don't look like that! Try to stop it!
      O why now, a reminder
      That I have gone too far to return. Oh, good-bye.

(The curtains part and the Eumenides appear in the window embrasure)

      Why do you show yourselves now for the first time?
      And here? I do not want you. I do not know you.
      When I knew you, I was not the same person,
      I was not any person. Nothing that I did
      Had to do with me. The accident of a dreaming moment,
      Thinking of something else, a moment of distraction
      Put me among you, and I woke to find the trap closed.
      I tell you, it is not me you are looking at,
      Me you are grinning at, not me your confidential looks
      Incriminate, but that other person
      You thought I was, let your necrophily
      Feast upon *that* body. They will not go.

                    .   .   .

MARY   Harry, there is no one here.

*(She goes calmly to the window, almost touching them, and pulls the curtain
across the window)*

                    .   .   .

HARRY   They *were* here, I tell you. They *are* here.
      Are you so imperceptive, have you such dull senses
      That you could not see them? If I had realized
      That you were so obtuse, I would not have listened
      to your pretentious nonsense. Can't you help me?
      You're of no use to me. I must face them,
      I must fight them. But they are stupid,
      How can one fight with stupidity?
      But I must speak to them.

(He rushes forward, and tears aside the curtain. The embrasure is empty)

      Oh.

                    .   .   .

The Family Reunion

MARY O Harry!
(*Enter the family severally*)

(*FR*/D5)

This scene shows the nature of the task ahead. Neither of its characters is quite a person; rather, they are speaking a 'duet' of the seasons and the mysterious forces beneath the surface of life; it is more a theme-song than a scene. The facts about Mary (whose acquisition of a name helps her to find her personality) stated in the 'Revise' scenario were elicited by the need for such a discovery. Harry, if he is to be real, must have real people to talk to; Mary and Agatha (who becomes the *youngest* aunt by the next draft, and is enabled thereby to be more of a person and less of a high-priestess) must necessarily be the ones to whom Harry can unburden himself; thus it is vitally important that they are as clearly defined, as clearly differentiated, as possible. We can watch this as it happens.

The scenario deals practically not at all with the relations between the three women in Harry's struggle, Amy, Agatha and Mary, and it has no ending. Between it and the full draft of the play's text must come a scenario (in the Houghton Library collection) for the final section, written in manuscript; this develops the scene between Harry and Agatha and goes on from there:

Scene: Harry and Agatha. My brothers will be going on the same as before—but I . . . Reverts to his wife. When *in*, he has no feeling of

That is the process of de-possession her being human being. When *out*, cannot connect. Stain, not guilt. But *here*, all horrors of childhood coming out and becoming legible. Never understood his childhood misery before. One thing led to another. Are we getting back to real source of trouble?

Great uncle Harry was cursed by a witch? Agatha on his father. Only looked through the little door.
Harry realises or re-incarnates his father's feeling towards Agatha. Agatha is the de-possessed. She however wavers for a moment. The Eumenides appear again—scene corresponding to that in Act I. Harry decides to go and Agatha agrees.

Scene: Amy enters and accuses Agatha of taking her son as she took husband. This *was* to have been reconciliation but now might as well spill the beans.
Harry reiterates intention to leave and goes to pack. While he is speaking Mary enters. After his exit she turns on Agatha and the 3 women rave at each other.
Amy totters out. Reconciliation of Mary and Agatha. 'You saw them too.'

Enter Downing to fetch Harry's attache case. 'I know about them.'
Exit.
Enter Family.
Amy's voice.
Telegram from Arthur.
Enter Doctor.

In January 1938 we went with *Murder in the Cathedral* to the United States. While we were at Liverpool, where we gave a few performances to 'run in' the new actors and try out the new set, I must have received an urgent letter from Eliot asking whether naked lights could in any circumstances be allowed on stage. I replied on 13 January 1938:

> The Adelphi Hotel
> Liverpool
> Thursday evening

My dear Tom,

I can't think how to explain this in a wire so hope a letter will do. Naked lights are allowed on stage *if they are part of the action* and can be shewn to be integral to it. E.g. matches for cigarettes are allowed: and a candle in the flame of which someone burns his aunt's will! I imagine you could easily make the lighting, or blowing out, of the candles an essential part of the scene, if not so already.

We've got a lot of good work done here and I feel more sanguine now. The new set is good.

Henzie sends her love and so do I.

> Yours ever,
> *Martin*

This enquiry had obviously been concerned with the candles on the cake in the final ritual; and a few weeks later, when we were in New York, the first complete script of the play arrived:

> 15 February 1938

Dear Martin,

I am sending under separate cover a copy of the complete text of THE FAMILY REUNION to you, and also to Ashley. I should be grateful if when you receive it you would send me a short wire, merely saying 'manuscript received', as if the manuscript went astray without my knowing of it, much valuable time would be lost.

I can imagine how little time you have at present, and I am very sorry to add to your burdens, but if the play is to be produced and published in the autumn, it is really important that I should have your and Ashley's criticisms at the earliest possible moment, especially if they involve any drastic changes.

I should like from you if possible both fundamental and minor suggestions for alteration. It is a pity that we cannot discuss points in conversation, as the play must really go to press early in June in order to be ready for publication. I want any criticisms therefore of the plot as a whole, of the characters, and of any inaccuracies or weaknesses that suggest themselves.

I am not certain of all of my entrances and exits. I have an uncomfortable feeling that some of the entrances may appear fortuitous and unmotivated, and especially the entrance of Mary in the last scene.

Incidentally, you are much more at home, naturally, in foxhunting society than I am, and you may find minor points which could be improved from this point of view.

You will notice that I have rewritten Act I Scene 2, and I think have improved it by giving it more relation to plot and character, and I hope relieving some of the slowness which seemed to me to afflict that Act.

If I think of any other points of detail, I will send them on later, but I must get this letter off to catch the Queen Mary.

I hope that you are keeping well in spite of the strain, and that you have not suffered from excessive hospitality in Boston.

In haste,
Yours ever,
Tom

The script was read both by ourselves and Ashley Dukes, who hoped to present this new play to follow up the success of *Murder in the Cathedral*. I have a carbon copy of this script, and will make detailed comparison of it with the final text. But first, I think it will be valuable to print in full the correspondence about the text, even though Eliot's letter has already been published by F. O. Matthieson,[1] for it enables the reader to see the whole process, often stumbling and devious, by which others come to understand what an artist is driving at, and how Eliot, by the exercise of patience and clarity of mind, discovered what he could use, and what evolve for himself, from the suggestions offered to him.

Hotel Great Northern
New York City
March 11, 1938

My dear Tom,

Our efforts to prolong 'Murder's' chances in New York have finally ceased after a week of frantic ups and downs, so I am free to write about the much-more-important new play. I am very tired, and it may not have had the best of my brain, so if you find some of my ideas about it trivial or stupid, don't be surprised or mind them, but just discard them. I think, though, that Ashley and I are in agreement about the main questions, and that these are what you most want to hear of now.

[1] *The Achievement of T. S. Eliot* (Oxford University Press, third edition, 1958), pp. 167–8.

The Family Reunion

We both feel the play to be weak in plot. Reading it again, one is once more enthralled as at the first hearing by the skill and wit of the versification of natural country-house speech, and by the strong and authentic atmosphere of the house, family and retainers. This is splendid, and so long as development is not called for, is good for the stage. But later one begins to feel the need of stronger on-stage plot, and at the end one is definitely disappointed for lack of it. Two or three ideas have come up which I put for consideration:—

(1) *Mary*. The scene with her leaves her indeterminate: and she fades out after it. This is a pity as she comes at so crucial a point: and also she can be of great use: she is or has been a *way of escape*. Henzie suggests that, as she is a distant cousin, to marry her may have been Harry's right way of nullifying the curse: there might have been a real love between them: then Harry, feeling the oppression of Wishwood and unwilling to face and overcome it, ran off with his alien woman and so was led from crime to crime—from desertion to murder. This would make material for real use of Mary, and would bring out the now-obscure genesis of the push (that *most* dangerous word!).

It is also possible to draw a parallel between the child—the next heir to Wishwood—that Harry did not give to Mary, and Harry himself whom his father tried to destroy in the womb. So can be established that struggle, so tragically typical of English county families, between the conscious need of an heir and the subconscious curse of barrenness in the soul which fears the power of the unborn generations. All this can be on-stage (tho' not contemporary) plot (like Ibsen).

(2) Gerald and Charles, Ashley suggests, should be Arthur and John. It is true that the accidents are impossibly weak, happening to people one never sees: they also don't develop the plot at all, and because we don't *see* those people, your effect in Amy doesn't register. You want, don't you, to show Amy unmoved by the physical disasters but killed by Harry's spiritual one? This needs defining far more clearly: and if Arthur and John appeared it would be easy. I don't think their part in the Chorus need be invalidated either.

(3) In this connection I suggest that the Winchell scene could be far more strongly planned, still preserving the wit of the dialogue. Winchell could come *to arrest* Arthur, unwillingly of course: and the matter could be arranged with him and hushed up—a contrast between the physical arrest which the power of the Manor can avert and the spiritual arrest by the Furies, which is unavoidable because Wishwood is itself one with them.

(4) *Ivy and Violet* are also nebulous, and it would, I believe, be of great value to get a *quarrel* between them, in which both characters would define themselves more clearly, about Harry and the future—we should see them jealous of Agatha as being closer to Harry, and afflicted by the sense of barrenness and isolation, yet feeling their roots strong in the family and house—this study of two of the thousands of such women could be very poignant. By reconstructing pp. 60–69 (the newspaper stuff will probably come out anyway now?) you could make a good join also between scenes 1 and 2—this is now a bad stage-join, with no motivated entrances or exits.

The Family Reunion

(5) Amy's death is brilliantly done: and I like the ritual enormously. I suggest two things:

(a) Amy's acceptance of Harry's going seems far too meek. If she is the strongest person in the play, she would either *fight* to keep him, or would expressly recognise his going as the working of the Fates (see below). There's a necessary scene here, and one of the strongest in the play, perhaps the *climax*.

(b) The *cake* should be carried on, unlit, on p. 93 (Charles' speech): the candles lit during the Chorus p. 97. So we get *time* to appreciate its significance.

(6) *The curse.* (a) What started it? *Surely* we need some indication of its origin or at least of its *deep* past.

(b) Is it a *curse* (doesn't some human *pronounce* a curse?) or a *fate*?

(c) If it is connected with house or family and not just with the two pushers, wouldn't all the family know it in some form? It needs this grandeur: and at the end we need to sense its expiation more definitely.

These are the big questions I see needing answers. I have noted smaller ones on a separate sheet.

You'll realise, I hope and think, that we all three feel this draft to have magnificent possibilities. I hope this analysis will seem constructively useful; and to be in tune with your aims. It is directed towards making the play the overwhelmingly strong work it *implicitly* is now, without destroying the quiet, witty, loving observation of character which makes it so valuable.

We are planning to stay here a couple of weeks anyway, but most likely shall be back in mid-April. I should *very* much like to know, however, when you've seen Ashley, whether it would be of material assistance to you to have me on the spot by that time, as I should try to make my plans accordingly. Could you send me a deferred cable saying 'should appreciate your presence' if you want me: I do want to help over this, more than anything else I might be doing, so *don't hesitate* to call on me, if Ashley wants to make an early production. I haven't told you how *enormously* we enjoyed your Boston friends and especially your brother Henry and his lovely wife.

Yours ever,

Martin

Notes on Minor Points[1]

16/17 [65, 66]   Harry is very abstract in these speeches.

28 [73]   The scene needs an end—this might be made out of the *car*, which needs to be made significant—the chariot that bears him away.

34 [80, top speech]   Harry's second speech is very hard to follow, as spoken.

43/4 [87, 88]   This for the end of Part I is going to be a bit flat on the stage: the Chorus' point of view is negative and the Rune is mysterious, and they follow a scene of several pages with no happening. Here is where revision of plot may be a great help. *Don't* cut the Rune!

48 ff. [89–93]   This excellent dialogue needs sharpening up—the dramatic point

---

[1] The page numbers given in square brackets refer to *Collected Plays*.

of each speech needs defining and they need to have more pressure and less reflection, so that one gets the excitement of conflict—the *reaction* on each other of two men each in a difficulty.

67   Is Amy's speech a little too resigned?[1]

69 [102, 103]   Could more concrete facts and pictures enliven this very important past history?

70 [105]   Could Agatha *discover* on the stage 'you have not known what crime you expiate'? If this were *new* it would be thrilling: and it should be explicitly connected with his father etc. for the audience to grasp it.[2]

71   The description of father has a few phrases like 'common realities' which need sharpening.[3]

74/80 [106–8]   This scene seems to stand still here—to deal with *states*, rather than *developments*, of mind: and some of the very fine abstract phrases need linking to the story. They tend to seem almost absurd if there are too many, spoken by two characters only, in close continuity.

83 [112]   Amy (bottom of page)—does she speak too elaborately for so single an emotion?

90 [115]   The house is suddenly called 'damned'—we ask why? Here would come in the advantage of some history of the curse.

Do reflections of 'Murder' matter:

'seven years'.

'end or beginning' (75)

'wait and witness' (88)?

Hotel Great Northern
New York City
March 8th 1938

Dear Tom,

Martin will have told you something of our sad history, and I will let you have the whole tale in London about March 22, for I am sailing with about half the company on Thursday by the Antonia for that port, Martin and others remaining for a few days.

We are both eagerly interested in the new play, which I have read several times. First the title. I wanted to suggest something like pursuit or horizontal doom—rather than the perpendicularity generally associated with doom, and asked why you could not have a hunting metaphor implicit in
(1)   the name. Martin then thought of *Meet at Wishwood Manor*, which was a development of an old suggestion about the name of the house. I think on reflection *Meet at Wishwood* would seem to me expressive enough. Does it not also contain the same basic idea as *A Family Reunion*, or would not *The Meet at Wishwood* say the same thing in a satiric way as *The Family Reunion*? And still bring in the Furies as a pack?

---

[1] Part of this speech was cut, the rest transferred to a position immediately after Harry's final exit (cf. *Collected Plays*, p. 117), where the resignation is entirely appropriate.

[2] This has been done.

[3] These were cut.

(2)   Martin and I both feel that the controversy bound to centre in the poetic use of the word 'push', and the image conjured up by 'push', especially in the case of the well,[1] will be disturbing to the play. This is almost certainly the word dearest to you, and we have no hope that you will give it up, but think you ought to. And Martin does not quite see the chorus yet but will write to you himself on that matter.

Meantime it is all deep and exciting and must go on to the stage soon.

Yours
Ashley Dukes

[Note by T.S.E.:]
For consideration.

I don't hold with (1) at all. As for (2) I think that the push into *the well* might go out, but I hold to the pushing in Part I sc. 1.

24 Russell Square
London, W.C.1
19 March, 1938

Dear Martin,

Your good letter arrived yesterday, and I cabled at once, as there was no point in waiting for Ashley. The fact is that after Easter I am going to Lisbon (I do not yet know the exact date) to sit on a jury to decide the award of the 'Camoens Prize'—at the expense of the Portuguese government! This sounds rather silly; but I had thought of taking a short holiday after Easter, as I found it beneficial last year. Then when I got this invitation I had the opportunity of enquiring about it in a very high quarter, and was urged to accept—to contribute my mite to the Ancient Alliance! I shall have to be back early in May in any case, as I have to speak in Salisbury. I thought you ought to know at once that I should not call upon you to change your plans: it was good of you to offer to return sooner.

Your examination of the play was no more painful than I had anticipated—I had been looking forward to the moment with dread. I shall try to do some work on it before I see you; but first I have to sort out, of course, the criticisms I can accept from those I can't! And where I think you may have misunderstood me, that is significant too, as indicating that I have not made the meaning transparent. First, I am ready to admit my own apprehension that the play has not enough plot, or that what plot it has is too much in the background. That must be remedied somehow. Second, I confess that some of your criticism seems to me tantamount to asking me to write a new play: but if I do that I shall start with quite another situation and another set of characters! This includes, first, the suggestion that I should substitute Arthur and John for Gerald and Charles. But, apart from my affection for Charles (as the character most like myself) and apart from the fact that we are meant to realise that Arthur and John, though we never see them, are weaker images of Gerald and Charles, I mean Gerald— John; Charles—Arthur, I still feel that there is a good deal of point in their not

[1] In Part II of this script, Agatha tells Harry that his father planned to push his mother into a well; see below, pp. 115, 131.

being there. This needs a lot of thinking about; all I am quite sure of at the moment is that if I re-write the play in this way it will not be finished until next year. That does not matter in theory, but political events make one feel that one is working against time, and may lose the race anyway.

Next, as to Mary. I do feel that there is a weakness in having her turn up only for two big scenes, and disappear in between. Of course, if I accepted Henzie's suggestion, I should have to make her much older, because as it is she was hardly more than a child when she last saw Harry, and he could hardly have been interested in her then. This could be done, but altering her age would mean altering her character. And there is meant also to be some point in the parallel between her starting life now as a teacher, and Agatha's debut in that profession.

Now, as to Harry's marrying Mary as the right way of ending the 'curse', here I feel on surer ground. The point of Mary, in relation to Harry, was meant to be this. The effect of his married life upon him was one of such horror as to leave him for the time at least in a state that may be called one of being psychologically partially desexed: or rather, it has given him a horror of women as of unclean creatures. The scene with Mary is meant to bring out, as I am aware it fails to, the conflict inside him between this repulsion for Mary as a woman, and the attraction which the *normal* part of him that is still left, feels towards her person-ally *for the first time*. This is the first time since his marriage ('there was no ecstacy') that he has been attracted towards any woman. This attraction glimmers for a moment in his mind, half-consciously as a possible 'way of escape'; and the Furies (for the Furies are *divine* instruments, not simple hell-hounds) come in the nick of time to warn him away from this evasion—though at that moment he misunderstands their function. Now, this attraction towards Mary has stirred him up, but, owing to his mental state, is incapable of developing: therefore he finds a refuge in an ambiguous relation—the attraction, half of a son and half of a lover, to Agatha, who reciprocates in somewhat the same way. And this gives the cue for the second appearance of the Furies, more patently in their role of divine messengers, to let him know clearly that the only way out is the way of purgation and holiness. They become exactly 'hounds of heaven'. And Agatha understands this clearly, though Harry only understands it yet in flashes. So Harry's career needs to be completed by an *Orestes* or an *Œdipus at Colonus*.

Mary understands nothing, and is in a fair way to having to follow exactly the footsteps of Agatha, in order eventually to reach the point that Agatha has reached.

Amy also understands nothing: she is merely a person of tremendous person-ality *on one plane*. What happen to Arthur and John are not meant to be 'disasters', but minor accidents typical of each: she *is* affected by these. But I admit that her behaviour on Harry's departure needs clearing up. But Harry's departure is not a disaster for *him*, but a triumph. The tragedy is the tragedy of Amy, of a person living on Will alone.

There is one point which is meant to be left in doubt: did Harry kill his wife or not? This is the justification of the word 'push'. In what other *simple* way can one person imagine that he has killed another, except by pushing? Suppose that the desire for her death was strong in his mind, out of touch with reality in her company. He is standing on the deck, perhaps a few feet away, and she is leaning over the rail. She has sometimes talked of suicide. The whole scene of pushing her over—or giving her just a little tip—passes through his mind. She is trying to play one of her comedies with him—to arouse *any* emotion in him is better than to feel that he is not noticing her—and she overdoes it, and just at the moment, plump, in she goes. Harry thinks he has pushed her; and certainly, he has not called for help, or behaved in any normal way, to say nothing of jumping in after her.

Harry therefore is really expiating the crime of having wanted to kill his wife, like his father before him. Only, his father did not succeed; he only dragged out a miserable existence first at Wishwood and then abroad. So the crime, and the necessity for expiation, repeat themselves. But Harry is still not quite conscious. At the beginning of the play he is aware of the past only as *pollution*, and he does not dissociate the pollution of his wife's life from that of her death. He still wants to *forget*, and that is the way forbidden. (It is not I who have forbidden it, I see it as Law.) Only after the second visit of the Furies does he begin to understand what the Way of Liberation is: and he follows the Furies as immediately and as unintelligibly as the Disciples dropping their nets.

As for the pushing, I had already felt some doubt of the advisability of the second pushing ('into a well') and I am ready to drop that. But I thought I had made things clear enough to the audience by having Harry say, in his dialogue with Agatha, that perhaps he only dreamt he pushed her.

I do attach a good deal of importance to Charles, and what I get out of him (a different attitude from that of any of the other choral figures) I could not get out of a younger man. What just saves Charles is his capacity for being surprised by the bulldog in the Burlington Arcade.

Of course there is meant to be a marked difference between Amy's attitude towards her eldest son and towards the two younger sons whom she 'created', whom she has already recognized to be second-rate, and who, ironically, take after the less interesting members of her husband's family. She is as near to real affection for Harry as she is capable of being. Not that I mean her to be a terrifying stone image, but her capacity for love has been atrophied by a loveless marriage, a humiliating marriage as it turned out to be, and that humiliation working on a character whose great sin was pride. I mean her to be pathetic as well as powerful and jealous.

Well, I think this must do for the present. I can imagine what 'scare' headlines the New York papers have been printing. Of course anything may happen, but no one seems to expect war in the immediate future.

With many thanks, and love to Henzie,

Yours ever affectionately,

Tom

Following this correspondence, Eliot wrote a memo to himself of

What *I* think must be done:
1. To introduce Mary at beginning and send her out to arrange flowers.
2. To make Amy's farewell to Harry more convincing.

The Family Reunion

3. To break up Harry's long speech at beginning of Act II sc. ii.

4. To motivate Mary's entrance later in this scene.

5. To deal with definite article in Harry–Agatha duet [this refers to a criticism of the excessive number of 'the's in this passage].

6. Harry's father etc.

7. To alter newspaper paragraph.

He then sent the whole collection to Frank Morley, an old and close friend who was also a partner in Faber and Faber. Morley replied with a 'Memo' which he kindly allows me to quote:

MEMO to TSE from FVM 20.iv.38

When I consider how difficult it is to feel anything in N.Y. except distracted, Martin Browne's letter seems 1st. rate. I mean that I would qualify it very greatly, but that it is document A among the criticisms. Your own letter of March 19 to MB is document B. Dukes' letter I don't think worth considering, except as indicating that he may be hard to handle.

I don't hold with much that Browne *says*. I disagree with all of his detailed points, and most or all of his rationalisations. But *behind* what he says seems to me 1st. rate dramatic criticism. His good points—those your document B admits—are in reality pleas for more attention to time: speaking time, acting time, audience-reception time. That is what he seems to me to mean by 'weak in plot'. It is *not* weak in plot: it is if anything surcharged with too much plot: but too much remains hidden, especially to the hearer who cannot change the pace of his reception, as a reader can.

There is this general difficulty, that the pace on different planes is different, and while you do shift gears in a way that is marvellous, there are some corner-ings not yet (I feel) perfect. I feel that because Martin B and Ashley failed to get you and had too much excuse to fail.

MB suggests that your most trouble to come is Mary. Your own *statement* (document B, p. 2) is 1st. rate (ça va sans dire) *conception*. MB's conceptions of Mary are out of tune. But in the text your conception is apparent only if one can read shorthand. I'm not man enough to say how, but you must somehow give more time to expose that scene. I don't mean that you need prolong the actual Harry–Mary contact at that spot: but if not prolonging it there, must *prepare* for its importance: for on seeing more in that scene than MB saw, depends seeing more in the Furies than a mere pack of hounds: more in Harry–Agatha: etc etc, I needn't go on so clumsily. At present that Scene II, all-important in its place of importance, *doesn't* mean all it should. Isn't explicit.

I had the feeling that what I called a short 'Willow Willow' passage between Mary and Agatha might replace most of Mary's speech at the beginning of Sc. II: Agatha coming in there might give more aid to the 'following' relation-ship (document B, 3rd para) and if she hit Mary with a sort of 'you're pretty, child: ought to get married' shot it would help (in its untruth as well as truth) in suggesting Harry's temporary what shall I say. Having scored such a point, Agatha off, Harry on with only some little slowing, maybe, of the existing text:

and (about p. 35, 36) either some action or some acting such as some of the audience might indistinctly resent, to make the Furies more *evoked*. I don't mean wholly or mainly or mostly evoked: but I do mean *partly* evoked. (In part a resolution of discomfort in a hearer's sensibility.)

My own suggestion perhaps much more feeble than those I castigate in MB! But I feel *some* Willow Willow passage needed: which I call Willow Willow because of Desdemona: meaning that was the perfectest example I think of, of how sensitive he was at knowing when and what and how to do. How he knew to put that there, in all simplicity and touching every plane of feeling.

You cannot, must not, touch the Agatha–Harry scene later on (except do as you please with the article-criticism, which I wouldn't take too seriously *in that place*) because that is too delicate to tamper: I wouldn't know yet, or perhaps ever, if it is just right, but I suspect so. But by that same token, you should improve the Harry–Mary reception.

In general, that is, you can afford to expose more of your plot. You have a good hand, a tremendously full hand: show it a little more boldly. As to your 7 points as to what *you* think must be done, I castigate the expression of point 1: it isn't enough (as you know) merely to introduce Mary at beginning and send her out to arrange flowers. I feel you *could* leave her *appearance* to Scene II and get away with it, if you wanted: I mean appearance earlier, and arranging things, is not enough. I don't myself worry about your point 2, Amy's farewell to Harry. When I first read Act I, in scraps, Amy seemed to loom large: now I feel MB is making too much of her—I think she's pretty well OK as is—overdo her farewell and you give too much emphasis to a sub-phase of the plot. Your point 3, breaking up Harry's speech: just as you like: and so with point 4—not difficult— though if MB gets you too agitated you'll be having Mary doing nothing but rush in and out with flowers! Your point 5, would be of more importance anywhere *except* in that Harry Agatha duet, where the *the*'s have point in the frenzy. Don't know what you mean about yr point 6; and point 7, keep if you can get around the mechanical difficulty. There are one or two trivial age-questions: Harry's age, Mary's age—don't *matter*, but better juggle to fit if need be. Harry's mental-age (as the psychologists say) seems to me about 40! But what the hell. Another trivium: p. 49, Agatha *never* came? Is that so? Another: in your letter (document B, para 2, you refer to '*there was no ecstasy*'. In the text, doesn't this come later on: I mean, a *listener* wouldn't hear that to help him with Harry–Mary scene?

Since I am getting reckless, let me say that if you want you might change gear more slowly between bottom p. 5 top p. 6 [*Collected Plays*, p. 60], by having Gerald say he never understands Agatha, and so give her more springboard for this first high dive.

p. 14   I wondered if the Harry–Agatha speeches: mean particularly Agatha at bottom of the page: might not be better if shorter–more rapid dialogue.[1]

p. 87 top: the question to Mary more telling if Agatha makes it?[1]

p. 88 top: Amy's first two lines—is that Amy, or better Agatha, speaking?

---

[1] These were transferred to a later position.

If Agatha, more point to Amy's 'that woman there'. If Amy, a little weak, not proud?[1]

But these are foolish. My own main feeling is it will act *damn* well if the actors can obtain comprehension of the main idea: if where you feel right you dilute for them, for you can't deny you do nacherly tie yr knots pretty tight. Which is swell too . . .

. . . I think that's all that occurred to me, if you call it occurring. Oh yes, keep Push 1, not Push 2.

Huzza: bravo the Portugooses

FVM

Having looked at these comments, we can examine the play's progress through the various drafts we have. These are:

'D5' first draft of Part I in the John Hayward collection.

'Harvard' draft in the Houghton Library collection.

The draft of March 1938 in my possession.

'D4' in the Hayward collection, dated 28 September 1938, with many notes in Hayward's hand.

Hayward was an astute observer of manners, and acutely conscious of social niceties. He also suggested re-ascriptions of speeches; and all these, together with his exact sense of the sound and meaning of words, were much-valued aids. Eliot, however, could firmly go his own way from him as from all of us when he felt it to be better.

The matter of the play's title was an instance of this; Ashley Dukes's alternatives had no appeal. In the Houghton Library draft, the play is sub-titled 'A Melodrama'; but the line is crossed out, clearly by Eliot himself when he wrote the words 'vernal equinox' on the title-page. But it is worth remembering that this description had been in his mind. 'Vernal equinox' recurs in other notes, and indicates how much the seasonal pattern influences his thought.

The setting is described thus in my draft:

The action takes place in a country house in the North of England.

Part I is placed in the drawing-room, between tea and dinner; Part II is in the library of the same house directly after dinner on the same day. The two rooms may be conceived as lying on either side of a central hall; so that the disposition of doors and windows is symmetrical.

Each part is in three scenes, which are played without intermission.

(*FR*/EMB)

The detailed second paragraph was dropped from the next draft. The purpose of shifting across the hall for Part II was to give Harry

---

[1] This scene was remodelled.

and Warburton the most plausible setting for their after-dinner conversation. But it was less plausible for the rest of the Part, and the style of the play was better matched by a single monumental setting to depict the brooding power of the classical mansion.

The opening scene remains almost unaltered from the first draft to the final text. This can be observed also in *Murder in the Cathedral* and in *The Cocktail Party*. It seems as if the opening of each play came to Eliot along with its framework, and that to write this was the necessary way to establish the pattern of characters whose lives would provide the action. The alterations made later are of single words, or the cutting of a couple of repetitious lines. The only one of special interest is in the last line of Amy's speech, on page 62 (*Collected Plays*) which is drafted as:

> Please behave only
> As if he had returned from a long holiday
>
> (*FR*/EMB)

But one addition has been made to the scene: the passage with Mary. This character, as will have been noticed from the discussions above, is the one who was least clearly conceived at first. In the scenario, she does not appear till her scene with Harry; and her age (which is afterwards altered) and antecedents are only defined when that scene is revised. Her relationship with the family is not developed at all until the final scene with Agatha. Yet she is one of the most important people in the pattern of Harry's redemption,

To establish her the passage on pages 58–9 (*Collected Plays*) was inserted. In the drafts, the scene runs straight on from

CHARLES   The younger generation
    Are not what we were. Haven't the stamina,
    Haven't the sense of responsibility.

to

GERALD By the way, Amy,
    When are those boys of yours due to arrive?

Mary's new passage, though short, is of immense value to the actress. It lets us see her living among a family in which she has no standing, because of her youth and her poverty. This creates sympathy for her, so that her next, rather edgy scene with Agatha is made easier.

The Family Reunion

Agatha's first dialogue with Harry[1] contains in the drafts some lines which were transferred to the end of the scene, where they are more useful. At this moment, Harry is obsessed by the lack of understanding shown by the family, and is not ready to listen to the one who does understand. The draft contains also some lines, which, though afterwards cut, give the student some valuable indications of how Eliot conceives Agatha:

```
                 shall
HARRY   I should be less embarrassing to you. Agatha?...
AGATHA   I think, Harry, that people must be taken
                                      can exist
    On the level of consciousness on which they choose to live
    If you have the strength to do it. I am afraid you haven't.
    If not, you must proceed on the way of destruction
    On your own responsibility. Half measures are no kindness.
    But you cannot go on living in a private world
    Unless you can reconcile it to the public.
    You cannot go on living in a double nightmare.
```

.   .   .

```
HARRY   I think I understand what you mean, though I cannot explain it;
    As you once explained the sobbing in the chimney,
    The evil in the dark closet, which they said was not there,
    Which they explained away, but you explained them
    But I do not know how, and if I knew
    It would not be an explanation.
    But how can I explain? How can I explain to you?
    All that I can make you understand
    Is only events.
    And people to whom nothing has ever happened
    Cannot understand the unimportance of events.
```

.   .   .

```
GERALD   Well, you can't say that nothing has happened to me –
    I was a youngster in the Afghan War—
    Been in tight corners most of my life,
    And some pretty nasty messes.
```

.   .   .

```
CHARLES   And there isn't much that would surprise me, Harry,
    Or shock me, either.
```

.   .   .

[1] See *Collected Plays*, p. 65.

HARRY   You are all people
   To whom nothing has happened, at most a continual impact
   Of external events. You have gone through your lives in sleep,
       woken
   Never ~~waken~~ to the nightmare. I tell you, you do not know time.
   You only know the abstractions of past and present and future;
   You do not know what happens. You do not know
   The noxious smell, untraceable in the drains,
   Inaccessible to the plumbers, that has its hour of the night; you do not know
   The unspoken voice of sorrow in the ancient bedroom
   At three o'clock in the morning. I am not speaking
   Of my own experience, but trying to give you
   Comparisons in a more familiar medium. I am the old house
   With the noxious smell and the sorrow before morning,
   In which all past is present, all degradation
   Is unredeemable. As for what *happens*!
   Of the past you can only see what *is* past,
   Not what is always present. Which is what matters.

                .   .   .

AGATHA Nevertheless, Harry,
         us
   Best tell ~~them~~ what you can.   (*FR*/D5)

Harry's speech is interesting in several ways. The Time theme, which we met in *Murder in the Cathedral* in another form, is re-stated. The punctuation of the final lines is worth noting. And Agatha's introduction to Harry's revelation is briefer, without the understanding couplet added. The exchange between them[1] before he goes to have his bath was written in later, using some of the lines dropped from the scene quoted above: and the effect is to make the relationship between them much closer and Agatha more sympathetic. This is all part of the necessary process of bringing warm flesh round the bones of the plot, and mitigating Harry's inevitable isolation so that the audience too can get into touch with him. He must be able to talk to someone in order that we may share some of his experience.

   The climax of Harry's revelation is marked by the words

   When I pushed her over.

Dukes and I had been afraid that on the stage we might get a laugh in the wrong place, not on Harry's line but on what followed:

VIOLET   Pushed her?
IVY He means, gave her a push.   (*FR*/EMB)

---

[1] See *Collected Plays*, p. 68.

When Ivy's line was removed the passage worked perfectly. The second 'push' referred to in the letters came into Agatha's recollections of Harry's father in Part II:

>   I found he was thinking
> How to get rid of your mother.
> HARRY   To push her?
> AGATHA   Into a well. You would not have been born ...   (*FR*/EMB)

Eliot abandoned this as a result of the correspondence, leaving Harry's

> I only dreamt I pushed her

to stand alone in contradistinction to his 'I pushed her over' in Part I.[1]

We have seen in his letter what a particular feeling Eliot had for Charles, 'as the character most like myself . . . I do attach a good deal of importance to Charles . . .' He is built up, between the first and second drafts, by the insertion of the lines hinting at his own experience of the nightmare possibilities of life:

> There's a lot in my own past life that presses on my chest
> When I wake, as I do now, early before morning.
> I understand these feelings better than you know—
>
> > (*Collected Plays*, p. 67)

Now we come back to Mary, with whom, as Morley says, 'M.B. suggests that your most trouble [is] to come'. Her scene with Agatha is Morley's 'Willow willow' passage, and serves to tell us a great deal about both women. It replaces a soliloquy, 'about five inches',[2] specified in the Synopsis of the revise and actually written in the draft. While a soliloquy would not be ruled out by the style of the play, it contains no other, and the direct contact of this newly appearing character with the audience would have felt uncomfortable. The material is far better used in the duologue.[3]

The scene with Harry is, in the second (*FR*/EMB) draft, already far better than the one from 'D5' printed above. Mary has become a person with her own entity and point of view, and the relationship with Harry has begun to become clear. Even now, however, there is ambiguity, and more must be done. The suggestion in my letter, however wide of the mark, does make that evident. It is, by the way,

---

[1] Cf. *Collected Plays*, pp. 66, 104–5.   [2] See above, p. 92.
[3] *Collected Plays*, pp. 75–7.

the one comment which Eliot misunderstood; he speaks of 'Harry's marrying Mary as the right way of ending the curse' as if it were intended that this should take place *now*. The actual suggestion was that 'to marry her may *have been* Harry's right way of nullifying the curse'—that is, before he married his unsuitable wife. It still does not fit Eliot's conception; but it is not the one to which he replies.

All this discussion produced some good results. The first improvement was to change the ages of the two characters. In the drafts, Harry is 29, Mary is 22; and she is too young to fulfil her role. Her value in the final analysis is that of the buoyant spirit which has suffered a long period of conscious frustration but still believes that the spirit's problems can be solved by will. To speak at all to one who has endured what Harry has, her suffering must have been long; seven years since she came down from Oxford to be incarcerated by Amy is the necessary discipline. And Harry, too, whose 'mental age seems to be about 40' to Morley, gains from becoming 35.

On the last page of Eliot's letter I have scribbled

Mary and Harry re childhood at Wishwood: should this theme be more definite?

Obviously this was taken up: and it resulted in one of the most moving passages in the scene,[1] the shared memory of the hollow tree. One wonders whether it is a personal memory of American childhood; for the terms 'wilderness' and 'stockade' would have been unknown to English children. The revision has also given the scene a far better line of development; it now starts with their common memories and goes on to Harry's despair, which Mary recognises to be 'an experience I have not had'. She tries to help him back to hope —and almost succeeds; and their empathy is expressed in the first of the two 'lyrical duets'.

This passage differs entirely in rhythm from the final text,[2] and considerably also in content. The use of rhythm *different* from that of the rest of the play is common to both, and is essential to the effect aimed at, of allowing the characters to escape from conscious thought into a shared subconscious state, almost of trance. Eliot himself criticises this device rather harshly;[3] and it is true that actors have a real difficulty in preserving its quality without allowing the play's progress to seem entirely suspended. But I think that the instinct

[1] See *Collected Plays*, pp. 78–9. [2] *Ibid.*, p. 82.
[3] 'Poetry and Drama' in *On Poetry and Poets*, pp. 82–3.

which inspired the duets is a right one; they prepare both actors and hearers for the imminent incursion of the supernatural Eumenides.

'The appearance of those ill-fated figures, the Furies' is amusingly described and castigated by Eliot in 'Poetry and Drama'.[1] 'Their failure', he says, 'is merely a symptom of the failure to adjust the ancient with the modern.' This part of the problem—for it is only a part—is illustrated by the stage directions. In the scenario: 'one man and two women, in evening dress'. The first draft ('D5') says only 'The Eumenides appear in the window embrasure' . . . but to this, in the draft at Harvard (FR/H), is added in Eliot's hand:

Evening dress. Black ⎫
                 ⎬ tie?
        White ⎭

In my draft, the black tie has won.

The other part, and theatrically the more important, is the effect on the chief actor. In order to *show* the Eumenides in the window embrasure, the director must place the window in the back wall of the set. This means that, in each act, Harry must be facing upstage, with his face away from the audience, for the climactic moment. He faces a group of figures who neither speak nor move; who have in fact no life for the audience. This is a grave mistake; and Eliot is right in saying that none of the devices that either he or I have used or seen others use has overcome this handicap. The Eumenides, whatever they look like, however eerie the sounds or lighting effects which accompany them, cannot involve the audience in an experience which cannot be seen upon the face of the character who alone can mediate it.

Here then is the draft of the scene with Mary:

SCENE II (MARY, *alone, with vases of flowers*)

MARY   The spring is very late in this northern country,
      Late and unconfident, clings to the south wall,
      Deprecating, with thin apologetic bloom.
      I always forget how late the spring is, here.
      Yet I would rather wait for our windblown blossoms,
      Such as they are, than have these cultured strangers
      from the greenhouse, that do not look at you
      And have no language; that do not know
      The wind and rain, as I know them.
      I wonder how many we shall be for dinner?

[1] *On Poetry and Poets*, p. 84.

It is very trying, having to plan
for uncertain numbers. How can I stand it?
I must remind Hardy. There are six already.
Arthur and John eight—Harry perhaps—
None of them here yet. We shall have to keep the dinner back.
Is there anything more formal than a family dinner?
An official occasion of uncomfortable people
Who meet very seldom, to make conversation.
I shall have to sit between Arthur and John.
Which is worse, thinking of what to say to John,
Or having to listen to Arthur's chatter
When he thinks he is behaving like a man of the world?
I wonder what Harry is going to be like.
It won't be too easy talking to Harry
After all that's happened. Oh how can I stand it?
Can I stand another season in this house?
What does this place mean? Where everybody
Has always seemed to be waiting, waiting,
Waiting. I think this house *means* to keep us waiting.
(*While* MARY *has been speaking,* HARRY *has entered unnoticed by her*)
HARRY   Waiting for what?
MARY (*turns*)   Why, Harry! No one told me you had arrived!
When did you get here? Do you remember me?
I must have changed a good deal since you saw me last—
But you look just the same.
HARRY   And you look just the same, Mary,
Except for being seven years older.
And now you're at Oxford. I remember,
This must be your last year.
MARY   Why, Harry!
You don't remember as well as you think.
I came down last summer.
HARRY   And took your degree?
MARY   Yes.
HARRY   With honours, I suppose?
MARY   Only a second.
HARRY   Well, that's better than I did.
MARY   Oh, you could have, if you'd wanted to.
But I hope you are glad to be back, Harry;
It was good of you to get here for your mother's birthday.
Are you glad to be at home?
HARRY   I don't know at all.
I certainly looked forward to it. All these years
I'd been longing to get back. It seemed to be a place
Where one would feel safe, where one could stop and think,
Where life would become substantial and simplified—

But the simplification took place in my memory,
I think. It seems that here I shall get rid of nothing,
Of none of the shadows that I wanted to escape;
And at the same time, other memories
Earlier, forgotten, begin to return
Of unhappy childhood. I can't explain—
But I had assumed that I had had two different lives
And that I could escape from one to the other.
And it seems that perhaps it is all one life,
And there is no escape. Tell me, you must remember
Better than I, because not so long ago for you—
Were you happy here, as a child at Wishwood?

MARY   Happy? not really, though I never knew why—
It always seemed to me as if it must be my own fault,
And never to be happy was always to be naughty.
But then, there were other reasons—I was only a cousin,
Only here because there was nothing else to do with me;
And besides, my childhood wasn't yours: I mean
You were so much older. We were rather in awe of you—
At least, *I* was.

HARRY   And are you happy now?

MARY   That is not a simple question.
On the surface, there is always the perpetual struggle
With difficult circumstance, unrealised ambition,
And waking in the morning, the reminder of the ceiling
Of something more for which it is too late.
Oh, I know how silly that must sound!
But you can feel like that as well at twenty-two
As at forty-four, and youth is not happiness:
It is only harder now to understand unhappiness
And that makes it harder.
Why should I be talking like this?
You are only thirty, and you have as much future
Or more than I.

HARRY   One thing you do not know:
The sudden extinction of every alternative,
The unexpected crash of the iron cataract,
And that single instant of realisation
Is an eternity, for it is out of time.
I say, you do not know what hope is, until you have lost it,
In that way, and joined the legion of the hopeless,
Unrecognised by other men, though sometimes by each other.

MARY   I know what you mean. That is an experience
I have not had. Nevertheless, however real,
However cruel, it may be a deception
Just as truly as mine. You may confuse yourself

119

Like the man convinced that he is paralysed
Or the man who believes that he is blind.

HARRY   What I see
May be one dream or another; if there is nothing else
The most.real is what I fear. The bright colour fades
Together with the uncapturable emotion,
And the eye adjusts itself to a twilight
Where the dead stone is seen to be batrachian,
The aphyllous branch ophidian.

MARY   You bring your own landscape
No more real than the other. And in a way you contradict yourself:
That instant comprehension of the death of hope
Of which you speak, I know you have experienced it,
And I can well imagine how awful it must be.
But was that not a vision of another world?
You looked over the edge of things, into the pit.
But in this world another hope keeps springing
In an unexpected place, while we are unconscious of it.
You hoped for something, in coming back to Wishwood,
Or else you had not come. Perhaps that is a cheat—
As you feel it is. But you have gone on hoping!
So, if this hope goes, you may find another
Growing in some corner. Do you think I am right?

HARRY I have spent many years in travel;
You have been in England, yet you seem
Like someone who comes from a very long distance,
Or the distant waterfall in the forest,
Inaccessible, half-heard.
Or I hear your voice as in the silence
Between two storms, one hears the moderate usual noises
In the grass and leaves, of life persisting,
Which ordinarily pass unnoticed.
Perhaps you are right, though I do not know
How you should know it.
But is the spring not the time for deceptions?
The early spring, now, brings recurrent delusions?
Is the spring not an evil time, that excites us with lying voices?

MARY It is a time to be humble, accepting whatever is living.

HARRY But to what end but another autumn, repetition of issue of
blood and congealing?

MARY We lose and we gain, or it would not be life, our life.

HARRY But then do we move except in identical circles, between the
dark and the light of the moon?

MARY But also in a spiral we move, and tomorrow will not bring
What we wanted yesterday, but a different desire,
So the gain and the loss of tomorrow have a different meaning

120

From the loss and the gain of to-day. For each stage of the journey
A new signification of sorrow and joy.
And we never pass twice through the same door
Or return to the door we did not open.
HARRY   So I have to study a new joy and sorrow.
Whether you know what you are saying, or to whom you say it—
That does not matter. You bring me news
Of a door that opens at the end of the corridor,
Sunlight and singing; when I had felt sure
That every corridor only led to another,
Or to a wall, and that one kept moving
Only so as not to stay still. Singing and light.
Stop!
What was that? did you feel it?
MARY   Feel what?
HARRY   That apprehension deeper than all sense,
Deeper than the sense of smell, but like a smell
In that it is indescribable, a sweet and bitter smell
From another world. I know it, I know it!
More potent than ever before, a kind of odour, a vapour dissolving
All other worlds into its own reality. O Mary!
Don't look at me like that! Stop! Try to stop it!
Oh why now, a reminder
That I have gone too far to return. Good-bye.

(*The curtains part, revealing the Eumenides in the window embrasure. Evening
dress, black tie*)

HARRY   Why do you show yourselves now for the first time
And here? I do not want you. I do not know you.
When I knew you, I was not the same person.
I was not any person. Nothing that I did
Had to do with me. The accident of a dreaming moment,
Of a dreaming age, in which I was someone else
Thinking of something else, put me among you—
A passage of distraction, and I woke to find the trap closed.
I tell you, it is not me you are looking at,
Not me you are grinning at, not me your confidential looks
Incriminate, but that other person, if person,
You thought I was: let your necrophily
Feed upon that carcase. They will not go.
MARY   Harry, there is no one there.

(*She goes to the window and pulls the curtains*)

HARRY   They were here, I tell you. They are here.
Are you so imperceptive, have you such dull senses
That you could not see them? If I had realised
That you were so obtuse, I would not have listened

121

To your pretentious nonsense. Can't you help me?
You're of no use to me. I must face them.
I must fight them. But they are stupid.
How can one fight with stupidity?
Yet I must speak to them.
(*He rushes forward and tears apart the curtains, but the embrasure is empty*)
                    Oh!
MARY   O Harry!

                                                    (*FR*/EMB)

After this, Mary needs a good exit-line to escape from the family, who intrude upon her state of shock. But it is not given her until the final text; and the excuse, of dressing for dinner, is there prepared for, first by Agatha's exit line[1] then by Mary's attempts to get away from Harry, motivated by shyness[2] and later[3] by defeat.

By the time the script has reached this final stage, Mary has become one of the most living people in the play, and one of those who has most hold upon the audience.

The Part ends with Agatha's cryptic rune. Eliot had a delight in incantations, and could not resist introducing one into *The Cocktail Party*, where it arrives with something of a jolt. In this play, with its atmosphere of ritual tragedy, they are much more at home; and Agatha gives from the first an impression of arcane knowledge. But in this, as in many aspects of the play, Eliot is experimenting; the mystic number, for instance, is different in the early versions:

There are five together
May the five be separated.   (*FR*/H)

The drafts all contain variations of an extra stanza, following that which brings the curtain down in the final text. It shows, more clearly than it can be seen elsewhere, the way in which the Christian pattern of purgation is interwoven in Eliot's mind with the Greek; the commendation of Amy's soul at the end of the play, which is parallel to it, does remain in the final script. Here is the stanza as in 'D5':

Who called down the curse
Let him make the purgation
But where does the curse begin
And where does it end?
Not in the stony corridors
From one dream to another   (. ?)

[1] *Collected Plays*, p. 77.   [2] *Ibid.*, p. 78.   [3] *Ibid.*, p. 81.

May the curse be withdrawn   (Till the curse is)
Till the knot is unknotted
The crossed is uncrossed
And the crooked is made straight
By intercession
Of the Virgin Mary
At the centre, in the abyss
To the Father, to the Son
And to the Holy Ghost.

In *FR*/EMB, some alterations have been made:

Who called down the curse
And who shall make the purgation?
Where does curse begin
And where does it end?
Not in the stony moor-path
From one dream to another
Or at the ford in the burn
Where the young men come stepping with their horses, proud walkers,
Shall the curse be withdrawn
The knot be unknotted
The crossed be uncrossed
And the crooked made straight.

Eliot criticises the first scene of Part II as an overlong continuation of the exposition:

When the curtain rises again, the audience is expecting, as it has a right to expect, that something is going to happen. Instead, it finds itself treated to a further exploration of the background: in other words, to what ought to have been given much earlier, if at all.[1]

It remains in the same form, however, throughout the development of the script; and it does contain the essential information about Harry's father which is to be built upon in his scene with Agatha. Then come the scenes related to the accidents to the two absent brothers. To what Eliot says about their value to him, in his letter, may be added the fact that, as remodelled thereafter, they provide the best comedy in the play; and this, as the audience is about to be asked to listen very hard to the scene with Agatha, is of great theatrical value. It is intertwined with speeches for Harry which keep us aware of his groping progress. The changes made between the drafts and the final text are sufficiently interesting to make it worth while

[1] 'Poetry and Drama', in *On Poetry and Poets*, p. 84.

preserving the earlier version. The draft which follows should be compared with the passage in *Collected Plays* from Harry's re-entrance on page 98 to the end of the scene.

(*Enter* HARRY)

HARRY Engaged in discussing my brothers' characters?
    Engaged in predicting the minor event,
    Engaged in foreseeing the minor disaster
    On which people depend, to keep their minds distracted.
    You go on trying to think of each thing separately,
    Making small things important, so that everything
    May be unimportant, a slight deviation
    From some imaginary course that life ought to take,
    That you call normal. What you call normal
    Is merely the unreal and the unimportant.
    I, too, was less conscious, so long as I could think
    Even of my own life as an isolated ruin,
    A casual bit of waste, in a normal universe.
    But I see it is just a part of some huge disaster
    Which is the world, which I cannot put in order.
    O God, the things that I have seen in this house,
    Since I came home, a few hours ago, to Wishwood.
VIOLET I will make no observations on what you say, Harry;
    My comments are not always welcome in this family.
AGATHA Whatever you have seen, Harry, you might remember
    That there is always more; and what one has to see
    Is not merely that which is outside oneself
    Though there is a great deal to see: but we must also
    Try to penetrate the other private worlds
    And pass beyond the knowledge which is still our own
    To undertake the burden of others' stupidity,
    Malice, deception, ignorance, misery.
VIOLET   Really!
HARRY I might have understood you, if I had not seen them.
    It is something of the nature of a private puzzle
    Which I have to solve first. Were they simply outside
    I might escape, somewhere, perhaps. If merely inside,
    I could cheat them perhaps with the aid of Dr. Warburton—
    Or any other doctor, who would be another Warburton—
    Do you think that I believe what I said just now?
    That's only what I have been trying to believe,
    As the only way out. It is not being alone
    That is the horror, to be alone with the horror:
    What matters is the filthiness. I can clean my skin,
    I can clean my life, I can clean my mind—

But always the filthiness, that lies a little deeper
Than what can be cleaned . . .

(*Enter* IVY)

IVY   Where is there an evening paper?

GERALD   Why, what's the matter?

IVY   Somebody, look for Arthur in the evening paper.
That was a friend of Arthur's, ringing up from London.
It seems that Arthur too has had an accident,
But I gathered that he has not been hurt.
The connection was so bad, I could hardly hear him,
And he spoke very queerly, whoever he was.
But I heard him say it was in the evening paper.

VIOLET   What's the use of asking for an evening paper?
You know as well as I do, at this distance from London,
Nobody's likely to have this evening's paper.

HARRY   Stop, I think I bought a noon edition
On the way out of London. If I did, it's in my overcoat;
I didn't look at it. I'll see if it's there.

(*Exit*)

GERALD   Well, I said that Arthur was every bit as likely
To have an accident as John. And it wasn't John's fault,
I don't believe. John is unlucky,
But Arthur is definitely reckless.

VIOLET   I think these racing cars ought to be prohibited.

(*Re-enter* HARRY, *and hands a newspaper to* CHARLES)

HARRY   Here it is. See if there's anything in it.

CHARLES (*turning the pages*)   Yes, there is a paragraph . . . I'm glad to say
There isn't very much . . .

GERALD   There'll have been more in the later editions.
You'd better read it to us.

CHARLES (*reads*)   'Peer's Brother in Motor Smash'.
'While being pursued by a police patrol, at 7 o'clock this morning, the Hon.
Arthur Gerald Charles Piper, younger brother of Lord Monchensy, ran
into and demolished a roundsman's cart in Ebury Street. The milkman,
Percy Hopgood of 14 A, Bethesda Grove, East Sheen, was removed to St.
George's Hospital with two broken ribs. A friend who was travelling with
Mr. Piper was treated on the spot for minor injuries.
'In trying to extricate his car from the collision, Mr. Piper reversed into a
shop-window. When challenged, he appeared slightly confused, and said:
"I thought it was all open country about here"'—

GERALD   Where?

CHARLES   In Ebury Street.—'The police state that when pursued, Mr. Piper
was travelling at 66 miles an hour. When asked why he did not stop when
signalled by the police car, he replied: "I thought you were having a game
with me". He was taken to Gerald Road Station for further examination.'

GERALD   This is what the Communists make capital out of.

CHARLES That's not quite all. 'It will be recalled that six months ago Mr.
    Piper's name was freely mentioned'. . .
    No, we needn't read that.
VIOLET   This is just what I expected. But if Agatha
    Is going to moralise about it, I shall scream.
GERALD   It's going to be awkward, explaining this to Amy.
(*Enter* AMY)
AMY   You can spare yourselves the embarrassed explanation.
    I have been listening; and have heard nothing to surprise me.
    I am too old for sudden surprises. I might die at any moment,
    But not of this sort of news, you may be sure.
    At my age, one either does not understand,
    Or if one understands, there is nothing to say.
    At my age, I begin to apprehend the truth
    About things too late to mend: and that is to be old.
    Nevertheless, I am glad if I can come to know them.
    I always wanted too much for my children,
    More than life can give. I only twisted nature—
    You cannot change it.
(*Exit* AMY)   (*FR*/EMB)

In this *FR*/EMB version, Harry enters with an abrupt attack on the busybodies; in the final text, he begins with a few lines which show that he has established some sympathy with his mother. In *FR*/EMB just before their exit together[1] she has an extra line:

You looked like your father
When you said that. He sometimes spoke
In a different language.

After Harry's speech at re-entry, in which one may note[2] changes for the better, there comes in the final text Denman's entry to summon Ivy to the telephone. The exchange with Agatha has undergone revision. Ivy's account of the telephone conversation is more effective when it is Arthur himself who speaks to her; and the newspaper paragraphs have also benefited from the elimination of unnecessary material about the injured man and the police station.

Amy's re-appearance in the draft, and her exit, are unmotivated, and Eliot, with his customary economy, made the double saving of eliminating her scene here and using the last half of her speech where it is far more valuable, after Harry's final exit.[3]

Instead of this, he provides a lead-in to the chorus.[4] As one would

[1] See *Collected Plays*, p. 97.   [2] *Ibid.*, p. 98.
[3] *Ibid.*, p. 117.   [4] *Ibid.*, p. 100.

expect, he uses Charles for the purpose. This little passage provides a particularly good example of the way in which I believe the Chorus should be approached, and it may be useful to discuss it here.

As we have seen, the chorus was one of the first conceptions in the poet's mind and one which changed least. The changes were not in the choral passages but in those given to the individuals composing it, as they became more living and more idiosyncratic people. And this development seems to have had the effect on directors, including myself when I first worked on the play, of impelling them to mark the shift from scene to choral passage by changes in convention so definite as to compel the audience to notice them and to say to itself: 'Now we have a chorus.' As I have lived and worked with the play, I have become convinced that this is the wrong approach; and when I have seen it made by other directors recently my conviction has been reinforced. This play should not be made to conform to the conventions of its Greek ancestor, but should be taken at its own face value. These minor members of the Monchensy family, under unusual stress in the stiff atmosphere of the ancestral home, might well find themselves seized, as they sat in the drawing room, with common emotions of fear and dread, or assailed by common memories. In naturalistic drama, these thoughts would remain unspoken; but the poet, one of whose tasks is to increase the scope of 'the dialect of the tribe', can find the words for them.

So the director should find ways of bringing these characters into positions in which they can slide almost imperceptibly into concerted speech; and should allow such a mood as Charles creates:

In my time, these affairs were kept out of the papers,
But nowadays, there's no such thing as privacy

to evoke common memories. The 'Chorus' speech does not necessarily have to be begun in unison, and the lines are meant to be split up among the individual speakers, so that only at moments of strong common emotion do all four speak together.

Changes of lighting at the beginning and end of a chorus are only justifiable if imperceptible; their only purpose is to help the actors to establish the reflective mood, probably by concentrating attention upon the area where they are. But this device may well be dispensed with. Music, concrete or otherwise, is, I am sure, misleading.

Just as Eliot has provided for a natural flow into the choruses, so he has provided ways out from them, either by the intervention of another character[1] or by making the members themselves 'come to', their conscious sense of the immediate penetrating through their reverie. The last five lines on page 101 (*Collected Plays*) were added at my suggestion to achieve this effect and to make an exit. At the end of Part I[2] the obligation to go into dinner breaks each one's spell; at the end of the play[3] there is the even stronger obligation to pay homage to the deceased head of the family.

We now come to the climax of the play, the scene between Harry and Agatha. The most interesting version to show, I believe, will be that in Harvard's script from the Houghton Library collection. This is slightly earlier than *FR*/EMB and the revision done afterwards is therefore more evident by comparison with the final text; and it contains some readings which cast light upon the origin of certain thoughts there expressed.

The re-arrangement which placed 'I only dreamt I pushed her' at a later and higher point in the scene[4] is a manifest improvement; and it makes an additional reason for eliminating the pushing into a well.

Agatha fought for many years to win her 'dispossession'. Eliot used the form 'de-possessed' in the scenario of this scene.[5] It presumably relates to the passage from St John of the Cross which Eliot placed alongside Orestes' line as epigraph to *Sweeney Agonistes*:

> Hence the soul cannot be possessed of the divine union, until it has divested itself of the love of created beings.

Harry has only four words in which to register the effect of his aunt's revelation that he was born of a loveless marriage. For the actor, it is a short ration. Eliot quotes 'there was no ecstacy' in his letter to me as if it applied to Harry's own marriage. It could do so, but the parallel is not suggested in the play itself.

The 'lyrical duet' in this scene is already in the verse pattern which Eliot eventually used also for the duet between Harry and Mary. The excess of definite articles, discussed in the correspondence, has been considerably pruned in the final text. While Harry and Mary emerge from their 'trance' before the Eumenides appear, Harry and Agatha pass from reflective empathy to a closer sympathy which the Eumenides interrupt;[6] and they are not recalled to the transient world until

---

[1] *Collected Plays*, pp. 63, 74.   [2] *Ibid.*, p. 88.   [3] *Ibid.*, p. 121.
[4] See *ibid.*, p. 105.   [5] See above, p. 100.   [6] See Eliot's letter, p. 107, above.

after her 'somnambular' rune. The description of the Eumenides'
appearance here corresponds to that given in Part I and, like it, is
eliminated after *FR*/EMB.

In printing the following passage from *FR*/H, I have incorporated
readings inserted in the author's hand, except where he has marked
them as questionable or gives more than one possible choice. In these
cases I have shown them in footnotes.

HARRY   John will recover, be what he always was;
      Arthur again be sober, though not for very long;
      And everything will go on as before. These mild surprises
      Are all in the routine of normal life at Wishwood.
      John is the only one of us I can conceive
                  find
      As settling down to ~~make~~ himself at home ~~again~~ at Wishwood.
      Make a dull marriage, marry some woman stupider—
      Stupider than himself. He can resist the influence
      Being ~~quite~~ unconscious of it, living in gentle motion
      Of horses, and right visits to the right neighbours
      At the right times: and be an excellent landlord.
      As for me, there is this I want to tell you:
      ~~I am interested in hell, and I must think it out.~~
      I still have to learn exactly what *their* meaning is.
      Now, this whole past year was a kind of oscillation.
      —But before, at the beginning, seven years ago,
      There was, for months, that sense of separation,
      Of isolation unredeemable, irrevocable:
      It's eternal, because it feels eternal while it lasts;
      That's one hell. Then the numbness came to cover it.
      That was the second hell of not being there,
      The dull quiet pain of being parted from oneself,
      The self
      /Which persisted only as an eye, seeing, ~~watching.~~
      But this last year—nothing will fit together,
      There are two things that will not fit together:
      When I am *inside* the old dream, I am again the same emotions
      I felt, or was, while in it; the same loathing
      I was, I not a person, in a world not of persons
      But only of† contaminating shapes and noises—
      And I can feel no horror at my action,
      I only feel the repetition of it
      Over and over. When I have been outside,
      I could associate nothing of it with me

† contaminating *contacts . . . touch and noise . . . skins*

Though nothing else was very real. I thought foolishly
That when I had got back to the door here, as I left it,
            to
Everything would fall in/place—I would begin again.
They will not let me do it. Here I have been finding
                               torture
An old sorrow long forgotten, and a new ~~torment~~—
The shadow of something behind our narrow childhood;
The origin of evil. How far behind us?
Perhaps the later things have only been the dream
Dreamt through me by the minds of others. Perhaps
I only dreamt I pushed her. Why does the reality,
If so, seem a deeper nightmare?

AGATHA   It may be
                            torment
That this is the real purgatorial ~~torture~~:
Passing from the smaller to the larger punishment
Thinking that each is forever, while it lasts.
It seems possible that you do not know what crime
You expiate, or whose, or why. You will know hereafter.
Passing alone through chilly fires, chosen
To resolve the enchantment under which we suffer.

HARRY   That brings me to asking questions about my father.

AGATHA   If you knew what you were asking, what you are asking
   Is dangerous for you to know, dangerous for me.

HARRY   When I know, I know that in some way I shall know
   That I have always known it. That will be better.

AGATHA   I have fought many years to win my dispossession
   And many years to keep it. What people see me as:
   The hard efficient mistress of a women's college—
   That is only part. There is a deeper
                              could
   Organisation, which your questions ~~will~~ disturb.

HARRY   That is not how I see you now. I mean
   I thought of you before as ~~the~~ completely liberated
   From the human wheel. As the wholly dispossessed.
       turned
   So I ~~looked~~ to you for strength. Now it is rather
   A common pursuit of liberation. Speak.

AGATHA   Your father also, sensitive to influences
   Grew up at Wishwood. Untaught in common reality
   Could not control its ghosts. Yet he might have spent his life
   Like   very
   ~~As an exceptionally~~ cultivated country squire
   Reading Greek, sketching, playing upon the flute
   And not neglecting public duties. Inexperienced
   He hid unusual strength beneath unusual weakness.

Where he was weak he recognised your mother's strength
And yielded to it.

HARRY   There was no ecstacy.
   Tell me now, who were my parents?

AGATHA   Your father and your mother.

HARRY   You tell me nothing

AGATHA   The father whom you have assumed to be your father,
   And my sister whom you have known to be your mother:
   There is no mystery there.

HARRY   What then?

AGATHA   You see your mother as identified with this house—
   It was not always so. It was many years
   Before she succeeded in making terms with Wishwood,
   Before she took your father's place, and reached the point where
   Wishwood supported her, and she supported Wishwood.
   At first it was a vacancy. A man and a woman,
   Married, alone in a lonely country house together.
   She wanted always to have a sister there.
   I was the †eldest of the three. I was then
   An undergraduate at Oxford. I came
   For one long, (too long) vacation. I remember
   The summer day of unusual heat
                    Well?
  For this cold country. Need I say more? of that?‡

                                   Yes.
HARRY   No.

AGATHA   There are hours when there seems to be no past or future,
                        It only comes
  Only a present moment of burning light. They only come once,
   Thank God! that kind. Perhaps there is another,
   I believe, across a whole Tibet of broken stones
   That lie fang up, a lifetime's march. I hope there is.

HARRY   I have known neither.

AGATHA   The autumn came too soon, but not too soon,
   With a high wind. It had not shaken your father
   Awake yet. §One night he told me his designs
   To get rid of your mother.

HARRY   To push her?

AGATHA   Into a well. You would not have been born in that event.
   You were due in three months time. And I stopped him.
   I take no credit for a little common sense:
   He would have bungled it.

† youngest?
‡ The first question mark was deleted before the deletion of the whole sentence. (EMB)
§ He had been making plans.

HARRY ~~Either way. I am under no obligation.~~
    ~~It's indifferent to me~~.

AGATHA   I did not want to kill *you*!
    You to be killed. What were you then? only a thing called 'life'
    That should have been mine—as I felt then.
    That was the way I felt. *I* wanted you.†

          you
HARRY And/have me. That is the way things happen.
    Everything is true in a different sense—
    A sense that would have seemed meaningless before;
    Everything tends towards reconciliation,
    As the stone falls, as the tree falls. And in human lives
    That is the completion which at the beginning
    We could only have envisaged as the ruin. Look, I do not know why,
    It seems quite irrational, but now
    I feel quite happy, as if happiness
    Did not consist in getting what one wanted
    Or in getting rid of what cannot be got rid of,
    But in ~~seeing~~ a different vision. This is like an end.

AGATHA Or a beginning. Harry, my dear,
    I feel very tired, as only the old feel.
    The young feel tired at the end of an action,
    The old, at the beginning. Beginning all over!
    (I see that) I thought that living was like saving up capital:
    A period of discipline, then living on the interest—
    And
    ~~Then~~ one day you wake up, and the capital has vanished.
                  my own
    (~~You see,~~ I have had to think about/investments!
    So I talk in these terms). Living's not like that:
    One has to earn one's spiritual income daily,
    And I am old, to start again to earn my living.

HARRY But you are not unhappy, now?

AGATHA   That word does not mean much.
    Relief from an artificial burden
    And the brittle strength of pride, weak and wondering
                   must
    As when the headache stops. I/begin to learn
    To be alone with myself, without the company
    Of an invented self, between myself and me.
    But I am a little frightened. If there is another strength
    I do not know where it is to come from. Not in me.

HARRY You, frightened! I wish I had known
    But to have known, I should have had to have come already
    To the point where I am now. That was impossible—

† ? 3 or 4″ more for Agatha?

The Family Reunion

One cannot rearrange the past, that would mean going
Back to the beginning of time, the original chaos.
Yet if I had known—I think I could be fonder of my mother
By understanding how she came to be herself—
But she would not like that. Family affection
Was a kind of formal obligation, a duty
              by its
Only noticed ~~in the~~ neglect. One had this part to play,
After that training,
~~That was why~~ I could endure, those seven years,
Playing a part that had been imposed upon me—
And I return to find another made ready,
The book laid out, lines underscored, and the costume
Ready to be put on. But it is very odd:
When other people seemed so strong, their apparent strength
Stifled my decision. Now I see
I have ~~only~~ been wounded in a war of phantoms,
             who have
Not by real people, ~~with~~ no more strength than I.
The things I thought were real are shadows, and the real
Are what I thought were private shadows. O that awful privacy
Of the insane mind! Now I can live in public.

AGATHA   I only looked through the little door
When the sun was shining on the rose-garden.
             tiny
And heard in the distance the ~~little~~ voices
And then the black raven flew over.
I was only the feet walking
Away, down the concrete corridor
In a dead air. Only the feet walking
Sharp heels scraping. Over and under
Echo and noise of feet.
I was only the feet and an eye
               unwinking
Seeing only the feet. The ~~terrible~~ eye
Which sees the dream, is always real
Fixing the horror. Over and under.

HARRY   In and out the ceaseless movement
Of the shrieking forms in the circular desert
Weaving contagion of putrescent embraces
On
~~Of~~ dissolving bone. In and out the movement
Until the chain breaks, and one is left ~~alone~~
Under the terrible eye in the desert.

AGATHA   Up and down, through the stone passages
Of an immense and endless hospital,
Pervaded by a smell of disinfectant,

133

Looking straight ahead while passing the barred window.
Up and down, Until the chain breaks.

HARRY   To and fro, dragging the feet
Among the inner shadows of the smoky wilderness,
Trying to avoid the clasping ~~cactus~~ branches
And the giant lizard. To and fro.
Until the chain breaks.
                                    The chain breaks,
The wheel stops, and the noise of machinery;
And the desert is cleared, under the judicial sun
Of the final eye: and the awful evacuation
Cleanses. *I* was not there, *you* were not there, but only our phantasms.
And what did not happen is as truthful as what did happen.
O my dear, and you walked through the little door,
And I ran to meet you in the garden. And this is the next moment.

AGATHA   Only for a moment. The chain reforms, the wheel resumes, and the
noise of machinery;
And the eye is clouded but menacing. This is only the beginning
Of a new journey. We do not pass twice through the same door
        Or
~~And we do not~~ return to the door through which we did not pass.
I have seen the first stage: release from what happened
Is also release from the unfulfilled craving
Flattered in sleep, and deceived in waking. You have a long journey.

HARRY   Oh, not yet! please! This is the first time I have been free
From the ring of ghosts with joined hands, circling around me,
And come into a quiet place.
                                    Why is it so quiet?
Don't you feel a kind of stirring below the air?
Do you? *don't* you? a communication, a scent
Direct to the brain? Just as before,
But not quite like—

(*The Eumenides appear as before; but are now dressed as for travel, with luggage,
shawls etc.*)

                        —and this time
                        am surprised
You cannot think that I ~~did not expect~~ to see you.
And you shall not think that I am afraid to see you.
This time, you are real; this time, you are outside me,
And just endurable. I see that you are ready,
Ready to leave: and I am going with you.
You followed me here, where I thought I should escape you—
Or much more likely, you were here before me.
Now I know for certain that I am following you,

134

The Family Reunion

can be
And I know that there ~~is~~ only one itinerary,
One destination. Let us lose no time.

(The curtains close. AGATHA *goes to the window, in a somnambular fashion, opens the curtains, disclosing the empty embrasure. She steps into the place which the Eumenides had occupied)*

AGATHA   A curse comes to being
As a child is formed.
In both, the impossible
Becomes the actual
Without ~~our~~ intentions
Knowing what is intended.
A curse is like a child, formed
In a moment of unconsciousness,
        accidental
In an ~~unwholesome~~ bed,
Or under an elder tree
According to the phase
Of a determined moon,
A curse is like a child, formed
To grow to maturity;
Accident is design
And design is accident
In a cloud of unknowing.
O my child, my curse,
You
~~(They)~~ shall be fulfilled,
The knot shall be unknotted
And the crooked made straight.

(She moves back into the room)
Where have I been? I was just saying
That you have a long journey. You have nothing to stay for.
Think of it as something like a children's treasure hunt:
Here you have found a clue, hidden in the obvious place.
Delay is complication of minor evil.
What you have wished to know, what you have been told
Make impossible what this party was summoned for.
What was an interment has become an exhumation.
You did not intend this, I did not intend it,
No one intended anything. Go.

HARRY   Shall we ever meet again?

AGATHA   Shall we ever meet again?
And who will meet again? What is meeting?
Meeting is for those who do not know each other.
I think that this is only the kind of question
That is never answered, but merely superseded.

135

HARRY   I know that I have made a decision
    In a moment of clarity, and now I am dull again.
    I only know that I made a decision
    Which your words echo. And I know
    What you do not know, that these beings are real now,
    Real and outside me, and just endurable. I am still befouled.
                        defilement
    But I know, the only way out of ~~befoulment~~
    Is by a final agony of separation
            in me
    From that/which is defiled. I know this:
    I do not understand it. But I no longer fear her.[1]
    And I know that I must go.
AGATHA   You must go.
(*Enter* AMY)   (*FR*/H)

On page 110 (*Collected Plays*) occurs the largest addition to the second act; everything from the end of Harry's first speech, 'Until I come again', to the end of the scene is new. This was in response to our strong plea that neither the nature of Harry's experience nor his destination was at all clear, and that an audience wants at least sufficient clues to enable it to speculate on this all-important subject. Richard Findlater, in his biography of Michael Redgrave, who played the part of Harry in the first production, tells how Redgrave tried to elucidate the matter with Eliot and what answer he got.[2] But when he suggests that Eliot wrote in other lines than those of pages 110/111, he is mistaken. Harry now knows that those whom he formerly regarded as pursuers are really his guides; and that he is to seek a life of expiation through service, following 'the bright angels' from whom he had hitherto fled. This is enough; and though Eliot could say privately to Redgrave 'I think he and the chauffeur go off and get jobs in the East End', he certainly would not want to incorporate any such precise suggestion in a play which was meant to retain, at least in respect of its central theme, a universal and timeless quality.

In production, Redgrave was handicapped by the positioning of the Eumenides upstage at the moment when he had to communicate his fresh understanding of their nature. I have only recently found what I believe to be the solution to this problem. Eliot has said that 'They [the Eumenides] must, in future, be omitted from the cast, and be

[1] 'her' is presumably his wife. Note that in the *Oresteia* it is the Ghost of Clytemnestra who sets the Eumenides in pursuit of Orestes.
[2] *Michael Redgrave, Actor* (Heinemann, 1956), pp. 49, 50.

understood to be visible only to certain of my characters, and not to the audience'.[1] Accordingly, the last time I did the play, I set it as follows: the window, in the stage left wall, the door in the right. Both are classical in design and are strong features balancing each other.

When the Eumenides appear in Part I, they are seen by Harry through the window: we see nothing except a change of lighting, and Mary who is looking at Harry does not see them when he does. She *does* of course see them (as she reveals later to Agatha): but only at the moment when she makes the supreme effort of drawing the curtains and denying their existence.

In Part II, Harry and Agatha both see them at once in the window. At

I know that you are ready,
Ready to leave Wishwood, and I am going with you.

(*Collected Plays*, p. 108)

both characters see them moving through the room between the actors and the audience. When Harry says

No! you were already here before I arrived

they are downstage centre. They then move towards the door and go out of it, leaving Harry, who follows them, at the door at the end of his speech. Agatha has been upstage of him during the Eumenides' progress. She delivers her 'rune', not in the window embrasure but upstage centre, looking at Harry as 'my child, my curse'. When she breaks the spell with

What have I been saying?

he comes away from the door.

This plan lets us see the Eumenides, not in visible shape but through the imagination of the actors, and allows to the actor playing Harry the full opportunity of registering the change wrought in him by their appearance and of responding to their summons.

I now proceed with the comparison between the drafts and the final text. The quarrel scene is strengthened in the latter by the addition of the opening lines:

I was a fool to ask you again to Wishwood;
But I thought, thirty-five years is long, and death is an end,

[1] 'Poetry and Drama', in *On Poetry and Poets*, p. 84.

And I thought that time might have made a change in Agatha—
It has made enough in me.

(Collected Plays, p. 112)

It has not been altered otherwise until the entrance of Mary. This, in
the drafts, leads to a confrontation between Amy and Mary who
offers her 'resignation'. Eliot finally prefers to let Mary concentrate
her thoughts upon Harry, and gives her dialogue with Agatha,[1]
ignoring Amy until she breaks in with

So you will all leave me!

Amy's explanation

Harry is going away—

the intentionally lame explanation that he is to become a missionary
evoking comic responses from the uncles and aunts,[2] is inserted to
afford relief and bring the scene down to earth.

Downing's long speech on page 118 was put in for another reason:
it adds to Harry's picture of his future. The manuscript of this
passage is in the Houghton Library collection, but undated.

I print Harvard's draft from the entrance of Mary while Amy is
speaking:

AMY   And now at the moment of success against failure,
    When I felt assured of his happiness and settlement,
    You who took my husband, now you take my son.
    You take him from me, you take him from Wishwood,
    You take him from Mary.
MARY   I am very much obliged to you, Cousin Amy,
                    most
    It would have been ~~very~~ useful for your designs
    To have a tame daughter-in-law with no money,
    A housekeeper-companion for you and Harry,
    But you might have gone through the form of consulting me
          no one can
    Though ~~one cannot~~ say that you disguised your plans:
    I suppose *my* feelings were not worth the trouble of that.
               burden
    You can spare yourself at least the ~~trouble~~ of grieving
    Over what would not have happened. Do you really think
    That I have enjoyed my life so much at Wishwood
          on
    As want to assure myself of staying ~~here~~ forever?
    I am very glad to offer my resignation.

[1] *Collected Plays*, pp. 114 f.   [2] *Ibid.*, p. 116.

AMY   What will you do, Mary, if you leave here?

MARY   I can be a school-mistress too, as well as Cousin Agatha.
    If she is so successful, as they say she is,

does
    Well, I have learned from her, and I know how she ~~did~~ it:

college
    I suffered three years under her at ~~Oxford~~
    That gave me time to study all her gentle methods
    Of dominating frightened girls. And I can do it.
    When I have had as many years of bossing women,
    I may like men as much as she does. At present, I don't.
    And I have had enough of being petted, patronised and bullied
    By older women. Now I want my own turn.

life
AGATHA   When you have shaped ~~yourself~~ (by stubbornness and pride—)
    Your hands are on the clay now, I have seen them,
    I see you about to put it in the oven
    To bake it to a brittle hardness, may be broken
    But cannot be remoulded . . . If I could make you see!
    The agony of words that carry no meaning:
    One day, walking down a heedless passage
    Or in a strange room, in an unexpected mirror,
    You will meet yourself, and catch the altered look of eyes
    That you do not know. And you will have to begin again
    When you are old, to try to *be*, beginning as nobody.
    If I could spare you that!

MARY   You are very kind.
    I did not think you had so much compunction in you;

batch
    Please keep it for your next year's ~~lot~~ of pupils.

AMY   Mary, Mary, you forget that at this moment,
    Harry is preparing to leave us. That woman there,
    She has persuaded him; I do not know how,

him such   as
    I had not thought ~~he was~~ a weakling ~~like~~ his father,
    Apparently he is; or she has some spell
    Which works from generation to generation. Can *you* not stop him?

MARY   Is Harry really going?

AGATHA   He is going;
    But that is not my spell, it is not my doing;
    I have only waited and witnessed. In this world
    It is inexplicable, the resolution only in another.

MARY   Oh, but it is the danger comes from another!
    Can you not stop him? Cousin Agatha, stop him!
    You do not know what I have seen and what I know!
    He is in great danger, I know that, don't ask me,

You wouldn't believe me, but I tell you, I know.
You must keep him here, you must not let him go.
I do not know what must be done, what can be done,
Even here, but elsewhere, everywhere he is going to death.
I will stay or I will go, whatever is better,
But Harry must not go. Cousin Agatha!

AGATHA Here the danger, here the death, not elsewhere;
Elsewhere no doubt is agony, dispossession,
But birth and life. Harry has crossed the frontier
Beyond which safety and danger have a different meaning,
And he cannot come back. That is his privilege
                    in this world
(And possible (sanctification)) For those who live ~~here, who belong here~~,
In this world only, do you think I would take the responsibility
Of tempting them over the border? No one could, no one who knows,
                  is to be found
No one who has the least suspicion of what ~~one finds~~ there.
But Harry has gone, has been led, and he must follow;
For him, the danger is now only on this side;
    him,
For/danger and safety have another meaning.
They have made this clear. And I who have seen them must believe them.

MARY Oh!...so...you have seen them too!

AGATHA We must all go, each in our own direction,
You, and I, and Harry. You and I,
My dear, may I think very likely meet again,
In our wandering in the neutral territory
Between two worlds.

AMY   So you will all leave me!
An old woman alone in a damned house.
I will let the walls crumble. Why should I worry
To keep the tiles on the roof, combat the endless weather,
Resist the wind? fight with increasing taxes
And unpaid rents and tithes? nourish investments
With wakeful nights and patient calculations
With the solicitor, the broker, agent? Why should I?
It is no concern of the body in the tomb
            the
To bother about ~~its~~ upkeep. Let it go.

(*Enter* HARRY, *dressed for departure*)

HARRY But, mother, you will have always Arthur and John
To worry about: not that John is any worry—
He is the ideal occupant of Wishwood,
Sober and somnolent and vegetative:
The ideal son for any mother. As for Arthur,

The perpetual minor worries that he causes
Will keep you from worrying over me. And as for me,
I am the last you need to worry about,
I have my course to pursue, and I am safe from normal dangers
While I pursue it. I can not account for this,
But it is so, mother. Until I come again.
AMY   †I shall not see you again, if you go now.
CHARLES   What, is Harry leaving? What's the matter?
AMY   Ask him.
GERALD   But what's the matter? where is he going?
AMY   Ask him.
VIOLET   I cannot understand at all. Why is he leaving?
AMY   Ask Agatha.
VIOLET   Really, it sometimes seems to me
That I am the only sane person in this house.
Your behaviour all seems to me quite unaccountable.
What *has* happened, Amy?
AMY   Put your questions to Agatha.
HARRY   I tell you, it has nothing to do with Agatha.
When I was mad you refused then to believe it,
And now I am sane you would say that I am mad.
I would tell you, but I know you would not believe me,
Or if you believed me you would still not understand,
No, none of you; you none of you know or can know
Why I am going; you none of you have seen or can see
What I have seen. I only want, please,
As little fuss as possible. You have just got to get used to it.
Only let me tell you this:
That if you understood you would be quite happy about it.
There is much less to worry about than there was four hours ago.
So I will say good-bye, and wish you all
As direct a course as mine until we meet again.
AMY   That will be never.
GERALD   Well, if you say so, Harry, I suppose we must accept it.
But it's a bad night, and you will have to be careful.
You are taking Downing with you?
HARRY   Oh yes, I'm taking Downing. You needn't fear for me
Such accidents as happen to Arthur and John:
Take care of *them*. My address, mother,
Is care of the bank in London till further notice.
Good bye, mother.
AMY   Good-bye.
HARRY   Good-bye.

† A sign made in ink by the author directs that the two halves of this line be reversed, to
   read as in the printed text:
      If you go now, I shall never see you again.

AGATHA   Good-bye.

HARRY   Good-bye, Mary.

MARY   Good-bye, Harry: take care of yourself.

(*Exit* HARRY)

AMY   Gerald, you are the stupidest person present,
     Violet, you are the most malicious in a harmless way:
     I prefer your company to that of any of the others,
                             next
     Just for a moment, to help me to the ~~other~~ room,
     Where I can lie down. Then you can leave me.

GERALD   O certainly, Amy.

VIOLET   I do not understand a thing that's happened.

(*Exeunt* AMY, VIOLET, GERALD)

CHARLES   It's very odd, but I am beginning to feel
     That there is something I could understand, if I were told it.
     But I'm not sure that I want to know. I suppose I'm getting old.
          softly up to
     Old age came ~~quietly till~~ now. I felt safe enough,
     And now I don't feel safe. As if the earth should open
     Right to the centre, as I was about to cross Pall Mall.
     I thought that life could bring no further surprises,
     But I remember now, I am always surprised
     By the bull-dog in the Burlington Arcade.
                were   if   were
     What if every moment ~~is~~ like that, ~~when~~ one ~~is~~ awake?
     You both seem to know more about this than I do.

(*Enter* DOWNING, *hurriedly, in chauffeur's costume*)

DOWNING   Oh, excuse me, Miss; excuse me, Mr. Charles.
     His Lordship sent me back because he remembered
     He thinks he left his cigarette-case on the table.
     Oh, there it is. Thank you. Good night, Miss; good night, Miss Mary;
       good night, Sir.

AGATHA   Downing, will you promise never to leave his Lordship
     While you are away?

MARY   Never to leave him.

DOWNING   Oh, certainly, Miss. His Lordship couldn't get on without me,
     If I may make so bold. He's been like a brother to me.
     I'd never leave him. Nor he wouldn't leave me.

AGATHA   And, Downing, if he seems a bit unaccountable
     At times, you mustn't worry about that.
     He is every bit as sane as you or I are;
     He sees the world as clearly as you or I see it:
     It's only that he has seen something more than we see,
     And now I have seen it too. So we know.
     And what he does is only what he must do.

DOWNING   Oh, I understand you, Miss. And if I may make so free,
    Now that you've raised the subject, I'm most relieved.
    Relieved I am. I thought that must be the reason
                    half
    We were off tonight. In fact, I ~~have~~ expected it,
    And I had the car all ready. You mean them ghosts, Miss:
    I'd wondered when his Lordship would get round to seeing them;
    And so you've seen them too! They must have given you a start!
    They did me, at first, nine months ago. You soon get used to them.
    Of course I knew they was to do with his Lordship,
    And not with me, so I could see them quite objective,
    If you take my meaning. There's no harm in *them*,
    I'll take my oath. Will that be all, Miss?
AGATHA   That will be all, thank you, Downing. We mustn't keep you;
    His Lordship will wonder that you've been so long.

(*Exit* DOWNING)

                      (*FR*/H, cf. *Collected Plays*, pp. 113–19)

The telegram from Arthur has been improved in the final text; nothing else in the last action is altered except two stanzas of the rune around the cake, which in *FR*/H contain some interesting alternatives:

MARY   Not in the day time
    When we know what we are doing
    Or think that we know
    There it has no operation
                  Follow follow
AGATHA   But in the night time
    When the subtile meshes
    Confirm responsibility   or   Divide us from our friends
    One for another   Unite us to our enemies
                    Follow follow

I should like to quote one more page of manuscript from the Houghton Library collection, since it sums up in Eliot's own hand the conclusions reached about ages and the reasons for them:

TIMING

Amy	65 to 70
Ivy	62
Violet	58
Agatha	50 to 56

Harry	32/35	With a line to explain that Amy had no son for several years after marriage.[1]
Mary	29	

Harry married for 7 years, wife died a year ago.

Having traced the development of the text, I return to our diary for 1938. We were not all in London again until late in May, and the first meeting was 27 May, when Eliot came 'to dine and discuss new play in detail'. We do not seem to have met again until 10 August. The summer had been a full one for us, with a Festival at Tewkesbury and Miss Fogerty's Summer School of which I was director for the stage classes; and Eliot was doubtless working on the play in the time he could spare from Faber and Faber. (He was a working director of the firm through all his playwriting life, giving at least half his time to publishing.) We were by that time at Stratford-on-Avon, living at a quiet private hotel a few miles from the town. There Eliot came to tea; and the diary says 'play discussed and postponed'.

The original aim had been production in the autumn of 1938. As the letter of 19 March shows, Eliot was already troubled by the looming clouds of war and anxious to get the play finished and on the stage before they broke. So this decision for postponement must mean that we all felt that revision was still imperative. But he was determined to press on, and on 9 October I received the following letter with a text:

9 October 1938

Dear Martin,

The reason why I am anxious to get the play right without delay, is that I have to look at it from a publisher's point of view. If (as I hope) the play is to be produced at the beginning of February, then we want to have it on sale at the same moment—not before or after. The point being that the production will in any case stimulate sale of the book: if the play is a success we lose nothing by having the text on sale from the start; and if it fails, then we shall get some additional sale at the beginning anyway. On the other hand, I especially don't want the literary critics to review it before the performance.

Two things in particular for you to scrutinise: (1) the chronology, which is improved, but as you will see not yet quite cleared up—I mean the ages etc. (2) exits and entrances, also improved but not perfect. And, of course, anything else.

[1] *Collected Plays*, p. 104. 'For three years childless'.

The Family Reunion

What I should like to hear from you on Wednesday is, whether the text is right enough to go to the printers, or whether it needs some drastic re-casting anywhere, which I should try to get done within a week.

Yours ever,
T.S.E.

This is the last time that Eliot went in for publishing a play at the moment of production. For *Murder in the Cathedral*, the agreement with Canterbury included a Festival edition printed locally, so naturally Faber and Faber wanted the full text to appear on the day of production. We have seen how much alteration this involved in later editions. *The Family Reunion* was not so altered, but I know that its author regretted not being able to learn from the experience of rehearsal and audience-reaction. Thereafter, he declined to send a play to press till after the opening night.

Meanwhile John Gielgud was interested:

Queen's Theatre, W.1
September 23rd, 1938

Dear Martin Browne,

Now that this play [Dodie Smith's *Dear Octopus*] is safely launched I am very anxious to see the Eliot script if it is ready. Perhaps you could come and see me one day during a performance or have supper with me after the play one night— provided all this trouble [i.e. Munich] blows over . . . I'm sorry to hurry you but the B.B.C. have approached me about doing a Shakespeare play in November, and I have been asked to appear for one or two charities; I'd like to know whether there is any question of doing the Eliot play for matinees instead, as if it seemed possible I'd rather do that in my spare time than anything else.

Yours sincerely,
John Gielgud

Queen's Theatre, W.1
30th September, 1938

Dear Martin Browne,

I am enormously interested in the Eliot play. I think it will be better if we don't discuss it in greater detail until the final revision has been done, as I agree with the letter I found in the back (which you may or may not have meant me to read) that the play is far more lucid and easy to understand in the early part. I do certainly think the thing needs a good deal of clearing up, and I am very troubled about the Furies, as I cannot quite see them, as he has conceived them, making anything but a comic effect. But as soon as you have talked again with him, and had the revised script, do let me have it and we can talk in detail about the play. Meanwhile I will read it again more carefully: my first perusal was done on Tuesday when one wasn't at one's most receptive about anything. [*That Tuesday, we were waiting for news of the Munich meeting.*] It seems to me that if the financial aspect could be arranged it is the kind of play which would do better for a series of matinées than in an evening bill, but of course Eliot may feel that this is not giving him much chance of making any money out of it. But if it was to be kept for a regular run you might have to wait till next autumn, which does seem rather a pity. From my own point of view it would amuse me very much to do it for matinées while this present play is running, because (a) I should love the interest of the extra work and (b) I am sure it would be fun to point the contrast between the two plays; this one of Dodie's has so many of the same main characteristics— the family theme, and the return of the prodigal etc.—but how differently treated. I think this would intrigue people very much.

Anyhow let me know when we can meet, and thanks so much for letting me see it.

Yours sincerely,

John Gielgud

This opened up a most attractive prospect. Gielgud agreed to co-direct the play with me. He was to play Harry; and he pencilled into my draft his suggested casting for other parts: May Whitty as Amy, Sybil Thorndike as Agatha, Margaret Rutherford, Martita Hunt, Frederick Lloyd as aunts and uncles, Ernest Thesiger as Downing. I do not know why it never came to anything. Of course it is true that a production for matinées during the run of a very successful play would have given *The Family Reunion* a limited showing. I find that as late as 12 December, John Gielgud dined with us, so it is possible that we were still discussing the project. He found the play particularly compelling, and later did a number of broadcasts of it.

Meanwhile, revision was going on. We 'worked on the play' with Eliot in October; it was not until 15 February that we read the final text. By that time, the play is 'settled for Westminster'.

The Westminster Theatre was in the hands of a very enterprising management, the London Mask Theatre, of which the directors were J. B. Priestley, Ronald Jeans and Michael MacOwan. They had, since 1936, produced an unusually fine series of plays for short runs of four to eight weeks, and notable among them had been MacOwan's production in 1937 of Eugene O'Neill's *Mourning Becomes Electra*. This trilogy, in which the Orestes story is re-told in terms of American life at the period of the Civil War, was compressed by MacOwan into a single evening and scored a success. It was therefore appropriate that another and very different adaptation of the Aeschylean material should be staged at the Westminster, and the management welcomed

Dukes's offer to produce it there in association with him. Negotiations must have been going on for some time before February, for rehearsals began on 20 February.

The part of Harry was entrusted to Michael Redgrave. This young actor—his thirty-first birthday occurred on the day of the final dress rehearsal—had already made a name for himself at the Old Vic, with John Gielgud in his season at the Queen's, and with Michel Saint-Denis at the Phoenix.

Helen Haye, noted for her playing of aristocratic parts, was Amy, and Catherine Lacey made a personal success as Agatha. She was a member of Michael MacOwan's company that season, as also was Ruth Lodge, who played Mary. Henzie Raeburn was asked for by the author to play Ivy, the aunt who was modelled upon a relative of his; Marjorie Gabain played Violet; Colin Keith-Johnston, who as the first modern-dress Hamlet in the 'twenties had suggested an uncanny resemblance to the Duke of Windsor, was Gerald, and Stephen Murray Charles. Murray had taken a whole series of leading parts in MacOwan's season, and when he came to me was very tired indeed. At the last dress rehearsal, with an invited audience of about 300, the curtain had been up only ten minutes when he began to sway on his feet. We put the curtain down and begged indulgence of the audience; I went on and finished the part, while the doctor came and pronounced that pneumonia had supervened on exhaustion and Murray would have to take a month's rest. So I found myself playing Charles for the first four weeks of the five-week run.

It was to be Eliot's first real first night in a London theatre. A week before the day, at rehearsal, my wife, who was playing Ivy, asked him: 'Have you thought of flowers for the ladies of the cast?' He had not known of this custom, and he felt out of his depth. 'Would you arrange it for me? And please include yourself.' 'Of course,' she said, 'if you will write the cards.'

After the first night, Michael Redgrave and his wife Rachel Kempson were giving a party at the new house into which they had just moved. During the next few days my wife contrived to engage all the ladies in talk about what they were going to wear for it. Having acquired this information, she chose flowers for each actress, carefully graded (from orchids at one end of the scale to violets at the other) according to her standing in the company, and carefully selected to go with her dress.

147

The Family Reunion

At the party, the author was greeted with amazed thanks: 'How could you have guessed I was going to wear *this* colour?' He answered with an enigmatic smile. It all added to the delight that all of us felt that night; for, whatever the response, we knew that we had shared in the creation of a major work of art.

Two days afterwards, I received this letter:

23 March 1939

Dear Martin,

I have been in bed with my cold ever since the party, but if tomorrow is fine I hope to get out for a bit and see the notices. I expect very little in favour of the play, but I hope at least that the papers will give due marks for the fine acting and for the production, about which I was completely happy. It seems to me that you have far surpassed even *Murder* at its best. All I want is that the play should pay for itself, that it should run for the whole month and not throw the company out of work, and that it should not raise any prejudice that might make it more difficult to get the next one—which I hope to make free from some of the more obvious weaknesses of this—produced equally well. This letter is merely to thank you for all you have done for the play, from the time when you read the first draft until now.

If I feel fit, I should like to come in and look on Saturday night, sitting somewhere at the back of the pit in order to study the audience (a first night audience is never interesting). What do I do when I want to see the play again? ring up the box office?

Yours affectionately,
T.S.E.

The notices, as he anticipated, were mixed; incomprehension was common to most, respect was mingled with delight in a few and irritation in more; the first impact of so difficult a work, produced at a time when acute political tension[1] made it hard to free the mind for it, was not unnaturally dulled. It took the Second World War to make us aware how immediate are the truths the play tells.

Charles Morgan in *The Times* speaks first, as one distinguished literary man to another, about the play's craft, and agrees with Eliot's subsequent judgement that his success in this respect is the principal value of the piece:

Mr. Eliot's dialogue is in verse which seeks in large measure the freedom of prose. And it succeeds in capturing the cadence and rhythm of our everyday conversation and in passing, without breaking its own texture, from small talk to the statement of truths which illumine the inner lives of a family of landed aristocrats. In a theatre still struggling gamely to stretch conventions that have

[1] Hitler had just annexed Bohemia and Moravia.

148

become oppressively rigid so bold an experiment in language, an experiment with nothing Expressionistic about it, must command much good will. Yet, sad to say, the good will just fails in this case to get warmed into enthusiasm . . .

There is not a great deal of narrative, and perhaps Mr. Eliot has imperfectly realised how little there really is. Hence the impression of lifeless smoothness much of the second part of the play produces. Much more adroitly handled are incongruities inevitable in the transference of the legend of Orestes to a contemporary English setting. The Eumenides are strange figures in an English drawing-room, and all the stranger when they come hard upon the droll news that a son of the house, having drunkenly reversed his car into a shop window in Ebury Street, has told the police: 'I thought it was all open country about here', which is almost a Wodehouse joke.

But these and other incongruities are wonderfully well interwoven with the fabric of what begins by seeming to be a story of detection, and swiftly and fascinatingly reveals itself as a story of sin and expiation . . .

The play as a whole, though it lacks something of stage force, is still one which Mr. Eliot may be proud to have written.

(*The Times*, 22 March 1939)

W. A. Darlington in the *Daily Telegraph* finds it 'a deeply interesting, though difficult evening. . . The play has literary qualities as high as those of *Murder in the Cathedral*, but its stage effectiveness is nothing like so good. . .

'The story halts . . . It is not Mr. Eliot's theme that has defeated him, but the theatre, which forgives no dramatist if he drops the tension as he approaches his climax.'

Lionel Hale in the *News Chronicle* is angry with the poet who 'proceeds intolerably to confuse the stage . . . you can claw out of these people the purpose of the play. But the effort leaves you vexed and exhausted'.

James Agate of the *Sunday Times*, the most influential critic of the moment, fills his column with a pastiche of Eliot's verse; I quote some paragraphs from it:

The Eumenides At Home
Audience at Sea

It does not worry me that this verse has three stresses,
Why should it since the glass in my car is triplex?
One must move with the times,
As the old maid said in the musical comedy
On meeting a young gent Oxonianly debagged.
Nor does it worry me that this verse does not tinkle.
I do not expect modern art to sound nice.
Or even to look nice . . .

149

The Family Reunion

What does worry me about this play is something altogether different—
The sneaking suspicion that I may not be intellectually up to it.
Il est si facile, said Balzac, de nier ce que l'on ne comprend pas.
Meaning that the fool sees not the same tree that the wise man sees.
Perhaps it might be easier if I had the Eumenides nearer my finger-tips,
In which case I should know whether moaning becomes Agatha as mourning
     becomes Electra . . .

CHORUS

Twice two are four
But twice three are not five
Cows neigh in the byre
Herb-o'-grace looks for Sunday
Octaves wilt
Fifths grow consecutive
Moon and green cheese
Have come to terms
Fog horns summon
The household to supper
The bones of the majordomo
Rap out curses
Methylated spirits
Wait round the corner . . .

Will someone, for example, tell me exactly where
Harry is going to when he puts on Johnson's overcoat.
Is he for the police station to give himself up,
Or lankly starting on an introspective, cis-Jordanian trek?
Where, where, where, where, where, where?
And as the author didn't know,
Nor Aeschylus nor even the Libraries,
We in the audience must pretend to be wabe-conscious,
Some gyred, others gimbled. I did neither.
But nothing could stop foyer-cluttered Bloomsbury
From explaining *en deux mots* what the play was all about.
It baffled me but did not in the least baffle them
To read a B.C. cross-word by an A.D. light.
Yet try as I would I, a modern Englishman, could not see why
Because a man's aunt ought to have been his mother
He must push his wife overboard
And I just could not accept the explanation
That it was all because Harry's soul
Had got mixed up with the Wishwood drains.
And here I have to say quite firmly
That what was good enough for Aeschylus is by no means
Good enough for me!

(Sunday Times, 26 March 1939)

The Family Reunion

Archie de Bear, in the *Daily Sketch*, is the one who, unexpectedly in that place, avers that 'the poet T. S. Eliot has made a new and important and profoundly interesting contribution to English drama' which he thinks is a better play than O'Neill's and 'strikes an entirely new note in the theatre of today'. And Ivor Brown in the *Observer*, who characterises the people of the play as 'Forsytes who will suddenly speak in chorus, like the elders of Argos', prophesies that 'Mr. Eliot might write an excellent light comedy'.

5

War Interlude

Ivor Brown's prophecy was ultimately to be fulfilled after its fashion: but it had to wait a long time. *The Family Reunion* was, as the theatrical phrase goes, 'put to bed' by the onset of war and was not to wake again for seven years: and its author's playwriting talent likewise went into hibernation. But our relationship through the war years remained as close as ever.

As soon as the war started, I saw how great a need there was for entertainment in smaller places, particularly those to which people had been evacuated from the big cities; and I formed a small professional company, The Pilgrim Players. We started work in October 1939 under the friendly roof of Kent College, Canterbury, and Miss Babington got us plenty of bookings for the first seven months, until with the German advance into Western Europe the school was evacuated and we took permanently to the road.

Kent College
Canterbury
6.11.39

My dear Tom,
    Would you become a Patron of the Pilgrim Players? The others will be:

> The Archbishop
> Bp of Chichester
> John Gielgud
> Sybil Thorndike
> Marie Tempest (?)

We start next week, and have a good company and keen, and lots of bookings, with *Tobias*[1] followed by the Wakefield Shepherds-cum-Charles Williams Nativity programme. I *hope* so much that I can't tell you, that an idea is being born to you that may follow in 1940, while the chance is there! . . .

Yours ever,

Martin

[1] *Tobias and the Angel* by James Bridie.

War Interlude

Almost every letter in our war correspondence contains this hope for a new play. In arranging to meet Eliot in London in April 1940, it comes out again:

Has light been shed upon the theme or plot of a new play? I do hope so.

But such hopes were frustrated by the German victories. The following letter may serve to recover something of the atmosphere of those days:

THE PILGRIM PLAYERS

May 22, 1940
at Benenden School
Cranbrook
Kent

My dear Tom,

One of the few things that have relieved our minds in the present tension is the thought that you will not have been able to go to Italy. I hope it has not left you with an empty feeling, but has given you a little freedom, especially to enjoy the wonderful weather of the past weeks.

We are in the most idyllic spot, a village with the most beautiful green sloping up to a fine XV century church and a school to rehearse in which occupies a magnificent mansion set among parkland and may-trees. I am now writing in the little old pub where we have lunch. We actually live at the house of an ardently Catholic schoolmistress (it is called 'Our Lady's Dowry' and painted bright blue). Here we rehearse Morna Stuart's new play, which has turned out very pleasantly. It all seems an acute contrast to the news, but one is grateful beyond telling to be creatively busy.

Which brings me to your new poem.[1] It has given us much pleasure to read and re-read. To me its atmosphere is very familiar. And the variety of aspects, and of rhythms, is a great delight.

We have been wondering whether we could possibly do an emergency version of *Murder in the Cathedral*. The company is 5 men and 4 women. What would you feel about this? It would, as far as I can envisage it without working on it, involve beginning with a Chorus and then Becket's entrance (only one priest): rest of Part I would stand: Part II would have to run much as at the Mercury, but almost doing away with the 'To vespers' scene and ending with Meeting and Chorus only. It would frankly *be* an emergency version and billed as such: but it would enable us to present the play in a lot of places where it will never otherwise be seen, and to give its most essential values. And I *badly* want some Eliot in our repertory! Lawrence[2] isn't wearing well, and we need some Christian work of first quality more than anything.

We are here till the 31st and then go to Dorset for a strenuous tour. At present

[1] *East Coker*, published in the *New English Weekly* (Easter number, 1940).
[2] *David* by D. H. Lawrence.

people are carrying on with bookings and we hope to keep alive, especially going Westwards. But who can tell?

Our love and every good wish to you,

Yours ever,
Martin

The author replied (5 June):

Of course you may knock *Murder* about as you think best and use it in the Pilgrim repertory for the during of the war. I shall be happy to see it serve that purpose.

We played the emergency version for three years in every setting from cathedral to air-raid shelter and from theatre to village school-room. I myself played Becket, and made many discoveries, especially of his close ties with the Chorus. These women, the ordinary, faithful Christians, are his anchor. His long, silent struggle with despair as the Tempters surround him is carried on in isolation until the women succeed in breaking through to him. It is their intuition that 'the Lords of Hell are here' which reveals to him the nature of his danger. It is their plea:

> O Thomas Archbishop, save us, save us, save yourself that we may be saved;
> Destroy yourself and we are destroyed.

(*Collected Plays*, p. 30)

which calls forth from him the power to banish the Tempters. And later, it is because they take upon themselves the shame that Christendom must suffer at his murder that he is enabled to face death with calmness:

> Peace, and be at peace with your thoughts and visions.
> These things had to come to you, and you to accept them.
> This is your share of the eternal burden,
> The perpetual glory.

(*Ibid.*, p. 43)

A six-month gap follows, when our pilgrimage took us to the north. Early in 1941, we spent a day at Shamley Green, near Guildford in Surrey, at the house where Eliot had a temporary home with friends: and a few days afterwards he came to see *Murder in the Cathedral* in Guildford's pro-cathedral. Before Easter we had gone northwards again.

War Interlude

July 3rd, 1941
St. Hild's College
Durham City

My dear Tom,

We should be really glad to hear from you, even if only on a postcard, for we have thought so very often of you for so long while seeming to be cut off from news of you. So we have lived on hopes of your wellbeing without any evidence on which to found them.

Life with us has pursued its usual winding route. After we left you in Surrey, we had a week both profitable and pleasant in Cambridge, thanks to the generosity of Keynes[1] and the Arts Theatre governors who gave us the use of the theatre for MURDER and TOBIAS, and, since the Cambridge public liked them, enabled us to strengthen our resources to an extent unthought of before. The next week we spent some of them in playing in London shelters, including a memorable performance of MURDER, given without a break, in the basement of Lloyds in Leadenhall Street, to a deeply stirred audience mostly hailing from Hackney.[2] After that we started northwards again: Passion Week in Sheffield and Holy Week in Leeds playing THE WAY OF THE CROSS, and then Bradford, Ilkley, the Lakes and now a month of Durham mining villages. In Ilkley we ran MURDER for a week in the local Playhouse, small but much alive. We follow our stay here with an excursion into Scotland, to play a fortnight in St. Andrews as a kite to attract bookings for Scotland next year. Then a holiday, and then, we think, Tyneside, and so gradually southwards again by the eastern route.

We have been lucky enough to remain unchanged in personnel for all this time. I doubt whether the lull will continue much longer, though there is a sort of 'reserved occupation' label attaching to the Players in some quarters and we may be left alone. It certainly is good for the quality of the work, and enables us to do far more than when we had continually to rehearse new people. We are about to start on Obey's NOAH (in English) produced by Mme. Alice Gachet, and I think we shall all benefit from a fresh touch upon us.

The other day I was in a church in West Hartlepool. I was meditating in a wandering way on the Incarnation, and I found myself trying to see it from the point of view of Simeon. The one man who could have had any idea of its significance at the time of its happening in time. One whose mind must have been full of the riddle of the two kinds of Jewish expectation—of the King and of the Suffering Servant—and who must have seen them both in the light of the political

---

[1] Lord Keynes, Chairman of the Council for the Encouragement of Music and the Arts (soon to become the Arts Council of Great Britain) and of the Arts Theatre, Cambridge.

[2] 'The whole basement of the great building was fitted with bunks and held over 200 sleepers; it was comfortable as the heating plant was there. We dressed in the men's lavatory. I felt a little startled for the moment, but a Pilgrim's adjustment to new conditions was by this time almost swift enough to appear spontaneous . . . For the first ten or fifteen minutes the form and language of it [*Murder in the Cathedral*] seemed strange to them; then they got caught up by it, and it was one of the most "shared" performances I have ever known.'

(Henzie Raeburn, *Pilgrim Story*, Frederick Muller, 1945, pp. 71–2)

situation of an occupied country. One whose age made him wise enough to accept a humble-looking salvation, even if not strong enough to do any more than accept. Which—acceptance—is the first thing required, and enables the salvation to shine forth.

Later on I thought of A SONG FOR SIMEON, which means much to me. And I thought that perhaps the play about Christmas from a completely adult point of view, which is so much needed and doesn't exist, might be here.

It would be Elizabethan in its dependence for continuity upon plot and people, not place or time, and in its direct approach to the audience.

Simeon was doubtless spiritual counsellor to a good many people, rich and poor. At first a fellow-rabbi might bring the news of Zacharias' dumbness: then Elizabeth might come for counsel as to the meaning of it. Meanwhile one might know, meeting Joseph and Mary, of Mary's waiting—a kind contrasting with Simeon's in many respects: perhaps might see the Annunciation in her alone— the reception of a spiritual experience too deep to be witnessed in material form of an 'angel'. (In this scene one should have been conscious of the turmoil of the world outside—of the crucifixion of the Zealot rebels by Pilate, for instance, so that the house at Nazareth is not a retreat from the world around it but a place where everything is brought into relation with God's will.)

Shepherds come to Simeon: how are they to behave in face of Roman soldiery: perhaps they have men billeted on them, how are they to treat them? extortion of stock and crops is going on, the Jewish tax-collectors are siding unfairly with the Romans against their own people, and so on. What is really the Jewish hope? what will the Messiah really be and do? This is where Simeon's own knowledge of and view of the problem comes out.

Mary visits Elizabeth.

In the winter: the Shepherds come to Simeon with the news of their vision and of what they found. Somehow they are convinced this is the Messiah, against all their hopes in the previous scene.

The Presentation in the Temple, gathering all these threads and forming the resolution of the theme. 'Now lettest thou thy servant depart in peace.'

These ideas are only rough, as you see. One might put the matter in another way, by seeing four houses on the stage: each house going through a similar process of thought:

SIMEON	MARY AND JOSEPH	ELIZABETH	SHEPHERDS
			(Jewish people)
Expectation .	. . . .	. .	. Expectation
	Vision . .	. . .	. Vision
	Fulfilment		

for clearly all are in the final scene.

Does it appeal to you at all? Because it came to me as it did, and so closely linked with A SONG FOR SIMEON, I hope it may. Or that it may suggest something—more likely it may do that. For I do feel desperately the need that we meet, and that we have ourselves, for something of you in our work. Length doesn't matter. Depth is the thing! (And if meanwhile you have been germinating a farce, that's just as true). At any rate, if this means anything to you, I should be very, very glad . . .

9th July 1941

My dear Martin,

Thank you very much for your long and good letter of July 3. I am very much aware of owing you a letter to account for myself since I saw you. I have been perfectly well for some time past, that is to say, since the week before Whitsun, and have been profiting in health from the sunny weather. Otherwise, I have nothing particular to report.

I am very glad to hear of your plans though I am never sure that you and Henzie allow yourselves enough holiday in the summer.

I shall not attempt to comment on your generously elaborate suggestion for a play until I have given myself time to absorb it. The question, however, of when I shall get time for anything of the sort presents itself at once. I am at present struggling to get on paper the fourth of my series of poems and that attempt, if successful, is likely to occupy my spare time for several weeks more. After that I have several prose engagements ahead of me: I have to revise my Shakespeare lectures to deliver again in Bristol in the autumn, and I have to prepare for the early spring a lecture in Glasgow and an address to the Classical Association. There is also another literary job, the arrangements of which are not quite settled, but which will take some time and must be finished this season. I don't think I shall want to write any more poems in the immediate future and therefore my next attempt at anything interesting to myself will probably be a play. Whether it will be this one or not I can't tell. My first impression is that it is a very fine theme but I am not sure whether the topical reference which people would read into it would be quite suitable for the present time. At any rate, I shall consider it as seriously as I should any suggestion of yours . . .

July 13, 1941
St. Hild's College
Durham City

My dear Tom,

Many thanks for your welcome and pleasant letter. We are greatly cheered by your good report of yourself.

I am glad you will think about the suggestion for a play; through which perhaps something useful may come to your mind. Of course I understand the other demands on your time: but I always feel that God will call all of us to account if your supreme gift as a creator is not fully used owing to more ephemeral interruptions! I hope the last poem of that fine series is shaping as you would wish it to . . .

We were playing in Scotland for most of 1942, so contact was very occasional. The one chance of meeting was missed, as was sadly so often the case, because Eliot was taken ill.

157

7 October 1942
Glasgow

My dear Tom,

That was very bad luck for me, but it distresses me much more that you are continuing to suffer ill-health. I do beseech you to take ruthless steps to look after yourself this winter, and particularly to avoid travelling. I know you will feel that I am the Pot, and that I have said all this before: but I can't help that. If you could hear all the hundreds of people who speak to me of your creative work as of supreme value to them and the society they live in, you would understand that I don't speak for myself alone, though I am urged by my personal affection for you. You know, better than any of us, that even the fiercest struggles of today are ephemeral: let us tell you, if you can't believe, that you bring us and those who come after us something more lasting and of deeper significance . . .

20 October 1942

Dear Martin,

I was bitterly disappointed not to see you: my illness also prevented my going to Iceland and addressing the Central School as I had promised Gwynneth Thurburn. It should have been only a week, but I had a slight relapse and was kept in bed for a fortnight altogether. I am just getting back into the routine. You will be up again, I suppose, round about Christmas tide? And if there should be an opportunity of meeting in November, I shall be zealous not to miss it. Your encouraging words gave me great pleasure (and I hope that you may like *Little Gidding*). This sort of encouragement is really needed. It is one thing to see what was best worth one's while doing, in a distant retrospect: but in the midst of what is going on now, it is hard, when you sit down at a desk, to feel confident that morning after morning spent fiddling with words and rhythms is a justified activity—especially as there is never any certainty that the whole thing won't have to be scrapped. And on the other hand, external or public activity is more of a drug than is this solitary toil which often seems so pointless.

Affectionately and regretfully,
Tom

Early in 1943, I made a production of W. B. Yeats's *The Resurrection*. This was the last play to be put on by the company which had toured together since 1939. On 21 March, we had lunch at Shamley Green and Eliot came with the family to see *The Resurrection*:

24th March 1943

Dear Martin,

In the somewhat pressed and confused conditions in which we met on Sunday, I forgot to ask you a question which I promised to ask on behalf of someone else. I thought that you might know something about present conditions in Canterbury and I have been too long out of touch with the place to know whether there is still anyone whom I know on the spot. Can you tell me anything about existing hotels in that place. If you could merely give me the names of any that you can remember which are still doing business, or alternatively suggest somebody to whom I could write, I should be very grateful. The information is wanted for a lady who would like, if possible, to spend her Easter holidays in Canterbury.

It was also stupid of me not to extract from you your next address.

It was a great pleasure to the household as well as to myself to see you and Henzie though we all felt that you both needed a period of rest and relief from locomotion, and I want to say that my doubts about the suitability of *Resurrection* were quite reassured. I thought it an admirable production, your own appearance quite satisfactory, the costumes[1] most lovely. I didn't think the Greek and the Syrian made quite the best of their parts, but knowing that you have to do the best you can with the material available, I was altogether delighted with the performance. It was really very moving and you may be interested to know that judging from the comments of the children from Shamley Wood it was successful from the juvenile point of view also.

Yours affectionately,

Tom

4.4.43

My dear Tom,

I have a horrible fear that your last letter has not been answered. Henzie said she would write as I was busy, but I do not feel sure that we ever settled this, and the letter may have fallen between our stools.

So to make sure, and with apologies if my fears are justified, I write now. At Canterbury, most of the Western half of the city is standing. This leaves the Fleur-de-Lis and County Hotels (the former the less expensive) in the main street. The Cathedral Guest House (next to Christ Church Gateway) is also intact and may be open again: it was recently closed for lack of staff. (Communications to the Proprietress at the Dutch Tea House, which is open for meals.) I don't know of anything else, but if it exists, of course Miss Babington (3, The Precincts) would.

I was truly glad of your kind words about *The Resurrection*. It was a risk, and I am relieved that it succeeded. The performance has matured somewhat since you saw it, though the actors' imaginations still fail in part to transport them into the moment of shepherdless grief at which the play opens. Yeats has not made that easy: but we are getting towards it a little way. That day with you was a joy to us both.

I don't think I told you that the Archbishop of Canterbury,[2] inspired by a sight of some pilgrim work, has conceived the idea of an hour's meeting of Church and Stage (at Lambeth on May 13th at 11.30 a.m.) to discuss the possibility of organising church support for tours including distinguished Christian actors. He has asked me to suggest names. You know that I always avoid involving you in talking about plays when you might be using the time to write one. But would this hour be well spent to that end? Would the sight and hearing of those concerned in the business help you? If so, I should like to suggest you.

---

[1] Again by Stella Mary Pearce. [2] William Temple.

War Interlude

Pilgrims are about to undergo reorganisation: a rise in pay,[1] a governing committee of 3 or 4 wise folk outside the company, a change in the relationship between the companies, and some change of personnel.

I shall have a really serious need of a new play by the autumn, for all the above reasons. And seeing that your biggest success was written as a commission, I was inclined to ask you to discuss with me the acceptance of a commission for a play. Length, an hour or longer, preferably longer. Treatment suitable for production without a front curtain or a realistic setting, and in church if desired (though this could be waived). Cast not above ten, and preferably smaller: it is not advisable to make more than half of it male, if you want the best quality of performance, at present.

Subject: here's the rub, of course: but if you haven't anything even remotely in mind I would try to make a few suggestions, hoping to start a train of thought. I do not feel that it need be a conventionally religious subject, even for church, since if you write it it will be a Christian play.

Money: £100 advance for a play that can be played by itself, and thereafter the usual $5-7\frac{1}{2}-10\%$ royalty for a new play.

The above is presumption in a way, and I ask forgiveness for that. I am urged by the belief that this is a moment which should not be lost. Most of the world's best art has been made to order. So I dare to ask you to accept a commission. It is urgent, and perhaps a Christian commission may take priority even over Government ones?

Henzie, I know, would join her love to mine.

Yours ever,
Martin

29th April 1943

My dear Martin,

I have been very slow in answering your excellent letter. I could come to Lambeth on March 13 at 11.30 if you wish but I don't know what I could contribute to the discussion. If I do come I should like to see you beforehand if possible to get a notion of the agenda and decide what we are to say.

Now as to the play. Of course, I should like to write a play, and I should like to write a play for you, but I dare not give any promises. At present I am devoting all the time I can spare to the South India scheme for Church Union and associated matters and shall probably have to do a job for the British Council which will take three weeks and some preparation in advance. I started early in the winter the first draft of a small book I want to write but I had not got further than one version of two chapters when it had to be laid aside for other things. There is also the worthy Mr. Hollering ever at my back and I have not even faced the problem of whether I can do anything for his film or not. Finally, there is the question of whether even when I got down to it I should be able to turn out a possible play or not and I will try to think about it a bit this summer, especially

---

[1] Up to now, one guinea a week plus board and lodging (see Henzie Raeburn, *Pilgrim Story*).

if I get off for a fortnight's half-time harvesting in Sussex. But it is clear that even if I think to any purpose I could not set to work until the autumn. When shall I see you?

Yours ever
Tom

During that summer we moved into a London flat, a home again after three and a half years as vagabonds, and our two boys returned to us from their evacuation in the U.S.A. Before they arrived I took a period of rest. Touring began again in the autumn, but now only for me alone (my wife keeping house for the boys) and for spells of not more than ten or twelve weeks. As the war drew towards its end, I planned to lease the Mercury Theatre from Ashley Dukes, who was going to Germany with the Allied Control Commission, and to establish a policy of New Plays by Poets. These would be produced under the Pilgrim Players' management, which would have the support of C.E.M.A. for this, and also for continued tours. Most of the poets whose work I contemplated producing were published by Faber and Faber, so Eliot was involved on more than one count, and he and I had fairly frequent discussions on these matters. The project was launched in September 1945, and thanks to the success of Ronald Duncan's *This Way to the Tomb* I was able to run in repertory with it plays by Norman Nicholson (*The Old Man of the Mountains*) and Anne Ridler (*The Shadow Factory*); and shortly after these, to give Christopher Fry his first London production with *A Phoenix Too Frequent* which he wrote for me.

In the autumn of 1946, Fry's delicious little play was to move to the Arts Theatre; and I planned to revive *The Family Reunion*. Having broached this to Eliot, I took *This Way to the Tomb* to Paris in June 1946:

Paris, on the
fourteenth of July 1946

My dear Tom,

They have danced till dawn in the Place du Palais Bourbon outside our windows. Paris is wonderfully gay. A storm cleared the hot air just before dark, and though it wetted the chairs and tablecloths of the Bar, also stimulated the people to enjoyment. It is grey this morning, but bright sky is behind the cloud, to come through later.

You are soon to be back from America, and we from Paris. We hope very much to see you. We shall be in London all August, from the 17th at latest, and thereafter. I have agreed to do Peter Yates' play on Booth, *The Assassin*, at the

161

War Interlude

Lyric, Hammersmith, while Harry Latham does *Tangent*[1] at the Mercury for the opening of the season. Then I look forward to turning to *The Family Reunion*.

You said when we last met that I might write to you about this, and that you might try to mend the flaw in it. I am sure that if the moment of 'conversion', so to call it, could be made clear and become the unmistakeable climax of the play, it would gain immeasurably. The question is, how to do this.

The first problem is, how far does Agatha know the experience through which Harry passes? because the scene as it is now is dramatically difficult through lack of contrast. If she goes the whole way with Harry, it is difficult to take the development in their scene further than the present:

'I feel happy for a moment, as if I had come home.'

But if, as I suspect, she knows *about*, but has never *known*, his ultimate experience, you might be able to get the scene to a point, just before the Eumenides' entrance, at which he attains to a knowledge she cannot share or even understand—for I think you want his experience to be more than a resolution of the old problem, an unknotting, a lifting of the curse: he comes into a new country in which everything looks different. Can he best explain the experience to her in these terms? by looking at the wife's death, the family, his mother, and seeing something in each case *startlingly* different—surprising to himself? This would serve to *dramatise* the experience. Take for instance the passage in which he thinks he could now get on with his mother—at present dramatically flat, this could be heightened by surprise. And Agatha's point of view regarding the mother–son relationship could be developed in contrast.

Now to come to the Eumenides. They are, as we know, most difficult to deal with anyway. May I take first the problem of whether they should be seen and if so how. Your last word to me was that they had best not be seen—be in a side window, so that the effect on Harry was the predominant thing about them.

After a lot of reflection I think you are probably right. The loss of the classical shape of the scene is a pity; it might be possible to put the *door* centre back and so preserve it to some extent. But as no-one can find any satisfactory solution of *what they look like*, we are clearly better with imagination. But here one need imposes itself: seen or unseen, there should be a perceptible difference in them for the audience as well as for Harry, between Parts 1 and 2.

If they were seen, I should want furies in Part 1 and angels, gradually seen in an increasing light, in Part 2. If they are not seen, I suggest a strong light of greenish tinge in Part 1, golden in Part 2, perhaps throwing a shadow on the wall, perhaps not: but a beam of light as opposed to the general blue-white radiance of the moon when no Eumenides are present. I should like your reaction to all this, as much to tell me your sense of the Eumenides' character as for technical reasons.

Now for the speech to the Eumenides in Part 2. If they are at the side, we shall have the great advantage of being able to see Harry's reaction to them, which dramatically is what matters. So in this speech can come the top of the climax, presumably at 'I am following you'. I have, as you know, always felt this to be right and a true climax. But it is at present difficult for an actor to make, because

[1] By Gilbert Horobin.

162

the tension before it is too strong. I wonder whether you could profitably reconsider the passage where Harry senses their coming, which is now similar in tension to that in Part 1. Should the coming be more of a surprise to him? since he *is* achieving the new orientation and the appearance is in the nature of a ratification of that (though it is also a call to something further).

I also think the drop from the climax is a little too quick for Harry. Agatha's lifting-of-the-curse speech interrupts his flow, and when it is over he is already down 'on the flat' again. This is a little hard, perhaps, unless the next rise can be improved, given more of conviction and less of exposition, and the difficult exit: 'I must follow the bright angels' can be made easier by being given more emotional momentum. Dramatically, in fact, the post-conversion moments are as hard to act as to live—a tribute to their truth, but not to their efficiency in conveying the truth to an audience.

One other suggestion, of which I am less sure, though at least I am sure of a need. The audience never knows, till Downing's last scene, anything at all about what 'THEY' are. Is it possible that some *clue* (for that is all it should be) could be inserted earlier in the play? Remembering that the Eumenides-idea is unknown to a modern audience, some clue for them to follow would make the play far more satisfying to see. It could come from a quite unlikely quarter—a chance question from an uncle or aunt, for instance, that hits on the truth, or Mary might supply it. This becomes all the more important if they are not seen by the audience.

All this means quite a bit of thought for you, I'm afraid. But seeing the play again convinced me that it's so *nearly* right that it's worth a lot to try and bridge the small gap. You will, I think, be pleased to know that Sybil Thorndike is really keen to come to the Mercury and play Amy, if her engagements should permit. I don't think we ought to wait about for her—the play should be done this autumn: but it is a pleasant if remote chance and her keenness at least is gratifying.

We spent an hour yesterday at an exhibition of relics and models of Charles le Foucaud's life—'The death in the desert'[1]. . . I am right, am I not? A moving presentation of a great life, about which I know very little. The French still have the gift of bringing Christian living home to one in the most direct and simple manner: one *felt* the *difference* that Christ had made so vividly.

27 August 1946

My dear Martin,

I know that a long time has elapsed since you wrote your very good letter from Paris. But I did not arrive until August 2, and since then I have been busy with arrears, chiefly in the publishing business. I have meanwhile read your letter several times, and the days have slipped by. I am now spending a week at Shamley. The two months in America was a very beneficial change, but re-adaptation to a business routine, especially as these three and a half weeks have been consumed in matters not very stimulating to me, has proved rather tiring. Now, I meant to bring the Family Reunion with me, but I forgot, and I find that my hosts have not got it here, so I must write without study of the text.

[1] *Murder in the Cathedral, Collected Plays*, p. 54.

I think your suggestions are very good indeed. My difficulty is that they both go too far and not far enough. Not far enough, I mean, because, as soon as I start thinking about the play, I have inklings of altering it still further. Greater emphasis upon the reconciliation with the mother (which would be true enough to human nature, and would show Harry as more human) means a corresponding balance of the relation with Agatha, which is thus doubly concluded; and this involves further examination and development of that character, who must however not be made any more important, and somehow her eventual separateness must, in being the measure of how far she can get, be also another measure of the distance Harry goes. And I want a different concluding scene, possibly the tardy entrance of John and Arthur, to restore everything to where it was before (but the part of Fortinbras is not a very great prize for even a raw recruit from a dramatic school). And so on.

I put all this as a warning, to myself more than to you, that when I start rearranging I dont know where it may lead me. The question there is, whether I can do what you want without doing a great deal more. The other question (to which I have little doubt of the answer) is whether I could do even the minimum that you ask (and reasonably ask) without giving several months to it. That precludes an autumn production: but the effect of your suggestions is to make me loth to see the play produced again without at least this much work done to improve it. It will be extremely hard to settle down to a job like this: first, because I have two small books which have been half written, clogging my digestion, for the last two or three years, and which I need to get rid of; second, because my goal has been to clear away this stuff, slip out of as many committees and odd jobs as possible, and start a new play—for it is hard to get up the enthusiasm now, after seven years, to settle down to a winter's work on the Family Reunion. So I don't know what to say to you. I feel that it would be healthier for *me* to leave it alone.

I shall be back in town on Monday. Could you give me a ring and arrange for us to meet and talk at some time during the week?

Affectionately,
Tom

Sept. 1. 1946

My dear Tom,

Many thanks for your letter. I am glad that you are safely back, and shall enjoy hearing more of your trip when we meet. Arrears will of course have piled up in your absence, and I didn't expect to hear before this.

Regarding *The Family Reunion*, I agree that the best course is to leave it alone. If you find, as I can well understand you may, that one change inevitably leads to the necessity of another, it is not worth expending a long time on such a revision. People are constantly asking for the play and its production this autumn will certainly be attractive: and I think we shall find that the mental climate of today is so much clearer for it than that of 1939 that many of its difficulties will be resolved by a more sympathetic audience (not including Mr. Agate). I expect to get to it in October or at latest November, unless *Tangent* proves a bigger success than I anticipate. That opens on Sept. 9th, and I hope you will come and look at it (Stuart Latham's production, by the way).

I am the more willing to agree that *The Family Reunion* stays as it is if that brings the new play any nearer. I confess to some bitterness when I read of two other books half finished, and the promised play not begun. That I am constantly assailed about this, by the Arts Council and others, and that the continuance of our Poets' Theatre does depend to some extent upon it, is not the main point. What I do press is this: you are the father and the master of modern English poetry and in particular of poetic drama: all the poets and all those in the theatre who are trying to help them need, not so much your advice, as your creative leadership. This, being a matter of creation, is a more important use for the years of the creative master's life than exegesis in even the profoundest subjects of literary or theological criticism. We need your poetry and your drama: don't put off giving for too long! Immediate things are also ephemeral: leave them to those whose minds are of ephemeral quality.

Ronnie Duncan, whom I gather you are seeing today, will be telling you of our gamble on the *Tomb*, which we open at the Garrick for matinées from Sept. 16th. It is worth trying, I think, as we have some backing for it. To bring the Mercury into the West End again is quite a good thing, and should help us to expand later. Our 130 seats make the Mercury itself, of course, permanently uneconomic: but what it has created has a value bigger than itself.

If you can do anything to help us on at the Garrick, please don't forget us.

The tour of *The Old Man*[1] has been cancelled: transport was the main difficulty, and the Arts Council couldn't rescue us from that. I hope to do the play at the Mercury this winter with the new last act: and am also giving it to Sladen-Smith for the Manchester Unnamed Society in the hope that Nic can get to it there.

We both want very much to see you: and perhaps after *Tangent* has opened we could have a meal together. Henzie is playing in it, and I am rehearsing Peter Yates' *The Assassin* for the Lyric, Hammersmith, so we are very full up this week.

Our love to you as always.

Affectionately,
Martin

3rd September, 1946

My dear Martin,

Thank you very much for your kind and thoughtful letter of September 1st. If you feel that *The Family Reunion* is worth risking again in its present form, God bless you. Even if I sat down to improve its chances I know that it would not be ready for some time after you want it, and that eases my conscience a little bit.

[1] Norman Nicholson, *The Old Man of the Mountains*, the first in my season of Plays by Poets at the Mercury.

War Interlude

I shall certainly want to come and see *Tangent*. I have promised to go next week to see Duncan's adaptation of the Cocteau play.[1]

What you say about relative importance for me of several kinds of work is certainly true and I have no resistance to put up except just this: that these two essays have got stuck in my digestive system and I feel at present that I must clear them out before I can concentrate on anything else. I shall, however, try to do the minimum rather than the maximum.

I hope you will let me know as soon as you and Henzie are a bit freer as I should love to come and have a long talk.

Affectionately,

Tom

The Family Reunion was revived at the Mercury on 31 October and ran until 1 February 1947. The critical reactions this time contain a fresh note. Charles Morgan and W. A. Darlington represent the stability of the experienced critics who have seen it before; but there is a new awareness among most of the others that, though imperfect, this is a play that will last. Eric Keown in *Punch* is worth quoting at length:

Strictly speaking this is a revival, since the play had a short run in 1939 which was spoilt by the war, but to most of us it comes fresh. From every point of view this is a notable production. Mr. T. S. Eliot is one of the few serious critics of the drama who has justified original views in works of his own. What he did in *Murder in the Cathedral* was to bring back ritual to the theatre, finding expressive use for a chorus against a background of history and employing verse of unorthodox rhythm in simple and powerful patterns. Here he has gone after something even more difficult, a moment in the journeying of the universal spirit set within the narrow framework of a family party in an English country house. The play is dramatic and exciting, but it seems to me to be less important for itself than as a new and fascinating experiment.

That a group of moribund uncles and aunts politely sipping sherry in an atmosphere of feudal melancholy should suddenly speak their inner thoughts in chorus may at first appear shocking, but the fact that it is a chorus and not an isolated psychological bid such as O'Neill played in *Strange Interlude* quickly makes it seem perfectly natural. A novelist barred from revealing what was going on in his characters' heads would consider himself hamstrung, and the messages which Mr. Eliot sparingly allows his family hierarchy to flash to us are so well observed that they have great value in setting off the serious core of the play:

Charles: I might have been in St. James's Street, in a comfortable chair rather nearer the fire.
Ivy: I might have been visiting Cousin Lily at Sidmouth, if I had not had to come to this party.

[1] *The Eagle Has Two Heads.*

166

War Interlude

Gerald: I might have been staying with Compton-Smith, down at his place in Dorset.
Violet: I should have been helping Lady Bumpus, at the Vicar's American tea.
Chorus: Yet we are here at Amy's command, to play an unread part in some monstrous farce, ridiculous in some nightmare pantomime.

The nightmare pantomime is the return of *Harry, Lord Monchensey*, after an absence of eight years spent, until one night when she was washed from the deck of a liner, travelling with a wife of whom his family bitterly disapproved. He is the Greek tragic hero, the victim of the age-long curse of sin, pursued in his mind by the Furies. *Amy*, his frail but tremendous mother, is celebrating her birthday with a glacial gathering of the clan. With characteristic family feeling she has preserved the house unchanged for *Harry*, and she issues orders that no one shall refer to his unhappy adventure. *Harry*, however, has changed. He declines to play the pretence-game and informs his horrified relations that with his own hand he has pushed his wife over the rail. Now for the first time he not only hears the Furies but sees them, and so do we, clamouring dreadfully at the drawing-room window. He is extremely distraught and it is assumed that he is mad. Only two of the party understand him, a cousin, *Mary*, who goes all the way in sympathy, but can only grope at his meaning, and his aunt, *Agatha*, who has come through her own special purgatory to a knowledge that, whether or not the murder is imagined, he must no longer run away from his tormentors but must face them and find expiation from the curse by following them, not as the Furies but as the Kindly Ones leading him back to peace.

That is a very bare account of what happens. It is in the passages with *Agatha* that the play rises to its heights. Mr. Eliot has an extraordinary power of evoking in a few words a crisis in the life of the spirit. Here he is demonstrating an essentially Christian doctrine on an essentially pagan foundation. *Agatha* is not a character in the usual sense but a kind of summing-up of how far the human intellect has succeeded in reaching in its effort to meet the divine. Nor are the others, the elderly philistines, fixed characters—though they are sufficiently dramatic—but rather representative types, a fact which is emphasized by giving them only Christian names.

The language is absolutely free from verbal boloney. It is crisp, pure English, geared to modern usage and set in verse forms which combine flexibility with impelling rhythms of their own which go on ringing in one's head . . .

(*Punch*, 13 November 1946)

The greater sense of naturalness about the Chorus was partly due, I suspect, to my having learned how to treat it: as Stephen Potter put it in the *New Statesman*:

The chorus of uncles and aunts is full of individuality, yet with the slightest side-step they fall naturally into the function of Chorus.

From Philip Hope-Wallace in *Time and Tide* comes this confession:

167

It seemed to me more than ever a great and important play (perhaps that only means that I have grown up to it?)

and I think that Leila Davies, in the *New English Weekly*, is probably right in her fuller formulation of the reasons for such an estimate:

Over seven years ago—in another age, as it seems to one looking down the inverted telescope of time—I went to the first performance of *The Family Reunion* at the Westminster. I came away from it, I remember, deeply impressed but not sure how successful it was in the theatre . . . Now, after a second European war, and much beside, I have seen the play again. This time there was no shadow of doubt; it is incomparably the best modern play now running in London; more, it is beginning to stand the test of time and is slowly rearing itself above all its contemporaries and moving quietly to the niche it will occupy in the long future . . . There is a sense of elation in watching it beat its heavy wings on the upward flight.

(*New English Weekly*, 30 January 1946)

That summer, the Edinburgh Festival was begun. Rudolf Bing, who had helped John Christie to start the Glyndebourne Opera, succeeded in persuading the elders of that staid northern capital to embark upon what seemed an equally hazardous venture directly after the end of the war, when everything was rationed and restricted to the greatest possible extent. The instinct which led them proved triumphantly right; people who had suffered a long strain, and who were still hemmed about with frustrations, were ready to take great gulps of the fresh air of artistic excellence, especially when the air of Edinburgh itself was at its most sparkling.

The Gateway Theatre invited me to take the two Eliot plays in repertory for the Festival. Speaight came back to play Becket; and for *The Family Reunion* I had Patrick Troughton as Harry, Henzie Raeburn as Agatha, Yvonne Coulette as Mary and Eileen Thorndike as Amy. Sybil Thorndike, who had in the end been unable to play Amy at the Mercury, came to a number of her sister's rehearsals, and had gained a deep understanding of the part when Peter Brook secured her for his revival in 1956.

The success of the Edinburgh season created what seemed to me a suitable opportunity for 'the new . . . the promised play':

Sunday, 28.9.47

Dear Tom . . .

I want to put before you a result of the Edinburgh Festival. As you know, the season at the Gateway was a very great success, most of all in the kind of reception accorded by the audiences. It struck me as the ideal place in which to launch a new play by you. They want us back: and if you were able to agree to provide a play for the 1948 Festival (Aug: 22–Sept: 12), it would be part of the official Festival programme, and a much honoured part. People were more deeply interested by your plays than by any others performed, and there's no doubt that the Festival needs such a new work as only you could provide. It also strikes me that the Gateway is the ideal place in which to start a play for you: it is of 500 seats, with a good and large stage, yet a friendly and intimate atmosphere. From it, one could go to theatres either bigger or smaller, as the play's effect demanded.

I put this on paper that you may think it over . . .

Hard as it is to realise now, such opportunities were not then easy to come by: the commercial managers had not yet experienced the drawing power of modern verse drama. Eliot had not got far enough in the conception of his new work to take up the Gateway offer (which I accepted instead for the première of Christopher Fry's *The Firstborn*). But the idea of opening his new play at the Edinburgh Festival had been put into his head.

He became a British citizen in 1927, just 300 years after his ancestor, Andrew Eliot, left East Coker for the New World. Twenty-one years later, he received the highest honour that his sovereign could bestow on him, the Order of Merit. My wife planned a party:

> 56 Portland Court
> Great Portland Street, W.1
> Jan. 11, 1948

My dear Tom,

Martin and I feel very proud that we are giving this small 'home-made' party to celebrate your honour. The date is settled I think to suit you and other guests as Wednesday, February 4th at 7. And we thought the 'black tie' would give a festive note! or perhaps the glint of the dress-shirt. The party almost comes within the limit of our dining table—yourself, George Chichester, Mrs Bell, Stella and Eric Newton, Ashley—(Bobby if free), Denis[1] and our two selves.

Our love,

> Yours ever
> *Henzie*

> 14th January, 1948

My dear Henzie,

Thank you for your letter of the 11th. I shall look forward with great pleasure to your very select party on February 4th, and my secretary has entered in my diary that I am to wear a black tie!

> Affectionately,
> *Tom*

---

[1] Our elder son.

War Interlude

19th. January 1948

My dear Tom,

I don't want to mix the mention of business with the pleasure of our party to you on Feb. 4th, so I write now ... regarding your new play. It is of course possible that recent events have held back its progress towards mental formulation, but I hope they may not. If it is on the way to being born this year, and will not be interrupted by your visit to Princeton, the Edinburgh invitation will still, probably, be open: but an answer of some kind will be wanted in the first week of February ...

I hope you are pleased about Princeton: it should provide a welcome change and opportunity.

Looking forward to the 4th,

Yours ever,
Martin

25th January 1948

My dear Martin,

I am sorry for the delay in answering your letter of the 19th. I certainly expect the play to be born this year. I do not know how long it will be before it learns to walk, to say nothing of an acrobatic turn worthy of the theatre. Knowing how slowly I work and the amount of time it is likely to take up to get up a head of steam with an engine which has been out of action for so long, I know that the thought of working to a date for this summer would throw me into a panic. I should be quite happy with the prospect of Spring, 1949, and if, as I hope, I can break the back of the new born infant during the summer, I should be able to do polishing work even while at Princeton. I hope to be able to start work—or more exactly perhaps I should say sit down morning after morning with nothing else to do—in two or three weeks ...

Meanwhile, the Pilgrim Players' stay at the Mercury was coming to an end. I had been appointed Director of the British Drama League; and Ashley Dukes was back from Germany. Morley had been right in judging him 'difficult to handle'; and he had given the company notice to quit. Yet he was one of the architects of Eliot's success in the theatre, which was what we were especially to celebrate, and must be invited to the party.

To make a happy evening of it required some delicate diplomacy on the part of the hostess:

Ash Wednesday, 1948

My dear Henzie,

I have been meaning to write to thank you for your dinner party: to express my appreciation first of the intention, then my appreciation of the compliment and of the testimony of friendship, then my recognition of the way in which the intention was realised—the goose was memorable—and finally my happiness—no, not finally that, though there is always that in any meeting which includes yourselves and the Bells and the Newtons—but finally my appreciation of the 'total situation' and the way in which you dealt with it . . .

Affectionately and gratefully,

T.S.E.

6

The Cocktail Party

1st June 1948

Dear Martin,

Here is the first draft of three scenes which I promised you to examine at your convenience. When you are ready for a preliminary talk about it please let me know and we will arrange a meeting.

You will understand of course that this is only a first rough draft and that everything, including a good deal of the actual dialogue, is subject to revision. The verse is still in a very rough state and will in any case need a good deal of polishing. On the other hand I understand how little you can say about what is not more than a third of a play. Possibly no more than whether you think it is worth pursuing or not.

I should also like to talk to you when we meet about the Drama League in relation to this curious festival of Britain in 1951, of which I find myself on the Council.

Yours ever,

Tom

It must have been evident from the accompanying pages, of which I have no copy (they would have been returned with my note in reply) that the new play was something very different from what had gone before, and from the ideas which I had put forward in the meantime. But I at once replied:

6.6.48

My dear Tom,

I have read the three scenes twice, and certainly think you should go on. More when we meet, and you tell me more of the rest. This, written in the train, is just to say 'yes' to that question. Looking forward to Tuesday week,

Yours ever,

Martin

Eliot acknowledges this on 'Sunday', probably 13 June:

The Cocktail Party

Dear Martin,

Thanks for your note. That's all I need for the moment, though if you have any detailed suggestions I shall be glad to hear them when we meet. I am doubtful of many things, down to the false teeth—perhaps that is too near a stale music-hall joke. If so, something else could be substituted for teeth: though it is really based on a true story.

Since then I have drafted the second act: that is to say about half the play. I don't think it is worth while sending you any more until I can put into your hands the whole of this draft. I ought to finish it during the summer, get your criticism; and then, if the play is still worth going on with, work on it while I am at Princeton . . .

On 15 June, the diary tells me:

TSE to dine in gay mood, to discuss first draft Act I *One-Eyed Riley*.

A month later I received a further and fuller draft. The title page read:

ONE-EYED RILEY
A Comedy

It was accompanied by the following letter:

18 July 1948

Dear Martin,

Having finished the first draft of three acts, I think that I might as well let you have a copy now. The original scheme was for three acts and an 'epilogue'. I have not changed this scheme, but I propose to call the Epilogue 'Act IV'. I think the term 'epilogue', read in the programme, is discouraging for the audience: it suggests that everything will be finished by then, and the epilogue might be omitted.

Act IV, as I now propose it, will repeat the scene, and most of the personages of Act I. The only person absent will of course be Celia. It should be a year, or perhaps two years later than the rest of the play. Some indication of the fate of Celia will be given in the conversation: this is tricky, but I don't want to leave her in the air like Harry. The interesting problem, however, is that of the behaviour of the several persons while Celia is being discussed.

In order to use the same set for Act IV as for Act I, I have put in a final scene at the end of Act III, which was not contemplated in this form when I last saw you, so as to get Julia, Reilly and Gibbs together with all the others out of the way. This is a kind of scene which I, naturally, rather fancy; and which, equally naturally, I fear you will disallow.

You don't need to give your attention to this at once: I hope to sketch out Act IV during August. But as I shall want criticism to work on in America, in October and November, it seemed to me that you had better have the material for as long as possible before I leave; and I don't think that any opinion you

The Cocktail Party

form, after digesting the first three acts, will be materially altered by reading the fourth.

I should think we might allow another 20 pages for the last act. One question will be whether this will work out at anywhere near the right length. On the one hand, there are probably passages where there are more words than necessary to carry forward the situation, and others where there are gaps. I don't feel that I can myself judge whether I have plotted the emotional curve of the important scenes successfully. One sees the situation at the beginning of the scene, and the situation one wants to arrive at, at the end; but it is, I feel sure, only too easy to leave out indications of significant changes, in the course of the dialogue, which the audience must have. I suspect, for instance, that the transformation of Edward and Lavinia, and the development of Celia, in the hands of Reilly occurs too abruptly to be convincing. At the same time, I believe that there is always a way of solving the problem *within the time limits of the form*, if one selects the essential words which will do the work within that time. I suppose it is the business of the dramatist to be able to give, in ten minutes on the stage, the illusion of an operation which in life would take at least half an hour.

Yours ever,
Tom

P.S. I am inclined to think that a better title would be THE COCKTAIL PARTY. A cocktail party of guests whom the host didn't want, corresponds very well to a family reunion from which part of the family was absent.

I acknowledged this on 21 July:

Many thanks for more of *The Cocktail Party*, which I agree is the better title of the two.

The attraction of *One-Eyed Riley* was quite understandable: it reflected Eliot's affection for the music-hall and made an intriguing suggestion about the psychiatrist which was borne out by his song in the first scene, allying him, as Eliot afterwards pointed out, to the Heracles of the *Alcestis*, in which the germ of the play was found. But *The Cocktail Party* was calculated to give a truer impression of the play's *milieu* and mood, as well as being a good 'selling' title for those days. This choice set the mould for subsequent titles; *The Family Reunion* had begun what *The Cocktail Party* now carried on, a pattern of three words beginning with the definite article.

The draft consisted of the material which makes the present Acts One and Two; 'Act Four', which was not yet written, was finally to become Act Three. Before sending a detailed letter of analysis, I sketched out for myself a scenario:

174

The Cocktail Party

I.1	Cocktail party of guests he couldn't put off.		Edward
			Julia
			Celia
			Peter
			Gibbs
	Interview Ed/UG	Unidentified Guest =	Reilly
I.2	Interview Ed/Peter		Ed.
			Peter
	'Phone to Celia		
II.1	Interview Ed/Celia		Ed/Celia
II.2	Interviews Ed/Reilly		Ed.
	Ed/Lavinia		R
			Lav.
III.1	,, Ed/Sir H. Reilly/Lav.		Ed
			R
			Lav.
III.2	,, Reilly/Celia		Reilly/Celia
	Council: Reilly/Julia/Gibbs		Julia/Gibbs

On 31 July, I wrote fully, a letter of which I have only the MS draft, the ending of which is missing; but the draft has been carefully corrected and doubtless represents what Eliot received:

My dear Tom,

Now for a couple of hours, at last, to discuss *The Cocktail Party*! We have both read it, and besides greatly enjoying its beauties and pleasantnesses of detail, feel that it promises well as a whole. A summary of the general impression is that it needs *amplifying*—which is the best possible state for a play in first draft.

To analyse this need more in detail:—

(1) From Act I scene 2 to the middle of Act III scene 2 the play consists of a series of interviews. Each is of great interest in itself, but they do not seem to me to be sufficiently integrated into a pattern of action. The solution of this problem seems to lie in the use of Julia and Gibbs.

For (2), these two characters do not have sufficient chance to develop. *Julia* is vivid in scene 1: but her reappearance in an entirely different capacity in III.2 is hard to accept at present, since one has not seen her at all in the capacity assigned to her in the later scene. If she intervened at times throughout the play, the trail could be laid in such a manner that, though the audience were not allowed to perceive where it led to, they would recognise, when the destination was made clear in III.2, that this destination had been implicit all along.

Gibbs is only a shadow at present, and you could most profitably work him up into a complete character, again by means of interventions between and during the interviews.

(3) There are some chances to exhibit *action* which could with advantage be

The Cocktail Party

taken. The play at present is a little static. Most notably, one would like to *see* the resolution[1] of Celia's affair with Edward. Also it would perhaps be possible to witness something of her relations with Peter (who up to date is another shadowy person, tho' one gathers we are to see more of his development in Act IV). The more of Celia's growth we can actually see the better we shall be satisfied: description, however clear and vivid, is never the same as seeing. (Let me remark in passing how *extraordinarily* clear the writing is.) We need every possible chance to learn, by seeing it, the difference between her and the others—her struggle, her surrender, and whither that surrender will lead. She is the character whom above all we want to love—the heroine, the play's necessary focus of sympathy.

(4) There are some questions, on the realistic plane, which it would be well to answer. To do so will have the double advantage of expanding the play and of quieting the nagging voice which can break the illusion by asking the awkward question. I note the chief ones that strike us:

I.1. Edward seems to accept the UG (when he says 'you shall see her again—here') without asking 'Who are you? How do you know?' If he asks these questions he will also make the audience curious and increase the dramatic value of the later revelation.

I.2. Why didn't we see any trace of *Peter*'s love for *Celia* in scene 1? and what becomes of it afterwards?

II.1. How did *Celia*'s relations with *Edward* develop? Who began it? And the same about that uncomfortable *Lavinia–Peter* affair.

III. How and why did all these people *start consulting* this *Reilly*?

Celia/Reilly interview: we do need to know more about 'the circumstances'—perhaps not here but at an earlier stage (this is covered by question under II.1.) . . .

As you will see, all this is excellent material for the expansion which the play needs: I think there's enough to make it complete, and long enough, without bringing in any more characters, or any extraneous plot.

Now as regards FORM. This may of course alter with the expansion, but as it looks at present I should recommend that it becomes a play in two parts. *Part I* to consist of Prologue (Cocktail-Party—this, I realise, is to be called Act I scene 1) and everything up to the end of Act II; joining up Act I scene 2 to Act II (the time it takes for Celia to arrive would be filled by a Gibbs/Julia interlude) and going straight on from II.1 to II.2 with no curtain.

Part II would similarly consist of a continuous Act III and then a return to the Prologue-group. There could be a curtain after Prologue, and a curtain before Act IV.

Then as to the FINAL SCENE OF ACT III (*the 'libation' scene*). I think the validity of this depends on what development Julia and Gibbs undergo between the Prologue and this point. In itself, I find it most attractive: but it can hardly be unique in the play, can it? I think the problem of these characters is a single whole and needs solving for the whole play. May it perhaps be that some contact

---

[1] A note amends this to 'development', the course of which was made clear in the opening and 'telegram' scenes. See *Collected Plays*, pp. 128, 130–1, 158–63.

176

between them and Celia will give you the occasion for the establishment of their deeper significance?

Eliot acknowledges this on 4 August:

Dear Martin,

This is to thank you briefly for your very valuable letter of the 31st, which I shall allow to guide me in my re-writing. On a first reading, I recognise some points of which I was already aware, others which I accept at once, others which I do not at once see how to deal with, and perhaps a few which I do not understand. At the moment, I cannot proceed further with the study, as I have been obliged to interrupt my labours ... This may mean that I shall be unable to finish Act IV of the present version before I leave for America—there is turning out to be more to it than I had expected, and the character of Peter is being developed more than I intended. But if I cannot do this in time to get your observations before I leave, I do not think that this need hold me up; as I believe that I shall be able to get to work on the re-writing of the first three acts while you are still meditating your criticisms of Act IV.

On 31 August, our diary tells us, Eliot came 'to dine and talk over his play (first three acts)'. This was the last meeting before he left for a semester at the Institute of Advanced Studies at Princeton, and I for Edinburgh to stage *The Firstborn*. Our next contact was a result of the award to him of the Nobel Prize for Literature in November:

November 13th, 1948

My dear Tom,

We add one more to the thousands of messages of congratulation which you have received, but it is a very loving and heartfelt one. We rejoice once more that you have been honoured as you deserve for a work without compare in this century's literature. And also because of what that work *and its creator* mean to us personally.

I have delayed a few days in writing because developments are taking place about the play, and I wanted to wait to see Rudolf Bing, the impresario of the Edinburgh Festival, which I did yesterday at his request.

I had already had a talk with Bronson Albery, owner of the New, Wyndhams and Criterion, who took HAPPY AS LARRY[1] to the latter theatre last Christmas. This was of course quite a confidential talk on my own responsibility. What I was trying to do was to discover how we could secure that the play, if produced at Edinburgh, would be certain of a London home to await it afterwards. Theatres being as difficult to get as they still are, this should be settled before a commitment is made to Edinburgh.

---

[1] A verse comedy by Donagh MacDonagh, the last new play produced at the Mercury under my management.

The Cocktail Party

The situation is now like this:

Albery would like to do your new play (though he rather naturally wanted to read some of it, but I have shewn the first draft to no one). He is worried by the idea of an Edinburgh premiere, as it involves coming to London at the busiest time and he might not have a theatre (the Old Vic occupying the New, he has only Wyndhams and the unsuitable Criterion left). He asked what chance there would be of the play being ready, and of your being willing to consider a London opening, for the New when the Old Vic go out for the summer (early June). I said I doubted this but would ask you. He does not of course exclude the October date, but could not pledge a free theatre at that time.

Bing would welcome the play at Edinburgh as part of the official Festival and is sure the Festival Society would too. They could not finance it, but this is not, I am sure, a difficulty. He thinks it would have to be at the Gateway, not at the Lyceum, as the Old Vic are likely to return to the latter: and of course the smallness of the Gateway (500 seats) makes finance more difficult: but again I am quite sure this is not impossible. There are some domestic problems to be cleared up here, but that could be done.

Bing also suggested an approach to Tennents (Hugh Beaumont) about managing the play. This would be likely to exclude the Pilgrims from the presentation, even if they accepted me: but might well be the only way of getting a theatre. I did not of course do anything about it as I feel that whatever you may think about an approach we ought to give Albery first chance.

Bing also indicated that if we wanted to get the play into the Festival programmes we had not long to decide in, as the first circular will go to press within the next month; and the matter would have to go through the Festival Society and the Gateway management before it was announced.

So the next thing is for you, if you will, to write me as quickly as possible on the following points:

Do you want me, either personally or as Director of the Pilgrim Players, to act for you officially in negotiation for the play?

Could you consider having the play ready in time for the New at the end of May or early June, and if so would you want it launched thus to the exclusion of Edinburgh?

Do you want it presented by the Pilgrim Players or do you not mind about this?

Do you feel satisfied with the conditions so far suggested by Bing for Edinburgh?

We hope that your American stay is proving as pleasant as it promised to, and that you have been able to do what you wanted. Of course there will be added unto you Nobel celebrations: and I expect you have to go to Sweden to receive the prize?...

Our love to you as ever,
Martin

Entrusted by Eliot with the task of negotiating for the play's production, I talked further with Rudolf Bing, who asked me to propose to Hugh Hunt, the newly appointed director of the Old Vic, that they should do the play at the Lyceum Theatre, which he was trying to arrange that they occupy during the Festival:

4th January 1949

Dear Martin Browne,

May I say at once how very interested I am in your suggestion that Eliot's new play should be done by the Old Vic and how much we would like to present it at the Edinburgh Festival. But there are two major worries about it.

The first is that I cannot agree that the play be tied to a particular producer. Mr. Rees[1] agrees with me in this decision. Were we to allow this we should lay ourselves open, as I am sure you will readily appreciate, to similar conditions on other occasions which would gravely interfere with the freedom of choice that the Old Vic must have if it is to build up any consistent standard of theatrical policy.

The second difficulty concerns the script. Obviously the bare outline which you give is insufficient for me to be able to cast the play. This naturally must be done in relation to other plays in the season. Moreover, although I have the very highest opinion of Eliot's genius, both Mr. Rees and I would have to know a little bit more about the particular merits of the new play before we could confidently recommend it to the Governors.

I feel the latter question is not insurmountable and that Eliot himself could probably give us some kind of rough draft before we finally agree to do the play. But the former difficulty is one which must concern you and the author very closely, and I am afraid it would be necessary for Eliot to allow the Old Vic to make its own decision on the matter of the producer before we could contemplate a production.

I do hope that you will understand our feelings in this matter, and that you will not take it as a reflection upon yourself. When planning a season for the Old Vic a great many intricate questions arise regarding both producers and artists which must be solved by the Management of the Company. Perhaps you will have a talk to Eliot and let me know his decision. In the meantime I will drop him a line.

Yours sincerely,
Hugh Hunt

5.1.49

My dear Tom,

Here is Hugh Hunt's letter, and he says he is writing you a line so I expect you will be glad to see this in explanation. You will of course realise that I want to leave the matter quite open for you, and shall understand any decision you may make. I do of course see Hunt's point of view.

Will you very kindly let me know whether you want to talk it over or not, as I imagine we cannot delay long.

[1] Llewellyn Rees, the administrator of the Old Vic.

I am not going to Germany, so shall be available here.
With our love,

Yours ever,
Martin

6th January, 1949

My dear Martin,

I return herewith Hugh Hunt's letter to you of the 4th January. It has always been an understanding between ourselves that you should produce this play, and I should consider it turpitude to throw over my producer! I assure you also that from my point of view I think it might be grasping the shadow and dropping the substance since I should feel grave hesitation in putting it into any other hands. I assure you that self interest combines with loyalty to turn this proposal down without more ado.

Yours ever,
Tom

January 8th, 1949

My dear Tom,

Your letter of January 6th moved me deeply, both by reason of your loyalty and of your trust in me. I am very far from being worthy, but I am profoundly thankful for these great gifts of yours to me . . .

I communicated Eliot's decision to Hunt; but meanwhile, Bing informed me that the situation had changed, and that the Old Vic would not after all be occupying the Lyceum. He was in treaty with Henry Sherek who would, he hoped, undertake this instead. Would I go and discuss the matter with him?

Bing had already mentioned the matter to Mr Sherek when I asked for an appointment; and that same afternoon I went to his office at 40 Pall Mall. The first meeting with this very large, ebullient and powerful man was a shock; I was shy and hesitating in face of his assurance; but what I had to bring him was of immediate and absorbing interest. He read, while I was in the office, the draft of the first two Acts which I had brought; and despite the fact that all the joins were still missing and there was not even a sketch of a last Act, he agreed then and there to produce the play at Edinburgh under my direction.

Thus began a collaboration which was to last until the end of Eliot's playwriting life. I suppose it looked very strange to an outside observer. Eliot, the austere, quiet poet with the academic manner and reputation, was henceforth to be under the management of a real commercial showman, one who, following in his father's footsteps, had learned the hard way about every aspect of show-business. My wife and I asked them both to lunch for their first meeting, which was an occasion of acute embarrassment all round; but Eliot very soon came to appreciate Sherek, as I did, and delight in the size and warmth of his personality.

He took Eliot at one bound into the world of entertainment, giving him the opportunity he had always wanted, to offer his play-writing talent to the theatre-public on equal terms with other drama-tists, and to prove whether it was possible for a poet to make a success with plays in verse.

Sherek and I, starting almost equally far apart, found much in common; we were just of an age, and we shared a love of language, which was the reason why he had been immediately captivated by Eliot's writing that January afternoon. Both Eliot and I conceived a great respect for his theatrical judgement, which he was backing with his personal assets and reputation: here was no faceless com-bine, but an individual who staked all he had on his love and know-ledge of the theatre. It was Sherek who provided us with the finest actors, the best designers, and who undertook the infinite labour involved in achieving the presentation of the plays at the best theatres on both sides of the Atlantic. In the course of all this, we both enjoyed much of his companionship, and also that of his delightful wife Pamela.

Sherek has written his own account of the collaboration in his autobiography, *Not in Front of the Children*.[1]

Production being assured, the urgent necessity was to get a finished script to produce. By this time the last Act was in draft; but it passed through more changes than any other part of the play. Eliot came to lunch on 3 March to discuss it, and on the 15th the 'first version arrived'.

This brings us to the point where the development of the script may be plotted in detail.

SHAPING THE SCRIPT

THE FIRST ACT

We may take two questions raised in my letter of 18 July 1948[2] as a starting point for this study: the questions of the play's form,

[1] Heinemann, London, 1959. [2] See above, pp. 175–7.

and of how Gibbs and Julia could provide a framework for the series of interviews which constituted most of the first draft.

Since Eliot conceived the play as occurring in the solid type of setting which was usual on the stage of drawing-room comedy, this production would clearly be using the front curtain; but it was desirable to reduce the number of times it fell and rose again to the minimum. In *The Family Reunion* he had used the word 'scene' in the French manner, to indicate a change of mood or of characters on stage, not intending a visual break; but in the drafts of this play he puts the word 'curtain' at the end of several scenes. My letter already suggests how a smoother flow can be achieved; and the final shape of three scenes (two curtains) in Act One, a continuous Act Two, and a return to the first setting two years later for Act Three, was worked out by means of using the secondary characters to link the interviews.

In the first draft, Julia already makes a return after her exit from the cocktail party, to fetch her umbrella;[1] and at the end of Edward's scene with the Unidentified Guest, she comes back again[2] for her glasses. The curtain comes down while the search for them is going on: but we eliminated this in the Edinburgh Festival version by bringing Peter back with Julia, so that he is left with Edward, to seek his advice directly after Julia has gone.

During their talk, Alex is brought in, and insists on cooking Edward a special meal; this results in periodic incursions from the kitchen which interrupt Peter's self-revelations. When he has left, Edward tries to telephone Celia; and on this the curtain of what was originally Eliot's Act One falls.

He planned to have a day pass before the next scene; but we hastened the action by making Edward's call abortive because Celia was already on her way to him. As soon as the curtain rises again, she rings the doorbell. Hardly has the conversation got going when Alex rings up to know how his dish, which Edward has forgotten, turned out. This leads to Celia finding the burnt saucepan, which she has in her hand when Julia appears saying

> Celia! I see you've had the same inspiration
> That I had. Edward must be fed.

(Collected Plays, p. 148)

---

[1] See *Collected Plays*, p. 131. [2] See *ibid.*, p. 136.

and plants herself in the kitchen while their conversation proceeds a little further. She emerges with champagne and makes them drink a disconcerting toast. She tries to carry Celia off with her, but Celia insists on staying and at last the momentous scene is finished. But Julia is still hovering; as Celia is making her confession to Edward, the telephone rings. Julia has left her glasses again—in the kitchen.

EDWARD   You're sure? In the kitchen? Beside the champagne bottle?
    You're quite sure? . . . Very well, hold on if you like;
    We . . . I'll look for them.
CELIA   Yes, you look for them.
    I shall never go into your kitchen again.
(*Exit* EDWARD. *He returns with the spectacles and a bottle*)
EDWARD   She was right, for once.
CELIA   She is always right.
    But why bring an empty champagne bottle?
EDWARD   It isn't empty. It may be a little flat—
    But why did she say that it was a half-bottle?
    It's one of my best: and I have no half-bottles.
    Well, I hoped that you would drink a final toast with me.
CELIA   What should we drink to?
EDWARD   Whom shall we drink to?
CELIA   To the Guardians.
EDWARD   To the Guardians?
CELIA   To the Guardians. It was you who spoke of guardians.
(*They drink*)
    It may be that even Julia is a guardian.
    Perhaps she is *my* guardian. Give me the spectacles.
    Good night, Edward.
EDWARD   Good night . . . Celia.   (*Exit* CELIA)
                          (*Collected Plays*, p. 155)

And Julia is still holding on.

These additions not only served to break up long duologues, and to sharpen their effect by doing so, but also to make clear the role of the three Guardians. We should now try to analyse this.

A short while before the scene quoted above, Edward describes to Celia the way in which he now sees his destiny as being shaped. In the first draft, the speech runs like this:

    I see that my life was determined long ago
    And that the struggle to escape from it
    Is only a make-believe, a pretence
    That what is, is not, or could be changed.
    The self that can say 'I want this—or want that'—

The self that *wills*—he is a feeble creature;
He has to come to terms in the end
With the real, the tougher self, who does not speak,
Who never talks, who does not argue;
And who in some men may be the *daemon*, the genius,
And in others, like myself, the dull, the implacable,
The indomitable spirit of mediocrity.
The willing self can contrive the disaster
Of this unwilling partnership—but can only thrive
In submission to the rule of the stronger partner.

(CP/1; cf. Collected Plays, pp. 153–4)

A note of mine as late as 10 July 1949, when the play was about to go into rehearsal, makes this suggestion:

The business of '*daimon*, genius, *guardian*' is worrying in two respects: (a) the unfamiliar word *daimon* is used nowhere else and will simply puzzle hearers; (b) the word *guardian* seems to have two different connotations on two nearly following pages: here it refers to the innermost self, (later) to another person acting in that capacity. Would it be possible, and in accord with your meaning to reshape the line . . . so as to take out the words 'daimon' and 'genius' and say something like
    'and who in some men may be the guardian'
so that we can see what I take to be the two various kinds of guardianship implied on the two pages referred to, clearly differentiated?

Eliot accepted this suggestion, because it expressed what he meant: influence of a spiritual kind may be exercised both within the self and by persons outside it.

I think that my own understanding was assisted by having, for a long time during the war, played the part of the archangel Raphael, who is disguised as Azarias the porter, in James Bridie's *Tobias and the Angel*. After leading the good, but timid and clumsy youth to recover a fortune and find a beautiful bride, Sara, Raphael has to cope with her infatuation for himself. He explains to her (Act Three, scene 1) that he is Tobias's *daemon*:

A daemon, spelt with an 'a' is a creature by whose agency you write immortal verse, go great journeys, leap into bottomless chasms, fight dragons, starve in a garret . . .
Sara: Strangle our husbands.
Raphael: Yes, that too. It is perhaps fortunate that daemons are much too occupied to visit, or to concern themselves with, the bulk of mankind.
Sara: It is very fortunate.
Raphael: When it is necessary to Jahweh's purpose, they make contact, often with extremely disturbing results . . .

and later:

Often, at odd times in the future, you will see me looking out of Tobias's eyes.
But you must look the other way and busy yourself with your household tasks.
For I have no pity for you . . .
Sara: But how can I help loving his daemon?
Raphael: You cannot love what you cannot understand . . .

I am not suggesting that Bridie's and Eliot's conceptions are the
same; re-telling a story from the Apocrypha, Bridie is concerned with
guardianship by angels rather than by human beings: but the idea
that the self of the person guarded may house the guardian spirit is
common to both. Eliot also conceives that there are people in the
world who are appointed guardians; and I think that David E. Jones[1]
is right in relating this to the Community of Christians in *The Idea of
a Christian Society*.

The group seems to have grown outward, so to speak, from the
final scene in the consulting room, where the three are left together
after Reilly has had the deciding interviews with Edward and Lavinia
and with Celia. In the first draft, as we have noted, only Reilly is
active until this scene, when for the first time Julia and Alex disclose
their part in the alliance. Julia's first appearance in the room is after
Celia has left: she has been cavesdropping. She finds the psychiatrist
lying on his couch (the fact that he is the only person to use it provided much amusement especially for American audiences):

JULIA   Henry! get up! You can't be so tired as that.
    You're just trying to feel important.
REILLY   It's a great responsibility,
    These decisions of life and death.
JULIA   They are not *your* decisions;
    You have no responsibility except to execute them . . .

(CP/1)

We agreed to eliminate the eavesdropping. It was seen by all of us
as overstepping the fine-drawn line between the guardian and the
busybody. It is a line which each critic of the play draws in a different
place; some have reacted against the whole idea of the Guardians on
the ground that such interference with the lives of others is in itself
unacceptable. But of course it is practised by everyone, and suffered
by everyone, in some way throughout their life. The difference here
is that the Guardians are not acting on their own initiative; and just

[1] *The Plays of T. S. Eliot* (Routledge and Kegan Paul, London, 1960), pp. 149 ff.

185

because of this they are limited both by the obligation to leave the ultimate decision to the person cared for, and by the boundary set on their own knowledge of the way. One is reminded of Agatha in relation to Harry. Julia, the most experienced of the three, tells Henry, later in the scene as drafted:

> You, for your part, must not take yourself too seriously.
> You are only an instrument.
>
> (*CP*/1)

And when she turns to discussing the case of Celia, she confesses her own limitations:

>   With the Chamberlaynes
> We are in a region you and I know completely—
> I am sometimes terrified by my own knowledge.
> But here, I am terrified by my own ignorance.
> We are earth-bound spirits, Henry, frontiersmen;
> We can help those who are elected, and we are allowed to know
> The moment when we can show them the first stages
> On the way which they themselves have freely chosen,
> But do not know that they have chosen.
> We can help them to know it. But what do we know
> Of the kind of suffering they must endure
> On the way to illumination?
>
> (*Ibid.*)

She sums up for all of them:

>   We must accept our limitations:
> That is the condition of the service.
>
> (*Ibid.*)

'The condition of *the service*.' Eliot is surely thinking of these characters as ministers: and he duly gives them, at the end of the Act, their special ritual. Here is the first draft of it, following directly the line last quoted:

ALEX (*enters*)   Well, and how have we got on?
JULIA   Everything is in order.
ALEX   The Chamberlaynes have chosen?
REILLY   They accept the wheel.
ALEX   She has made the choice?
REILLY   She will be fetched this evening.
JULIA   When the full moon has risen.
ALEX   When the full moon has risen.
       And the prayer of protection?

The Cocktail Party

REILLY   It has not been spoken.

JULIA   We awaited your coming.

ALEX   Proceed to the libation.

(SIR HENRY *rises and produces from a cupboard a bottle and three champagne glasses, which he sets on a low table in the centre*)

REILLY   Je suis de si bonne disposition que c'est moi qui vous verserai à boire.
     What a relief it is to be talking prose.

JULIA   Henry! When have you ever talked anything else?

ALEX   Your task is now ended. (*They raise their glasses*)
     The prayer for the building of the hearth:
               Let them build the hearth
               Under the protection of the Moon,
               And place a chair on each side of it.
               Who shall surround the house?

J AND R   The four higher protectors.

ALEX   Who shall watch over the roof?

J AND R   The two winged ones shall watch over the roof.

ALEX   Under what sign shall it be erected?

J AND R   Under the sign of the seven stars.

ALEX   Who shall cast influence upon the bed?

J AND R   The Moon shall influence the bed.

ALEX   In what name shall she act?

J AND R   In the name of the fructifying Sun.

ALEX   The prayer for those who go upon a journey:
               Protector of travellers

J AND R   Bless the road.

ALEX   Protector of travellers

J AND R   Watch over them in the desert.

ALEX   Protector of travellers

J AND R   Watch over them in the mountain.

ALEX   Protector of travellers

J AND R   Watch over them in the labyrinth.

ALEX   Protector of travellers

J AND R   Watch over them in the sucking sands.

ALEX   Protect them from the Voices
          Protect them from the Visions;
          Protect them in the silence,
          Protect them in the vacancy.
                    what
          In ~~whose~~ name is this protection?

J AND R   In the name of the Name which is not spoken.

(*They drink*)

REILLY   But there is one for whom we do nothing.

JULIA   It is Peter whom he means.

ALEX   Peter? What Peter?

187

The Cocktail Party

REILLY The young man Peter Quilpe.
ALEX There are things beyond our powers
    Which must be left to the mystery and the mercy.

(Curtain)

(CP/1; cf. Collected Plays, pp. 192–5)

In the correspondence about the first draft,[1] Eliot had expressed both his affection for and his doubt of this scene; and its progress thenceforth is one of the best illustrations of how the play came to its final form. It underwent three kinds of change. First, the very large (and in itself fascinating) amount of mystic symbolism was greatly reduced. But this remained a stumbling-block to some people, who found it still 'unique in the play' and destructive of the reality of these characters. So constant was this protest, especially about the word with which it is introduced, 'libation', that I later suggested the substitution for Reilly's

    And we now are ready to proceed with the libation

of the line:

    And now we are ready to drink their health.

Eliot's comment on this (25 May 1950) was characteristic:

I will perpend the libation problem for the next few days, only it does seem to me that every step in simplification brings me nearer to Frederick Lonsdale.

Secondly, the parts were redistributed. In the draft, Alex, whom we have not seen since the opening scene, is the master of ceremonies at the libation ritual. This was of course deliberate, to emphasise that no one of the Guardians is above another, and all are servants of a power greater than themselves. Each is therefore successively displaced or deflated. But in the theatre it is necessary to give the audience a focus of attention within the group; and Reilly is the only choice for that purpose. So it is Reilly who finally acts as the master of the ceremony, while Alex and Julia have the speeches which preserve what remains of the mystic symbolism.

But Alex has his moment, at the curtain of the Act. He is the lightest of heart among the Guardians; he provides much of the comic element which, it became progressively clearer, was essential to set the right mood for the play and to bind it together. In the draft, Alex gives a mystic answer to the question about Peter Quilpe:

[1] See above, p. 173.

The Cocktail Party

There are things beyond our powers
Which must be left to the mystery and the mercy.

But in the final version, he has 'connections, even in California'.

We may now return to the beginning of the play to look in detail at some of the differences between the drafts and the final form.

The opening scene remains substantially the same but there are interesting changes. In *CP*/1, the Unidentified Guest never speaks; those repeated single-sentence replies to the challenges of his fellow-guardians, which produce so good a comic effect and also establish the sense of a secret understanding between them, are added in the final version. Lady Klootz is at first Lady Kahn, and has the false teeth referred to in Eliot's second letter:[1]

JULIA   Lady Kahn was very lovely, once upon a time;
        Before she lost her teeth—I mean, the first time she lost them,
        And before she had three husbands . . .

                    .   .   .

PETER   But aren't you going to tell us about Lady Kahn?
JULIA   What Lady Kahn? Oh, you mean the Lady Kahn
        Who dropped her teeth from the leaning tower of Pisa?
PETER   I thought she left them in a wedding cake.
JULIA   Oh, that's another story.
FARQUAHAR-GIBBS   And another Lady Kahn.

                              (*CP*/1, cf. *Collected Plays*, pp. 126, 130)

The first few lines of the play were added at my request, to allow more time for the audience to take in the characters at the rise of the curtain; in all the drafts it begins at

> Do tell us that story you told the other day about Lady Kahn and the wedding cake.

At the end of the play[2] is printed the music for Reilly's song.[3] There is a first verse which is not in the final text. This originally stood early in the scene between Edward and Reilly:

    May I take another drink?
EDWARD   Whisky?
UNIDENTIFIED GUEST   Gin.
EDWARD Anything in it?

[1] See above, p. 173.   [2] *Collected Plays*, p. 213.   [3] *Ibid.*, p. 137.

189

U.G.   Nothing but water.
   Sings: 'As I was a walkin' around and round
            And round in every quarter;
            I walks in to a public house
            And orders up me gin and water.'
   You may be astonished at my levity,
   But I have had experience of such cases,
   And, I assure you, it's a mode of treatment.
EDWARD   Shock treatment?
U.G.   To find out whether it is a shock;
   Or rather, to find out, what kind of a shock.
   Let me put a hypothetical case.
   How long married?

             (*CP*/1; cf. *Collected Plays* p. 132, where the giving of a drink to
             Edward has replaced the above passage)

The line 'Let me put a hypothetical case' calls attention to a marked change which took place in the development of the play. Raymond Williams, in *Drama from Ibsen to Eliot*,[1] described the writing in *The Cocktail Party* as 'verse of the surface, although not superficial. It is conscious, lucid statement'. This is far more true of the final version than of the first draft, which is apt to indulge in argument, hypothesis, generalised philosophical reflection. These are eliminated in favour of direct address to the other person in the scene, related to the matter in hand. The Unidentified Guest, whom Edward in the draft suspects of being Lavinia's solicitor, acquires the teasing and very significant passage about letting 'the genie out of the bottle'[2] to give us a hint as to the real nature of his influence. But at the end of that speech,[3] *CP*/1 has a passage which may typify the difference in style between it and the final text. It goes on:

EDWARD   If you are not a lawyer, you should have been one—
   Drawing the most convincing conclusions
   From the wrong premisses. It is not like that at all.
U.G.   The only way I can get at the truth
   Is to proceed from general to particular
   And observe the residue of several hypotheses;
   And to probe where I find resistance the strongest.
   You don't pretend you love her?
EDWARD   What does that mean?
   Love is merely a comprehensive term
   For a great variety of attitudes

[1] Chatto and Windus, London, 1952, pp. 239–40.
[2] *Collected Plays*, p. 133.   [3] *Ibid.*, p. 134.

Of different men in different situations. We presume
An ecstatic beginning. But if two people
Gradually come to take each other for granted
And are not too aware of what they don't understand
And if each life facilitates the other
And neither thinks he would be any happier
With another person—then we say they are well suited.
Of course I was often irritated by her
And she by me. That's nothing to do with it.
I saw nothing more. So her going away
At a moment's notice, without explanation,
Only a note to say that she had gone
And was not coming back—well, I can't understand it;
And I do not like what I can't understand.

U.G.   Ah, that leads us to the next hypothesis.
We think of ourselves as something positive,
Always the subject of the sentence;
As having arranged, having been responsible
For the part we play in every scene.
Suddenly to find oneself merely an object
Is never pleasant. But is often happening;
Only, we contrive to forget about it quickly,
The ignominious aspect which is always reappearing.
When you are dressed for an evening party
Walking down the stair, and everything about you
Is your own set of peculiar stage properties
Until you come to the bottom, and
There is one step more than you expected
And you walk into space . . . there is a moment
In which you are aware that you are only an object
Among others, like a broken cup
Or a stalled engine. Or, consider an operation.
In consultation with the doctor and the surgeon
In going to bed in the nursing home
In talking to the matron, you are still the subject,
The centre of will. But, stretched on the table
You are a piece of furniture in a repair shop
For those who surround you, the masked actors,
You are merely your body, merely an object,
And *you* have been withdrawn. We identify ourselves
With our action, and are lost when we do not act.
Discipline yourself to be the observer
Of yourself as well as others. Cupbearer, fill.

In talking of the play afterwards,[1] Eliot says

[1] 'Poetry and Drama', in *On Poetry and Poets* (Faber and Faber, London, 1957), p. 85.

The Cocktail Party

I laid down for myself the ascetic rule to avoid poetry which could not stand the test of strict dramatic utility.

This led to a 'rationing' of the poetry so strict that, as some feel, it has diminished the peculiar contribution which Eliot as a poet could have made to the stage. But the test of dramatic utility was usefully applied, in consultation with Sherek and myself, to those disquisitions which, however interesting in themselves, held up the action. Edward on love, in the passage just quoted above, is an example; another from later in the scene, comes also from him. The speech[1] is directed towards one of the cardinal ideas of the play; that one's belief in one's own identity is dependent on one's sense of the identity of those closest to one: Edward finally goes to consult Reilly because

> I have ceased to believe in my own personality.
>
> (*Collected Plays*, p. 174)

But before reaching this seminal subject, the draft of Edward's speech contains a fascinating but irrelevant reflection on another topic:

> Stop! I agree that much of what you've said
> Is true enough. I know the feeling
> Of wanting to be left entirely alone,
> A recurrent feeling of curiosity
> To know what it is like to find oneself alone
> And discover whether solitude could be something positive
> Instead of the merely negative condition
> It was before one married. The experience of loneliness
> Living with another person, one wants to compare it
> With physical loneliness, after one knows it.
> But now, it seems to me merely different
> And in no way preferable. As for what you said
> About the embarrassment, the inconvenience—
> That is one of the first responses,
> I agree. And the interruption of habit,
> That, and the consequent exasperation,
> And finally, the sense of humiliation—
> That is strong enough. But that is not all.
> There's something else that lies much deeper,
> Too obscure to rise to conscious emotion
> Or to have a name. And that's what really matters.
> Since I saw her this morning after breakfast
> I no longer remember what my wife is like.

[1] For its final form, see *Collected Plays*, pp. 135–6.

I am not quite sure that I could describe her
If I had to ask the police to look for her;
I'm sure I don't know what she was wearing
When I saw her last. And so I want her back;
I *must* get her back, to know what has happened,
To know anything about the last five years;
I must find out who she is, to find out who I am ...

(*CP*/1 and, with minor alterations, *CP*/2)

Peter, the central character in the next interview, is the least fully realised of the quartet whose destiny the play traces. His interview with Edward was first written without the interruptions of Alex; and it contains some passages which, though perhaps not dramatically justifiable, are indications of Peter's personality. Edward asks the direct question, which is modified later:

EDWARD   And you became lovers?
PETER   Oh no, no, never.
    But I thought that she really cared about me,
    And I was so happy when we were together—
    So ... contented, so ... at peace; I can't express it,
    I had never imagined there could be such quiet happiness.
    I had only imagined the excitement, the delirium,
    The desire for possession. It was not like that.
    It was not like anything I've ever heard of.
    The ordinary passion—I think I know about it,
    The mixture of motives that poison each other,
    The leaping vanity, the recoiling disgust
    And all that sort of thing. This was such ... simplicity.
    As if some chaotic noise had been suddenly resolved
    And you heard the one pure note which had always been there
    Unheard, and timeless. I never thought ahead,
    It seemed like eternity, the question meaningless.

(*CP*/1)

Here it is possible to feel, what became obscured in the growth of the play, that Peter has, in an embryonic form, the same nature as Celia, and may be destined to share her vocation. Perhaps there was not room for two such, in a play which started as a comedy of the ordinary married couple; and it would surely have made impossible Peter's liaison with Lavinia, which is needed to complete the plot, but which remains hard to believe in. In the draft, Edward's handling of Peter is so unprepossessingly cynical as to make it very hard to accept that Celia could love Edward. Yet the scene in *CP*/1 contains much revealing writing. Here is what follows straight on from the above:

EDWARD   And what interrupted this interesting affair?
      Perhaps you discovered that you, or she,
      Had other concerns than with eternity?
PETER   No. She just . . . faded
      Into the distance. She doesn't want to see me;
      Makes excuses, not very plausible,
      And when I do see her, she seems preoccupied
      With some secret excitement of another life
      Which I do not share.
EDWARD   She's lost interest in you?
PETER   You put everything just wrong. I think of it differently.
      It is not her interest in me that I miss—
      There have been women interested in *me*—
      But the moments which were not of her or of me
      In which we seemed to share some perception,
      Some feeling, some indefinable experience
      In which we were both unaware of ourselves.
      In your terms, perhaps, yes, she's lost interest in me.
EDWARD   This is all very normal. But what did you expect
      Was going to come of this? Only two things could happen
      And this is one of them. If you could only realise
      How lucky you are! In a little while
      This would have become an ordinary affair
      Like any other. As the fever cooled
      You would have found her a different woman
      And found yourself a different man,
      Naming the elements of your infatuation
      As the mixture disintegrated. The common ambition
      To penetrate a world so different from your own
      Which you had endowed with fantasies of brilliance,
      And which would remain forever impenetrable,
      Forever alien, incomprehensible
      And yet a disappointment, because the differences
      Are different from the differences you believed in
      And the similarities only too evident
      As the surface tarnishes. The common vanity
      Distended by the gluttony of power
      To dominate a woman who might have ignored you
      And who, for that reason, you would never trust.
      The greed more desperate as habituation
      Makes clear that you have nothing together
      That you could not have had with much less trouble

With a girl encountered in a cinema,
And without disappointment, because without illusion.
You have been spared the coming to awareness
That the superficial is the substantial
And that nothing else is left you but the yearning of the loins
As full of concupiscence as a weasel of eggs—
Fry, lechery, fry! I congratulate you
On a timely escape.
PETER   I should prefer to be spared
    Your congratulations. I don't know what I expected.
    And I don't suppose I really thought that you could help me
    But I had to talk to someone. I did not expect
    That you would deny what I know to be true.
    Everything else may be a delusion
    But I have been telling you of something real—
    My first experience of reality
    And perhaps it is the last. And you do not understand it.
EDWARD   My dear Peter, this is quite irrelevant.
    I am willing to concede the revelation
    Which I cannot understand. But what do you know
    About yourself? We only know
    About ourselves, the feeling of the moment
    And that is not knowledge. We have a little information
    Also, about the immediate past.
    What we never know about ourselves
    Is the man that one will be next year,
    Next month, next week, in another fifteen minutes.
    Here, at least, I speak from experience.
    About other people, we can judge the probabilities
    Not from knowledge of their souls, some supposed inmost secret,
    But from knowledge of their general situation
    And from what we can see of the external forces
    Governing their lives. I have only told you
    What would have happened to you and Celia
    In another six months' time. There it is.
    You can take it or leave it.
PETER   But what am I to do?
EDWARD   Nothing. Wait. Go back to California.
PETER   But I must see Celia.
EDWARD   Will it be the same Celia?
    Better be content with the Celia you remember.
    It is often better to lose a person
    To preserve an imaginary portrait. There are cases,
    Of course, where we must cling to a person
    Because that person has become a habit.
    But the Celia who could become simply a habit

195

Is not the Celia you remember.
Remember! I say she's already a memory.

PETER   But I must see Celia at least to make her tell me
What has happened. Until I know
I shan't know the truth about even the memory.
Don't you see, already I begin to doubt it.
Did we really have those interests? Did we really feel the same
When we heard certain music? or looked at certain pictures?
There *was* something real. But what is the reality
Of experience between . . .

(*The telephone rings*)

EDWARD   Excuse me a moment.
Hello! . . . I'm afraid I can't talk now . . .
Yes, there is . . . Well then, I'll ring you
Within the next half hour.
                              I'm sorry. You were saying?

PETER   Of experience between two unreal people?
If I can only hold that reality
I can bear any future. But I must find out
The truth about ourselves, for the sake of the memory.

EDWARD   There's no memory you can wrap with camphor
But the moths will get in. Every memory
Goes on changing. Everything you do,
Everything you discover about yourself—
That is to say, everything you discover
About your past self, for the present,
Like the future, you cannot know—
Everything you think and feel, accept, deny,
Is altering the past . . . So you want to see Celia.
I don't know why I should be taking all this trouble
To protect you from the fool you are.
What do you want me to do?

PETER   I wish *you* would see Celia.
You know her in a different way from me,
And you're a good deal older.

EDWARD   So much older?

PETER   Yes, I'm sure that she would listen to you
As someone disinterested. I wish you would find out
First, whether there is some misunderstanding;
If not, whether she cannot explain
What has happened; and explain it to me
So that I shall know what is left me to keep
And what I must reject as having been an illusion.
You could do that.

EDWARD   Well, I will see Celia.

196

PETER (*rising*) Thank you, Edward. It's very good of you.
I've taken up too much of your time.
Oh . . . and give my love to Lavinia
When she comes back. But, if you don't mind,
I'd rather you didn't tell *her* what I've told you.
EDWARD I shall not mention either you or Celia.
PETER Thank you, Edward. Good night.
EDWARD   Good night, Peter. (*Exit* PETER)

(CP/1)

I have a second draft of 'The First Act of a new play by T. S. Eliot' which is later than the July 1948 draft and much nearer to the printed text. In this, Alex's cooking incursions in the Peter scene[1] are introduced, and also Julia's into the Edward/Celia scene. But the balance of the latter, as between the two protagonists, remains more nearly what it is in the first draft. Celia is more positive, urging Edward to 'take action' for a divorce, more firmly imbued with belief both in Edward's love for her and in her power, through her position in society, to affect his career. The passage in *CP*/1 from which derive pages 146 (bottom)–147 (top) of *Collected Plays* typifies this difference:

EDWARD It has only brought to light the real difficulties.
CELIA But surely, those are only temporary.
I always thought you were a man of action:
But it's just like a man, to lose his head
When his own affairs are involved. A woman
Sees things more clearly. You must accept my judgement:
What you are afraid of won't happen just yet.
EDWARD What am I afraid of that won't happen yet?
CELIA Why, of course, the private detectives.
EDWARD The private detectives!
CELIA   Yes, of course, the private detectives.
If Lavinia comes to change her mind,
Or if the man should get cold feet—
She may want to prevent you from taking action.
EDWARD Taking what action?
CELIA   Really, Edward,
This is more than my patience can bear:
Anyone would think you had lost your memory.
You know that I accepted the situation
Because a divorce would ruin your career,

[1] Note that egg-rationing was still in force when the play was produced; hence Edward's dismay at Alex using 'all those eggs', piquantly recalled in Lavinia's curtain-speech (*Collected Plays*) pp. 144, 170.

Because there were people only too eager
To find an excuse to keep you out of politics;
And we thought that Lavinia would never let you go.
But now that it is Lavinia who has left *you*—
Surely you don't hold to that silly convention
That the husband must always be the one to be divorced?
EDWARD   I see. But it is not like that at all.
Lavinia is coming back.

A little later, Celia is still bent on galvanising him into action:

I think it is just a moment of surrender
To fatigue. And fright. You can't face the trouble,
The explanation, the reorganisation,
The interruption of the world you are used to,
The interference with your public life—
But only a temporary interference, Edward.
I must shake you out of this weakness.
This is not the man I thought I loved,
So cowardly, so spineless . . . But perhaps it is;
Perhaps it is because you are weak that I love you
And want to protect you. You must be advised by me.

(CP/1; cf. Collected Plays, p. 150, middle)

In the second draft, Julia's parting shot to Celia before leaving her with Edward, is

Poor child, you look as if you'd seen a ghost.

Indeed Celia has seen a ghost—the ghost of what was left

Of what I had thought you were.

(CP/2; cf. Collected Plays, p. 154, middle)

The end of the scene, which in the final version is heightened dramatically by Julia's telephone call,[1] is in the first draft much more fully written out; and though, as in other instances, the shorter version 'plays' better, one learns much about the author's point of view by studying his first attempt to commit it to paper. Here, then, is the end of the scene in *CP*/1.[2]

CELIA   Edward, I see that I was merely making use of you
        And I ask you to forgive me.
EDWARD   You ask me to forgive you!
CELIA   Yes, for two things. First, for making use of you—

---

[1] See *Collected Plays*, pp. 154, 155.
[2] Cf. *ibid.*, pp. 154–5. Note that it *is* Reilly who rings the bell, as in this draft the Edward–Reilly scene follows 'immediately after'.

The Cocktail Party

EDWARD But perhaps . . . it is I who was making use of you—
    If you choose to put it like that.

CELIA   In a different sense,
    And a way that does not matter. You have gained nothing by it.
    A weak man in a state of confusion
    Bored and baffled, and ready to accept
    Whatever was offered, craving admiration
    Because he clutched at illusions of strength;
    This is what you were, and this is what I leave you.
    I wanted to be freed from the limitation of self:
    You, only to escape from the knowledge of yourself.
    I could not have understood this half an hour ago.
    Edward, I see you only as a human being—
    For the first time, as a human being—
    For whom I feel sorry. And that is the second thing
    For which I want you to forgive me—for feeling sorry for you.

EDWARD I do not want you to feel sorry for me.

CELIA Yes, that is hard to bear. Have we both changed,
    Or were we always utterly different
    From what we felt ourselves to be? I stand apart from you
    And I shall never stand any closer again,
    And I see you as someone merely pathetic.
    I wish that I could comfort you.

EDWARD   A moment ago
    I expressed a concern about your future,
    And you, quite rightly, resented, and rebuked me.
    I know now that this is not my business.
    Perhaps I am incapable of loving anybody—
    But I wanted to love *you*: and to lose you
    Makes the craving desperate. That will be numbed.
    I have had a vision of my own mediocrity;
    But I shall return shortly, I suppose,
    To my proper dimness. Now while I am awake,
    For the first, and for the last time,
    Goodbye. It is time you left.

CELIA Oh no, Edward, do not condemn yourself
    To darkness which may be the darkness of self-pity
    So near as it is to self-accusation.
    Perhaps you will still have just enough light
    To proceed, however slowly. As for myself,
    I look into the darkness of the future
    More gladly than into light . . . Would *anybody*
    Make head or tail of what we have been saying?

(*Door bell rings*)
    What's that?

EDWARD   That will be Riley—and Lavinia.

CELIA   Oh, Lavinia! I had forgotten Lavinia.
EDWARD   I am afraid that I must see you out
    Into the mews—by the tradesmen's entrance:
    I hope you don't mind?
CELIA   Why should I mind?
    I should not have come—by the front door:
    It's right that I should leave by the tradesmen's entrance.
(*Exeunt*)

Into *CP*/2, there have been introduced Julia's interruptions and the business of the champagne. The ending here contains the toast, as in the final script; but the wording is different:[1]

CELIA   What should we drink to?
EDWARD   Whom shall we drink to?
CELIA   To the daemons.
EDWARD   To the daemons?
CELIA   To the daemons. It was you who spoke of daemons.
    It may be that even Julia is a daemon.
    Perhaps she is *my* daemon . . .

The short scene between Edward and the Unidentified Guest which follows when the curtain rises again is a good example of the shift towards comedy during the development of the play. The mood became much lighter; Alec Guinness, in playing it, made amusing passes with his walking stick, reflecting the gaiety of Reilly's success in the case so far. He is enigmatic and provoking; and he does not tell Edward when he is going to produce Lavinia. In the first draft, with this knowledge quickly communicated, the argument between the two is on a less piquant level of equality:

    (*The same room, immediately after.* EDWARD *answers the door bell and returns with the* UNIDENTIFIED GUEST)
EDWARD   So, after all . . . but why I should have depended
    So confidently on the word of a stranger
    I do not know. However—some gin and water?
U.G.   No, thank you. This is a different occasion.
    First, are you still sure you want your wife returned to you?
EDWARD   Why do you ask again? for what do you think I was waiting?
U.G.   The man who you were yesterday has been waiting;
    The man of twenty-four hours ago is waiting:
    But what of the man you are tonight? You see, my friend,
    It is one thing to want what is lost. Quite another thing
    To be able to rejoice over what is restored.

[1] Cf. *Collected Plays*, p. 155 quoted above, p. 183.

The Cocktail Party

EDWARD But you have not restored her. Where is she?

U.G.   Waiting,
    Of course, in my car outside.

EDWARD   Waiting? For what?

U.G. We must have a word together. I should impress upon you—
    It is a serious matter, to bring someone back from the dead.

EDWARD From the dead?

U.G.   From the dead

EDWARD   The figure of speech
    Seems rather forced.

U.G.   Oh, there are degrees of death.
    We die to each other daily. When it's friends
    We rarely meet, we do not know, it hardly matters
    How dead we are. We meet in a common past
    Or in a superficial present. That's good enough:
    The memories pleasant to recall, the common affection
    Lingers and revives. Unless the present reality
    Of one, affronts the memories of the other,
    It's very well. But think
    Of those you loved in childhood—if you loved them:
    The elder generation who surrounded, folded
    The early years in warmth, in mirth, security;
    The gentle maiden aunt, the merry bachelor uncle
    At the Christmas party. Above all, perhaps, the nursemaid
    With whom best terms of all—terms of equality.
    I speak of childhood, only to point my meaning
    More clearly. You still love them. But do you see
    The difference: love that's now, and love that's only memory
    Of love. The loved ghosts, if they returned now,
    Would you not be most fearfully embarrassed with them?
    What would you say to them, or they to you?
    Sustain a common pretence, that you were still
    The little boy they left, and they the same adults
    They were. You would find the insuperable barrier
    Of the past between you and any possible present.
    Better meet strangers. Intimacy is an accident
    Or a habit. A day, an hour, a moment
    Of separate experience can annihilate it.

EDWARD I tell you, all this is utterly irrelevant.
    I explained the situation yesterday
    And the same explanation is true tonight.
    There was nothing at all like that in the past *we* had,
    Nothing at all to look back upon with longing.
    It's nothing positive I want to get back to—
    It's something negative I need to escape from:
    Five years of nothing! That's come to an end,

But at least, nothing should not lead to nothing.
If it could have ended in something that was more real,
That would have been an end. But what can be the use—
What can be the use of escaping from a prison
If outside the prison there is no reality?

U.G.   And there is no use in returning to a prison
If, on returning, you still regard it as a prison:
To renew the old resentment, more resentful
For knowing that you are incapable of freedom.

EDWARD   I cannot argue with you. You may be right
But I see only the one way. I cannot justify it
By reasons. There may be every reason against it,
And the only reason for it—that there is no reason.

U.G.   Well and good—if that is the only reason.
But at the same time, in thinking of yourself—

EDWARD   Oh, myself! I have learned too much about myself;
That is what I want to escape from.

U.G.   The desire to escape from yourself
May be only your particular form of egotism.
But remember, you are to ask no questions
And give no explanations. The questions you would ask
And the questions you would answer, would be the wrong questions.
It is for each of you to question yourself
And not the other. Unless you take this advice
You will only begin to stifle yourselves again
Each in his own self. I have told her this.
I shall go now.

EDWARD   And will Lavinia come?

U.G.   I shall send her to you. For the present moment
It is better that I should not be of the company.

EDWARD   Shall I see you again?

U.G.   Very likely, very likely. Good night.

(*CP*/1; cf. *Collected Plays*, pp. 156–8)

In *CP*/1, 'the Unidentified Guest leaves. A short pause. Lavinia enters'; and the two plunge straight into their duologue. The intervening scene in the final script is the largest single addition to the play. This is the 'telegram scene'.[1]

The complexities of the telegram-device appealed to Eliot, and may be seen as a miniature parallel to the mix-up of the babies in *The Confidential Clerk*. I note from the prompt script that we reduced some of the detail, which remains in the printed script, when the

[1] *Collected Plays*, pp. 158–63.

play was staged. But this is a quite minor point. The scene serves many important purposes.

It brings the whole cast together in the middle of the play; and it establishes an intriguing presumption of common action by the three Guardians. It affords Lavinia an 'entrance' and shows her relationships with the others, particularly with Peter and, most important, with Celia. The little scene between these two[1] reveals their rivalry in a brilliantly succinct way and, in Lavinia's rebuff to Celia's overtures for peace—born of her new-found understanding of herself and Edward—prepares for one of the best moments in the last Act, Lavinia's repentant sorrow for Celia.[2] Earlier, the scene between Edward and Celia[3] marks the biggest step that we see on stage in Celia's growth. The day after her tragic parting with Edward, she has recovered her sense of humour: Edward is embarrassed at her appearance, but she is amused. Her image of Edward:

> You look like a little boy who's been sent for
> To the headmaster's study; and is not quite sure
> What he's been found out in

reveals that she has 'learnt a lot in twenty-four hours'; and the result is that she can see Edward 'at last as a human being'. It is the beginning of spiritual health. One of Eliot's recurrent themes is the danger we all run of making use of people by seeing them as 'projections' of our own desires. No true relationship can exist unless we see them as they are, as human beings; and until we are ready to say we are sorry, as Celia does to both Edward and Lavinia, for the damage we have done by our self-centred view of them.

The other function of the 'telegram' scene is recognised by Lavinia at the end of the interview with the psychiatrist:

> They had to tell us, themselves, that they had made their decision.

(Collected Plays, p. 183)

This was an absolutely necessary step in the action, which was not provided for in *CP*/1. Peter has to be 'going to California' not only in order to break the links with Celia and with Lavinia, which have no future, but also so that Bela and Alex can 'oblige each other'[4] in regard to his development. His new job is obtained from 'a man Alex put me in touch with', so that we already perceive the beginning

---

[1] *Collected Plays*, p. 161. [2] *Ibid.*, pp. 210, 221. [3] *Ibid.*, pp. 158, 159.
[4] *Ibid.*, p. 203.

of the influence further suggested at the curtain of Act Two, whose result is seen in the last Act.

Celia too is 'going away', though she does not know where nor for what purpose until she has consulted Reilly. But it is she who has already made the decision that her old way of life has reached its end, and that she must seek a new one.

At the end of the scene, Lavinia asks Julia and Alex to 'explain the telegrams'.[1] When they refuse, she says:

> I am sure that you could explain the telegram[s].
> I don't know why. But it seems to me that yesterday
> I started some machine, that goes on working,
> And I cannot stop it; no, it's not like a machine—
> Or if it's a machine, someone else is running it.
> But who? Somebody is always interfering . . .
> I don't feel free . . . and yet I started it . . .
>
> *(Ibid.,* p. 163)

This speech crystallises the sense of danger that all the three characters who arrive in Reilly's consulting room have at some time about what is happening to them. His speech to Edward suggests a reason analogous to Lavinia's:

> But let me tell you, that to approach the stranger
> Is to invite the unexpected, release a new force,
> Or let the genie out of the bottle.
> It is to start a train of events
> Beyond your control.
>
> *(Ibid.,* p. 133)

All three feel this sense of being in the grip of what Agatha calls

> powers beyond us
> Which now and then emerge
>
> *(Collected Plays,* p. 77)

and all three in their fear speak of one or other of the Guardians as devils. In reality, however, they have no sinister intent; we all feel this way when we are confronted by the truth about ourselves, especially through the agency of someone over whom we have no means of control. Eliot's Guardians appear in a pattern which suggests a symbolic meaning, but they do only what anyone who influences us does: they show the way towards a choice by which we may solve our problems.

---

[1] In the prompt script, this word is in the plural, as seems natural in the context, but it is printed in the singular.

The Cocktail Party

The others depart to leave husband and wife together. Their quarrel scene is one of the best-defined in *CP*/1. But it has undergone, in revision, a change more significant perhaps than any part of the play. In *CP*/1, the quarrel is bitter without much humour, and there are analytical speeches in the latter part of it. In revision, a great deal of humour has been allowed to develop, making the characters more interesting people, and the intimacy between them acquires the quality of tensile strength which living together creates, and which is hard to destroy when they want to break apart.[1] I print here two extracts from *CP*/1, to illustrate these comparisons:

LAVINIA ... That's what came of always giving in to you.
EDWARD I was unaware that you had given in to me.
It struck me very differently. As we're on the subject,
I thought it was I who had given in to *you*:
And that was what I found so oppressive.
LAVINIA I know what you mean by 'giving in to me':
You mean, leaving all the practical decisions—
To decide where we lived, and how we lived,
To choose all our friends, to take every initiative,
Do all the entertaining. You were always so polite,
So very considerate, people said!
Some of them thought you the perfect husband.
You thought you were unselfish. It was only passivity;
You always wanted to be bolstered, encouraged—
EDWARD Encouraged? to what?
LAVINIA   To think well of yourself.
You know it was I who made you work at the bar,
You know it was I who forced you to do something
About your political ambitions. But for me
They were only a day-dream. And it meant inviting
The dreariest of dreary people
To dinner and the dreariest of conversations.
It was so that you might believe in your own existence.
I thought, that if you had some reason
For thinking well of yourself, it might appease you,
Make you more human. But all in vain:
Everything I tried only made matters worse,
And the moment you were offered something that you wanted,
You wanted something else. I shall treat you very differently
In future.
EDWARD   Thank you for the warning ...

Comparing this with the printed text,[2] it will be seen how greatly

---

[1] *Collected Plays*, pp. 163 (bottom)–70.   [2] *Ibid.*, pp. 165–6.

the passage has been both lightened and sharpened by such touches as 'Peacehaven' and the lines about the Thursdays and the 'butler'.

The central part of the scene is the least altered. There is a good example in *CP*/1 of Eliot's recurring interest in the stage—someone ought to make a study of his theatrical references.[1] It occurs in a longer version of Edward's speech at the bottom of page 166 (*Collected Plays*):

> You wished to be the centre,
> Not only the producer, but the leading lady.
> Well, I played my part as a useful background.

More interesting is the improvement in the final section. The over-long draft of this was much curtailed, but a vital addition was also made to it in the printed version. The passage beginning

> I've often wondered why you married me
>
> (*Collected Plays*, p. 168)

is new; and both in its humour and its penetration of the relationship is extremely valuable. The draft contains quite a lot of material which was used in the remodelling, but it also relies on some of Eliot's most familiar imagery, notably the beloved metaphor of the door. We are reminded of the

> door that opens at the end of a corridor

and

> the little door
> When the sun was shining on the rose-garden[2]

by the opening of this scene, which I quote in full:

EDWARD   There's only one door out,
> Though it opens into the dark, though on the other side
> There may be nothing—just nothing—vacancy;
> No corridor, no stair, only the brief moment
> Of surprise, of stepping into nothing
> Before annihilation. Only that one way.

LAVINIA   Really, Edward, what *are* you talking about?
> Talking to yourself. Could you bear, for a moment,
> To think about *me*?

---

[1] The most extended example can be found in the first chorus of *The Family Reunion*, *Collected Plays*, pp. 62–3. See also *The Elder Statesman*, *Collected Plays*, pp. 340–1.
[2] *The Family Reunion*, *Collected Plays*, pp. 82, 106–7.

The Cocktail Party

EDWARD   Why was the other way
Impossible? There was another door
Ajar, and a beam of sunlight through it,
The warm spring breeze, the smell of lilacs ...

LAVINIA   I'm afraid you are mistaken about the smell:
'Lilacs' is not the trade name for it.[1]
But really, Edward, I'm very sorry for you—

EDWARD   And I knew I could not take the one step to cross it:
And I *must* go out through the dark door.
What is hell? hell is oneself,
Hell is alone, the other figures in it
One's own projections. But one cannot escape
From a ghost to a ghost, from lemur to larva;
One must fight with the ghost, until it becomes real,
Flesh and blood. One can part from the living
But not from the dead. But what is the next thing?

LAVINIA   I think you are on the edge of a nervous breakdown.
I know—I know of a doctor who might possibly help you—
But Edward, why do you think that I came back?
You are not interested. You have only been interested
In inventing for yourself interesting reasons
For wanting me back. But the true reason
For your wanting me, is the reason for my coming.
Edward, I should like to be good to you—
Or, if not that, at least to be horrid to you—
Anything but nothing, which is what you wanted of me.
But I am very sorry for you.

EDWARD   Don't say that again!
I have had enough of people being sorry for me.

LAVINIA   Yes, it's hard to bear, but you have got to bear it.
I thought that there might be another way out for you
If I went away. Then I saw that there was none.
I had already found that there was no way out for me
So that did not matter. I thought that if I died
To you, I who had been only a ghost,
You might be able to find the road back
To a time when you were real—for you must have been real
Up to a certain time—long before you knew me,
Perhaps; perhaps when you were still a child,
And start again. But you cannot do that, I see,
And ghosts *have* ghosts. And you can only go on
From where you are. But I knew that there was danger
In coming back. Every way is dangerous.

[1] In this draft, Celia has been in the room just before Lavinia arrives.

EDWARD I do not want you to explain me to myself;
When another person explains you to yourself
It is a self that is different from oneself,
And the less the difference, the more important the difference,
And the more it interferes with knowledge of oneself
Which is what I have to find. It is not by explanations
That we understand ourselves, but in a kind of vision
For which there are no words. If I ever understand *you*,
It will not come from trying to dissect you:
That merely leads to a new misunderstanding.
You are trying again to construct a personality
Which would only obscure me from myself.

LAVINIA   Now, Edward,
You are trying to complicate what is really very simple,
And escape in the confusion. I shan't let you escape.

EDWARD I have learned some things about myself since I saw you last,
And they are not things that could be put into words;
They lie much deeper than you can see
And are much more humiliating discoveries
Than anything that you could find the words for.

LAVINIA Humiliation again! I wonder what you have been up to,
And whom you have been talking to—for I'm sure
You would never make any discoveries by brooding.
No doubt it can all be very simply explained.
But it's one thing, Edward, to be humiliated,
And another to profit by it—to refuse the two evasions:
That of allowing oneself to be crushed by it
And revelling in being the worm one is,
Or that of forgetting all about it.
And both ways mean, you take yourself too seriously.
I said that I had always taken you too seriously,
And that was because you took yourself so seriously,
And I was hypnotised by your solemnity.
I mean to cultivate in you a sense of humour:
The first time I can make you laugh at yourself
I shall have hopes of you, and hopes for us.

But, Edward, I have something more important to say—
Something which has been forming in my mind
Ever since I came into this room. Now that I am back,
We are *not* to relapse into the same life we left
Yesterday morning. And that is what *you* want.
Oh, I know you're too divided to know just what you want,
But, being divided, you will tend to compromise,
And the easiest compromise is the old one.

EDWARD   I don't quite understand you. Haven't I made it clear
That in future you will find me a very different person?
LAVINIA   Really, Edward? Then why, may I ask,
Were you entertaining another visitor
Just before we arrived? How long ago had she left?
EDWARD   What makes you think that I have had a visitor?
LAVINIA   Really, Edward! I have my sense of smell,
And there are a good many kinds of scent
Besides the one I use. This one is quite identifiable
And I could name it. And now, I should be re-assured
If you could burst out laughing. But you won't.
EDWARD   O God, O God, if I could return to yesterday
Before I thought that I had made a decision.
I was too pleased with myself—for making a decision;
There was only the wish to come to some decision,
There was no decision that formed itself and took me.
So we do not experience utter blindness
Until we think we have had a moment of vision.
There is something to laugh about—for the devil
Who can make the last abyss of indecision
Look like the resting-place towards which we have been struggling.
And then you came, you, the angel of destruction:
In a minute, at a touch, there is nothing but ruin.
O God, what have I done? The python. The octopus.
Must I become, after all, what *you* would make me?
LAVINIA   I see no need to comment on what you have been saying,
Except to repeat, that you should have burst out laughing.
I must leave a note in the kitchen for Betty,
To tell her I am back, and to bring my morning tea.
Meanwhile, Edward, there's my luggage in the hall;
I'm afraid I must ask you to carry it up for me.

(*CP*/1; cf. *Collected Plays*, pp. 168–70)

THE SECOND ACT

Now we come to the consulting room. In *CP*/1, this is Act Three (in two scenes) and begins with Edward's entrance. All the dialogue between the Nurse-Secretary and Reilly was added subsequently, and Alex's appearance at the beginning was part of the reinforcement of the character which I had recommended, as was Julia's appearance between the scenes.

The Edward/Reilly duologue, and the three-handed scene with Lavinia which grows out of it, undergo very much the same kind of development as the Edward/Lavinia quarrel. All three characters

become wittier, more belligerent, and the dramatic points are made
with greater pressure. A good instance is the following passage from
CP/1:

SIR HENRY   There are some things
That you do not need to tell me. Your parentage,
Upbringing, education, social background—
All these I know enough about, for the moment.
I do not want your recollections of infancy,
And I am not at all interested in your dreams.
EDWARD I always understood that these things were significant.
SIR HENRY My profession, Mr. Chamberlayne, would be very much easier
If my patients had never read any psychology:
They always have, or have heard people talk about it.
With a person who has a history like yours
I always begin from the immediate situation
And go back as far as I find necessary.

This is so compressed in the final text that one half-line does the
work of eleven:

EDWARD   I remember, in my childhood . . .
REILLY I always begin from the immediate situation
And then go back as far as I find necessary.

(*Collected Plays*, p. 174)

This kind of dramatic compression can be seen throughout, and
is balanced by the insertion of new and telling points, such as Reilly's
direct challenge to Edward to confess the liaison with Celia—the one
thing in 'the immediate situation' which must be brought into the
open before a cure can begin.

REILLY You have nothing else to tell me?
EDWARD   What else can I tell you?
You didn't want to hear about my early history.
REILLY No, I did not want to hear about your *early* history.

(*Collected Plays*, p. 176)

One speech from *CP*/1 is worth presenting here, not for its dramatic
quality but for its descriptive power. It became the bottom speech of
page 175 of *Collected Plays*.

EDWARD When I learnt that my wife had gone away from me
I felt like a man, going about his business,
Walking the street, intent on his affairs,
Who becomes suddenly aware that he is in a different city,
In another country, where the streets are unfamiliar,

The Cocktail Party

Where the people are talking an unknown language,
Where he is completely lost. Or perhaps a man
Is travelling alone, and loses his memory,
And all he retains is the urgent conviction
That he was about some pressing errand
Of vital importance. It was something like that.
It was not regret for anything positive, lost—
Regret of lost happiness, or contentment, or security—
But myself I had lost. I was utterly sure
That if she returned, I should find myself again,
And be: for how can I act, unless I am?
But she had not been with me for ten, five minutes,
Before I felt again, still more acutely—
Indeed, acutely, perhaps, for the first time
The whole oppression, the unreality
Of the role she had always imposed upon me
With that obstinate, unconscious, sub-human strength
That women have. I was leaving vacancy
For unreality, nothingness for negation—
Am I talking nonsense, or really trying
To express the inexpressible? Which is more anguish:
To be nothing, or be nothing with the feeling
That one is positive at least in the denial
Of the part one plays? I know only
That in a minute, a moment, even while I speak
I may suffer some ultimate annihilation.
But I cannot go back. There is nowhere to go
But into solitude. I must be alone
And alone without responsibility.
So I want you to put me where I shall be alone,
In your sanatorium. I could be alone there?

The following lines, omitted from Reilly's speech in the middle of page 179, are also worth noting as a clue to his thinking about the case:

> You have, both of you,
> Moments of understanding, which give you the torment
> Which you choose to pretend is the disease from which you suffer—
> But what causes your suffering is incipient health
> Which needs rough nursing. You have both of you pretended . . .

The way in which the dénoucment has been sharpened is interesting. Here is *CP/1*:

LAVINIA Then what can we do
When we can go neither backwards nor forwards?

REILLY   You have just spoken it,
    Though you did not know the meaning of what you were saying.
    You said 'What shall *we* do?' The common action
    In the commonplace life.

EDWARD   The best of a bad job.

REILLY   When you find, Mr Chamberlayne—and I think you will discover this
    In time—that that is all that anyone can make,
    You will forget this phrase—and in forgetting it
    Will alter the condition.

EDWARD   Well, Lavinia—

LAVINIA   Yes, I think we have taken enough of his time—
    And besides, we are several days behindhand . . .

REILLY   Not wasted, I think

LAVINIA   Oh no, it was the time before
    That was wasted.

Comparing this with the longer but much more effective final version,[1] we see the turning-point far better defined and the comedy strengthened. Note Lavinia's appeal to Edward by name; the hotel in the New Forest (and Alex's hand in it); the shirts, the shared taxi. These distinctive touches sometimes appear at first writing, as for instance that 'piece of furniture in a repair shop':[2] and the dross of verbosity has to be refined away to let them shine. Quite as often, however, the felicities are the result of that careful reworking which Eliot always expected to do: no craftsman was ever more diligent in polishing his artifact than he.

The Reilly/Celia scene is the most deeply felt in the play, and the *CP*/1 draft should be printed in full. Revision gives it a firm basis in the actual doctor-patient relationship, which in the draft is shadowy. Reilly starts by talking about his work; then he asks for a description of symptoms, and with them, of Celia's way of life and the point of view of her family. Only then does he suddenly demand an account of the man in Celia's life. And only after that has been examined does he present the choice with which he has from the beginning planned to face her. This gives the scene a clearer shape, and the writing is shorn of unnecessary generalisations.

The nature of the 'sanatorium' becomes more apparent. This is not, I think, an entirely satisfactory symbol, as is proved by the amount of explanation it requires, and the awkwardness of having

[1] *Collected Plays*, pp. 182–3.   [2] See above, p. 191.

The Cocktail Party

to establish a second institution—'a house for transients' in the draft, finally

> A kind of hotel. A retreat
> For people who imagine that they need a respite
> From everyday life.
>
> (Collected Plays, p. 178)

But the obscurity with which the sanatorium is surrounded is lessened by Reilly's explanation to Celia of what will happen there. Eliot would have been more exactly served by the symbol of a religious order—Alex says that

> She had joined an order. A very austere one
>
> (Collected Plays, p. 205)

But he was anxious to keep religious terminology out of the play up to as late a point as possible.

ACT III. SCENE ii

(The same room. SIR HENRY *seated at his desk as before.* CELIA *enters)*

SIR HENRY Good afternoon, Miss Coplestone.

CELIA Good afternoon, Sir Henry.
It's kind of you to see me. I mean, I hope it will be.
I may have no excuse for taking up your time.
I suppose most people, when they come to you,
Know they have an illness, can give good reasons
For claiming your attention. Well, I can't.
I only know that something has happened to me—
No, I don't even know whether it has happened to *me*
Or to the world I live in: but if it is the latter,
Perhaps you can at least diagnose the world for me,
Though you cannot cure it. I am talking rather wildly,
I know. But I shan't be offended
If you simply tell me to go away again.
You must have enough people come to waste your time;
But on the other hand, no doubt most people
Know when they are ill. I don't even know that.

SIR HENRY Most of my patients begin, Miss Coplestone,
By telling me exactly what is the matter with them,
And what I am to do about it. And the first part of my treatment
Consists in convincing them that they are wholly mistaken
About the nature of their illness, and that probably
It's less interesting than they thought; and then I must persuade them
That the treatment required is something wholly different
From that which they had intended me to give them.

CELIA   I have no such belief. I am only quite sure
    That there is some fault much deeper in myself
    Than anything that I have ever heard named
    As disease or sin. Shall I explain the circumstances
    As best I can? As well as I can understand them.
SIR HENRY   I had rather you tried first to express your desolation.
CELIA   I have become aware of my own solitude.
SIR HENRY   The solitude, Miss Coplestone, is what we all grow into
    And what we must grow out of. ·
CELIA   Oh, I don't mean simply
    That there has been a crash: though indeed there has.
    It is not simply the feeling of being *left*—
    Or ditched, if you like, or having had the bird.
    Of course that is something that is always happening
    From which most people recover, more or less.
    I mean that what has happened has made me aware
    That I have always been alone. That is what is frightening.
SIR HENRY   That is the solitude I meant.
    The only difference between one person and another
    Is between those who are aware of the solitude
    And the greater number who are unconscious.
CELIA   And I have had a vision of my own emptiness.
SIR HENRY   That is the second revelation of oneself
    Which follows on the other. So far, so good.
CELIA   Some people would say I had done very wrong—
    But I know that I did nothing to hurt *her*—
    And most people would say that I had played the fool.
    No doubt both points of view are right.
    My bringing up was fairly conventional—
    I had always been taught to disbelieve in *sin*:
    I don't mean that it was ever mentioned,
    But anything that was wrong, from my parents' point of view,
    Was either bad form, or was something psychological.
    When everything is bad form, or else mental kinks,
    I suppose you become either bad form, or kinky.
    But however it is, it is not the things
    That people used to call sinful, that worry me;
    And yet I find myself with a sense of sinfulness!
    Much worse for not knowing what it's all about.
    It's something which must be an hallucination
    And yet, at the same time, I'm terrified
    That it is more real than anything I believed in.
    Can you treat a patient for that.
SIR HENRY   First the diagnosis.
    The immediate occasion. So will you tell me
    What you had *supposed* were your relations with this man?

The Cocktail Party

CELIA Oh, you had divined that, had you? that's clever.
Do you want me to tell you what his name is?
SIR HENRY No, I do not.
CELIA   But perhaps I'm only typical.
SIR HENRY If I thought that you were typical I should not be interested.
CELIA I thought that I was giving him so much!
And he to me, and the giving and the taking
Seemed so *right*—not in terms of calculation
Of what was good for the persons we had been
Before we met, but for the new person. If I could feel
As I did then, it would still seem right.
But then I found that we were really strangers
And that there had been neither giving nor taking
And that we had merely made use of each other
Each for his own purpose. That's horrible. Can we only love
Something that is created by our own imagination?
Are we all in fact unloving and unloveable?
Then one is alone, and if one is alone
Then the lover is no more real than the beloved—
And the dreamer is no more real than what he dreams.
SIR HENRY And this man—what does he now seem to you?
CELIA Like a child who had wandered into a forest
Playing a game with an imaginary companion,
And suddenly discovered that he was only a child
Lost in a forest. I was sorry for him.
SIR HENRY Compassion is already a clue
Towards finding the way out of your own forest.
CELIA But even if I find *my* way out of the forest
I shall be left with the inconsolable memory
Of the treasure I went into the forest to find
And never found, and which was not there,
And which is not anywhere.
SIR HENRY   The experience of disillusion
Can be a new illusion.
CELIA   I cannot argue.
It is not that I am afraid of being hurt again.
And I almost think that the ecstasy is real
Although those who feel it may have no reality
For what has happened has been like a dream
In which one is consumed with such intensity of loving
In the spirit, with no adulteration
Of desire, as one knows one is not capable of
When one is waking. But what, or whom I loved,
Or what in me was loving, I do not know. What can you do for me?
SIR HENRY You have a choice. There are two doors which would open.
But it must be a conscious choice. First, if you will,

215

I can reconcile you to the human condition,
The common world of those who have had the vision,
The world where there are many who have gone as far as you
And then returned, remember, and no longer feel,
Regret no longer, take the imposed routine,
Learn to avoid excessive expectation,
Becoming tolerant of both themselves and others,
Accepting, giving affection, taking, in the usual action,
And giving what can be taken and given. Not repining,
But contented in the morning that separates
And in the evening which brings together
Only for casual talk before the fire
Two people who know they do not understand each other,
Breeding children whom they will not understand
And who will never understand them.

CELIA   Is that a good life?

SIR HENRY   It is good. Though you will not know how good it is
     Until you reach the end. You will want nothing else,
     And the other life will be only a book
     You read, and then lay down. In a world of lunacy,
     Violence, stupidity, greed—it is the good life.

CELIA   What other good life is there?

SIR HENRY   The other path?
     The one I could describe in terms you understood
     Because you had seen it, as we all have seen it,
     Seen, not understood, in lives about us.
     The second is what you have experienced but not seen.
     Its destination is not conveyed by description;
     You will not know where you are going till you get there;
     You will journey blind, in faith. But it will give possession
     Of what you have grasped for, seeking in the wrong place.

CELIA   That is what I want. But which way is my duty?

SIR HENRY   Whichever you choose will impose the duty,
     And therefore duty is not to be considered.

CELIA   Which way is better?

SIR HENRY   Neither way is better.
     Both ways are necessary.

CELIA   I choose the second.

SIR HENRY   It is a terrifying journey.

CELIA   I am not frightened
     But glad. And I suppose it is a lonely way.

SIR HENRY   There are only different ways of loneliness
     And of communion. The only final loneliness
     Is to be alone in the phantasmal world
     Of your own imagination, shuffling memories and desires,

CELIA   That is the hell I have been in.

The Cocktail Party

SIR HENRY   It is not hell
Till you become incapable of wanting anything else.
Now! are you sure of what you want?

CELIA   I want your second way,
Though I do not know what it is, or why I want it.
But I cannot pretend to give you any reason.

SIR HENRY   There is no reason, one way or the other.

CELIA   And what do I do ?

SIR HENRY   I shall send you to the sanatorium.

CELIA   Oh, what an anti-climax! I have known people
Who have been to your sanatorium, and come back again.
I don't mean that they weren't very much better for it—
That's why I came to you. But they returned as . . . normal people.

SIR HENRY   Yes. The friends you have in mind
Had not been, Miss Coplestone, to my sanatorium.
Those who go to the sanatorium do not come back.

CELIA   It sounds like a prison. But they can't all *stay* there!
I mean, it would make the place so over-crowded.

SIR HENRY   Not very many go there. But I said, they do not come back:
I did not say they stayed there.

CELIA   What becomes of them?

SIR HENRY   They choose, Miss Coplestone. Nothing is forced on them.
Not at all. They come to very active lives,
Each in his own way.

CELIA   How soon will you take me there?

SIR HENRY   Go home, and make your explanations to your family.
Oh, there need be no concealment about it!
I will give you the address for you to give them.

(Writes on a slip of paper and hands it to her)

Let them expect you back in a few months' time:
I will answer to them. As to the future, after that
You will not return, simply because you will not want to;
But as you do not understand that yourself,
You cannot explain it to others. When you are ready
I shall send my car to take you.

CELIA   Won't you come with me?

SIR HENRY   No, Miss Coplestone, you will have no need of me;
My use to you is ended. Where you are going,
They will know all about you.

CELIA   Well . . . good-bye.
I do not know in the least what I am doing
Or why I do it. But I know it is *my* decision:
I tell you that, Sir Henry. I have never felt freer.

SIR HENRY   Go in peace, my daughter. Work out your salvation with diligence.

(CP/1)

217

The Cocktail Party

The last Act was not written when *CP*/1 was made, and the earliest script I have is that used at Edinburgh. This differs widely from the published text, and indeed was worked over both between the Edinburgh and New York productions and between the New York and the London one.

Eliot was setting out to do an exceedingly difficult thing. The characters were to meet again after two years without the one who had most deeply involved us; and we were now to concentrate on the reactions of the other characters to her painful death. There was an obvious danger that this would become, in effect if not in name, an epilogue—and this danger was not entirely avoided.[1] It was also necessary to hold a most delicate balance if this Act were to justify the appellation of 'comedy' and at the same time be attuned to its content.

Another problem was to show Edward and Lavinia living a married life of peaceful understanding without making the relationship boring or banal. The state is essentially an undramatic one. Sherek, in a note about it, says:[2]

I have always felt that during the Lavinia-Edward scene, some indication should be given that during the 2 years, they have got together gradually and happily. In spite of programmes, many people don't seem to realise that 2 years have elapsed. [I] even think they might refer laughingly to the unhappy episode, to show they are so sure now that they can laugh at it.

This produced one of the best bits in the scene:

LAVINIA   ... But all I rang up for was to reassure you ...

EDWARD (*smiling*)   That you hadn't run away?

LAVINIA   Now Edward, that's unfair!
        You know that we've given *several* parties
        In the last two years. And I've attended *all* of them.

(*Collected Plays*, p. 196)

We had discussed whether the Act had better occur before or after the party. As soon as he had finished roughing it out, Eliot wrote to me:

[1] Cf. 'Poetry and Drama', in *On Poetry and Poets*, p. 85.
[2] 9 September 1949.

The Cocktail Party

Dear Martin,

I think it might be possible for me to devise a better opening for Act IV rewriting the first few pages, and especially if you could allow me a couple of caterer's men to be present at the very beginning. It seems to me that a little business would enliven the opening and stimulate the interest of the audience instead of the mere dialogue. Besides I am not sure that that light comedy dialogue doesn't go on too long and perhaps give the impression of being rather forced.

On the other hand having now worked the thing out to an end I incline to revert to the view that this act works out best timed in this way—*before* the cocktail-party—rather than if I tried to reset it to take place just *after* all the other guests had left. I don't mind in the least writing quite a different opening to indicate that the party is over, but if I made that change I wonder whether the conclusion might not be less effective. It seems to me to add to the point of the scene for the audience to have in mind that my people have got to go on with their party in spite of everything; and this ending also seems to provide an effective exit for the other three. I shall be glad if you will think about this carefully. Of course I appear to be assuming that the centre of the scene is all right, and I am certainly not confident about anything.

Yours ever,

T.S.E.

The last sentence is a true summary of the author's feelings during the process of creation. Humble in his approach to his art, aware that he was treading so much new ground—at once that of the commercial theatre and that of the newly reborn poetic drama—he was 'certainly not confident about anything'. Sherek and I had probably been expressing the analytical doubts which usually accompany the making of a play, and at the end of the month I got this letter:

Mid Lent 1949[1]

Dear Martin,

... I was not questioning your readiness to proceed with the play. But I should not like either you or Mr. Sherek to go on with a play about which you were half-hearted: it would be no kindness to me to do so. And I am very doubtful whether any play of mine would be likely to gain immediate applause: it might be better for it to appear more modestly, in some little theatre. The publicity I have had in the last few years only means that anything now of mine will be judged more severely than ever.

My experience as a publisher is, that we never succeed with a book (unless

[1] I.e. 27 March 1949.

219

sometimes when it is by an author with an unfailing public) which no member of the firm really believes in. And I don't want anybody to produce a play of mine unless he really believes in it. As for me, I can wait.

I note that you will be away from April 7th; and I hope that you will have a good and restorative holiday. I have re-written the fourth act up to the point at which there is a question of doing more with Peter (you might make a prayer for him to St. Peter if you get to Rome); but I can't promise to find a solution of that problem before you leave. My new opening demands two caterer's men (one of them has a short speech) but it cuts out the rather laboured fun about the delinquencies of caterer's men and about drinking. I shall hope to have a script as final as the first three acts are at present by the time you return.

Yours,

Tom

It was not difficult to assure him that I wholeheartedly believed in the play; as also did Sherek, whose original enthusiasm for the writing never wavered. On his advice, the two Caterer's Men were later reduced to one.

Reilly originally came in with Julia. I have a pencil note from Eliot, headed merely 'Thursday' but clearly coming from a time when Alec Guinness had accepted the part of Reilly but was still uncertain about playing the Edinburgh week:

Dear Martin,

Enclosed scheme for revision. I don't want to work on lines until scheme is approved. If something like this suits Guinness I am quite ready to do it. It's about a day's work with the typewriter when I get back . . .

I assume that Guinness will still be unable to come to Edinburgh, but will join us in January for a London run?

Yours,

T.S.E.

This does seem to me to promise a considerable improvement.

This led to the present text, in which Julia enters, followed a moment later by Alex, and Reilly has a much later entrance, at the end of the scene with Peter about the casting of his film.

The casting was originally treated at much greater length, with Reilly on stage, and with detail which, although it was wisely omitted because it was irrelevant to the main point of the Act, is worth preserving here both to show Eliot's intentions about Peter and as giving some character indications about the others. It would have stood immediately before the top of page 204 (*Collected Plays*):

The Cocktail Party

LAVINIA   I'd love to know what sort of parts he'd give us.
What would you do with Edward, for example?
Could you make him the Duke's legal adviser?
PETER   He wouldn't do. Not for a part like that.
Edward doesn't look secretive enough.
Dear Edward, don't feel hurt. That's the way it is:
Very few people can act the thing they are,
And I'd never cast *you* for the part of a lawyer.
You see, you look at people in a very special way
In my sort of business. For instance, you learn
That nobody ever looks just what he is
If you see him apart from all you know about him:
You have to *learn* to see what people look like.
REILLY   You should be a good judge of faces, Mr. Quilpe.
JULIA   I'd love to know just how Peter *would* cast us.
You won't have Edward for the duke's man of business:
What *could* you give him to do?
PETER   There's a minor part
Which I believe Edward could make a good thing of,
Though the ordinary filmgoer wouldn't appreciate him.
There's a poacher in the story, who's the first suspect—
So of course he has to behave suspiciously;
Though in the end he turns out to be innocent
Of everything—except poaching. I don't know why,
But I do think Edward could catch the expression
Of furtive simplicity, which is what I want.
JULIA   There's a very nice part for you, Edward!
Now haven't you a part for the poacher's wife?
PETER   Oh, you mean for Lavinia? Pan-Am-Eagle doesn't do that.
They would never cast a husband and wife together
Unless, of course, they were both famous stars
Who had just been married—you can build that up.
As a rule, they know far too much about each other
To act well together—at least, in minor parts;
Much better have strangers. No, for Lavinia,
I would give her a character part, the housekeeper—
Mrs. Blenkinsop, her name is. Husband deceased,
One son, whom she's pining for, who went to America,
And reappears again, having made a fortune,
And astonishes the villagers. He has a good scene
In the local pub.
EDWARD   That sounds the part for you, Peter.
PETER   Oh, but that's the star part in this film:
It's Spud M'Guffie, because he plays the bnajo.
JULIA   But now Peter, haven't you a part for me?
I'm the one who's keenest to go to California.

221

PETER You'd be awfully difficult to write in, Julia.
　　　I have a feeling, whatever part was written for you,
　　　You'd turn it into something else. You don't mind, do you?
　　　I should be afraid of your stealing everything—
　　　Like child actors and performing animals.
　　　That sounds rather crude . . .

REILLY　　　　　　　　　　　Not at all, Mr. Quilpe;
　　　It is simply that the artist's eye is merciless.

PETER But what I feel is, Julia, that any part we gave you—
　　　If it was comic, you'd be the great tragic actress,
　　　If it was serious, then you'd gag it.
　　　We should never know where we were, with you.

JULIA Goodbye to my hopes of seeing California.
　　　But if I'm rejected, what about Alex?

PETER Oh, Alex, that's easy. He could make himself useful.
　　　In fact, I wrote a part that makes me think of him.
　　　I have a visitor staying in the house
　　　Whom nobody seems to know much about
　　　Except that he's lived a great deal in the East—
　　　And he's always round the corner when anything happens.
　　　He turns out in the end to be very important
　　　In the Secret Service. He's known as the Colonel.
　　　It's not a part that anyone would think of
　　　For Alex, I dare say—and yet it would suit him.

REILLY You have a real gift for casting, Mr. Quilpe.

PETER It's not my work, but I'd like to try my hand at it.
　　　Of course, as I say, it's a matter of appearances—
　　　Not of what people are: but all the same
　　　There's a difference between the way people appear to us
　　　And their *real* appearance. And what we have to learn
　　　Is a certain detachment, to get their real appearance.

JULIA But now that you're giving a part to everybody—
　　　Except me—and whisking them off to California:
　　　Tell us, Peter, what could you do with Sir Henry?
　　　You see, Sir Henry is a famous consultant.
　　　You must want a doctor in a story like this—
　　　Though I haven't a notion what it's all about

PETER Oh, of course there is a doctor in this film:
　　　Where you have a murder, you must have a doctor—
　　　At least, for a full dress country house murder.
　　　But you want a country doctor. It's to be his first murder,
　　　So he doesn't recognise the cause of death.
　　　Now Sir Henry does look something like a doctor—
　　　That's the odd thing—but some other kind of doctor.
　　　I've been observing you, Sir, while we've been talking:

I hope you don't mind? It's become a habit
To look at everyone with a professional eye ...

REILLY   I don't mind at all. I observed you observing me.
We have some habits in common.

PETER   Well then, I should say,
That Sir Henry could never look the part of a doctor
Who was deceived about the cause of death.
He looks, if he doesn't mind my saying so,
Like a man who would know quite a lot about murder
And couldn't be taken in. Of course you realise
I'm only talking of appearances.
But it's easier for me to catch Sir Henry's appearance
Because of my never having seen him before
And because of my not knowing anything about him.

JULIA   I've always wondered what it was about you,
Henry, that made you so intimidating.
Still, I'm glad I know you well enough
Not to see you just as Peter does.
But, Peter, if he's not right for the doctor,
What sort of a part do you think he *could* play?

PETER   I simply don't know. He's something like you, Julia.
I don't see how he could be used in a film
Except by building the film around him.
Anyway, this film is an ordinary thriller—
Murder, spy work, and the banjo chorus;
And with you or Sir Henry in a film like that
I'm sure the chorus would never come off
Unless you led it. That's an idea!
Can you sing, Sir Henry?

REILLY   Only old-fashioned songs.

PETER   But that doesn't solve it. It's the murder I'm thinking of.
I can't see Sir Henry in a murder play—
Not an ordinary murder. I'm not sure what I mean.
The murder would come to seem ... rather unimportant.
He has the face of a man who knows about things
More important   more terrible perhaps—than murder.
That's what I get from *your* face. But, whatever they are,
They don't make the sort of story that can be told in pictures.

JULIA   Well, Henry, you must stay behind
To keep me company. I'm partially appeased.
But Peter, since you're so frightfully choosy,
How would you ever get a cast together?

PETER   Oh, but we've only been pretending.
I'm not a casting director yet.
And I know very well not one of you would come
If you were invited. So what does it matter?

But there is one person I'm serious about
And I'll get our director to give her a test
If I can find her. It's Celia Coplestone.
You know, she was always keen about films,
(And I believe I'm now in a position to help her.)
I wrote a part with Celia in mind—
It's a part that belongs to her completely
And could make her reputation over night.
I was waiting for a chance to ask you about her.
Is she at her old address?

JULIA   Not at the old address.
But what was the part you had created for her?

PETER   It's the duke's daughter. That's the part for her.
She's misunderstood and neglected at home.
She nearly falls for the villain, of course,
Not knowing that he's plotting murder all the time
And in the pay of a foreign government.

JULIA   Does she have a happy ending?

PETER   A very happy ending.
In the end she marries the housekeeper's son—
That's Spud M'Guffie who plays the banjo.
He's a millionaire: not that it matters,
But the audience likes a wealthy husband—
If he's good looking, and can dance like Spud.
Is Celia in London?

                                          (*CP*/Edin.)

When Reilly's entrance had been transferred to a point later than this passage, he was treated to some banter by Julia in place of the casting episode. After Reilly has asked for a glass of water with nothing with it[1] follows this passage:

JULIA   I was starting to say—
I was starting to say, when you *all* interrupted me,
That Sir Henry *can* be very good company,
And he *can* be most amusing. And a very good singer!
You should get him to sing.

REILLY   After remarking
That my appearance is not in my favour
Julia now presents me as a music-hall comedian.

JULIA   Well, you *are* a comedian, Henry!
But he's really a very great doctor as well,
Though you might not think so. Perhaps you know it.
You know, my friends are all clever people.

[1] See *Collected Plays*, p. 204.

The Cocktail Party

But that's enough in the way of introductions,
Considering that you know each other already.
Tell me about yourselves. It's so long since I've seen you:
But I've been hearing about you everywhere.
EDWARD Nonsense! It's our turn now, Sir Henry:
If she's been giving a false impression of you,
You must believe she's doing the same of us.
We lead a quiet life.
JULIA   But a very active one—
And a very useful one, I'm sure.
I said that all my friends are clever—
I never say that all my friends are good:
And that's why I won't let either of you drop me.
Now how's that for giving a good impression?

(CP/Edin.)

Lavinia then introduced Peter to Reilly. This was found dispensable when the play had to be shortened after Edinburgh.

'I appear to be assuming that the centre of the scene is all right', Eliot had written. He was indeed taking great risks here. One might liken the 'act' demanded of Alex in this scene to the walking of a tightrope. I remember very well my fears lest the walker should fall off, as the play was given for the first time at Edinburgh to an audience including critics from all over the world. My nervousness at opening 'cold' to such a house grew to fever pitch as we approached the news of Celia's death. The audience, which had received the play up to this point extremely well, was laughing heartily at the absurd story which Alex was telling about monkeys on that tropical island he had just been visiting. Peter's arrival from California diverted the conversation to an equally absurd plea from Julia that she and the others should take part in his forthcoming film. The amusement continued: and every moment, we drew nearer to the announcement which should bring it to an abrupt halt. But the author had not miscalculated. In a dozen lines he made the change of mood with perfect control.

The description of Celia's death caused quite a furore at Edinburgh. Eliot's first draft of Alex's speech had left it as vague as Harry's future in *The Family Reunion*. My wife urged that it was unwise to take refuge a second time in cryptic hints, and that the audience would share her own curiosity to know exactly what happened. Once convinced of the necessity, Eliot produced a picture of stark horror:

ALEX   ... But Celia Coplestone, she was taken.
 When our people got there, they questioned the villagers—
 Those who survived. And then they found her body,
 Or at least, they found the traces of it.
EDWARD   But before that ...
ALEX   It is difficult to say,
 At such a stage of decomposition:
 Bodies disintegrate quickly in that climate.
 But from what we know of local practices
 It would seem that she must have been crucified
 Very near an anthill. They smear the victims
 With a juice that is attractive to the ants.

                (*CP*/Edin.)

This proved to be too great a shock. In my notes to the author after Edinburgh, I wrote:

'JUICE ATTRACTIVE TO ANTS' and 'DECOMPOSITION' have, as I prophesied, caused a general reaction of strong distaste. Do you mind? I imagine you don't, but thought I should mention it.

Sherek pressed the point in his notes to me:[1]

There is universal distaste and criticism of the juice line. Surely the horror is enough without this? It seems unnecessary to me and why fight *everybody*? I *hate* the decomposition line.

It was evident that the physical details which the author intended to reinforce the authenticity of Celia's suffering were having the effect of distracting from what he wanted to say about its meaning: and they were modified to give the present text.[2] The introduction of physical violence into a work of art demands very careful judgement; and the effect varies with the time at which the work appears. The reaction today might be different from what it was in 1949, when Weiss's *Marat/Sade*, Rudkin's *Afore Night Come* and Bond's *Saved* had not been thought of. What Eliot wanted was certainly not to shock for the sake of shocking, but to make sure that the martyrdom should be realised as actual suffering—hence Reilly's replies to Edward.[3]

 Another question about this passage arose in my mind before Edinburgh. It suddenly introduced, what had been sedulously avoided up to this point, some overt religious words and symbols. Alex's account of what Celia was doing in Kinkanja ran as follows:

---

[1] 9 September 1949.   [2] *Collected Plays*, p. 206.   [3] *Ibid.* pp., 209–10.

The Cocktail Party

ALEX She had joined an order. A very austere one.
And as she already had experience of nursing . . .
LAVINIA Yes, she had been a V.A.D. I remember.
ALEX That was appointed as the way of sanctification.
We need not concern ourselves with *that*. The point is
That she was directed to Kinkanja . . .

(CP/Edin.)

And this was followed by 'crucifixion' as the way of martyrdom. I wrote in some notes dated 9 July 1949:

'That was approved as the way of sanctification.' I find that this religious word strikes me as out of place every time I read the line, as you have not used such terminology before (except 'sin' with a lot of apology). Also I think that this line would be more effective if it were put in a more practical way: 'they thought it was best to use her experience'. Or by cutting the first two lines of Alex' speech, go straight on to 'She was directed to Kinkanja'.

This was the solution adopted; but Celia's crucifixion remained, and with it the necessity for making sure that it bore no relation to a romantic crucifix.

One other passage of a religious nature remained in the Edinburgh and New York script, but was finally dropped for London and from the published text, not without reluctance.

LAVINIA . . . Yet I thought your expression was one of . . . satisfaction!
Interest, yes, but not in the details.
ALEX There's one detail which *is* rather interesting
And rather touching, too. We found that the natives,
After we'd reoccupied the village,
Had erected a sort of shrine for Celia
Where they brought offerings of fruit and flowers,
Fowls, and even sucking pigs.
They seemed to think that by propitiating Celia
They might insure themselves against further misfortune.
We left *that* problem for the Bishop to wrestle with.
REILLY Yes, the Bishop's problem is certainly a detail.
Mrs. Chamberlayne, I must be very transparent
Or else you are very perceptive.

(Cf. Collected Plays, p. 208)

Do we hear echoes of 'the glittering, jewelled shrine' of Thomas Becket?

Peter's part in this Act raised pressing questions. We had been trying to build him up, and finding it difficult. The casting material, as we have seen, was an irrelevance we could not afford at this late stage of the play. Another idea was that Peter had been trying to write novels before taking up film-work; after Alex has given his news, Lavinia tells him, in *CP*/Edin.:

> your picture of Celia
> Was only a substitute for another picture—
> That of yourself as a famous novelist.
> It was bound to come a crash—better this way than another!
> And when that happens—better sooner than later!

The novel-writing which produced this rather heartless analysis was seen to be a red herring and was thrown overboard—a minor loss for Peter. But he needed a major gain. In *CP*/Edin., Julia, after she had finished her speech to Peter,[1] sent him off to Boltwell to get on with his job. This meant that he missed Reilly's exposition of the meaning of Celia's death, which, although he could not be allowed much of a chance to express his reaction to it, was certainly necessary to the completion of his part in the play.

Two weeks after I got back from the New York opening, I wrote to Eliot suggesting for this purpose some transpositions:

26.2.50

My dear Tom,

First of all, our thanks for the lunch-party. It was delightful, and the pleasure of talking over the triumph and prospects of *The Cocktail Party* with you and John was enhanced by Mme Prunier's succulent food. Thank you very much indeed . . .

I know you will groan at having to hear anything more of the script: but I feel bound at least to put before you the enclosed notes on the final scene, in case you feel that anything should be done before the play appears in London. The feeling about this scene was almost unanimous, that drama was lacking after the announcement of Celia's death: that it became just the summing-up of an argument, and gravely weakened the play. If what I suggest seems to you right, following the development of the characters and according with the ideas to be expressed, it might be worth the effort involved—indeed I am sure it would be.

The reception of the play was most exhilarating, because it was not just respectful: people were really carried away by it and enthralled by the characters, the ideas and the writing alike.

Last thing to say is about our return lunch-party: I know how hard you are to get so I make an early bid. The week of March 13 it had better be, as I am away most of the previous week. Monday (13th) or Tuesday (14th) are free for

---

[1] *Collected Plays*, p. 208.

me, at 1.30. Monday 6th is also free, and perhaps better? Will you consult with John and see if you can both manage one of these?

Meanwhile, I can come in an evening to discuss the script if you want me.

P.S. *The Shelley.* We have been playing without it in New York since about a week after the opening. No-one there knew it: and it confused them. 'Who is "my dead child"?' etc. Reilly's speech is complete without it. Sacrilege, I know! but at this stage of the play it may be wisdom.

THE COCKTAIL PARTY

Notes on the final scene

Among the hundreds of people who either in writing or by word of mouth expressed their delight in the play, there was an almost universal agreement that the last scene was not as completely satisfactory as the rest. I tried to sort out the reactions and their reasons, and arrived at this conclusion:

1. There were a number of people who disliked the shock given by the story of Celia's death, and a number more who disliked the flippancy of the introduction to it. These need not be taken notice of, because (a) the scene has the effect intended by the author, and (b) the audience are held throughout by it.

2. There were a number of people who said that the final scene was too long; and that it made the play too long. This is, I think, true; the effort made by an audience, even when mercifully delivered from coughing by the prohibition of smoking in the theatre, has to be great, and is slightly too prolonged.

3. It was evident that the attention of the audience was less complete during the passage after the story of Celia's death than anywhere else in the play. People raised certain objections to this passage which explain why they didn't find it convincing:

(a) The reaction of the three non-guardians to the story didn't seem violent enough.

(b) *Peter* in particular worried everybody. Why didn't he rebel actively against the Hollywood he only worked in for Celia's sake? How could he, after helpless protests, just go gaily back there?

(c) The death had no effect in *action*: the final section (after Peter went) seemed more like the author summing up than like anything developed from the hearts of the characters.

I have felt that it might be possible, and worthwhile, to make a slight re-arrangement which would tie the elements of this scene more closely together and would introduce action. It would work as follows:

Peter's speech about his job would end with the statement that he cannot now go back to it.

Lavinia, instead of answering this directly, would launch straight into her questioning of Sir Henry about his view of Celia's death, and be answered by his exposition.

Julia's speech about choice would end at the point where she speaks about Boltwell, and be addressed to Peter. He would have learned from Sir Henry's words to understand Celia to the point of being able to take up his Hollywood life in a new spirit, and his exit would follow.

Julia would then address Edward and Lavinia. They would react more violently than they do against the imminent party, but then see (probably helping one another to see) that this is their job: and so the end of the play would be as now.

This plan seems to me to have the merits of giving Peter a dramatic last scene, of making Sir Henry's exposition affect the action, and of keeping some suspense in the play to the end. I therefore submit for your consideration, humbly and with apologies for causing trouble.

I appended a typescript of the pages as they could be rearranged. This is so close to the printed text that it would be redundant here; Eliot altered my suggested plan only by simplifying, and it finally required only two or three lines of new writing.

The lines from *Prometheus Unbound* were restored for London. Most people find them puzzling, but their strange beauty assists in creating the right mood for what Reilly has to say.

Just before the final exit of the Guardians to the Gunnings', there was a farewell toast. Alex had briefly left the room, and returned as Julia spoke:

> And I think, Henry,
> That we should leave before the party begins.
> They will get on better without us. You too, Alex.
>
> ALEX Just a moment, Julia. There is one brief ceremony
> Before we go . . .
>
> (*Enter Caterer's Man with a tray and five glasses*)
> I took the liberty
> Of bringing a bottle of my own champagne—
> I thought it should be mine, for this occasion—
> And giving instructions to the man as I came in.
> I wish to propose a toast.
>
> (*They all rise*)
> EDWARD (*absently*)   To the Guardians.
> ALEX To one particular Guardian, whom you have forgotten.
> I give you—Lavinia's Aunt!
> ALL   Lavinia's Aunt!
> (*They drink, and the Caterer's Man takes out the tray*)
> JULIA Now, Henry. Now, Alex. We're going to the Gunnings'.
> (*Exeunt* JULIA, REILLY *and* ALEX)
>
> (*CP*/Edin.; cf. *Collected Plays*, p. 212)

Sherek noted to me:

I cannot see the point of Alex' toast to Lavinia's aunt. There is much ado about bringing in the drinks etc. which makes one anticipate a great surprise and then the toast seems anti-climatic.

Commenting on this to Eliot, I wrote:

I think the reason is that we haven't ever had it dinned into us that this fiction has been a principal weapon in the hands of the Guardians. Could Alex and Reilly have a word on it somewhere?

But Eliot thought it better to let it go; and though 'a great surprise' would certainly have been useful to build up the Guardians' exit, this one was probably too slender to take the weight.

The little scene between Edward and Lavinia also seemed slight as a preparation for the final curtain. I tried curtailing it; but Sherek proved right in his reaction:

I rather like some of the cut lines at the very end, especially
    One sometimes likes to hear the same compliment twice.
    Never mind, you're getting on.
It has a certain warmth and invokes the feeling that their comradeship (the essence of middle-aged marriage) will improve even more than the situation as we see it. It's not important, just the old sentimentalist coming out in me.

The curtain-lines had always been hopefully subject to revision:

2 July 1949

Dear Martin,
    The last half-line is the trickiest bit of all. One wants something very bright indeed; but it's much more important to avoid the wrong thing than to find the one right thing. One or two lines looked promising, but rather suggested that E. and L. didn't want to be left alone together—which would spoil the relation I had so laboriously built up between them. I should like to leave it open as long as possible, in the hope of what Julia would call an inspiration; but failing that, perhaps the enclosed is at least harmless.

This was the ending as it still stands.

FROM EDINBURGH TO NEW YORK

Sherek was to produce the play for one week only at the Edinburgh Festival. It was a gamble for him, and as great a one for the cast whom we set out to assemble. He asked me to make a list of every actor I could think of who was suitable for each of the parts. I still have my rough copy of this list: and it is phenomenal that for five of the seven parts the first name on the list is that of the actor who played it. We were supremely lucky to begin by securing Alec

Guinness to play Reilly. He had given a wonderful performance of Menenius in my production of *Coriolanus* for the Old Vic the previous year, and I was overjoyed to work with him again. His presence was also, of course, an encouragement to the other artists we wanted: and we ended up with the following cast for our week's run:

Edward Chamberlayne	ROBERT FLEMYNG
Julia (Mrs Shuttlethwaite)	CATHLEEN NESBITT
Celia Coplestone	IRENE WORTH
Alexander McColgie Gibbs	ERNEST CLARK
Peter Quilpe	DONALD HOUSTON
Sir Henry Harcourt-Reilly	ALEC GUINNESS
Lavinia Chamberlayne	URSULA JEANS

Meanwhile, we were busy considering the visual side of the production. Eliot had firm views about what he wanted. In a letter of 6 May he said:

The supernatural element, if we call it that, ought to be not at all evident: this play, it seems to me, needs a much more matter-of-fact and realistic setting [than *The Family Reunion*], and the costumes should not be too stylised and harmonious.

and on 2 July:

An *imposed* symbolism in the decor would be painful. What I want is something superficially at least purely realistic—the rooms what they would be in a perfectly naturalistic play. If the decor conveys any more than that, it should only come from the genius of the designer—and indeed be almost unconscious on the designer's part. But if the designer is TOLD to go symbolic, the only result will be a late imitation of 'experimental' theatre.

Accordingly, Anthony Holland produced for us two handsome realistic sets; and Mrs Sherek exercised her skill and taste to make the ladies look their very best in the latest West End creations. The results, and their bearing on the play, were noted by Mary Carson in the *Glasgow Herald*:

To reduce Mr. Eliot's play to a fashion parade would be unseemly; nevertheless this cocktail party was dressed in the newest styles by Angele Delanghe, and definitely reflected the coming trends. Moreover, one part depended upon a change in type of dress to convey to the audience its first inkling that there was something unusual here. This fell to the lot of Miss Cathleen Nesbitt who, wearing a floral-patterned, fluttering dress and fussy hat, is first of all the dithering guest who provides the light relief; when she appears in a later scene

The Cocktail Party

quietly dressed in a plain black frock, we have our first hint that she has a dual role in the scheme of things.

(31 August 1949)

The Edinburgh Festival, in this the third year of its life, was already established as a major international event; but this was the first time that an important new play was to be shown there. We therefore faced a mighty barrage of advance publicity. Yet we had to open under the same conditions as apply to a play on tour. The theatre would only be vacant at midnight on the Saturday; we had to move in during the week-end, dress rehearse in sets which we should be meeting for the first time, and play to our first audience on the Monday night—no previews. We rehearsed for nearly four weeks in London, ending with a run-through on Thursday and some touching up on Friday, and travelled to Edinburgh by train on Saturday.

I remember vividly one incident at the dress rehearsal. I was sitting in the front row of the dress-circle, and Eliot was immediately behind me. As Edward spoke the line

Hell is oneself

near the end of his quarrel with Lavinia, Eliot leaned over and whispered: 'Contre Sartre.' The line, and the whole story of Edward and Lavinia, are his reply to 'Hell is other people' in *Huis Clos*.

On Monday, 22 August 1949, T. S. Eliot watched the first performance of *The Cocktail Party* at the Lyceum Theatre, Edinburgh. It is a pleasant Victorian house with a warm atmosphere; and the packed audience was quick to respond to the excitement generated in anticipation. By the end, the play was evidently a success; argument for and against it was rife, but both sides had had a good evening in the theatre. The notices reflect every shade of opinion, as a selection will show.

The Times critic, now A. V. Cookman, sets the play in the perspective of Eliot's work:

In this brilliantly entertaining analysis of problems long since staled by conventional treatment Mr. Eliot achieves a remarkable refinement of his dramatic style. His earlier plays have been successive moves towards simplicity; and now his thought, wholly undiluted, flows with certainty and a new sparkle of wit along present-day theatrical channels. The framework of ritual sat a little heavily on *Murder in the Cathedral*. Greek props gave an air of embarrassing artificiality to the narrative of *The Family Reunion*. These he has now dispensed with; and

233

in lucid, unallusive verse which endows everyday speech with a delicate precision and a strictly occasional poetic intensity he presents in the shape of a fashionable West End comedy a story highly ingenious in its construction, witty in its repartee, and impregnated with Christian feeling.

(24 August 1949)

The play's 'lucidity' is upheld by some critics, such as A.D.M. of the *Edinburgh Evening Dispatch* who says 'there is little in this play that average intelligence will not grasp'. But to others, it is a puzzle. Cecil Wilson in the *Daily Mail* calls it 'a bewildering muddle of a play, but in many respects a brilliant one'. Perhaps the *Scotsman* in his *Log* found the wisest way of assessing the priorities in this controversy:

First Night

The first night of a play by a great poet is an occasion. It justifies and demands excitement. For it is bound to be some kind of message to humanity. Equally it is bound to affect different people in different ways.

This column was not present at the première of Mr Eliot's 'Cocktail Party', and it sought its first reaction from a housewife who was. This housewife doesn't get to the theatre very often, so she couldn't very well be blasé about it. She didn't have any preconceived notions, she was unversed in modern verse, and she gave us her comments over the clamour raised by a naughty child or two.

She said that she liked the play immensely. She didn't pretend to understand it all, but it had sent her away from the theatre with her mind in a furious state of activity and her heart aglow. It had been very hot and stuffy where she was sitting, but all the time she was very conscious of seeing a theatre put to its real purpose which she doesn't always feel.

A housewife's opinion may be of little critical value. But it is, in its way, an important opinion because it may be based on a comparative scale of values not always accessible to the professional critic. Mr Eliot is not a housewife's poet, but we thought that an entirely unsolicited word of praise from the kitchen sink would not altogether discountenance him.

(24 August 1949)

Most critics agree with the *Manchester Guardian* that 'this play pays its way very well as a play'. The *Aberdeen Press* points out one reason:

The play shows us in one way a new Eliot. He is witty and he 'wisecracks'—the wit reminiscent in its paradox of Oscar Wilde. There is more laughter to this basically serious play than I have heard for a long time.

W. A. Darlington in the *Daily Telegraph* adds to his appreciation the comment of several that it is hard work:

The Cocktail Party

Unless I am carried away by the excitement of the moment, this play is one of the finest dramatic achievements of our time.

One might complain of it that it is packed too closely—that it is so full of philosophy, wit and epigram and swings so quickly and so far between the deepest seriousness and the lightest of comic touches that the mind cannot grasp it. This is true to some extent. Yet Mr. Eliot contrives by sheer narrative skill to keep his tale simple amid all the complicated talk.

(23 August 1949)

Alan Dent puts the other view:

The week after—as well as the morning after—I take it to be nothing but a finely acted piece of flapdoodle.

(News Chronicle, 27 August 1949)

And one of the most eminent critics of the day, Ivor Brown, having got Mr Eliot's version of the 'light comedy' he had prophesied, is against it root and branch:

Eliot is one of those authors who divide the public sharply: either he commands you or he doesn't. There are no half-allegiances with him. The Eliotians were saying it was just too marvellous, and the Opposition were observing that it was all pretentious mystification and a blether of words. How subtle the rhythms, said the 'Pro' party, concerning this poetic chatter about first and last things round the short drinks! ('A nice Sin and Mixed, my dear?') Not poetry at all, growled the 'Cons'. What was it all about? Well, there at a party is Alec Guinness as a Mystery Guest, who might be Devil or Saint and turns out to be a psychotherapist remarkable for taking no fees and keeping a Lady Sneerwell (Cathleen Nesbitt) as an eavesdropper in his anteroom. His business seems to be mending other people's marriages or lack of them. He tells a quarrelsome couple some stinging truths, which apparently reconciles them, and sends a sad young woman to a death worse than fate in a way which struck me as purely sadistic. I have rarely disliked anybody so much as this icy Healer of Mr. Eliot's; though he is a medico in mumbo-jumbo and incantations, too, and is one of three self-elected 'Guardians' together with the Sneerwell and a strangely unpleasant young man. If these creatures be the forces of righteousness, then 'evil be thou my good' was my reaction to the long, vague sermon.

(Observer, 28 August 1949)

'Nevertheless', he prophesied next day, 'The Cocktail Party would be a tremendous success because it would be talked about' (Glasgow Bulletin, 29 August).

These were judgements on the author's view of life rather than of his competence as a dramatist. The Glasgow Herald sums it up well:

Mr. Eliot certainly appears to have produced an authentic incantation in his new play. It puzzled most people in Edinburgh, tantalising some critics and exasperating others—Mr. Ivor Brown among them. Yet at least one notice treated it as though it were the plainest piece of dramatic exposition in the world. Where there is room for such a diversity of reaction, a poet whose intentions are those stated by Mr Eliot in an interview in these columns last week is justified in declaring himself well satisfied.

(31 August 1949)

The interview referred to is worth preserving in full. Eliot had appeared on the stage at the end of the first performance and said a brief word of thanks. This was customary at the Festival, and he had overcome his shyness to do it. But once that ordeal was past, he talked quite freely to the press. This interview with the *Glasgow Herald*, was the most extended that he gave.

Mr. Eliot smiled when it was suggested to him yesterday that Festival audiences had not found his meaning very plain. 'Perhaps,' he said gently, 'I did not intend that they should.' Then he went on to outline the thesis that the meaning of poetry, in verse drama as in other forms, is that which each individual takes from his experience.

'All that one can aim at in a play of this type, which endeavours to combine the dramatic and the poetic in a somewhat new way,' he said, 'is to provide a plot and characters and action which are on the immediate theatrical level intelligible. That is, the immediate situation and the troubles and conflicts which agitate people should be obvious, the characters should not be on the surface unusual or different from ordinary human nature, and there should be perfectly intelligible things going on, with a reasonably intelligible conclusion.

'The first and perhaps the only law of the drama is to get the attention of the audience and to keep it. If their interest is kept up to the end, that is the great thing.'

But there was a more poetic side to it, treating it according to the way in which we treated poetry as distinct from drama. If there was any poetry in the play, and he hoped there was, then one could not explain it in the ordinary sense.

'No explanation in the ordinary sense of a poem is adequate. If you can completely explain a poem, with an exact correspondence between the deliberate intention of the author and the reception of the idea by the reader, then it just is not poetry. One of the things about poetry is that it does excite different reactions from different people. The main thing is that they should enjoy it; but they get different things out of it.

'I would not want to say to anyone that this or that is the meaning, because the whole interest of the process is in getting your own meaning out of it.'

One of the great struggles in the appreciation of poetry was to get people to stop asking the question of some one else—What is the meaning? 'They should not even ask that question too much of the literary critics', Mr Eliot added with a smile, 'because if you read an explanation by a literary critic and entirely

The Cocktail Party

agree, the thing is finished. One should never entirely agree with any literary critic.'

'In this case'—his final word on "The Cocktail Party"—'I think I am pleased.'

(27 August 1949)

However much the author insisted that each interpreter must be free to find his own meaning, those who penetrated furthest into the play's thought were the critics who were willing to recognise its Christian basis. Robert Speaight, in the *Tablet*, places the play both in the context of Eliot's work and in the repertory of its time:

The play is a masterpiece of theatrical contrivance. In the first act the trivial interventions of Julia and Alex, which seem an interruption of serious emotional business, prepare us for their critical intervention later. (Perhaps the Guardian Angels, whom they so amusingly symbolize, are more familiar than we guess.) The dramatist focuses his light, first upon Edward, who is our old friend J. Alfred Prufrock, and then upon Celia, who is already living the experience of the *Four Quartets*. Thus the play resumes, in its unstressed fashion, the long journey that Mr. Eliot has travelled. The loneliness of Gerontion is in Edward's definition of his dilemma:

> Hell is oneself,
> Hell is alone, the other figures in it
> Merely projections. There is nothing to escape from
> And nothing to escape to. One is always alone.

This is the other side of the Sartrian image which was dramatized in *Huis Clos*. The Lenten reminders of *Ash Wednesday* are in Sir Henry's parting words to the reconciled couple:

> Go in peace. And work out your salvation with diligence.

Just as the realism and humility of the *Quartets* are in his subsequent observation:

> The best of a bad job is all any of us make of it.
> Except, of course, the saints.

The gesture with which Mr. Alec Guinness took out his watch on these last words was perhaps the most imaginative moment in a magnificent performance. Sir Henry might so easily have become an ethical bore, sugaring his pills with whimsy. But with Mr. Guinness we are worlds away from ethics; this is the confessional and the choice is between the loss of personality and the love of God. Miss Irene Worth suggested, in a moving and vibrant study, the whole of Celia's capacity for sacred and profane love; Miss Ursula Jeans, with no sacrifice of natural charm, made Lavinia naturally unlovable, but yet made us realize, in the last act, how grace was doing its work; Mr. Robert Flemyng, young in years for Edward, gave us the authentic sag of middle age and a twinge of the Existentialist agony; and Miss Cathleen Nesbitt conducted Julia with both judgment and wit along the realistic and symbolic levels. This superb ensemble of English acting was so well directed by Mr. Martin Browne that you didn't notice it. But then Mr. Browne has been Mr. Eliot's theatrical *eminence grise* since the days of *Murder in the Cathedral*—and earlier. Author, actors and audience should be grateful that he has assisted into life a play which is among the rare masterpieces of the modern stage.

(3 September 1949)

But Desmond Shawe-Taylor in the *New Statesman* analyses the slightly forbidding quality which many who most admired it found in the play. The realisation that it made this impression may have influenced Eliot towards a mellower tone in his subsequent plays:

there is something about it which chills me: perhaps the lack of delight in the rich variety of human nature. Mr. Eliot's characters are admirably amusing puppets, he manipulates them as cunningly as the magician in *Petrouchka*, but, like the host at his own party, he seems incapable of love: of warmth towards the particular, as opposed to a diffused benevolence. The muddy adorable substance of life as it is lived seems curiously far from this fragile community, and I find something faintly repellent in the quiet smiles and antiseptic wisdom of Sir Henry and his two pals. Considered as moral teachers and 'guardians' (a key-word of the play), they suggest a group of infinitely superior Buchmanite leaders, out of the Upper Sixth instead of the usual Lower Fourth: but considered simply and solely as theatrical figures they are superb, just as the whole play is a superbly contrived conversation piece—lively, often cynical, sometimes profound . . . Mr. Guinness lends an extraordinary sort of comic authority to Sir Henry: with his long quizzical face, his long straight nose, his great searching eyes, his sardonic humour and his impressive delivery, he conveys (am I wrong who never saw the Great Man?) something of the magnetism of another Sir Henry.

(3 September 1949)

The author's own reaction to the stress of the opening can best be conveyed by quoting a letter to my wife.

28 August, 1949

My dear Henzie,

I got back from Edinburgh last night; this is the first opportunity I have had (apart from the fact that I did not take a typewriter with me) to thank you for your kind thought—the carnation posey for the Night, and the card and the thought that directed it. Well, it seems to have been a success. I had two days of chills-and-fever before the opening; I was terribly worried about those who had put so much into it—Martin, the cast, and last but least Mr. Sherek's financial gamble. Now I'm delighted to think that nobody will be the loser for it, and that perhaps one or two of the cast may benefit from it—apart from the benefit I hope they may get from the London run. And one thing is certain— that this is at least as great a triumph for Martin as for me. I know it was not an easy play to put over; it could not have been an easy matter to get even these actors to see what it was all about. I don't believe anyone but Martin could have done it. I'm more grateful than I can say—and to you too, who gave me the encouragement I needed when you read the first draft and said that I had got something in Celia. When the various drafts of the play are finally collated and studied by researchers in American universities, I think that my debt to you and Martin will emerge!

I hope to see you both soon.

Affectionately,

Tom

There were plenty of people to say, in print and otherwise, that the play must be seen in London. *The Times* critic says

London can scarcely afford to ignore entertainment of so much distinction, and it is to be hoped that when the play reaches a more permanent stage the company seen here at the Royal Lyceum Theatre will remain quite unchanged.

and T. C. Kemp concludes his enthusiastic notice in the *Birmingham Post* by speaking of *The Cocktail Party* as

a function which should be repeated in many theatres for many nights after the Edinburgh Festival has come to an end.

This consummation would in any case have had to be delayed, since Guinness had only come to Edinburgh on leave of absence from a film, and Robert Flemyng from another play. But when Sherek returned to London he found it impossible to secure a West End theatre for it when Guinness would be free at the end of the year. He therefore accepted Gilbert Miller's invitation to take it to the Henry Miller in New York at the beginning of 1950. Eliot was at first perturbed by this plan, but finally agreed to it, and the press announced it in the middle of October.[1]

Two members of the Edinburgh cast, Ursula Jeans and Donald Houston, were unable to accept the invitation to go to America, and we had to re-cast Lavinia and Peter. This, and the lapse of several months, made it essential to 'play in' the company before New York, and since Gilbert Miller did not want us to play other American dates Sherek arranged to go to the Theatre Royal, Brighton, for the two weeks over Christmas. With Eileen Peel and Grey Blake as the new members of the company, we opened there on 19 December.

The first-night audience was a glittering one. Ivor Novello brought Zena and Phyllis Dare down with him from London, and gave a

[1] See Henry Sherek's own account of the negotiations in *Not in Front of the Children*, pp. 142–3.

party for the cast after the show. Googie Withers and her husband John MacCallum were there, Dorothy Dickson, Hugh Williams—and the author, whose presence at the show had been unsuspected by the audience until the end. Gilbert Miller flew over from New York to see what he was getting.

Brighton had already become a significant theatrical outpost of London; and since London had no promise of when it might see Eliot's play, the Brighton audience was steadily reinforced from the metropolis. We had a very successful two weeks finishing on New Year's eve; and the scenery was despatched by ship. Most of us eschewed the January sea, and followed by plane on Sunday the 15th.

Irene Worth had not been so wise: with Alec Guinness she went by ship, had a bad voyage and arrived with a severe attack of 'flu. She was not allowed to play the two previews, but was able to appear for the opening on Saturday, 21 January.

Meanwhile, there were the toils of setting up the show in the Henry Miller Theatre. I wrote to my wife on Tuesday:

I'm sitting in what will be Alec Guinness' dressing-room, while the stage crew are setting up—a business which has gone on slowly and laboriously all day and won't be finished tonight. We are tremendously staffed: we have a *designer* to set and light, a charming man called Raymond Sovey, and a stage director (Bender) of great eminence as well as our own staff, who can't do much but stand around. It is all very amicable at present, and everyone is still patient with the very slow and poor stage-crew who are all that is left after Television has taken the cream. (Poor old Theatre, it's more nearly dead here than it's ever been in England!) No doubt it will all get sorted out, with much weeping and gnashing of teeth, by Saturday . . .

At the above point I was called for from the stage: various problems of pictures, etc., to be settled. Gilbert Miller and Henry [Sherek] both arrived; and we went on discussing these details for an hour and a half . . .

Miller is a most interesting character—the real old-fashioned *patron* in one sense, taking a very active interest in all the details of his show, laying down the law (often in the most unutterable language) with a high blood-pressure, running the theatre as his personally, meticulous and lavish in doing so. But this doesn't obscure the sharp commercial eye which is also characteristic of him.

The previews passed off all right, with the understudy playing for Irene Worth; and the setting and lighting jobs got done at last. On Saturday, as I was at lunch,

a long call from Henry, passionate about Friday night's performance—the speaking too quiet, the acting all 'down'. True: and we both spent various

The Cocktail Party

moments during the day in urging on our horses just as if they were running in the Derby! The result was the best performance the play has had—the strongest and most compelling.

This, January 21st, was the real first night; and as I wrote to my wife:

It was the queerest and most nerve-racking sensation. An audience which included the Windsors, Ethel Barrymore, Gladys Cooper and so forth. I was more nervous, and felt more exhausted afterwards, than I have ever felt. I didn't even see the Windsors or E.B. because I felt I couldn't and shouldn't be in front in the intermission. I spent the performance in various parts of the house and they were quite fascinatingly different. The Orchestra (Stalls) was quite unresponsive, few laughs (except for Gladys Cooper who I gather was a superb audience), but attentive. Above (i.e. in the Balcony) it was quite another thing: one felt strong reactions—laughter, tears, people hating and refusing it, people eagerly accepting it—much *keener* theatregoers than in England. That was the part that encouraged me. There were many curtains and a speech by Alec, the Orchestra being by this time almost empty. What it all means, no one will try to say: but at least not a complete flop.

I was rescued by Rosamund Gilder, whom I find the most wonderful friend, from a state of exhaustion in which I started introducing people by their wrong names etc. backstage. Everyone came round, of course, and talked for hours— what they all thought of it, who can tell?

Henry and Miller both seemed really pleased, and Henry was very touching about the direction—'noone else could have kept them on the razor edge where Eliot has placed them'.

By Wednesday, 25 January, I was able to write:

The play is a very big success . . . Yesterday's bookings totalled $8,000, and we were sold clean out both Monday and Tuesday. So the show is here for the season at least. Alec has made a very delightful personal success too.

At Brighton, Harold Hobson had written in the *Sunday Times* a prophecy which this success helped to fulfil:

Mr. Guinness is going to be one of our greatest actors. The triangle of Gielgud, Olivier, Richardson is visibly changing into a quadrilateral.

In those days, there were seven New York daily papers. Today, almost dictatorial power is wielded by a single critic on the *New York Times*; but in 1950 there was opportunity for healthy disagreement. As in Britain, *The Cocktail Party* readily provoked it, and gained heavily by becoming the talking-point of the season. But it would probably not have had the chance of doing so had not the majority of the critics used the most laudatory terms about it, enabling the publicity manager to splash in the next Sunday's papers an advertisement which quoted the word 'masterpiece' three times over and backed it up with other superlatives.

The advertisement had to resort, for a quotation from the most powerful of the newspapers, the *New York Times,* to W. A. Darlington's report from the Edinburgh Festival. For Brooks Atkinson, doyen of American critics and a deeply respected figure, was one of the two who were not in sympathy with the author's ideas. He found the drama 'verbose and elusive', though 'the performance is thoroughly intelligible and enjoyable'. Having described the psychiatrist, 'the father-confessor of modern people who have no basic religion', and what he does for his patients, Atkinson asks

Why? The reasons obviously lie concealed in the figured verse to which Mr. Eliot has confided his thoughts and religious faith. No doubt they are all there for theatregoers who are in tune with him, who can invade his spiritual privacy and who have faith in metrical abstractions. But today's report is written by one theatregoer who does not understand Mr. Eliot's dogma but recognises that it is genuine and worth understanding by means of the script, since it is too compact and too allusive to be assimilated from the stage.

(23 January 1950)

William Hawkins of the *World-Telegram and Sun* calls the play 'a didactic philosophical analysis, more suited to reading than to hearing' and can 'see little reason why the American public should attempt to embrace it in this form'. Howard Barnes of the *Herald-Tribune* finds that Eliot 'has written more eloquently than theatrically' but that the work in production has 'extraordinary and exhausting appeal . . . A great poet has employed the stage to magnificent advantage' in the first two Acts, but it is a pity that the events resulting from Celia's vocation 'inspire a morbid ending to a drama of high promise'.

If two of the seven voices speak against the play and one has a double tone, the other four are unstinted in their praise. Robert Garland in the *Journal American* makes no bones about beginning his review:

T. S. Eliot's *The Cocktail Party*, at Henry Miller's, is a masterpiece, worthily performed . . . Mr. Miller's importation takes its place as the one great comedy in town. A great comedy, as old as the theatre in its ecumenicity! And as modern as an atomic bomb in its method and motivation.

(23 January 1950)

The Cocktail Party

John Chapman in the *Daily News* likewise uses the word 'masterpiece' in his first sentence, and says later:

Within the framework of a fine drawing-room comedy he [Reilly] operates to give his patients—and the audience, who are also his patients—a glowing sense of the divine nature of the soul.

(23 January 1950)

For Richard Watts Jr. in the *Daily Post* 'the theatrical season took on stature' with this production:

The greatest of living poets has been trying to storm the drama for a long time, but at last he has mastered it, and his new work, which is technically in verse but hardly seems to be, is an authentic modern masterpiece, one of the two or three finest plays of the post-war English-speaking stage.

Watts deals faithfully, in the incredibly brief time allowed to a critic before he goes to press, with the question of obscurity:

It is a subtle play, but not really a difficult one, and although it demands a considerably closer attention on the part of its audiences than do most contemporary works in the theatre, it is absorbing on whatever level it is contemplated.

He makes an interesting comparison with Eugene O'Neill:

It appears that the author is expressing a point of view which is just the opposite of that eloquently stated in another distinguished post-war drama, *The Iceman Cometh*. While O'Neill told passionately of the world's need for illusion to sustain it, Eliot insists more urbanely that our illusions must be dropped and reality faced . . .

I must point out quickly, though, that the play is no mere discussion of philosophies, however interesting. It is also a drama of great emotional and theatrical effectiveness, and since its slightly complex text has been brilliantly staged by E. Martin Browne, it never ceases to be alive.

(23 January 1950)

Robert Coleman of the *Daily Mirror* calls it 'one of the great plays of our time' and 'a wonderful experience in the theatre'. Guinness, he says, is 'a great actor', and Watts thinks 'it is quite possible that he is the most accomplished actor extant'.

It is notable that all the enthusiasts write for the 'tabloids'; the reviewers in 'class' papers sit on the fence. Even then, it was rare that a play making intellectual demands should succeed without their support. But the alchemy of success is a mysterious thing; it was present on that first night.

243

The Cocktail Party

It is the custom of New York papers to print on the Sunday following a major opening an article appraising the play in more considered terms than can be expected when a reviewer is rushing for the deadline. It is a testimony both to the quickness of their judgement and to their ability to stand to their guns that none of the critics had much of substance to add. Brooks Atkinson's elaboration of his view raises a question which is still relevant to all Eliot's post-war drama:

The Cocktail Party is a remarkably provocative play—a fascinating experiment in the suitability of poetic drama to modern times and in the religious interpretation of modern life. But to me, it is insufficiently poetic. It needs more eloquence, passion and imaginative courage. Mr. Eliot is writing about things that cannot be adequately expressed in the earth-bound, cerebral style he has deliberately chosen for his experiment.

(29 January 1950)

Wolcott Gibbs, in the New Yorker made a characteristically sharp analysis of the play's content; and although 'its chances for success in the non-experimental theatre seem to me debatable', he finds that, as regards its comedy,

it is a fascinating performance, superior in style and intelligence to anything else being done now on either side of the Atlantic, and I like to dream that someday its author may so far demean himself as to write an entire play in this vein alone.

(25 January 1950)

For he finds much of the serious side of the play

almost unendurably provocative, but impossible to piece together into a coherent whole.

A review in Time (30 January) which calls it 'a major event in the theatre' is herald to the rare honour for a playwright of a 'cover story' on 6 March, ranging over Eliot's life and work with the play as central point.

Decca made a recording with the New York cast, which is still on sale at this writing. It was a hectic job; for various union and contractual reasons only a single day was allowed for recording the actors; and we worked flat-out from nine to five just getting it on to tape. The next day, and part of the following one, I spent with the technicians editing the several tapes of each scene that we had hastily collected. It was in a state of dazed exhaustion that I crawled on to the plane for home.

Sherek now found it much easier to gain the interest of theatre-owners in London; and he soon made an agreement with Bronson Albery, who had been well inclined in the beginning, to produce at the New Theatre when the Old Vic company (who were about to return to their old home) had finished there. This was expected to be after 1 June, when the contracts of the New York company would be open to re-negotiation and many of them in any case wanted to come home; so Sherek and I hoped to start with a majority of our original cast, whom he had promised that they should play in London.

However, the Old Vic business dropped and he had to put the opening forward to early May. This meant an entirely new production. Sherek assembled another excellent company:

Reilly	REX HARRISON
Edward	IAN HUNTER
Lavinia	ALISON LEGGATT
Celia	MARGARET LEIGHTON
Julia	GLADYS BOOT
Alex	ROBIN BAILEY
Peter (the original)	DONALD HOUSTON

We opened at the New Theatre on 3 May. By this time, the play was, I suppose, something of a legend; the Broadway success, with its attendant controversy, had come after months during which the export of the production had awakened advance interest; and then it had come out in print and become a best seller on both sides of the Atlantic. So it was assured of a large audience in the theatre. Meanwhile, too, attitudes had hardened, and the London notices are quite remarkably lacking in interest —except for the fact that, once more, the 'tabloids' unite to praise the show as a show while the more intellectual papers are about equally split in their attitudes towards the author's ideas.

Rex Harrison was at the first night in New York and was captivated by the play. Sherek took a bold risk in casting for London a star whose established image was so entirely different from Reilly's; and some thought it did not come off. T. C. Worsley (who disliked the play) gave perhaps the shrewdest analysis of the problem:

The Cocktail Party

That Mr. Harrison is miscast goes without saying. All the same he very nearly wins through in the second act. It is impossible to compare him with Mr. Guinness; they are opposites. Mr. Guinness was rigid, decisive, imperial; Mr. Harrison is soft, tentative, engaging; Mr. Guinness commanded his way through; Mr. Harrison charms his way along. But in the consulting room scene in the second act he does impose a kind of ascendancy. It would surely help if he could assert some authority earlier on. We want to feel a fist beneath his smart chamois leather gloves. In his first serious exchanges with the husband he should come down on top of the words, not slide smilingly up to them. Not only does the sense demand a harder and more authoritative note, but it is also demanded by the very fact of our finding Mr. Harrison here at all. An actor like Mr. Harrison who has traded on his personality in parts cut to measure, must assert his difference early when he is to be taken quite differently.

(*New Statesman*, 13 May 1950)

It was a performance of extreme skill, and also of sincerity; and I felt that on its own terms—in Harold Hobson's words, 'a man-of-the-world, not a man-of-another-world Reilly'—it was valid. Harrison had a constant desire to improve on his own success. We worked happily together to that end; and even when I went round to see him after his last matinée, he referred hopefully to a point we had been trying to make: 'I shall be able to do it this evening.'

The man-of-the-world aspect of the character naturally had its dangers, which Harrison was ready enough to fend off when realised. Eliot's acuteness about such things may be illustrated from a letter of 25 May:

there is one point which troubled me when I first saw this production, and still more when I went a fortnight ago. Towards the end of the first scene, when Edward goes to the door to admit Julia, Rex Harrison attempts to benefit by his absence from the room, by going to help himself to another shot of gin. You will remember that Edward returns and Harrison puts down the bottle without having been able to carry out his design. Now this is very amusing in itself, and Harrison does it very well, but I do feel it is a falsification of the character, and completely falsifies the nature of Reilly's drinking. It ought to be made clear from Reilly's behaviour in later scenes that the general drinking and singing—apart from their having been originally introduced to bring Reilly's behaviour into connection with that of Heracles in the *Alcestis*—are entirely an act put on by Reilly for the purpose of mystifying Edward. Rex Harrison's charming little gesture must tend to give the audience the impression that Reilly is a confirmed private drinker. I hope you will manage to keep his arms down at a certain point, to 45 degrees, and avoid the crucifixion suggestion.

246

The Cocktail Party

Harrison and Margaret Leighton, whose performance as Celia won much deserved praise, were available only for three months; and Sherek had tried to make arrangements where possible to allow the members of the original cast to take over their roles when they returned from New York. Most unfortunately, Alec Guinness could not do this; but Irene Worth, Eileen Peel and Ernest Clark rejoined the company in August. The changes disturbed the production for a time, as was to be expected, but with some special rehearsal and careful watching I was able to restore it.

The hundredth performance was given on 2 August, and Eliot entertained all the actors in all the productions who were in London at the time to a party afterwards. With over 200 performances chalked up in New York, and as many again to come in both cities, it was an occasion for rejoicing, since it represented not only a substantial sum of money but the achievement of an objective which the poet had aimed at for many years. One appreciates the effect of it best, perhaps, by the verses which *Sagittarius*, the sharpest-witted of current satirists, published in the *New Statesman*:

Nightingale among the Sweenies

I

(Total legit. grosses. 'Cocktail Party' Comedy Drama. Henry Miller Theatre. 20th Week. $20,300. *Variety*.)

This is the vulgarest success, blasting
A hitherto immaculate reputation,
The voice
Par excellence of the waste land and the wilderness.
Can the exalted oracle rejoice
Who, casting
Pearls before swine, wins swinish approbation?
Tereu, twit, twit, this metaphysical mime
That should have been
The most distinguished failure of all time
Proves quite the opposite.
Between the conception and the reception, between
The curtain calls the Shadow falls—
The deep damnation of a Broadway hit,
Groomed for some critic *coterie's* diploma,
Dear God, like *Oklahoma*!
(O what a terrible morning)
Seeing (let's face it) not alone the arty
But the dim rabble crash *The Cocktail Party*.
Has the hautboy of attenuated tone
Become the uncultured herd's unconscious saxophone?

247

The Cocktail Party

II

Author, author, take your bow,
Cocktail Party is O.K. now,
   Still it's a riddle how
   Lowbrow and middlebrow
Mix with the highbrow at this highbrow wow!

T. S. Eliot up in lights,
Hollywood angling for movie rights—
   Play for the study
   Clapped by the muddy-
Mettled hollow apeneck galleryites!

Cocktail, Cocktail, Cocktail clicks!
Connoisseurs, socialites, wise guys, hicks
   Quit for a poem
   Penned by an O.M.,
Radio, rodeo, vaudeville, pix!

Box Office total the shame completes,
Midsummer sag finds no empty seats;
   O sir, O sir,
   What glut is grosser
Than twenty thousand dollar gross receipts?

III

There is a prickly pear in the dry martini,
   But the poet must his private agony
  Transmute by intellectual discipline
   And welcome the sour cup of prosperity.
    Anything with it?
    Gin.

7

The Confidential Clerk

While *The Cocktail Party* was running, the pattern of a new play was taking shape in the author's mind. It proved to be a very complicated pattern, one which he had to work out pretty completely before it could be subjected to analysis by anyone else. Soon after the last night at the New Theatre on 10 February 1951, he was taken ill; meanwhile, I was occupied both with my job as Director of the British Drama League and with the first revival for nearly four hundred years of the York Cycle of Mystery Plays. After that my wife and I went on a lecture tour of New Zealand and Australia; and it is from Sydney that there comes the first mention in my letter of 21 October 1951:

I hope the new play has been moving along as you want it to, and *greatly* look forward to seeing a draft.

But it did not reach me for another year:

December 8, 1952

My dear Tom,

I have this moment received the draft of the first two acts of *The Confidential Clerk*. Directly I can snatch some time off I will eagerly sit down to them, and will ring you up before the week is out to suggest a meeting.

I take it that you have one more spare script? It would be a blessing if I could avoid parting with it to Hunter[1] and Sherek. But I'm going to read it before I let them know I've got it!

An exciting moment. Thank you.

Yours ever,
Martin

I do not know which of the many drafts was the one I got, and I have no copy of it. John Hayward, with whom Eliot had now been

---

[1] Ian Hunter, who had succeeded Rudolf Bing in the artistic direction of the Edinburgh Festival. The play had been promised to him, under Sherek's management, for 1953.

living for some years, collected all the synopses, notes, 'roughs' and drafts, which would indeed provide a job for 'researchers in American universities'. I shall only try to bring out the salient points in the progress of this most intricate play, and tell the story of its productions.

It is based, as is well known, on the *Ion* of Euripides. David E. Jones, in his chapter in *The Plays of T. S. Eliot*,[1] has given an excellent account of the relationship between the two. Euripides, with however ironical a twist, tells of the hidden son of a god and a mortal woman—a tale so common in Greek drama because it was related to the legend of Dionysus, from whose worship the drama sprang. Eliot, like Shakespeare in *The Comedy of Errors*, doubles the abandoned boys, and even adds for good measure an illegitimate daughter. The result has a smack of W. S. Gilbert or Oscar Wilde about it, with a suburban Pallas Athene to clear up the tangles.

The author's first task in such an undertaking was clearly to weave his threads into a satisfactory and plausible pattern. The first script preserved is dubbed (probably by Hayward) *Ur-Clerk*, on the analogy of Goethe's *Ur-Faust*. It has no date. With it are notes by him; and it is preceded by a descriptive list of characters, a cast list and a full scenario. We had better start from these, and then take from the script some passages which are remarkable either in themselves or by contrast with the final version.

The descriptive list is earlier, since the names in it are not those which appear in the cast list. It is a sketch-plan of characters, not all retained:

The Company Director	65	The C.O.[2]'s wife	40
The Young Man	21	The C.O.[2]'s Lady Friend	35
The Confidential Clerk		The Foster Mother	60
B. Sassnik		The Young Secretary	

When the Y.M. was born:

The C.D. was 44
His wife was 19
Mrs. Moss was 39

C.D. Married at 55 when his wife was 30

Underneath are some manuscript notes from a later date:

---

[1] Routledge and Kegan Paul, London, 1960; see especially pages 155–9.
[2] Presumably an error for 'C.D.'

Lady E. to be older   Lucasta younger?
Lucasta perhaps a natural daughter of Claude. This would make Ian's attitude towards her correct.

On another page, the cast list, with the names which remain largely unaltered:

Sir Claude Mulhammer
Lady Elizabeth Mulhammer
Eggleson
B. †Kogan
Mrs. ‡Gozzard
Miss Lucasta §Windibank (or Angel?);
IAN

and below in manuscript, tailed to 'IAN', 'Ian Sympkins'
                                        'Slingsby Mullin'
and a couple of experiments with spelling: 'Guzzerd'
                                        'Guzzard'
    There follows the synopsis, which I print in full as first typed, noting underneath the manuscript additions to each Act:

Act I. Scene i. Sir Claude's private office in his house.

Sir C. alone. Enter Eggleson to announce that the lady has come with the young man whom he is to interview as a possible successor for E. who is about to retire. Exit E. and enter Mrs. Gozzard and Ian. Mrs. G. makes clear that she has only come to effect the introduction and will then leave. Exit Mrs. G. Interview to elicit background etc. of Ian, and make plausible how Sir C. has known about him. He explains what I's position will be, and then calls in Eggleson again, who is to initiate Ian into his duties before leaving.

        Scene ii. The same room, several days later.

Eggleson with Ian. They have been going through papers. Conversation which gives character sketch of E. (enthusiastic gardener, lives in an outer suburb, Mrs. E). Also discussion of I's duties. B. Kogan is announced. E. explains who B.K. is (not too clearly). Enter B.K. fresh bustling young business man about Ian's age, obviously more knowing and experienced, having been in business world since 16 whereas Ian was at public school and university. Very friendly and obviously goodnatured, though sharp at business. Lucasta bursts in, and is greeted formally by Eggleson, more familiarly and offhand by Kogan. Ian is introduced. B. Kogan leaves. Lucasta obviously taken with Ian and makes a set at him. She leaves after hinting that she would like to see Ian again. Eggleson gives Ian a kind of explanation of Lucasta.

† Corrected in the author's hand to Kaghan.
‡ Corrected in the author's hand to Guzzard.
§ The former surname struck out and the latter underlined in the author's hand.

The Confidential Clerk

Scene iii. The same room, some days later.

Eggleson and Ian. E. has almost completed his instruction. Leaves early to do some shopping (gardening tools), looking forward to his retirement to his garden. Enter Sir Claude: more personal conversation with Ian, disclosing that Ian is Sir C.'s son.

In manuscript, 'and Lady E.' is substituted for 'alone' at the beginning, and her exit is suggested after 'about to retire'.

In scene ii, B. Kogan leaves 'after warning Ian against Lucasta, in a jocular way (I can cope with this type but you are too simple)'. Scene iii is 'a month' later; and 'perhaps Lady E. again here for a few moments'.

The name Eggerson is tried out, and 'Eggerson believes in compost' is written at the bottom of the page.

Act II. Scene i. Ian's sitting room. (He has been given a small but elegant flat in a mews behind Sir Claude's house?)

Ian alone. Enter Lucasta. She reproaches him for avoiding her and demands explanation. (While he is fending her off B. Kogan might burst in for a few moments. He feels a certain responsibility for Ian who although his contemporary is so much less experienced in the ways of the world.) Ian finally discloses that he has discovered that she is the mistress of Sir Claude. Lucasta does not see why this should make any difference. He does not reveal the secret of his birth.

Scene ii. The same, a little later in the evening.

Ian alone. Enter Lady Elizabeth (pretext?) She is obviously interested in Ian too, but in a very different way from that of Lucasta. This is the first opportunity for a private conversation with him. She asks him leading questions about his background, disclosing that she and Sir C. being childless she wants to take him in as a kind of adopted son. Ian tries to answer in such a way as to preserve Sir C.'s secret, but the information he gives her convinces her that he is *her own* illegitimate son. She tells him this. The effect is to leave Ian wholly bewildered as to whose son he is.

The one manuscript alteration here concerns Ian's disclosure to Lucasta. There is a note to the word 'mistress', 'perhaps some other objection to her'. Then the whole passage from 'Ian finally discloses' to 'make any difference' is scored through, and at the bottom is written the alternative which we have in the final script: 'Lucasta tells him frankly that she is Sir Claude's daughter. She knew he suspected that she was Sir C.'s mistress. She is baffled to find that this revelation puts him off completely.'

The Confidential Clerk

Act III. Scene i.

Same scene as Act I. This is perhaps the most difficult scene to contrive, because it must consist of a conversation between Sir Claude and Lady E. in which the secret of each is revealed to the other. Ian is called in. The situation is intolerable for him, as he now feels that it is far worse than being an orphan. It is agreed that Mrs. Gozzard must be sent for as she would know the truth.

Scene ii. Sir C., Lady E., Ian, Mrs. G.

Sir C. and Lady E. each put their case before her. Isn't it true that Ian is the baby whom each of them put away (before they had ever met)? Mrs. Gozzard perfectly composed. Says she will not speak until she knows what Ian wants. Ian now desperate says he doesn't want to be either. Mrs. G. then announces that he has his wish: he is not the son of either. Sir C. then in a rage asks Mrs. G. whether she is not Ian's mother. She admits it. Then is he not my son, as you told me he was? No, he is the son of Gozzard, who died before he was born. Gozzard left her penniless, so she naturally had to find a father to provide for Ian's education. Sir C. has no son. But, says Lady E. what about my son? whom I put with you to nurse. He lives, and the time has now come when he shall be delivered to you. He is B. Kogan. What, says Ian, my little twin brother who died, whom I recall dimly? He didn't die. The payments made by Lady E.'s lover were inadequate and finally stopped, so I let a childless neighbour adopt him. Sir C. reflects that B. Kogan is really much more his own sort than Ian, and decides that he will adopt *him*. Ian asks about his father Gozzard, and is told that he was a most respectable man, organist of a Baptist Church. That's my father, says Ian, I've always wanted to be an organist. B. Kogan is sent for, and everyone is happy.

(Perhaps Lucasta should be made rather more respectable, and marry B. Kogan) Query: is there any way of bringing Eggleson back at the end?

Here the manuscript alterations are small. For 'Baptist' read 'C. of E., St. Boniface'. The word 'nearly' is inserted before 'everyone is happy'. The parenthesis about Lucasta is scored through because after 'B. Kogan is sent for', Eliot has put in 'comes with his fiancée Lucasta'.

With the synopsis are two pages of notes by Hayward, asking many practical questions, about introductions, connections, consistency of one passage with another, and making points about names (e.g. Slingsby 'formerly used by Peter Fleming as pseudonym'), and social matters ('I can't place S. socially'). I shall refer to some of these in the following pages. There is also a letter from me of 1 March 1953, later than the *Ur-Clerk*, giving details of my search for information about how the cross-Channel services by air and sea would fit Lady Elizabeth's movements.

253

The Confidential Clerk

The script of *Ur-Clerk* is already a complete play. This has never happened before. It indicates, I think, Eliot's greater self-confidence as a playwright, and also is conditioned by the fact that such a plot as he has chosen must be worked out to the end by a single mind.

Act One is in three scenes set in 'Sir Claude's private office in his West End house'. The opening scene with Lady Elizabeth, as indicated in the manuscript correction of the synopsis, sets the tone of comedy which is retained during the whole of the play's progress:[1]

SIR C. ... I don't like your being in the clutches of an analyst.
LADY E. But I told you, Leroux is *not* an analyst:
    What he does is to teach you Thought Control.
    He's not concerned with what you think about.
SIR C. But what have you got to control, Elizabeth?
    I've always got along by thinking first
    And trying to control a thought when I've got one.

This is the end of the scene:

SIR C. It's time you were off.
LADY E.   There isn't any hurry.
    That's the advantage of travelling by air.
    They know I'm travelling on this plane
    And if I'm late, they can wait for me. Besides
    I've always found that they start an hour late.
SIR C. They may not be late, on this occasion,
    Especially if you don't turn up in time.
    And why on earth do you think they'd wait for you?
LADY E. Because they'll see my name on the list.
    They'll have to wait. And you can get Eggerson
    To telephone the airport and say I'm coming.
SIR C. They'll fly without you. You'd better be going.
LADY E. Very well, I see you want to get rid of me.
    Goodbye, Claude. And if you don't mind,
    When you say 'good bye', I will ask you, this time,
    Please, *not* to say 'take care of yourself'.
SIR C. I won't say that this time. I ought to know by now
    How pointless it is.
LADY E.   I'll send you a telegram
    From Lausanne or somewhere. If I have any trouble
    You can always send Eggerson out to help me.
(*Exit*)

Slingsby, who comes in with Mrs Guzzard, does not know that Sir Claude believes him to be his son. He is self-deprecating:

[1] I print extracts from *Ur-Clerk* as corrected in the author's hand.

The Confidential Clerk

I only got a Second.

I'm afraid, Sir,
I'm not so proficient as you seem to believe.
I haven't much experience of talking to foreigners.

After Sir Claude has engaged him and Mrs Guzzard has left, he has an introductory scene with Eggerson. The curtain speeches are significant:

s.s. It seems to me an awfully responsible position
    To be the confidential clerk
    Of anyone like Sir Claude Mulhammer
    With his vast business interests. A *confidential* clerk!
    I'd rather be a clerk without confidences.
egg You'll soon cease to worry about that, Mr. Simpkins.
    You'll come to know a good many secrets
    Of people with whom Sir Claude has dealings,
    But as for his own, he'll keep them to himself.
    At least, that's *my* experience as a confidential clerk.
                    (*Curtain*)

In the *Ur-Clerk* the second scene is taken up with introducing, to Slingsby and to us, the flighty Lucasta and the free-and-easy B. Kaghan. It registers Slingsby's bewilderment and Eggerson's steadying influence. Eggerson is the play's name-part and also the key to its meaning. He hardly opens his mouth without uttering a cliché, usually reflecting his inveterate habit of thinking well of people. At the end of the scene he is discussing Lady Elizabeth with Slingsby:

e. . . . But let's not be crossing any bridges
    Until we come to them: that's what I always say.
    And you'll come to like her. She's such a lady!
    And what's more, she has a good heart.
    Wasn't it the poet Tennyson.
    Who wrote of kind hearts and noble blood?
s.s. Everybody seems to be kind-hearted.
    I only hope that my own heart is strong enough
    To stand the strain of so much kindness.
    But there's one thing I do believe, Mr. Eggerson—
    That *you* have a kind heart. And I'm convinced
    That you always manage to think the best of everyone.
    In fact, too much so to be quite reassuring.
e. You'll come to find that I'm right, Mr. Simpkins.
    And now I'm going to take you out to lunch.
    By the way, Mrs. E. has asked me to tell you

That she hopes you'll come before long for the weekend.
But I said: 'he won't want to come
At this time of year. Better wait till the spring
When the garden will really be a treat to look at'.
s.s.   Thank you very much. Though you haven't said so,
I believe you're the one who really wants to protect me!

The third and last scene of the Act again opens with Eggerson inducting Slingsby into the mysteries of the household, this time concentrating on Lady Elizabeth and her idiosyncrasies to build up her surprise return, which was adumbrated in a manuscript note in the synopsis: 'perhaps Lady E. again here for a few moments'. At the end of the Act comes the *scène à faire* between father and son. It begins with a shrewd analysis of Lady Elizabeth by her husband:

... You mustn't be deceived by her vagueness,
It's a kind of game that she plays with herself
Partly, because she's bored. And partly, she believes in it.
She pretends to be observant because she's vague,
But the vagueness is a good means of observation.
It's when she's *not* looking at you . . . Slingsby,
That she's noticing you most.

Then he encourages Slingsby to talk about himself, and particularly his attitude to this new kind of work:

You don't find the work uninteresting, do you?
s.s.   Oh no, Sir Claude. In a way, it's exhilarating.
I mean, to find that one can do at all
Work so remote from one's previous experience
And, if I may say so, one's previous interests.
It gives me a kind of feeling of self-confidence
That I've never had before. And at the same time
It's rather frightening. I don't mean the work:
I mean myself. As if I was becoming
A different person. Just as I suppose
That if you learn to talk a foreign language fluently—
So that you think in it—you become
A rather different person when you are talking it.
I'm not quite sure that I like the other person
But he fascinates me. It's a kind of temptation
Of the understanding of material power.

This leads to Claude describing his own life with its parallel experience, and finally to the revelation that Slingsby is his son. Since this does not occur in the course of the play as finalised, but has taken place before it begins, it will be well to present this passage complete. It is interesting to note that here once more the image of the actor finding himself on stage in the wrong part[1] comes to Eliot as the expression of a climax of disturbance. This is the actor's classic dream, and its recurrence shows, I think, how strong was Eliot's instinct for the stage.

s. Sir Claude, you're being awfully kind to me.
   But you've been so very kind ever since I came here.
   But . . . how did it happen that you sent for me?
   It seems to me you must know a lot about me.
SIR C. I had a son myself. Tell me what you know
   About your parentage.
s.   Nothing at all.
   To be quite frank. And to tell the truth,
   I have no curiosity.
SIR C.   Oh, why not?
   Surely, that's unusual.
s.   It sounds extraordinary.
   It's impossible to explain to other people,
   Who have had parents, not only those
   Who have known their parents, but even to those
   Who have only heard of them, what it is like
   To have been brought up without the *idea* of parents!
   You see, I never was even adopted.
   Mrs. Guzzard brought me up to call her Mrs. Guzzard.
   And when I first began to play with other children
   I couldn't understand what they meant
   When they spoke about their 'father'! As for their mother,
   Well, that seemed another name for another Mrs. Guzzard.
   It didn't seem normal for children to have parents.
   And later, when I came to ask questions,
   Mrs. Guzzard told me that I had no parents.
   I just accepted that; but at a later stage
   I understood what it meant. And then she told me
   That my parents had been unfortunate
   And hadn't been married. That they both were dead,
   And that she would tell me about them one day.
   But I have never asked. In fact I suspect
   That what I believed when I was a child—
   That I had come into the world *without* parents—
   Is something that part of my mind still believes.
   It takes the form of not wanting to think about it.
   I had much rather not know who were my parents.

[1] Cf. the first chorus in *The Family Reunion, Collected Plays*, p. 63.

SIR C.   But tell me, how did you think you were provided for?

S.   I understood that there was a sum of money
In the lawyers' hands, that was just sufficient
For my education, and to get me started.

SIR C.   Did it ever strike you that your education
Was on a rather more expensive scale
Than Mrs. Guzzard's way of living?

S.   Yes, there was a contrast. Both my schools
Must have been expensive. Of course I got a scholarship
To Oxford. But I had my allowance as well.

SIR C.   But did it never strike you that if the funds you speak of
Were so limited as that, it might have been more sensible
To have had a more . . . frugal education—
Say, at a grammar school—and have something left over?

S.   No, I never thought of that. Mrs. Guzzard always talked,
From as long as I remember, about the importance
Of the best education for a good start in life.

SIR C.   But did it never occur to you
That there might be no point in such an education
With advantages more than just a good education
Unless somebody had made further plans for you
When you went into the world?

S.   No, that did not occur to me.

SIR C.   And did you never draw any comparison
Between the kind of life you had at school
And your life in the holidays with Mrs. Guzzard?

S.   No. I think I just took everything for granted.
Of course, when I first went to stay with other boys,
I noticed a difference. But I never took them home with me.
Not that I thought of being ashamed of it:
But I was naturally rather a solitary.
I got on well enough with other boys,
But I wasn't really very interested in them.

SIR C.   And if you learnt your parentage, would it be a shock to you?

S.   I had rather not know.

SIR C.   You are afraid, I think,
Because you want to know. Because you want to pretend
That you do not want to know. You *must* want to know.
You have no reason to be ashamed of it.

S.   You've no reason to say that I might be ashamed of it!
You think I want parents, because you had parents:
But if you've never had them, then you don't want them.

SIR C.   When you are married you will want to have parents
For the sake of your children.

S.   I haven't thought of marriage.

The Confidential Clerk

SIR C. I'm very glad to hear it. But the time will come.
Believe me, Slingsby, it's best that you should know.
It's impossible now to leave you in the dark.
Otherwise, everything becomes completely senseless.
Slingsby, haven't you realised that I am your father?

S. No! No! You mustn't be my father!
Has all your kindness been just a cunning trap
To lead me into a doubt and deception
For the pleasure of torturing me! Leave me alone!
Why did you get me here?

SIR C.   You are not responsible
For what you say now. And you recognise
That what I have told you is nothing but the truth.

S. Yes, I believe you. Of course, I believe you.
And I apologise, sir, for what I just said.
But a little while ago I think I told you
That I seemed to be turning into another person
Through your work, and your world, and I wasn't sure
That I liked becoming somebody different
Though it rather fascinated me. But now
I see that was only a figure of speech,
That the experience I thought I was having
Has only just happened. I *am* a different person!
No, the same person with a different identity.
We can go on changing, we do change of course,
All the time, but against the same background.
I suppose we never recognise ourselves
Except in relation to something that is permanent.
But now I'm like an actor who's walked on to the stage
And finds that he is in another theatre,
With a different setting and a different company
And a different play. And it's just too much for me.
I beg your pardon. I'm sorry to offend you.
You see, I haven't learned the words for my present part,
I shall have to learn them. Meanwhile . . .

SIR C. Meanwhile, I think I had better leave you.
I am sorry, Slingsby, to put you to this—
What you call torture. I imagined this scene
A long time ago. I believe I have been repeating
Words that I composed for the imaginary scene.
It's a shock for me too, to get another answer
That [sic] the one I had assigned to you. That's my own fault.
But we know the position, and we must both face it.
Slingsby, I'm sorry. But remember this:
That your new identity is your true identity;
You will have to live in it, as I have lived in mine,

259

And you will be content with it, as I . . . have been content.
For the moment, I must ask you not to speak of this
To anyone—and not to Mrs. Guzzard.
s.   Whom have I to discuss this with?
I shall not speak to Mrs. Guzzard—or anyone.
SIR C.   You had better go now. To the piano.
And I shall go and sit in front of a Chinese jar.
(*Exit* SLINGSBY)

(Curtain)

(Ur-Clerk)

I also print in full the scene between Lucasta and Slingsby at the beginning of the second Act. This scene is emotionally the most powerful in the play, and it is of absorbing interest to compare the earliest version with the final one. In the *Ur-Clerk*, the relationship has not advanced so far, and is less delicately treated. Slingsby has thought that Lucasta was Claude's mistress. She is less profoundly studied; and her reaction of hurt pride when Slingsby is so taken aback by finding out that she is Claude's daughter is harsher because not preceded by the discovery of their mutual loneliness. More, I think, is added to the play at this point than at any other, by the subsequent revisions.

Act II. Scene i.

(The flat in the mews. Late afternoon. SLINGSBY is seated at the piano. Enter LUCASTA.)
L.   Good evening, Slingsby.
s.   Good evening, Lucasta.
L.   Miserable weather, isn't it?
s.   I suppose it is. But I haven't been out,
Except to cross over to the office and back again.
L.   Well, Slingsby, if you can't say you're *pleased* to see me,
You might at least say you're *surprised* to see me,
As this is the first time I've ever been here.
I *had* been waiting to be invited—
But as the invitation has never been issued
I've given up expecting. And so I've just come.
s.   But of course I'm delighted.
L.   I heard you playing,
So I crept up quietly. And then you stopped.
You must have heard me coming. Don't you care for an audience?
s.   I didn't know who it was. But I would have stopped anyway.
I'm not really used to playing to an audience:
I've never played except to . . . amuse myself.

260

The Confidential Clerk

L. Then it's time you learned how to amuse other people.
Why do you want to keep your music to yourself?
I'm afraid you're not used to having ladies visit you—
I believe you're quite shocked! But it's perfectly proper;
And it's time that somebody took you in hand
And taught you how to behave. For instance,
After saying how delighted you were to see me—
And you shouldn't have forced me to drag that out of you—
You should instantly have offered me a cocktail.
And then you should have asked me if I was free for dinner.

S. Oh. Are you free for dinner?

L.   No, of course not, stupid.
I'm engaged this evening. But what about the cocktail?

S. I'm sorry. I'm afraid I haven't the materials,
And I shouldn't know how to mix them if I had.
But I have got some sherry. Would you like some sherry?

L. Well, that's better than nothing. Even a glass of sherry
Will create an illusion of hospitality.
You know, Slingsby, the first few times I saw you
I thought you very charming. You've disappointed me.

S. I'm awfully sorry. Tell me what to do about it.

L. The annoying thing is that you're still very charming
When you forget yourself. But that's not enough!
A man ought to know how to appear to be interested
All of the time. Perhaps you're just lazy.
But I don't think it's that.

S.   But you've lunched and dined with me
Several times.

L.   Yes, and who proposed it?
You've always waited for me to ask you;
And you left it to me to choose the restaurant,
And then you expected me to do the ordering . . .

S. But I wanted you to have what you liked.

L.   The wrong approach.
You ought to pretend that you *know* what I like,
That you'd planned the whole dinner out beforehand
To give me what I liked. Don't you understand
That it doesn't matter whether I like it:
What matters is that you should choose it *for* me
Or make the waiter think so. You must try to remember
That a woman is always very conscious of the waiter
And how the man with her impresses the waiter:
The food doesn't matter, so long as you pretend
To be very critical.

S.   I've a great deal to learn.

L. If you took me to the same place twice a week,
    You'd still look as if you'd never been there before.
    Some men can behave as if they owned the place
    On their second visit. And the waiters like that.
    But that's enough for the present about restaurants:
    I'll not dine with you again until you invite me
    And choose your own restaurant. And remember
    That when you ring up to reserve a table
    You'd better pretend to be your own secretary—
    It'll give you more confidence.

S.   Are there many other things
    That I ought to try to learn?

L.   Oh yes, thousands.
    For one thing, because you're so mad about music,
    You should have urged me to come with you to concerts,
    Or ballet or opera.

S.   But only last week . . .

L. You offered me an American musical.

S. Because you said you were keen to go and see it.

L. Yes, of course I wanted to see it,
    But not with you.

S.   Why not with me?

L. Because you don't like them. Do you think it's any compliment
    To take a woman to something she likes
    When she knows you don't like it? That's not a compliment,
    It's just being . . . patronising. You ought to try
    To educate me.

S.   But it didn't occur to me
    That you wanted to be educated.

L.   Of course I don't.
    And you can't educate me. But you ought to want to try.
    You know I haven't a note of music in me.

S. But don't concerts bore you?

L.   Of course they bore me.
    But there are compensations for that kind of boredom.
    The flattery makes up for it, full and brimming over.
    The fact is, you're not interested in me.

S. That's not true. You interest me very much.
    I've never known anybody like you.

L. The smallest compliments thankfully received.
    I suppose you'll say next, I'm an interesting *type*.
    Well, if I'm a type, that's not very interesting.

S. No, I don't regard you as a type.
    One knows by instinct when a person's not a type,
    Even when one doesn't know the type
    To which they would belong if they were typical.

262

L.   What a lovely way of putting it. Wonderfully highbrow.
     I dare say it has no meaning, but I like it.
     Well, I can return the humble compliment:
     I [*sic*] never known anyone like you, either.
     And I'm sure *you're* not a type. You're too odd a fish for that.

S.   We're getting on very well with the compliments.
     But seriously, I think you are very unusual—
     Not in the way that you *think* you are:
     That's only a pose—a kind of self-defense.
     I'm sure you're clever—but not when you think you are.
     I think you're brave—because you're frightened—
     Or else you've been terribly hurt at some time.

L.   What makes you think that?

S.   Because you take the lead.
     Because you never wait for anything to happen.
     You're afraid of what would happen if you left things to themselves.
     You jump—because you're afraid of being pushed.
     I remember very well the first time we met,
     You immediately wanted to give a false impression
     Because you thought I'd get a false impression anyway
     And you preferred it to be one of your own creation
     Rather than wait to see what happened. I hope you don't mind
     What I'm saying—it must seem awfully impertinent.

L.   Slingsby, this is the very first compliment
     You've paid me yet. You're more of a man
     And a cleverer man, than I thought you were.
     I'm beginning to believe that your schoolboy diffidence
     Is only *your* self-defense—against yourself!
     Because you're afraid that if you let yourself go
     You'd smash up everything.

S.   I sometimes want to.
     But I know I never shall.

L.   Some day perhaps you will.
     Oh dear, I'm beginning to like you more than ever.
     Perhaps you'll smash *me* up.

S.   God forbid!
     You shouldn't say such things.

L.   I'll say what I like,
     And it's not in self-defence, on this occasion.
     You know, you did like me very much at first.
     In fact, you've just admitted as much:
     Because I don't think you'd have been so observant
     If you hadn't been interested. The queer thing is
     That when I was *trying* to rattle you
     You weren't frightened, really. But when I was nice to you

263

You began to shy off. *Something* frightened you,
And I'm determined to get to the bottom of it.

s. Perhaps I see what you mean. But you mustn't think . . .
I mean, you don't quite understand the position . . .
I mean, it's nothing personal, to do with you . . .
Well, not exactly. What I've never understood
Is my own situation in this household:
Why I'm here—and what is expected of me.

l. You know you're Claude's white-headed boy. He's all over you.
Anyone can see that. As for your situation,
It's a great deal more satisfactory than mine,
If you only knew. Excuse me, Slingsby;
I don't want to hurt your feelings—
But there's such a lot you don't know, Slingsby.
I know what you *think*: I guessed that at once.
I'm going to tell you what you've been thinking;
But what I want to know is, how you came to think it.

s. I don't know what you're driving at.

l.   Oh yes you do.
Something gave you the idea that I was Claude's mistress.
Now, don't bother to deny it! *I* don't mind!
It rather amused me to let you think it,
And then see how you would behave. Very nicely.
Oh, of course I could see you were horrified
To find yourself involved in such a wicked world.
You have such a respectable background
And you've lived a sheltered life. Anyone can see that.
I've had to fight my way. So I didn't mind.
And also, of course, you were terribly anxious
To be loyal to your kind employer.

s. I've never been so pleased with this employment
As you seem to think. It's very different
From any sort of life that I had wanted.

l. I'm sorry. I'm afraid that sounded rather beastly;
But I didn't mean, I really didn't, Slingsby,
That you cared so much about holding your job
And keeping on the right side of the boss.
But I think you did feel a sense of loyalty
Even to Claude. He's not at all your sort.
I don't know anything whatever about you,
But you do seem to come from a decenter world
Than I've ever known. But what really matters
Is that this has put you off me completely.
You don't want to touch the sort of person
You think I am. Now answer yes or no—
I can tell if you're lying.

This *is* what has made you shy away from me.
But *why* did you think that I was Claude's mistress?
Was that the only way in which you could explain me?

S. Well, I didn't think . . . I mean, I didn't know
What to think . . .

L.   Was it due to anything
That Claude said about me?

S.   Nothing he said about you.
In fact, he's said almost nothing about you —
Except in connection with your finances.

L. Well then, it *was* due to something he said.

S. Sir Claude did certainly make it clear to me
That he didn't approve of my seeing too much of you.
He didn't say why. But I got the impression
That he was embarrassed because he couldn't tell me.
But please don't think I drew any conclusions.

L. Oh, Slingsby, how absurd you are!
It's one of the traits that make you rather lovable.
But it makes me very angry with Claude:
What right has he to be ashamed of me?

S. I don't understand. It never struck me for a moment
That he was ashamed of you.

L.   So Claude considers
That I'm not good enough for his . . . adopted son—
For that's what you are, for all practical purposes.
Well, if I'm not good enough, whose fault is that?
But Slingsby, tell me, now that I've told you
That I'm *not* Claude's mistress, and never have been,
Does that make things any better? Do you think you could like me?

S. You know I like you. You know I've been miserable,
Under this constraint. It's such a relief
That it makes me feel a little light-headed.
But there's still the problem of why Sir Claude
Doesn't want me to see too much of you.
Lucasta, can you explain that?

L.   I can, indeed.
It makes me laugh. And at the same time
Very angry with Claude. What a hypocrite!

S. What do you mean?

L.   You'd have to know eventually.
Aren't you supposed to be the confidential clerk?
Now, Slingsby, be prepared for the worst.
Anyway, I'm sure that everyone else knows—
Except for Lizzie, and if she doesn't know
It's because she's not interested. If she ever knew,

It would have slipped her mind. No, Slingsby;
I'm not Claude's mistress. I'm only his daughter.

s. His daughter!

L.   Really, Slingsby!
You are the most extraordinary creature!
I believe you're more shocked to learn I'm his daughter
Than you were when you thought that I was his mistress.

s. Oh, no, not shocked . . . but I am surprised.
And I begin to see . . .

L.   You begin to see
Why Claude doesn't think me good enough for his boy.
Claude's ashamed of me. Now *you're* ashamed of me.

s. I, ashamed of you?

L.   Yes, ashamed of me!
It's a pity you haven't a little more imagination,
And a little less sense of respectability.
You've never thought what it's like to be a bastard,
And wanted by nobody. My mother didn't like me—
She's dead, now, anyway. I didn't like her.
I can't imagine why Claude ever liked her,
Or why she liked him. I don't believe they did.
Claude has just accepted me like a debit item
Always in his cash account. I don't like myself.
I don't like the person I've forced myself to be;
And I liked you because you didn't like that person either,
And I thought you really liked the real kind of person
That I know I am. I suppose that flattered me.
It had never happened before. And I thought:
Now perhaps, if someone else sees me
As I am, I might become myself.

s.   Oh, Lucasta.
I have seen you like that. I . . . do want to help you . . .

L. I don't want your help. I don't want to be pitied.
I thought, when I told you what I did just now,
That everything would become all right.
Why, I *postponed* telling you, just for the fun of it,
Because I was so happy in anticipation;
I thought, I will go on letting him think it
Just a little longer. It will be so wonderful
All in a moment. And now there's nothing,
Nothing to look forward to. It's worse than ever.
Just when you think you're on the point of release
From loneliness, then loneliness swoops down upon you
And in getting out you go further in,
And you know for the first time that there's *no* escape.
Well, I'll be going.

266

S.   You mustn't go yet.
Lucasta, believe me, there's something else
That I want to explain. Only, I can't, yet . . .
Something about myself . . . I mean, I promised Sir Claude—
L. I don't believe you have anything to explain
That could explain anything away. I shall never
Never forget the look on your face
When I told you that Claude was my father.
I may be a bastard, but I have some self-respect.
I think I told you I have a dinner engagement.
S. But don't go like that! . . .

(Ur-Clerk)

In the *Ur-Clerk*, Sir Claude does not appear in the second Act. Its latter half, after B. has come in and taken Lucasta away with him, is a duologue between Slingsby and Lady Elizabeth. This leaves too much of the plot to be unravelled in Act Three, which has three scenes, and even so leaves Lucasta entirely out of the picture. I remember that many of the discussions which Eliot and I had in his little study at the back of the flat in Carlyle Mansions, Chelsea, where he lived with Hayward, were concerned with keeping all the characters alive throughout the play. We finally managed to have every member of the household in every Act, with the exception of Eggerson in Act Two; and he was kept in the audience's mind by Colby's references to his garden and Sir Claude's plan to have him at the meeting next day.

The first scene of Act Three, in the *Ur-Clerk*, consists of the rapprochement between Sir Claude and Lady Elizabeth; they agree to adopt Slingsby as son of one or the other. Next day, in scene 2, Slingsby is presented with this situation, but does not find himself able to accept their solution:

S. I'm afraid I don't yet understand either of you,
Or what you want. If I am the son of either of you—
I take it that there is no doubt
In either of your minds, I am either your son
Sir Claude, or else I am Lady Elizabeth's—
There is no doubt of that?
C.   Yes, that much is certain.
S. Then I am not the son of the other.
And in either case, there is a parent missing.
Please don't think that I want to make matters
Any more difficult than they are. Already

The Confidential Clerk

It's difficult enough for me, who have never had parents
And, if I may say so, never wanted parents,
To find myself suddenly having two parents
And having to try to prepare myself
For two more parents.

C.   That is just the situation
Which we wish to avoid. The two other parents—
From your point of view, I mean: a debating point—
For of course there is really only one third parent . . .
One of them is real and one imaginary.
But Lady Elizabeth . . . my wife . . .

LADY E.   "Your mother."

C.   Quite right. Your mother and myself . . . your father
Want to regard you as our son.
We propose to adopt you as our son:
Because, after all, you would have to be adopted
To be the son of whoever is not your parent.

S.   But don't you want to know whose son I am?

C.   But I do know. And . . .

LADY E.   So does your mother.

S.   But don't either of you want to know which is right?

C.   I know which is right.

LADY E.   And so does your mother.

S.   And which must I believe?

C.   Believe us both.
That is the sacrifice we both are making;
That is the sacrifice that you too must make,
For the sake of all our happiness.

LADY E.   Oh Slingsby!
You can so easily make *three* people happy
Or three people desolate.

S.   But somewhere in the darkness,
Crouching to emerge, at the inconvenient moment,
There must be the truth.

                                      (*Ur-Clerk*)

The last long scene of the play brings Eggerson back to Sir Claude and Lady Elizabeth, and heralds the arrival of Mrs Guzzard. While Eggerson is fetching her, there is a touching moment in which husband and wife decide that

                    if we cannot share a son
We can share the desolation.

The desolation which they do in fact share is caused, not so much by Mrs Guzzard's denial to both of them of the physical paternity

268

of Slingsby as by his denial of any meaning to such a relationship.
This was later transferred to the end of Act Two, where it assumed
a form less harsh than Slingsby's speeches in the *Ur-Clerk*:

s. Whose son do I want to be? I will tell you.
    I was brought up to be nobody's son:
    I was used to that. I was perfectly contented,
    I wasn't ashamed, and I wasn't interested.
    I was ready to make the sort of life I could
    With the sort of brains I had. I know, Sir Claude;
    I suppose I ought to be more appreciative
    Of all that you did for my education,
    And I hate to be ungrateful. But it seems to me now
    That my education was not for my own sake
    But for yours—for what you wanted to make of me!
    Someone like yourself. If that was what you wanted,
    How do you think you could make me like yourself
    When I had never known you as a child?
    A few months ago, I had never even heard of you!
    You brought me into a world that was then strange to me
    And where I don't belong. And now, at twenty-five,
    You want the relationship of father and son—
    When it is much too late. Sir Claude, I am sorry,
    But, whoever I am, I cannot feel that I'm your son,
    And I know I never will. And somehow, that's worse:
    To know I am your son, and to know that it's *meaningless*.
LADY E. But a mother, Slingsby, that is different.
    There is always a tie between mother and son
    Even when they have lost each other.
s. No, Lady Elizabeth, the position is the same
    Or crueller. Suppose I *am* your son.
    It is merely a fact. It is better not to know the fact
    Than to know the fact and know that it is meaningless.
    Twenty-five years ago, then you might have been my mother,
    But you chose not to be. We must take the consequences.
    Twenty-five years ago, the fact that you were my mother—
    If that is the fact—was a living fact:
    Now it is a dead fact, and out of dead facts
    No relations grow. You were my mother,
    Or Sir Claude, perhaps, was my father:
    I don't care which it was. If you want me now:
    I can only say, you both began from the wrong end.
    You should have made me *feel* what it was like to be your son
    Before you laid claim to me as a son.
    Now, all that you have done, between you,
    Is to make me aware that I am fatherless

And motherless. And if either of you
Is my parent, then I am fatherless,
And motherless, for always. And now, I *want* a father
And I know I shall never have had one. I even wish—
It came into my mind a long time ago—
I hope you won't mind my saying, Mr. Eggerson:
I wanted you for a father.

E.   I don't mind, Mr. Simpkins.
In fact, you made me think, sometimes,
Of Harold . . . I mean, my son who died.

The lines in which Slingsby wants Eggerson as father are scored out; it was too crude a way of saying what was later conveyed more delicately; but it is a significant indication of Eliot's thinking.

Mrs Guzzard has been Sir Claude's mistress, and has positively affirmed, in writing, that he was Slingsby's father: she has 'tricked' them both:

G.   You are not his father.
C.   So you deceived me!
G.   So I deceived you. Yes, I deceived you.
C.   But why did you write to say I was his father?
     I have your letter still.
G.   Yes, I wrote that.
E.   Mrs. Guzzard, excuse me for asking the question;
     But it is relevant to our problem;
     Who *was* Mr. Simpkins' father?
S.   It is highly relevant to the problem.
     Now, I want to know who was my father.
G.   My husband, Guzzard.
C.   Then why did you trick me?
G.   Yes. I did trick you. I am sorry, Sir Claude.
     I don't ask you to forgive me. But I ask you to remember
     That my lifetime's plans have now come to nothing:
     So I have my catastrophe, as you have yours.
     My husband was a good deal older than I.
     I was not a very good wife to him, I fear.
     Somehow, we never expected to have children . . .
S.   What was my father?
G.   He was a verger.[1]
S.   A verger!
G.   Of St. Barnabas. In the suburb where we lived then . . .

                                (*Ur-Clerk*)

[1] The only mention; in the synopsis and all subsequent texts, 'the organist'.

So Slingsby wants to be a verger too; and there is a vacancy in Eggerson's parish at Joshua Park. The pattern completes itself; but the parallel between Slingsby and Sir Claude does not include the creative element. He sums it up:

c. *My* father made my bed for me, and I must lie in it.
    I wanted to be *my* father over again—to Slingsby,
    And he wants to go the way of *his* father:
    And I dare say he's right. Perhaps we're all right—
    In one context or another.

B., who has come in with Lucasta to announce their engagement, learns that he is Lady Elizabeth's son. Cheerfully, he takes everyone off for a luncheon party—except Slingsby and Mrs Guzzard who go back to Teddington.

So ends the *Ur-Clerk*.

The development of the plot can be followed, stage by stage, through the notes, in typescript with manuscript additions, which the author made on his various recensions.

THE FIRST ACT

First, there are notes for changes between the first draft (*CC*/1D, a re-typing with a few emendations of the *Ur-Clerk*) and the second rough (*CC*/2R). Lady Elizabeth is eliminated from the opening. The Act is in two scenes instead of three:

The Office

Act I sc. 1: Sir Claude and Eggerson. The conversation discloses (a) that E. had seen Lady E. off to Lausanne the evening before; the reasons for her going (b) the approaching interview, with hints that C. and E. know more about S. and Mrs. G. than appears (c) something of Lady E's character for which S. is to be prepared. S. and Mrs. G. are shown in (MAID). Organist: he must have had some lessons (should he have been away at school or at day-school (St. Paul's) so as to have been taught by local organist?) C. takes Mrs. G. away for a private conversation, leaving S. with E. Some preliminary conversation about teaching him his job... Enter Lucasta, and later Kaghan, as before; K. taking l out to lunch, and E. taking S. how long?

Act I sc. ii: The same room, ~~two weeks~~ later. Enter E. as before, as S. is studying some papers. Similar conversation as in previous draft. Enter Sir C. (new conversation.) Enter Lucasta, who has chucked new job (probably an out-of-town job). She expects S. to take her out to dinner. Sir C. disturbed. Hint that he has supposed she was *au mieux* with K., and not pleased to find that she is turning her interest to S. *Sur ces entrefaites*, enter Lady E. (same surprise). They are all to dine at the Herbal Restaurant?

> Can I at this point get rid of L. Lady E. (having sent E. away early in the scene) and have the conversation between C. and S.? In that case, Act II in S's flat as before.

The following notes in manuscript probably represent a later reconsideration of this rough. Note that Lady Elizabeth 'should be made less confused in mind in this version', which is doubtless the second draft.

I. i (formerly scenes i and ii)
Sir C. and Egg. conversation discloses (1) the new clerk about to arrive; (2) his paternity; Egg. not to let on that he knows. Lady E. not to be told yet who he is. This brings in (a) Lady E's absence, (b) her addiction to cures, (c) her oddities, (d) her maternal instinct and her lost son.
Enter S. who is treated so as to make him believe that Egg. does not know. Sir C. leaves.
Conversation as before. Lucasta. Kaghan. (omit discussion of nature of business between S. and Egg.). L. mentions K. casually as her fiancée [*sic*]

I. ii Egg. enters as before. Some indication of S's interest in L. Sir C. enters. Lady E. enters (she has merely changed her ticket—shows what Dr. Rebmann has done for her. She shd. be made less confused in mind in this version. Scene between S. and C. bringing out their similarity of tastes. But difficulty of regarding C. as his father.

N.B. Fact that Egg. knows S's paternity from *beginning* must alter his tone to S. somewhat.

There is a sheet of 'Suggestions' on the play made by me on 26 February 1953, of which the *Alternative Act I* must belong to this moment in the play's evolution:

Sir C. has sent for E. because of a mysterious telegram from Lady E. from Zurich (here comes in the Lausanne/Zurich passage); something about 'flying home' which is metaphorical not factual. Sir C. wants E. to meet her because Colby is not yet up to it, or cannot be expected to meet her alone for the first time. They fill in the time till E. must go to the airport in talking on how Lady E. will react to C. (N.B.: here it is revealed that Sir C. thinks C. his son). C. has been in office two months.

C. now returns from visit to the City office; surprised to see E.; confident on the business side—finding he can do that: but disturbed when he hears Lady E. is coming; the personal relationships are his difficulty. Sir C. leaves them, and C. asks E. about Lady E.

The Confidential Clerk

This is the first suggestion for making the Act a single continuous scene; the rest of the plan remains as in the second draft. The author makes his own notes in typescript for the third rough, in which Colby has acquired his final name:

Early afternoon. Sir Claude and Eggerson. Conversation discloses: Egg. (retired) has come up by appointment to go to meet Lady E. at Northolt at 4.25. Reference to its not being suitable to send Colby his successor whom she knows nothing about. Reference to how Colby has been getting on, to Egg's garden etc., to the flat in the mews. Has Egg prepared Colby for Lady E? (gives some indication of Lady E's character). Mrs E. and the Eggs' son must be mentioned. Finally, do you propose to tell her that C. is your son? Must also explain the disappointed musician. To Lady E's child. Adoption. Teddington? (Mustn't say 'Teddington' in front of Lady E.)

Enter Colby, who has been to the City. Sir C. leaves. Egg and Colby discuss Lady E. Perhaps some of the description of Claude can be woven into account of Lady E. Ref. to Kaghan's position.

Enter Kaghan and Lucasta. 'Enter B.K. Introducing Lucasta.' 'Eggy, I've lost my job.' Kaghan salutes Colby, showing that they are on friendly terms, have dined etc. K and L leave (for tea?) Colby and Egg talk briefly about Lucasta. Egg says it's time he was off (in the car) to Northolt. Enter Lady Elizabeth.

Conversation much as before. Lady E. leaves in same way. Egg says there is no need for him any longer, he will slip out and buy some gardening things on his way home. Ref. to Mrs. E's interest in Colby. Claude and Colby as before.

Meanwhile, in the second rough there has already been one fundamental change. Slingsby already knows that Claude is his father. The following passage which ends the Act will indicate the effect. Though much of it is afterwards modified or omitted, the study of the relationship has much bearing on the way the play is meant to be interpreted:

SIR C.   Some day, if you will,
    I will show you my collection.
S.[1]   Thank you, sir.
C. And some day, perhaps, you will let me hear you play.
S. I believe I could.
C.   You see, my boy,
    We have a lot in common. I am sorry
    That you should have to inherit from me
    The same defeated genius. But it draws us together,
    Doesn't it?

[1] In this scene I have incorporated the author's manuscript emendations.

s.   Yes, Sir Claude.
It's very strange. It was strange already—
Our relationship. But it's stranger now.
Stranger than you think. Strangest of all,
That I can only address you as 'Sir Claude'.

c. You cannot, even now, call me 'father'
When we are alone together. That's natural.

s. Somehow it has become still more difficult.

c. I shouldn't mind, if it's easier, your calling me 'Claude'
As . . . as other young people do. It wouldn't matter now
Even in public . . . well, in the household.

s. No, I couldn't call you 'Claude'. Not yet,
Or not unless the relationship were different.
I don't want to hurt you. But this is too important
For us, to be anything but honest.
I must try to explain. First of all,
I've only come to know you very recently . . .

c. But I have known *you* for a very long time:
And watched over you, though you did not know it.

s. I know, Sir Claude, I appreciate that.
But can that alone constitute a relationship?
No, is it really different on one side from the other?
As a child, I knew nothing about my . . . paternity;
And then, when I was told, and I knew I had a father,
'Father' was a kind of algebraic symbol
Which merely stood for some unknown quantity.
†Have I been more to *you* than a symbol in algebra?
Please don't think I bore any resentment
Against this unknown father—or against my mother
Whom I never knew. It was not like that at all.
The name stood for something mysterious and longed for;
But when we met, I was disappointed—
Oh, I don't mean disappointed in *you*!
You were what I expected, in a sense:
My disappointment was with myself,
The absence in me of all the feelings
I had hoped for, though I did not know what they would be.
I found that to me you were Sir Claude Mulhammer,
An important man in the world of business,
A kind man, anxious to advance my fortunes—
A patron, not a father.

c.   But the talk we've been having,
Doesn't the likeness of our temperaments,
And of our destinies, bring us together?

s. It brings us together—or *would* bring us together,

† This line is in the author's hand.

274

If it wasn't for the fact that you were my father!
I really believe I could love you as a patron
Or as a friend—if you were not my father.
There's something else—I don't know what it is—
Something lacking. The lost father
Who was missing in the years of childhood
When he was wanted, can't be replaced now.
Those years are gone for ever. And I believe
It has nothing to do with temperament and tastes,
With sympathy and understanding:
A man might never understand his father
And the father might never understand his son;
They might misunderstand each other cruelly—
And yet have the bond of father and son.
I am bound to you by gratitude
And . . . similarity of temperament:
But somehow, that is not what is essential.
I don't know what the essential is
Because I have never had the experience.
But I know, Sir Claude, and I am very sorry,
That I could only regard you as a father
If you were not my father.

C.   It's my own fault.
S.   I know that I'm hurting you, sir, and I know
That I hate myself for hurting you.
C.   You mustn't think of that.
It's I have hurt myself. You have, if you choose,
Your grievance against me
S.   No, sir, I have none.
C.   Let me try to explain what I mean by that.
I planned it all so carefully, from the beginning!
I had already abandoned the hope
Of becoming a craftsman. Had I the right to do that?
Perhaps I should have tried, and found my own failure
Instead of yielding to my father's pressure.
I did not want to follow the course my father took:
I wanted you to have your musical training
As that was what you wanted. If you could have had
A successful career in the world of music
I should have been happy. If you could not,
I wanted you to find it out for yourself
And make your own decision.
S.   That is what I did.
You gave me every opportunity. And then,
I found out for myself my limitations
And when you offered to take me into business

I made my own decision again and accepted.
You know that.

c.   I know it. *That* was not my mistake.
But had I not already gone into the business
I should have been free. Had I married your mother
It would have meant poverty for all of us—
I say, for all of us, though that wouldn't have prevented
Your mother's dying when you were born.
Had I married her, I should have been disinherited.
But your mother would not marry me. She said it was for your sake.
Or was it for my sake? I shall never know.
She persuaded me that it was better for you,
For your future, to be illegitimate than poor.
She knew I would provide for you. But was it better?
It seems that in giving you your education
And your career—for you *have* a career,
I am convinced of that—I have robbed you of a father.
Until this moment, I never had a doubt
That I had taken the right course.

s.   You couldn't have known.
Perhaps we shall never know what was the right course.
Perhaps life is like that.

c.   We must live in doubt.

s. Well, sir, perhaps you would prefer
That I went away—found a place for myself
In some other business—as it must be business.

c. Oh no, no, Colby, I can't part from you.
I can wait. Meanwhile our contacts
Will be such as you can bear—not such as I intended.
We can come to be friends, at least, Colby,
Since we have so much in common. We are both divided men.
We can meet, surely, in that understanding,
As successful men of business, and disappointed artists
We can form new ties . . .
                   I shall go to my room
And sit for a while with a Chinese jar.

s. Excuse me, sir, but I must remind you
That you have that meeting in the City
This afternoon. You asked me to prepare
Some figures for you. I have them ready.

c. Oh, yes, that meeting. We must run through the figures.

                        (*Curtain*)

                (CC/2R; cf. *Collected Plays*, pp. 238–40)

The Confidential Clerk

The notes for changes in Act Two at the same stage show the intention 'to represent the friendship of Colby and Lucasta as having developed rather farther'. The various explanatory parentheses all indicate movement towards the final version. But there is now no duologue between Colby and Lady Elizabeth, a complete reversal of the situation in the *Ur-Clerk*.

To represent the friendship of Colby and Lucasta as having developed rather farther, Colby should be shown as just having finished playing to her. It is to be assumed that this is not her first visit to his flat. Alternatively, if we are to introduce Lady E. on the pretext of making an inspection of the flat since its redecoration, this might be L's first visit also, but by invitation, to hear the new piano—so it will be the first time he has ever played to her. Purpose of each visitor: to see the new flat. Perhaps each should say so in almost the same words on entering: i.e. B., Lady E. and Claude in that order.

First, conversation between Colby and L. Cut down her advice on behaviour, and make it retrospective: 'You are beginning to learn how to behave' (but at the same time suggestion that he belongs in a better world than she does). Develop exchanges about their history and background. Increasing current of emotion: a more poetical bit of dialogue here. L. suggests that (diminuendo) Colby's first standoffishness might have been due to his suspecting her of being Claude's mistress. Colby says he never supposed anything at all: whole set-up so strange to him that he didn't draw any inferences. She then feels that they are getting on so well that its only honest to tell him the truth: a kind of test of Colby (seeing that he was so innocent that he didn't even suspect her of being Claude's mistress—as most men she knew would have done (but not B. who had guessed the truth long ago) to find out whether he will be shocked by that, or whether, although shocked (from her estimate of him she expects him to be shocked) he has fallen for her far enough for him to accept it.

(Here, there is a question of the order of the conversation: whether the exchange of information should not follow the more lyrical scene for which they are prepared, Colby by the discovery that he can play to someone (L. pretty ignorant of music, as she will tell us) and enjoy it, Lucasta by the implied compliment of his playing to *her*.)

Lucasta interprets the 'shock' of which Colby shows signs, as the kind of 'shock' that she feared. In humiliation, lashes out at him. *Sur ces entrefaites*, enter B. as before, and then Lady E. B. has come 'to see the new flat'; Lady E. to see whether the decorations and furnishings fulfil her requirements. She picks up a framed photograph, with some curiosity, and asks who it is. Colby explains that it is his Aunt, Mrs. Guzzard. (NOTE: Perhaps Colby's supposed mother was NOT Mrs. G's sister. This would allow him to lead Lady E. more plausibly to her mistake, by indicating that there was some mystery about his birth. It would also settle Mrs. G. more plausibly as a genteel baby-farmer, making it

277

more natural that B. also should have been under her care). Lady E. shows interest and excitement, but of course cannot announce her supposed discovery to Colby, because of the presence of other people. Enter Claude 'to see Colby in his new flat'. Lucasta and B. are dismissed as before, only Lucasta forces B. to give her dinner (no previous arrangement).

Finally: Colby, Lady Elizabeth and Claude. Lady E. announces to them both that she has found her long-lost son. Curtain falls on a tense moment.

Perhaps the arrangement for confronting Mrs. Guzzard should be made at the end of this Act, so as to prepare the audience for Act III. Colby, in a frenzy much intensified by his misery over Lucasta (n.b. she has pointedly not said goodbye to him on leaving) says a plague on all my parents.

Eggerson must be *mentioned* whenever possible, as he is never on throughout this Act, and everybody feels the need of him at the forthcoming interview. It is important that their dependence on Eggerson must be kept in the audience's mind.

†Why shouldn't Claude and Lady E. enter together?

These are the only notes for Act Two, though the duologue between Colby and Lady Elizabeth was restored when the 'Rough' was written.

THE THIRD ACT

On Act Three, there are several sets of notes, and it is not easy to be sure, as none is dated, in what order they should be placed.

One possibility that is explored is that the Act should open with a scene between Claude and Lucasta. One sheet of notes, directed to the problems which are troubling the author at this stage, reads as follows:

ACT III

Office as in Act I. Several days (how many?) later. Sir Claude alone.

Enter Lucasta. This is the only opportunity of showing relations between Claude and his daughter. She announces engagement to B. Kaghan. Suggests that perhaps Claude would have preferred Colby. Claude tells her Colby is her brother. 'Oh, so that's why...' She proposes to bring B. at lunch time and Claude lunch with them somewhere. Claude says yes, his business should be over by lunchtime.

Let us break off here and look at a fuller version of this section headed *Act III Third Scenario*:

Claude on stage. Enter Lucasta. She announces her decision, and mentions attraction towards Colby. Claude tells her he is her brother. Lucasta says what

† This line is in the author's hand.

a good thing. Otherwise, couldn't have forgiven him; as it is, must apologise to him. Claude admits remote possibility he isn't, and explains about the approaching meeting with Mrs. Guzzard.

Lucasta had come to speak to Colby. Had felt that the last occasion had been unfinished—perhaps there was something he couldn't explain. This leads to Claude's disclosure. Well, I'll be glad to have him as a brother. But what if he isn't my brother. No, we don't need each other—it makes no difference. Rapprochement between Claude and Lucasta.

After explanation of the meeting with Mrs. G. and analysis of Lucasta's feelings towards Colby and B. (neither Claude nor Lucasta takes Lady E.'s pretensions seriously) L. agrees to come back later. On her exit enter Lady E. Trio. Claude explains to Lady E. How should the latter behave?

Despite these detailed studies, the scene between Sir Claude and his daughter seems never to have been written: it does not appear in any of the drafts preserved by Hayward.

It will be noticed that the three scenes of Act Three which are separated by curtains in the *Ur-Clerk* are becoming dovetailed into a single whole. There would seem to have been some vacillation about where the Act-break was to come, for there is a synopsis headed *Act III 2nd scene*.

The opening of this corresponds with the second rough; but later, as will be seen, the alternatives concerning the paternity of Colby are being explored:

> Several days later. The office as in Act I. Claude is seen alone, arranging chairs. Enter Elizabeth. Both very nervous. How shall the meeting be conducted. C. proposes to appoint Eggerson Chairman Where shall every-one be seated? (In the end they probably sit quite differently.)
>
> Conversation between C. and Eliz. Each ready to surrender Colby to the other. But Eliz. mentions his resemblance in character to her, and Claude to him. They discover things about each other's temperament hitherto reciprocally unknown. Growing intimacy between them.
>
> Enter Eggerson. (Is the situation explained to him now, or has he been prepared by a previous talk with Claude?) Eggerson takes command.
>
> Enter Lucasta. (a difficult bit of dialogue here). She announces her engagement to B.—want to be married soon. This is again a different Lucasta from both Act I and Act II, but must cohere with previous appearances. She avows her temporary inclination towards Colby. Claude, startled, informs her that Colby is her brother. This effaces her resentment against Colby, but she explains why they were suited. Elizabeth friendly and almost affectionate towards Lucasta.
>
> Lucasta must then be got offstage: perhaps meeting Colby coming in, on her way out. Is B. waiting downstairs for her? Then some excuse must be prepared for L. and B. coming in again at the right moment.

Claude, Elizabeth, Colby, Eggerson. Enter Mrs. GUZZARD. Cold and dignified. Enquiry (led by Eggerson) must be conducted in a manner not offensive to Mrs. G. Roundabout questions, leading to exposure of possibility (for a moment) that Colby is Eliz. son. Then the question. In what order?

A.   Mrs. G. appears to support Claude. Revelation that B is Eliz. son. This would bring B. and L. back together, and the whole company present at final disclosure. Just as C[laude] is satisfied Mrs. G. asks Colby whether he is satisfied also. He first professes indifference, but then bursts out with the statement that he would prefer to be the son of neither. 'You shall have your wish.'

NO: A. WON'T DO START AGAIN

B.   After questions have made audience more and more uncertain whether Colby is son of Claude or of Eliz. Mrs. G. asks Colby which he prefers. He admits he would rather be son of neither. She grants his wish. Next, dialogue between Mrs. G. and Claude: why did you deceive me?

Difficulty here is weaving in three strands: Colby in search of a father, Claude–Mrs. Guzzard demelé, and Eliz. asking what's become of my child?

Should Colby be son of Mrs. G. or of Mrs. G's sister by the organist who was *not* Mr. Guzzard? He might prefer both of his parents to be dead, so that he could think of them as real parents.

In addition to these notes in synoptic form, there are three pages which wrestle with the problem of paternity, and arrive at the solution incorporated in the finished play. They show the evolution very clearly. The last, headed *Mrs Guzzard's Solution*, summarises the result.

NOTE

In scene ii of this draft[1] there is an intimation of a change which I propose to try out in the next draft of Act III, which ought to be explained.

I am sure that Mrs. Guzzard must continue to be the real mother of Colby, because Colby's attitude towards her should have a correspondence to his attitude to Claude as shown in this scene ii of Act I. Colby's inability to *feel* that Claude is his father, though he has no doubt that he is, is the first twist of the knife. There must be a second twist to drive the knife home, which comes from Colby's being unable to feel towards Mrs. Guzzard as anything but his aunt. Claude has to take his medicine and Mrs. G. must take hers.

BUT if it is Mrs. Guzzard who was the mistress of Claude, then I think the audience will expect some more interesting view of their relationship (what it once was, and how it came to be what it now is) than they can get.

†(I feel that version i of Act III is unsatisfactory in this respect.)

So I propose to try this. Claude believes Colby to be his son by a deceased sister of Mrs. Guzzard (dead in childbirth, probably). But, either the child died

---

[1] We do not know which draft this refers to.

† This sentence is in the author's hand.

with its mother or if preferable there wasn't one. (I think the former is preferable as simpler.) Mrs. G. was about to have a child herself. Mr. Guzzard the Organist having died during her pregnancy. So, as she was on the rocks, and knew all about her sister and Claude, she has the idea of pretending that *her* child was her sister's—in order to provide a supposed father who would support her and the child and give the latter a good start in life. Thus both Claude and Mrs. G. will be making a sacrifice for the future of the child, and in so doing forfeiting the natural relationship of parent and child which can never be recovered.

The problem then is to explain in Act III without taking too much time over it, and to make the substitution† as plausible as possible. Colby will of course have been registered at birth as the son of the Guzzards. Mrs. G. can if necessary provide proof by the fact that the death of Claude's child will have been registered (or what does happen when a woman gives birth to a still-born child and then dies—there must be some record of still-born babies).

B. Kaghan would be a few years older than Colby, and would have been taken in (not formally adopted, because it was the Kaghans who formally adopted him) by the Guzzards during the lifetime of Guzzard.

MRS. GUZZARD'S SOLUTION

Colby

The sister had convinced herself and informed Claude that she was going to have a child. After her death in hospital, the child unborn, a letter comes from Claude to Mrs. G. which makes it clear that Claude . . .

Claude, on hearing that Sister is ill in hospital, assumes that she is in child-bed. Arranges to return at once, finds Mrs. G. with baby (suddenly widowed) and takes for granted that child is his. This gives Mrs. G. the idea of allowing him to believe that it is. Never occurred to him to ask to see birth certificate. She did not deceive him; but allowed him to deceive himself.

Kaghan had been taken in by Mrs. G. several years before. Payments failing, alternative orphanage or the respectable childless neighbours.

Of the many textual variants produced by such a series of recensions it is impossible to give any idea in a single chapter. But it is also made less necessary by the nature of this play.

The Confidential Clerk differs from all the plays that have gone before it in that the poetry is not in the words but in the conception and the characterisation. There are very few moments at which one is aware of Eliot as the maker of immortal phrases; he is just as much the master of words as ever, but the mastery is used strictly for dramatic purposes and no other. The style is unified by the drama. The only time when Eliot the poet is consciously recalled is in the scene between Colby and Lucasta in Act Two—which I find

†Added in the author's hand: 'and the deception of Claude'.

the most humanly moving scene in all his drama; here, the image of the garden and its door, so familiar in earlier work both lyric and dramatic, returns with a new poignancy because of the contrast with the 'dirty public square' of Lucasta's sordid childhood. But we may note that this passage was totally absent from the scene in the beginning, and only appeared as the fulfilment of Eliot's suggestion to himself for 'a more poetic bit of dialogue' in the notes for *CC*/2R.[1]

The notes do not deal with one problem which remained with us right through the period of rehearsals—the ending, after Mrs Guzzard and Colby have left the stage. The lunch-party of the *Ur-Clerk* would certainly not serve to show what Eliot wanted to show—the beginning of a family unity created among these persons of so diverse backgrounds by the events of the play.

The Edinburgh Festival typescript on which we started work in rehearsal had a very brief ending indeed:

(*Exit* MRS GUZZARD, *escorted by* COLBY)
SIR CLAUDE   What's happened? Have they gone? Is Colby coming back?
LADY ELIZABETH   My poor Claude!
LUCASTA   Poor Claude! I'm going to call you Daddy.
       Would you like that, Claude?
SIR CLAUDE   Don't leave me, Lucasta.
       Eggerson! Do you really believe her?
                     (*Curtain*)

(*CC*/Edin.)

But bound among the papers of the third draft in the Hayward collection is a longer version, in typescript but with many corrections in manuscript, which I reproduce: it presumably follows Lady Elizabeth's 'My poor Claude!'

                 Why don't you
LUCASTA   B! ~~You ought to~~ say something!
KAGHAN   I'd like to be of help. But what can I say?
LUCASTA   You know, I think Colby is fonder of you
       Than of any of us. He'd listen to you.
KAGHAN   I don't think that's true. I thought for a time
                     seemed to understand
       That you and he ~~understood~~ each other.
              I've never understood
LUCASTA   ~~I don't understand~~ him at all. But he helped me
       To understand *you*, through not understanding him.
       I can't explain that.

[1] See above, p. 277.

282

KAGHAN   I know what you mean.
   I only saw one side of him really,
   And you saw another. I didn't understand *that*† side
   But I understand you better because of what *you* saw.
   ‡We all wanted him to be something he wasn't.
   Eggers is the only one ~~who knows how to handle him.~~
                              asked nothing
   ~~He's the only one~~ who ~~didn't *ask* anything~~ of him—
   The only one who left him free.
LADY E.   ~~I think that's true!~~
   I think that's true of you and me, Claude.
   We wanted him to be something he wasn't.
   Oh dear, between not knowing what one really wants§ to be
                                                    be
   And thinking that one knows what other people ought to ~~want~~
   One gets
   ~~I get~~ so confused! But I mean to do better.
   You know, Claude, I said I thought that sharing Colby
   Would draw us together? Now I think
        can come closer
   We ~~are closer together~~ through not having him at all!
LUCASTA   There's one thing you said the other day, B.—
                              was a help to me.
   I meant to tell you—which ~~helped me about Colby~~.
        Colby
   You said ~~he~~ was the sort who might chuck it all!
   And go to live on a desert island.
   I didn't understand him any better for that;
   But it told me something about myself—and you.

This evidently led to the version finally played at Edinburgh, which
contained further new material:

SIR CLAUDE   What's happened? Have they gone? Is Colby coming back?
LADY ELIZABETH   My poor Claude!
LUCASTA   B! Can't *you* say something?
KAGHAN   You know, Claude, I think we all made the same mistake—
   All except Eggers . . .
EGGERSON   Me, Mr. Kaghan?
KAGHAN   We wanted Colby to be something he wasn't.
LADY ELIZABETH   I suppose that's true of you and me, Claude.
   Oh dear, between not knowing what other people want of one
   And not knowing what one should ask of other people,
   One gets so confused! But I mean to do better.

† 'side' inserted in the author's hand.   ‡ This line was inserted in the author's hand.
§ 'to be' inserted in the author's hand.

LUCASTA   There's one thing you said the other day, B.—
            You said Colby was the sort who might chuck it all
            And go to live on a desert island.
LADY ELIZABETH   I don't understand about desert islands;
            But Claude, we've got to try to understand . . . our children
                        we should
KAGHAN   And ~~they would~~ like to understand *you* . . .
            I mean, I'm including both of you,
            Claude, and . . . Aunt Elizabeth.
            You know, Claude, both Lucasta and I
            Would like to mean something to you . . . if you'd let us;
            And we'd take the responsibility of meaning it.
LUCASTA   B. That's what I wanted you to say!
            Though I couldn't have told you what I wanted.
            Claude! I'm going to call you Father!
            Would you like that, Claude?
SIR CLAUDE   Don't leave me, Lucasta.
            Eggerson! Did *you* really believe her?
                        (*Curtain*)

                                                    (*CC*/Edin.)

This was slightly reduced in playing, to the version in the printed
text; it shows the effort to establish the new series of relationships
with which the play was to close. This strange family group—
husband and wife, the bastard son of one and the bastard daughter
of the other—is the result of their actions and the basis on which
they must build their future.

Eliot's preoccupation with names and methods of address is
noticeable here, and is insistent throughout the play. Colby in the
first Act refers bewilderedly to 'all those first names!' His puzzlement
about what he should call people is not only a matter of correctness;
names symbolise what they are, like Lucasta's final 'Daddy', changed
to 'Father'. Eliot displays his sense of the importance of names in
The Book of Practical Cats; perhaps he derives it as much from the
unsayable Name of God as from the niceties of the English social
code.

As we drew near to the time of rehearsals, our meetings in the
little study were concerned much with detail which affected stage
presentation. I find pencil-notes arranging that Kaghan and Lucasta
should not enter together for the first time,[1] and asking whether the
setting of Act Two should or should not reflect Lady Elizabeth's
views on colour. Eliot writes on 8 April:

[1] See the result, *Collected Plays*, p. 224.

The Confidential Clerk

I should like to have an afternoon or evening with you as soon as possible on your return. I have now made all the changes we discussed and some others, and I should like to go through the whole text with you from beginning to end and discuss these changes and make sure that our texts are identical.

The text which resulted was that which Sherek had copied for use in the Edinburgh production. During rehearsals, a certain amount of tightening and other alteration took place; and some cuts were made for performance.

It was a great pleasure to work with Eliot on this often difficult task. He would, as always, take his time in making up his mind: but once he was ready to give an answer it was definite and its reasons were clear. He was the last man to regard his lines as sacred; what he wished was that each should serve its purpose. This might not be achieved in quite the same way in performance as on the page, and he would sometimes give leave for a cut in playing which he would restore in the printed text; the reader has more time to look all round a point than the member of the audience. He was equally sympathetic to purely theatrical considerations—the need of each actor for adequate material to 'keep him alive' during a scene, the total playing-time which would be acceptable to the public, the differing conditions such as the 'twice nightly' shows that came into vogue at this time in London on Saturdays. At the same time, he would be firm about any passage which he felt essential to the play's effect or significance.

I have a page of pencilled notes on the characters, evidently taken down from Eliot's description of them in a discussion with me:

CHARACTERS:

Guzzard: grievance against herself and Sir C. Double role —*dea ex machina* and suburban respectable woman. Wants Colby to find himself as the fruit of her marriage, and defeat Sir C. Bitter. Black or dark grey dress.

Eggerson. 'Only real Christian'—innocent, simple, not at all superior. *Stronger in his way than Sir C.* Not in business clothes; dark grey suit. Antiquated bowler. ?Wing collar.

Sir C. Inherited his mastery, deflated in the play, *lived* himself into a role— squeezed himself into it with an effort. 3rd generation of German grandfather. Final line is the blow of losing the illusion. Audience *must* accept Mrs. G's story. Smart, sober. ?double-breasted grey suit—v. well pressed!

Lady E: imposing, yet uncertain of herself. Her strength is breeding, not personal. Dignity. Reserved (B)—therefore appears more matter of fact about him;

unsure of her own feelings, must behave properly in public. Smart or eccentric, expensive. Cameo Corner.[1]

Lucasta. 3 *different aspects.* I an 'act', II real, but fleetingly seen. III realistic, sensible. Up to last act, she and Lady E. have mistaken views of each other.
I tailor-made, hat not showy. II afternoon. III
B has had affectionate adoptive parents. The freest spirit. *Not* to be dressed flashy—correct, conventional City man—*stiff collar.*

Colby, a certain deliberate ambivalence. egotist and ascetic. More informally dressed (not Bohemian).

These were some of the ideas which I communicated to Henry Sherek when we came to cast the play.

Sherek had the ball at his feet in the match for *The Confidential Clerk*. On the front page of the *Sunday Times* for 21 December 1952 appeared the announcement that *The Cocktail Party* had played to close on a million and a half spectators, and that five theatres in New York had offered a home to the new play after its Edinburgh opening. Mr Eliot instantly denied that any such unpatriotic move would be contemplated; but the offers were proof enough that his new play would have a very good kick-off. In fact, before *The Confidential Clerk* opened at Edinburgh it had an assured home at the Lyric in London, with a week at the Theatre Royal, Newcastle-on-Tyne, to break the journey.

Sherek was assisted in this negotiation by the excellent casting which we had achieved. I cannot imagine a better team than the following:

Sir Claude Mulhammer	PAUL ROGERS
Eggerson	ALAN WEBB
Colby Simpkins	DENHOLM ELLIOTT
B. Kaghan	PETER JONES
Lucasta Angel	MARGARET LEIGHTON
Lady Elizabeth Mulhammer	ISABEL JEANS
Mrs Guzzard	ALISON LEGGATT

We started rehearsals on 27 July, and at the end of the fourth week moved to Edinburgh. This time we were to play two weeks at the Lyceum, and were allowed to open on the Tuesday, giving ourselves Monday for dress rehearsals instead of the over-Sunday rush we had with *The Cocktail Party.*

Hutchinson Scott had designed the settings, and had fulfilled to

[1] A shop in Bloomsbury which sold antique and exotic jewellery.

admiration the desire I had expressed, that they should allow freedom to the imagination of the beholder. Though agreeing as a matter of policy to Eliot's demand for conventional realism in *The Cocktail Party*, I had felt that the totally enclosed rooms did not give the play's poetic aspect its proper chance. Eliot's point, that the characters in these modern plays are of the same ilk as those commonly seen on the contemporary stage, having been made, it was now possible to allow scope for, so to speak, a look through or around the rooms in which the action takes place. 'Jay' Hutchinson Scott gave me a library round which one could see into a mysterious depth of shadow, and a mews-flat over the roof of which one could see the evening sky.

Few people were consciously aware of this, because it accorded with a change which was coming over the whole attitude to the theatre. George Devine began operations with the English Stage Company in 1954. This may be called the first wave of the tide that swept away the more rigid conventions of the naturalistic theatre, restoring the freedom of the imagination. Eliot forestalled this tide: he accepted the conventions because his audience would expect to start there, but carried it beyond them; and this was what we tried to reveal.

Against this background, the acting must likewise have a glitter more than naturalistic. The story, as I have said, was elaborated in a way reminiscent of Gilbert or Oscar Wilde, and the verse-rhythm, however unobtrusive as verse, heightened the tone of the dialogue in a way comparable with those writers. In order that the depths beneath should be sensed, the audience must look through this kind of glittering surface to discover them.

The actors were fascinated by this demand and responsive to it; and I regard the English production of this play as the most completely integrated of any that I have made of the modern plays of Eliot.

We opened at the Lyceum on 25 August, and the reaction both of critics and public was enthusiastic. All were entertained—even those who had found *The Cocktail Party* least attractive. And all were left with questions as to the meaning underlying the gay surface. It is characteristic of the reaction that A. V. Cookman's notice in *The Times* contains a whole long paragraph composed of questions. But he thinks that the play is likely to be found brilliantly entertaining even by those who are left wondering what it is all really about . . . Mr. Eliot uses the ancient, the Greek stuff of popular comedy, to his own serious ends. Real people are involved in fantastic situations, but the characters are carefully studied and we are made aware of a meaningful destiny working through their wishes . . .

(26 August 1953)

But Ivor Brown, who had so much disliked *The Cocktail Party*, thinks there is 'no need . . . to sit and ponder what it is all about'. This play is the fulfilment of his prophecy based on *The Family Reunion*:

a light artificial comedy which suggests Oscar Wilde at slightly below best form and reminds one of countless ancient classical plays about mistaken identity and mysterious children who arrive perplexingly on parents' doorsteps and have to be sorted out.

He is still as unsympathetic as ever both to Eliot's view of life and to his claim to be a poetic dramatist:

I am informed that this play like the previous Eliot plays was written in verse. But nobody need be frightened by that for the simple reason that they will not notice it. When the piece is printed for publication no doubt the text will be chopped to resemble poetry, but no poetic diction or poetic melody is discernible in the lines as spoken by the cast.

Brown is writing for the Sunday Theatre Section of the *New York Herald Tribune* (30 August 1953), since of course the play is hot news in the U.S.A. W. A. Darlington follows up his *Daily Telegraph* notice with a corresponding article for the Sunday *New York Times*:

Eliot . . . is now by common consent the most important contemporary writer for the English-speaking stage and from the point of view of technical achievement *The Confidential Clerk* is his best play. Not, let it be clearly stated, his most important play. It is a light comedy and though its undertones are deep they remain undertones. There is here none of the passionate intensity of the earlier Eliot plays and little of their poetic color. Indeed, the ear can hardly detect that the language is different from colloquial prose; only an occasional heightened phrase reminds us that Mr. Eliot's medium after all still is verse.

As a piece for the theatre *The Confidential Clerk* is contrived with masterly skill. Mr. Eliot brings off that miracle which only dramatists of the highest class can work—he takes a hackneyed and unreal theatrical situation such as no merely average writer could hope to get away with and makes us accept it as a basis for serious thought.

(30 August 1953)

The Confidential Clerk

On the way south, Peter Wilsher writes in the *Newcastle Journal* (8 September) of

a packed Monday night house (at the Theatre Royal) and bookings almost the heaviest for straight (and poetic!) plays that the theatre has had in ten years

and is 'struck by [Eliot's] new humanity and sympathy'. In London, a cordial reception heralded a long run at the Lyric in Shaftesbury Avenue; and the author, now 'assured in possession' of himself as a successful dramatist, gave a supper party, arranged for him by John Hayward, at the Savoy after the first performance on 16 September:

> 20 Lancaster Grove
> London, N.W.3
> September 18, 1953

My dear Tom,

The party was a hundred per cent success, as I'm sure you must have felt, and crowned the happiness of an evening which we shall all remember with gratitude. Henzie and I send you our thanks and love.

The reception of the play was so warm and understanding that one couldn't have wished for better: nor indeed did I hope for anything like it from a first-night house.

It has been the greatest joy to work on the play: and I do thank you for the privilege and for all you have done to help me throughout.

I enclose the promised script 'as played on the first night in London', for collation with your text for printing.

Please give John my love and thanks for all his beautiful party-planning. I hope to ring him up today.

> Yours ever,
> *Martin*

> 5 October 1953

Dear Martin,

I ought to have written to thank you for the copy of the text—and indeed for all the work you have done during the past year or two to bring the text, from the first rough drafts, to this condition.

I have, of course, restored some of the excised passages; but for the most part, the amputations seem to me permanently to the good.

You have done a very fine job of production—never anything better. But you know that; and no critic so far has been able to find anything but praise for production and casting and acting.

I should like to look in at the theatre from time to time informally—oh, say two or three times between now and Christmas: largely to avoid giving the company the impression that now the play has been launched successfully, I have lost interest in them. I had thought that I should like to see the play from the wings, as well as prowl about behind the stalls now and then, instead of going to the trouble of getting a seat. Is there any etiquette about that? I mean, do the actors object, having got to this stage, to having the author on their side of the proscenium?

Yours affectionately,

Tom

Shd. like to go some evening or afternoon when you expected to be there.

The play ran at the Lyric till 3 April 1954, and transferred to the smaller Duke of York's for another four weeks. Meanwhile, the author had been ill: he was to find the English winter increasingly hard to weather during the next few years.

Hotel Metropole
Leeds 1
April 30, 1954

My dear Tom,

We are happy to know that you are really better and are now in process of recovery by means of rest. It has been an anxious time, and I'm sure you have been aware of how surrounded you were by the love of friends wishing and praying you back to health. Miss Fletcher[1] has been very good about giving us news, until she herself succumbed to the 'flu: I imagine she must be back at the office by now . . .

We went to the Duke of York's for Wednesday evening, spending most of our time backstage talking to each of our charming company. I had been in earlier to see the show in to its new home. It has fitted in very well there, and the company were in great heart because the 'Last Weeks' notice has brought in excellent houses, composed of what one might describe as your own audience, rather than the type which came to the Lyric after the first few weeks because it is in Shaftesbury Avenue. They were obviously enthralled by the play that night, and the company were happy playing it. It is heartening too to be closing to such fine business, and one feels hopeful that a tour will be possible and successful later . . .

Yours ever,

Martin

But meanwhile, too, the play had been produced in the U.S.A.[2] Sherek had accepted the offer of association with a powerful new group, Producers Theatre, who owned the leases of several Broadway theatres; and he spent many weeks of the autumn in New York assembling a new cast. By this time, it had become impossible to bring over a complete English company, because American Equity had obtained an immigration ruling that not more than 40 per cent

[1] Valerie Fletcher, his secretary since 1950, afterwards his wife.
[2] On all this, see Henry Sherek, *Not in Front of the Children* (Heinemann, London, 1959), pp. 185–201.

of foreign actors would be admitted to the country for any production. Only two of our seven characters, therefore, could be played by British actors.

He started with a piece of great good luck. Ina Claire, most beloved comedienne of the sophisticated audience, had been away from Broadway for seven years. Innumerable offers had failed to tempt her from San Francisco where she lived with her husband William R. Wallace, a wealthy marine lawyer. But the idea of a T. S. Eliot play intrigued her into cabling Sherek in London. She was perfectly suited to the part of Lady Elizabeth, and Sherek had a prize that every producer in New York had been longing for.

Claude Rains as Sir Claude was as great a capture. He made his first successes as a Shaw actor in England, repeating them in America, notably for the Theatre Guild. Settling there, he made a great name in Hollywood films, and had long been an American citizen. Recently, he had been using his fine voice to read the poems of T. S. Eliot, and came to the play with a veneration for its author.

Sherek aimed at getting a cast entirely from the American stage, feeling that this would make for greater unity; but in the event two English players came over. Joan Greenwood, who had already made her mark through British films, had never been seen in person by the American public when she appeared as Lucasta. Newton Blick came over as Eggerson; while Sherek cast a Canadian actor, Richard Newton, as B. Kaghan and Aline McMahon, again a considerable name in films, as Mrs Guzzard. The Colby was Douglas Watson, a southerner who had made a series of successes in juvenile leads notably with Katherine Cornell.

On the morning before my wife and I were to leave for New York, Sherek's manager rang up to say that Ina Claire was coming to London for the day. She had decided that New York could not produce dresses adequate for her needs in the play, had flown to Paris to shop, and was visiting London on the way home in order to meet the author. As Sherek was in New York, would my wife and I entertain them both to lunch?

We settled for Prunier's in St James's. Eliot was somewhat overwhelmed by Miss Claire's voluble complaints about the difficulty of finding anything to wear—Paris had after all proved little more satisfactory than New York. But she had got a red lace dress for the studio scene: 'No man can resist a woman in red lace, can he?' Mr

Eliot said he didn't know. (In the event, the lace dress was replaced by an old favourite from her wardrobe.) But she is a witty talker, and after a while he began to enjoy meeting her sallies with his own quiet and courteous ripostes.

She took it for granted that he would come over for the first night. Eliot, who avoided all such occasions especially in America, said he was sorry, but he would not be there. She was horrified; he was firm. At last: 'If you really won't come, you must send me red roses.' 'That will be my pleasure', he replied. And the roses duly arrived. Miss Claire was touched to observe that they came from the florist who had been most fashionable when the young Eliot left New York thirty years before.

We started to rehearse on 15 December 1954. I quickly found that I had problems, both personal and theatrical, in attempting to create a unified production. Where the English cast had a common tradition which prompted all of them towards a style suited to the play, the American cast came from a variety of backgrounds. Ina Claire had studied with the Comédie Française and played authors such as Maugham and Lonsdale. Rains was an essentially serious actor in the English classical tradition. Douglas Watson was a solid, simple young man who found it difficult to respond to the complexity of Joan Greenwood's acting. Aline McMahon could well portray an oracle, but the paradox of her emergence from a London suburb was difficult to make credible. In short, there was a wide divergence of styles.

We first played New Haven, the home of Yale University, and moved on to Boston, where Harvard and the Eliot family were intertwined. On the Friday of our first week there (15 January) we went to a huge cocktail party given by the Signet Society of Harvard for the play. That day, the *Harvard Crimson* had come out with a review by a student, Michael Maccoby, which found the most elaborate Christian symbolism in *The Confidential Clerk*. We spent the evening in trying to convince the intellectuals of Harvard—not only the undergraduates but the tutors, one of whom backed up Maccoby with a long letter to prove that Lucasta was Mary Magdalene—that the author had no such symbols in mind. To one who averred that Mrs Guzzard was clearly the Virgin Mary because she was dressed in blue, my wife replied: 'I bought that dress for her myself; and I had to take blue because they were out of stock of it in grey.'

The Confidential Clerk

But this game of hunt-the-symbol is dear to Americans, and by the time we got to Washington the papers were averring that scholars had found 'an obvious Trinitarian significance in Mr. Eliot's new work. According to them Act One is the Father, Act Two the Son, Act Three the Holy Ghost' (*Saturday Review*, 13 February 1954). Eliot, of course, as a compatriot, is familiar with the game and knows how to parry the moves of the exegetes: but they do not do a play much good with the general public.

The three cities we had visited had been skilfully chosen, and the show won good responses from all of them. In New York, we were housed at the Morosco, one of Broadway's most comfortable theatres. Everything was done to admiration by the Producers Theatre management, and all the triumvirate—Robert Whitehead (later the first director of the Lincoln Center Repertory Company), Roger Stevens and Robert Dowling—could not have been more helpful. We opened on Thursday, 11 February and the audience seemed entertained and pleased.

The critics were as divided as they had been over *The Cocktail Party*; and the line of division was much the same. Those who went all out for it were from two of the mass-readership papers, Robert Coleman of the *Mirror* who called it 'superlative theatre' and 'the brightest and easiest to understand of all T. S. Eliot's plays' and John Chapman of the *Daily News*, for whom it was 'his best work in this medium' and who, declining to worry about underlying meaning, found that

The real value of *The Confidential Clerk* lies in the surprising realisation, after the curtain has come down, that one has been led to know a number of interesting people most intimately. That's what I mean by profound.

But two critics on similar papers talk about 'hard work' for the audience and 'an infinitely melancholy observation, revealed in the most flippant surroundings'. There is a split in the ranks which stood solid for *The Cocktail Party*; and as before, the two leading journals, *The Times* and the *Herald-Tribune*, are full of doubts. Walter Kerr, in the latter, feels that

the play as a whole gives off a curious double image, like a Sunday comic strip in which the colours have slipped.

The search is serious but the course is overlaid with a thousand near-slapstick booby-traps ... We are left to brood and to speculate on the more serious overtones. But here the impudent face of farce, the deliberate overlay of non-sense, stands in our way. The outline is light, the background is dark, and we have to look at both simultaneously—going just a shade cross-eyed in the process.

(12 February 1954)

And in the 're-cap' article on the following Sunday he speaks of Eliot's 'failing to fuse the farce and the feeling'.

Brooks Atkinson in *The Times*, voices disappointment of another kind. He sees the play as 'a deliberate attempt to be ordinary. Unfortunately, Mr. Eliot has succeeded'. He bemoans the 'consistent retreat from poetry' in Eliot's drama, and finds that

The Confidential Clerk is the logical result of his long attempt to shake off the shackles of his own genius. A gifted man has written a commonplace play.

Everyone agreed in welcoming and revelling in Miss Claire, and most of the comment on the acting was complimentary. But there was not the same air of excitement as about *The Cocktail Party*. New York likes the new thing, and this, however glamorously, was Eliot over again, and Eliot making it more difficult than before to combine the esoteric with the entertaining, to dine out on speculation after enjoying yourself at the theatre. And something of any antago-nism inside a company, does, I believe, always communicate itself to an audience. The play did handsome business when it was new, and ran until the summer.

Writing in May to the author, I said:

I can't help feeling that the *Clerk* has taken you as far towards naturalism as you will want to go: and as I live with it I find that, with all its skill and fun and its impeccable choice of words, it does not grow on my affections as the others do: there is inevitably a thinness in the tone compared with those plays in which the several levels could be more freely used. Some day, we must talk about all this. Perhaps if you are in London in July you could come and sit in our back garden . . .

8

The Verse of the Modern Plays in Performance

With *The Family Reunion*, Eliot embarked upon the task of creating a verse form for plays of contemporary life. His convictions about the necessity of a new form, because the blank verse which became established with Shakespeare has become alien in rhythm from our speech, and because verse alone can allow the actor to speak in his own character on all the levels required by a poet, are set out in the essays on 'The Music of Poetry' and *'Poetry and Drama.'* I do not propose to discuss them here, but to attempt an account of what Eliot's director and actors, whose task it is to carry out his wishes, have to do.

Eliot lays great stress on the whole play being in verse, and upon the reason for this:

We have to accustom our audience to verse to the point at which they will cease to be conscious of it . . . The verse rhythm should have its effect upon the hearers, without their being conscious of it.[1]

And he points out, in analysing the first scene of *Hamlet*, that

the verse is not merely a formalisation, or an added decoration, but that it intensifies the drama.[2]

These remarks indicate very clearly to the actors that they have to use the verse entirely as a medium for acting; they are not required to make the audience consciously appreciate it as verse—indeed, this will defeat the author's purpose. But they are required to establish for themselves, and subconsciously for the audience, the rhythmic pulse of the whole play as the movement of the characters' life, within which they will be able naturally to express themselves at every level of experience.

If this is what is to be conveyed to the audience, then it follows

[1] 'Poetry and Drama', in *On Poetry and Poets*, pp. 74, 75. [2] *Ibid.*, p. 77.

that for the actors, first of all, the rhythm of the verse must become 'second nature'. They must be thinking and feeling in this rhythm as they begin to create their characters. I have therefore asked every cast, when approaching an Eliot play, to spend the first few days sitting with me at a table, reading from their scripts. I urge them not to look as yet for the movement of the character within them, but to allow the rhythm of their lines and of the whole play to sink into their minds. Questions of where the stresses fall can be discussed at this point, so that the actor gets to feel that the poet's shape of phrase is the natural one for what he is saying. He can talk across the table to his fellow actors, so that they share the growth of the rhythm among them. They will be getting the further benefit of familiarity with the words, which will have to be studied with the utmost exactitude. But even greater will be the advantage of allowing the rhythm to become the play's inevitable speech, which can be taken for granted when movement and character begin to develop. During this development, the actors make their discoveries through the sharing of a common rhythm. Words are created not by the actor but by the poet: the actor explores them to find the life which he is to portray.

What are the actors to listen for during this period? Eliot has defined the purpose and nature of his verse form:

to find a rhythm close to contemporary speech, in which the stresses could be made to come wherever we should naturally put them, in uttering the particular phrase on the particular occasion. What I worked out is substantially what I have continued to employ: a line of varying length and varying number of syllables, with a cæsura and three stresses. The cæsura and the stresses may come at different places, almost anywhere in the line; the stresses may be close together or well separated by light syllables, the only rule being that there must be one stress on one side of the cæsura and two on the other.[1]

So the determining factors are the cæsura or mid-line break, the three stresses (sometimes increased to four) and, of course, the end of the line.

Directly you look at a page of the actual script, you realise the immense variety obtainable within this loosely defined structure. But you also realise how firm it is. This verse, like all good verse, is like a living body: the skeleton is articulated so as to permit the maximum of movement, for which it has been built. The life of the

[1] 'Poetry and Drama', in *On Poetry and Poets*, p. 82.

character, its sense and thought and feeling, is to move within the skeleton of the verse. It is to be capable of accommodating the small change of conversation and everyday thoughts, and of passing without break or jar to the highest and deepest levels of experience.

All this can be illustrated from Amy's opening speech in *The Family Reunion*.[1] I have marked the cæsuræ and stresses to make the working of the verse form more evident:

> (*Denman enters to draw the curtains*)
> Not yét! I will ríng for you. // It is still quite líght.
> I have nothing to dó // but watch the dáys draw oút,
> Now that I sit in the hoúse // from Octóber to Júne,
> And the swállow comes too sóon // and the spring will be óver
> And the cóckoo will be góne // before I am oút again.
> O Sún, that was once so wárm, // O Líght that was taken for gránted
> When I was yoúng and stróng, // and sun and light unsoúght for
> And the níght unféared // and the day expécted
> And clócks could be trústed, // tomorrow assúred
> And tíme would not stóp in the dárk!
> Put on the líghts. // But leave the cúrtains undráwn.
> Make up the fíre. // Will the spring néver come? I am cóld.

This speech is a perfect example, first of all, of the function of verse in the plays. In a single speech, Amy runs the whole gamut, from the prosaic orders to the maid, through complaints to her family sitting round her of the uselessness of old age, to the expression of her deepest fear: then back to the maid again. Every level of her experience has been revealed.

Rhythmically, it is very firm. There are no 'run-on' lines, in which the sense is carried over from one to the next. Though the number of syllables varies from 8 to 15, the pattern of cæsura and stresses is pretty regular. But it will be noted that, even in a speech which is one of the heavier in the play, an extraordinary lightness is obtained by the use of so few stresses. It would of course be possible to scan the lines with more stresses and thereby increase the weight, but this would be against the declared intention of the poet. He means that each stress should carry along with it a number of light syllables, and thus keep the lines flexible and easy-moving. When he wants finality, he gets it by making the stresses regular, as in

> And time would not stop in the dark!

where there is no cæsura and the beat is laden with doom.

[1] *Collected Plays*, p. 57.

297

The Verse of the Modern Plays in Performance

In such a speech, it may seem relatively easy for the actress to marry verse to sense; but what about the relaxed conversational passages? How much will the verse influence, how much will it inhibit an actor? To test this, I will print some lines of Warburton as prose. The doctor is telling Harry of his mother's condition:

I needn't go into technicalities at the present moment. The whole machine is weak and running down. Her heart's very feeble. With care, and avoiding all excitement she may live several years. A sudden shock might send her off at any moment.

If this is compared with the published text,[1] it will be seen that, while an actor in a naturalistic prose play might well feel it easier to run over what in the verse are the line-endings, these do not distort or inhibit the flow of the speech. Indeed, since the old doctor is delivering a grave diagnosis to a son on whom he wishes to impress its seriousness, the marking of such words as 'technicalities', 'weak', 'excitement', either by leaning on them slightly or pausing briefly, will add to the effect of the speech. If the actor has begun his study with the script in front of him as I have suggested, these markings will occur without his calculating them, because the line-endings will dictate them to him.

But *The Family Reunion* is from this point of view the easiest of the four plays. There is a higher proportion of writing which reaches a poetic level, and the sense of the universal significance attaching to the particular events is seldom absent. Technically, the verse pattern is firmer than in the later plays, quite apart from those moments (which Eliot himself later criticises as 'too much like operatic arias') that are deliberately poetic—the runes and the lyrical duets between Harry and Mary in Part I, Harry and Agatha in Part II. The lighter conversational passages shade into the choruses, which again create beneath the idiosyncrasies of the individuals a clearly poetic projection of the family image. Ivor Brown, that staunchest and most realistic of Shakespearians, is sympathetic to the verse of this play:

He uses, with very good effect, a series of metres in which the trochaic and anapaestic feet do more of the marching than the familiar iambic ... There is so much innovation of style and such skilled use of words and rhythms that the play is arresting and important.

(*Observer*, 26 March 1939)

[1] *Collected Plays*, p. 92.

298

The Verse of the Modern Plays in Performance

As we have seen, Ivor Brown has no use for the verse of the post-war plays. This, for an ardent believer in the blank verse tradition, is a correct reaction to the dramatist's new approach. Eliot abandons all poetic devices: 'no chorus and no ghosts',[1] no lyrical passages standing apart from the dialogue. Further, in attempting a purely contemporary picture of life, he loosens the verse structure to allow of yet more natural speech, and gives himself hardly any licence to allow his characters to express those deeper feelings which would not come out in conversation. He says of *The Cocktail Party*

It is perhaps an open question whether there is any poetry in the play at all.[1]

This last statement I vehemently dispute. It is true that there are passages where one wishes for poetry and is fobbed off with didacticism; but there are more, many more, in which the depths below the surface are revealed in powerful images. Celia naturally has the largest number of these: for an example, take the speech in which she describes to Edward the effect on her of the dryness she has found in him:

> I looked at your face: and I thought that I knew
> And loved every contour; and as I looked
> It withered, as if I had unwrapped a mummy.
> I listened to your voice, that had always thrilled me,
> And it became another voice—no, not a voice:
> What I heard was only the noise of an insect,
> Dry, endless, meaningless, inhuman—
> You might have made it by scraping your legs together—
> Or however grasshoppers do it. I looked,
> And listened for your heart, your blood;
> And saw only a beetle the size of a man
> With nothing more inside it than what comes out
> When you tread on a beetle.

(Collected Plays, p. 154)

But Celia is not alone in being given such power of expression. There are ironic images such as Reilly's of the jolt in descending the stair, or of the operation.[2] Julia has another of the many images drawn from the stage, in talking of the fate of Edward and Lavinia; and in contrast, she talks of Celia in terms of 'the scolding hills' and 'the valley of decision', mystical pictures which remind one of *Pilgrim's Progress*.[3] Lavinia has a remarkable image of bewilderment:

[1] 'Poetry and Drama', in *On Poetry and Poets*, p. 85.   [2] *Collected Plays*, p. 134.
[3] *Ibid*, p. 193.

> ... it seems to me that yesterday
> I started some machine, that goes on working,
> And I cannot stop it; no, it's not like a machine—
> Or if it's a machine, someone else is running it.
> But who?
>
> (*Collected Plays*, p. 163)

Stronger than any particular passage of poetic quality is the effect of the whole poetic scheme of the play. In terms of language and verse patterns, this is carried out within a framework of classic comedy. The opening of the play is very firm in rhythm and keyed well up into comic sophistication:

ALEX   You've míssed the point // complétely, Júlia:
    There *wére* no tígers. // *Thát* was the point.
JULIA   Then what were you dóing, // úp in a trée:
    You and the Maharája? //
ALEX   My déar Júlia!
    It's perfectly hópeless. // You háven't been lístening.
PETER   You'll háve to tell us // áll over agáin, Alex.
ALEX   I néver tell the sáme story twíce.
JULIA   But I'm stíll waíting // to know what háppened.
    I know it stárted // as a stóry about tígers.
ALEX   I said there were nó tigers. //
CELIA   Oh dó stop wrángling,
    Bóth of you. // It's yoúr turn, Júlia.
    Do tell us the story you told the other dáy, // about Lady Klóotz and the wédding cake.

The passage is cunningly brought to a halt by Alex's short line in his third speech; and started up again to erupt into Celia's long line which loosens the pattern to allow of more diversity afterwards.

Eliot is very fond of repetition, and uses it with great effect especially for comic purposes. A few lines later, talking about the same story, he exploits it with typical thoroughness:

JULIA   Well, you all seem to know it.
CELIA   Do we all know it?
    But we're never tired of hearing *you* tell it.
    I don't believe everyone here knows it.
    (*To the* UNIDENTIFIED GUEST)
    You don't know it, do you?
U.G.   No, I've never heard it.

The play is patterned on repetitions, structurally as well as verbally; and the actors have to be aware of the echoes in both respects. Their study of the play will bring them to be as alive to overtones and undertones as to the conscious life of their characters; and the rhythms of the verse will help a great deal to make these penetrate the subconscious mind of the audience.

This is how the poet means them to work. He is not interested in whether people think they are listening to verse or to prose—indeed, his object is to make them forget altogether to ask that question. It is difficult of attainment because people are still so self-conscious about verse in the theatre—and the publicists, seeing it as a news-item, tend to exploit it and so fight against the abolition of self-consciousness. But even so, I believe that not many people in an audience of *The Cocktail Party* pay any attention to it until the last quarter of an hour.

Here is the actors' most difficult problem. With Alex's story about Celia's death[1] the action of the play is over; with Sir Henry's explanation of what he knew about it the drama is over. The rest is exploration of the effect on the others: necessary to Eliot's purpose, but not inherently dramatic. So the characters tend to become stilted in their speech. Julia, who has bubbled for most of the play, has to force her way in to a conversation only to inject platitudes:

> Henry, I think it is time that *I* said something.
> Everyone makes a choice, of one kind or another,
> And then must take the consequences. Celia chose
> A way of which the consequence was Kinkanja.
> Peter chose a way that leads him to Boltwell:
> And he's got to go there . . .
>
> (*Collected Plays*, p. 211)

And in this kind of dialogue, the verse seems to increase the danger of pedantic utterance. The actors have a hard task to keep its shape without letting that happen.

Perhaps one of the reasons why *The Cocktail Party* could remain poetic, and the verse seem right even through occasional moments of discomfort, is that the three Guardians are figures outside the human action. In creating, for the last two plays, a cast of characters who are all within it, Eliot sets himself a new problem. He wants to use a diction which is natural to these people, all of them involved in a purely realistic action, and at the same time to keep the verse pattern. Does this then become an excrescence? or a limiting factor

[1] *Collected Plays*, p. 206.

301

for the players? Is it true that, as one critic says, Eliot has in these later plays 're-discovered prose' and that all the actors have to do is, as they would in a prose play, to speak in what seems to them and their director the natural manner?

Both of these plays have very low-toned openings. In contrast to the formality of Amy's family gathering or the vivid chatter of the cocktail party, *The Confidential Clerk* begins with a long scene in which employer and trusted, elderly private secretary discuss, in leisurely fashion, the affairs with which they are concerned. Nothing, surely, could be more prosaic than this. Does a verse pattern help the relaxed mood? or does it not rather militate against such an atmosphere?

The verse is more relaxed too. There are more run-on lines, and breaks in the flow of a phrase like the hesitations one makes in conversation. Sir Claude is talking about Colby:

> He's like mé, Eggerson. // The sáme disappóintment
> In a dífferent fórm. // He won't forgét
> That his gréat ambítion // was to be an órganist,
> Just as Í can't forgét . . . // no mátter.
> The gréat thing was // to fínd something élse
> He could dó, and do wéll. // And I think he's found it,
> Just as Í did. // I shall téll him about mysélf.
> But só far, // I've léft him to his own devíces.
> I thought he would fáll into this wáy of life // more quíckly
> If we stárted on a púrely búsiness basis.

(Collected Plays, p. 218)

There is a much larger proportion of dialogue on a purely prosaic level; so that at times one wonders whether the sense of a deeper level will not be quite lost. It is more difficult for the actors to establish their sense of the rhythm as they read, because there is so little to make it seem inevitable or to show what are the heights to which it is designed to rise. But if they trust to it, they find that it establishes something which is invaluable to them as actors—a style for the playing.

I have referred to this in the chapter on the play. One of the ways in which it helps is in defining the comic mask which each character has assumed; for instance Lucasta's description of how she lost her latest job:

> Twó mónths I'd gone on // filing those pápers
> Which nóone ever wánted— // at least, not till yésterday.

Then, just by bad lúck, // the boss díd want a létter
And I couldn't fínd it. // And thén he got suspícious
And ásked for things I'm súre he didn't wánt—
Just to make troúble. // And I coúldn't find óne of them.
But they're áll filed sómewhere, I'm sure, // so why bóther?

(Collected Plays, p. 224)

In the scene with Colby at the beginning of Act Two, she starts in the same mocking vein; but the revelation of her deep loneliness later in the scene is arrived at with not a suspicion of a 'gear-change', as Frank Morley called it; and there is no doubt of the value of the verse pattern as a unifying factor in such a case. It is perhaps somewhat firmer here as when Colby talks of his secret garden:

COLBY It's simply the fact of being alóne there
    That makes it unréal.
LUCASTA   Can nó one else énter?
COLBY It cán't be done by íssuing invitátions:
    They would just have to cóme. And I should not sée them coming.
    I should not héar the ópening of the gáte.
    They would símply . . . bé there súddenly,
    Unexpéctedly. Wálking down an álley
    I should become awáre of sómeone walking wíth me.
    That's the ónly way I can think of pútting it.
LUCASTA How afraíd one is of . . . being húrt!
COLBY It's not the húrting one would mínd
    But the sénse of desolátion áfterwards.
LUCASTA I know what you mean. Then the flówers would fáde
    And the músic would stóp. And the wálls would be bróken.
    And you would fínd yourself in a dévastated área—
    A bómb-site—wíllow herb—a dírty public squáre.

(Collected Plays, p. 246)

I have scanned this passage without trying to fit it to Eliot's specification of the verse form. He had freed himself from dependence on this, and his intention would seem to me to be better represented by marking only the stresses called for by the sensibility of the actors. It is all-important that the verse should not, by a multiplication of stresses, be made heavy or seem a burden on expression. In this delicate scene, which may be reckoned the most completely poetic of his post-war drama, the rhythmic pattern is as supple as the feeling of the two young people. Yet it is none the less strong. This is the achievement of Eliot's later dramatic verse at its best: a flexibility which yet never fails to maintain the underlying wholeness of the rhythmic movement.

From this scene, he dares to pass on to one in which some speeches are quite indistinguishable from prose, as Lady Elizabeth takes charge:

> I've come over to have a look at the flat
> Now that you've moved in. Because you can't tell
> Whether a scheme of decoration
> Is *right*, until the place has been lived in
> By the person for whom it was designed.
>
> (*Collected Plays*, p. 253)

Why print this as verse? Because this scene too rises from the commonplace to Lady Elizabeth's expression of her faith; and the verse becomes stronger accordingly:

> Of course, there's something in us,
> In all of us, which isn't just heredity,
> But something unique. Something we have been
> From eternity. Something . . . straight from God.
> That means that we are nearer to God than to anyone.
>
> (*Collected Plays*, p. 257)

This alternation between the conversational and the poetic, this movement from surface to depth and back, is assisted by the framework of the plot, with its farcical improbabilities which compel, as we have seen, a high style of playing. To this style the verse is an essential contributor. I remember a broadcast performance of the play, soon after its stage production, in which the director had obviously asked for complete naturalism. It was disastrous. The meaning of the play went out of the window with its style, and the result was an improbable bore.

The Elder Statesman again opens in a low key. The entering chatter of Charles and Monica about restaurants and staying to tea could not be more naturalistic, and the verse is deliberately unobservable. But in a couple of pages deep feeling comes out of it, as imperceptibly as the love that Monica describes:

> How did this come, Charles? It crept so softly,
> On silent feet, and stood behind my back
> Quietly, a long time, a long long time
> Before I felt its presence.

CHARLES   Your words seem to come
 From very far away. Yet very near. You are changing me
 And I am changing you.
MONICA   Already
 How much of me is you?
CHARLES   And how much of me is you?
 I'm not the same person as a moment ago.
 What do the words mean now—*I* and *you*?

           (*Collected Plays*, p. 298)

The verse is perhaps the most consistent of that in any of the modern plays. There are very few peaks; there is little variation in tone; there is no artificiality. Eliot, unlike Shakespeare, has not become more difficult in his late writings; but the price for this is that he has accepted a narrower range of diction. This is partly because the play contains less interesting characters: Lord Claverton is inclined to be prosy, and Monica to be colourlessly devoted. The sparks fly when the two Intruders come, and when son attacks father; then, the verse gains a sharp edge:

MRS CARGHILL You attracted me, you know, at the very first meeting—
 I can't think why, but it's the way things happen.
 I said 'there's a man I could follow round the world!'
 But Effie it was—you know, Effie was very shrewd—
 Effie it was said 'you'd be throwing yourself away.
 Mark my words' Effie said, 'if you chose to follow *that* man
 He'd give you the slip; he's not to be trusted.
 That man is hollow'. That's what she said.
 Or did she say 'yellow'? I'm not quite sure.

           (*Collected Plays*, p. 321)

And later in the scene, it deepens to the note we expect to hear at some point in an Eliot play:

 It's frightening to think that we're still together
 And more frightening to think that we may *always* be together.
 There's a phrase I seem to remember reading somewhere:
 Where their fires are not quenched.

           (*Collected Plays* p. 325)

In both these instances, the verse form is as strong as ever. But there is a great deal of writing which has not so firm a rhythm, and which does not rise above the naturalistic.

 Yet the actor will still find the verse to be the right basis of study. In this play, it will seem so natural, nearly all the time, that he may think he need not bother with it. But if he takes that attitude, he will be losing his main support. A very interesting analysis of the play and its verse has been made by Mr William V. Spanos.[1] He draws an analogy between the verse of Eliot's late plays, and this one in particular, and that of the medieval dramatists. We remember that Eliot, when he was shaping a verse form for *Murder in the Cathedral*, 'kept in mind . . . the versification of *Everyman*'. Spanos speaks of the 'low tone' of these medieval 'realists'. Having directed many of the Mystery Plays, I think this is a valid comparison.

It is true that their writers use certain devices such as alliteration in quite an elaborate fashion, and that because their verse is rhymed it is always noticeably verse. But most of their drama is couched in matter-of-fact language with no attempt at poetic diction, and many of its most telling strokes result from this. Further, the reason for this approach is that they believe what they show to *be* matter of fact: the gospel is to them an immediate part of life and they show it as such. In judging how to approach Eliot's verse, this is a useful guide. It wants playing as matter of fact, but also as matter of moment; and the structure of it will help in both respects if attention is paid to it from the beginning.

[1] *The Christian Tradition in Modern British Verse Drama* (Rutgers University Press, 1967), pp. 244–50.

9

The Elder Statesman

During the early months of 1954, Eliot had been ill; and from this time onwards he was to be troubled by the bronchial complaint which made the English winter a progressively greater danger to him. Though he succeeded each spring in re-establishing his usual routine of work with Faber and Faber, and in making an annual visit to America to see his family and friends there, his energy for creative writing was reduced by this exhausting disability.

Nevertheless, he began, in due course, a new play. The planning and writing of the first two Acts took place while I was myself in New York, where in 1956 I became Visiting Professor in Religious Drama at Union Theological Seminary for half of each year.

Oedipus at Colonus provided the play's basic structure. Many years before, when writing to me about *The Family Reunion*,[1] Eliot had mentioned Sophocles' last work as providing one way of completing Harry's story. The use he made of it did not turn out at all like that, but it had clearly remained in his mind as a source of creative ideas. Now they took shape in what was to be his own last play. I do not think he so conceived of it; but it has the mellowness of 'the aged eagle'.

The first stages of his work on it are preserved in John Hayward's collection. The earliest document is a synopsis on green paper, setting out Act One in some detail, Act Two in sketch form, while Act Three is represented only by a couple of sentences. This synopsis clearly precedes any writing of text. It is headed *The Rest Cure*.

GREEN SYNOPSIS

I. House or flat of the distinguished politician. Daughter and Secretary. Conversation indicates (a) relation between D and S. (b) sense of duty (rather

[1] See above, p. 107.

than affection) of D. to D.P. (c) Status of D.P.: retiring at moment of great success, on grounds of health—health must be discussed.

Enter D.P. Conversation merely to show his character (ambitious public man in bad health), his intention to take a long rest cure, his selfish attitude towards daughter. Background history could be built up here. Interruptions: business to be dealt with before his departure.

The Intruder. D.P. finally consents to see him. Friend of his youth, neerdo well, whom D.P. had allowed to go to prison for offence in which they were both involved. Has been living abroad since then. D.P. presumes intention of blackmail: Not at all, in no need of money, why should he indulge in such dangerous activities? Merely wants D.P.'s company from time to time—makes clear that D.P. cannot get rid of him. Leaves, promising that they will meet again before long.

D. returns after I. has left. D.P. parries her questions about I.

II. In lounge of Hotel-conv. Home? Arrival of D.P. and D. Met by Matron-Manageress. Conversation formal. D. withdraws (does she go home or is she staying to look after father?). Act ends with arrival of I(ntruder female) (I.(F) and I.(M) know nothing about each other?)

Should we introduce D.P.s son into this act?

Act III. A scene with D.P., I.(F) and I.(M). Must introduce D. and S. also.

[PENCIL NOTES:] Distinguished Person and Daughter
              and Young Man (D's fiancée)
              Intruder (Male)
              Intruder (Female)
              Son
              Matron
              ?Doctor (friend of D.P.)
              ?D.P.'s son?
              Photographer

The chief character, as here conceived, has been a 'great success' in public life; is 'ambitious' but 'in bad health'—great stress is to be laid on this: is 'selfish'. The relationship between him and his daughter shows no traces of warmth; if this is the Antigone of the Oedipus story, she cares for her father out of duty rather than out of love: and she herself is shadowy, the relationship with the Secretary who might (from the pencil notes) be her fiancé even more so.

The stress falls on the Intruder (Male), a ne'er-do-well who is strongly bound up with the Distinguished Person's past; both involved in offence for which D.P. had allowed I. to go to prison.

The Elder Statesman

This naturally leads to blackmail—but not for money, only for the D.P.'s company. Here is a new note: is this character—and presumably his female counterpart in the next Act—suggested by the Eumenides in the Oedipus story, but with a colour derived from their role in that of Orestes?

The son—a major character in Sophocles' play—is to appear. The last Act has two *scènes à faire*, but their nature is not yet clear.

This 'Green Synopsis' is bound by Hayward into the volume which contains all the typescript he had of this play, between the first drafts of Act One and Act Two (*ES*/1R). Into the front of the book is bound another, more detailed synopsis, on two sheets of white paper. In this, the principal character is called Elder Statesman, though the title of the play presumably remains *The Rest Cure*, as is borne out by the Male Intruder's snide reference to 'resting'. The second Act has been moved from indoors to out; and both this and Act Three have a fuller and clearer shape.

WHITE SYNOPSIS

ELDER STATESMAN: retired from politics to become Bank Chairman. Married somewhat above him. When given peerage took wife's family name. Wife dead. Relations with wife may be elicited in dialogue: anyway, some mention must be made of her.

DAUGHTER: At first, filial piety rather than affection. This to be brought out in her dialogue with YOUNG MAN—either fiancé or aspirant. Whether YOUNG MAN is to be Elder St.'s secretary or not—no, not as Bank Chairman. Probably better be promising young politician, which would give him his reason for admiring Eld. St. while objecting to his selfishness towards Daughter.

THE FIRST INTRUDER. Neerdowell friend of Eld. St. in youth—at University. To be elicited in dialogue with Eld. St. in Act I: he has served term in gaol for some financial trickery—probably forging cheques for it to have happened when he was young enough. Then Eld. St. had lent (given?) him money to go abroad. Had been in Central America, perhaps South Seas (Papeete?) rather like a Simenon scoundrel. (Might have been cheating at cards, instead of gaol offence—cf. *Le voyageur clandestin*). Eld. St. takes rather haughty attitude at first—not glad to see him again. He then reminds Eld. St. of the occasion on which he had been speeding, and ran over somebody and didn't stop. Eld. St. modifies attitude finally and asks whether he wants money. Int. laughs at this: no, he has done quite well for himself, thank you, and at the moment is taking a holiday—*resting*, in fact—merely wants pleasure of company of an old friend from time to time. Expects to stay in this country for some time—as long as he can bear the climate. Departs, saying he will see Eld. St. soon again. CURTAIN

The Elder Statesman

Four characters in Act I.

In Act II we are on the Terrace of the hotel—Convalescent Home (of the nature of which we have had some definition at the beginning of Act I). ELD. ST. [&] DAUGHTER to whom enter MATRON-Manageress. This is slightly comedy character—slight parody of manageresses and nursing home matrons. Exit MATRON. Eld. St. and DAU. sit and talk a little. Exit DAU. She is to be there with him—he is selfishly dependent on her and makes her act as nurse and secretary. While ELD. ST. is sitting (perhaps by this time he has been settled in Deck Chair (warm pleasant weather) enter INTRUDER FEMALE and sits beside him. Long conversation corresponding to dialogue with INT. MALE in Act I. Or MATRON might introduce them to each other. MATRON perhaps in and out to break up scene and give irony. Also perhaps NURSE (understudy for DAU.) could bring in bouillon for ELD. ST. and INT. FEM. sitting side by side as on deck of steamer. Enter INT. MALE. ELD. ST. introduces the two INTS. INT. FEM. leaves ('I am sure you have a lot to talk about'). CURTAIN

IN ACT III SON enters (unless we can get him into Act II without leaving too little action and surprise for Act III). He has got into a scrape—through an accident of speeding—injured a man. Might be able to settle out of court. Asks Father for money. Father reproaches him for his bad living—Son retorts— were you any better? Then should have passage with ELD ST. surrounded by SON and TWO INT. They must all be got off stage and DAUGHTER on. Here the ELD ST. begins to unburden his heart to DAUGHTER. She is happy to find him so changed, and instead of condemning him, as he expects, she exhibits a new protective affection. He is still further affected by her response. He feels the end approaching. Enough must have been said about his health to suggest (early on) that violent activity might be dangerous. But he feels released—wants to take a walk. Goes out. Dies offstage. Thunderclap? YOUNG MAN must be brought back at some point—come to visit DAU. They run off-stage, hand in hand, towards ELD. ST. who has obviously collapsed and died out of sight.

Certain developments may be noted. The Young Man has become a rising politician. The Elder Statesman has no longer been involved in the offence committed in the past by the Male Intruder, who is compared to 'a Simenon scoundrel'. The opening section of Act Two obviously presents a problem: it is thin, and the 'slightly comic' Matron will have her work cut out to give it sufficient body. The nature of the dialogue with the Female Intruder is still uncertain: the effect of sitting on the deck of an ocean liner, complete with bouillon, is as far as the picture has got. Eliot by this time thinks in terms of theatrical conveniences such as using the Nurse as under-study for the Daughter. The Act still ends without the appearance of the Son, though at the beginning of Act Three there is again a suggestion that he might be got into the second Act. The Elder

Statesman's confession has become the climax of the last Act and indeed of the play, but has still very little action to surround it. The death, Oedipus-style, is adumbrated.

Already, with the play in this embryonic form, we may see the author's main purpose, and compare it with that of Sophocles. Here again I would refer the reader to David Jones's admirable treatment,[1] which my few observations may serve to amplify.

However many correspondences there are, and however much Eliot has been 'sparked off' by the Greek masterpiece, the intentions of the two are totally different. *Oedipus* is a whole man, who belongs to an age which holds certain firm convictions about the nature of man; his experience of life, painful as it has been, has brought him steadily nearer to peace of spirit. He is a figure of majesty because he is completely himself. The process of the play is the final establishment of this completeness. Eliot is writing in an age of shifting sand, in which man yesterday and man today are two different beings. His protagonist is a hollow man, who wears 'a public mask', under which he fears that there is no identity. The process of his play is, by daring to strip off the mask, to find the identity.

Correspondingly, the action in Oedipus is large; the sins of the past are great sins, the conflicts of the present concern whole cities. The action in Eliot's play is small, and Claverton is aware of this:

> It's hard to make other people realise
> The magnitude of things that appear to them petty.
>
> (*Collected Plays*, p. 345)

For the small things *are* great in the terms of Eliot's play, where the true sphere of the action is the battle for a soul. Eliot has introduced the Furies, who are off-stage in Sophocles and faceless and immobile in *The Family Reunion*, as fully active participants in the conflict. The Intruders, who as we have seen are an integral part of the play's original conception, are Claverton's pursuers and challengers. The sins which motivate their pursuit may seem in material terms to have done them more good than harm; but the criterion of judgement here is that of the effect upon the real personality, and by this measure, sin has been committed and confession is the only way out.

All of which may be summarised by saying that the difference

[1] *The Plays of T. S. Eliot* (Routledge and Kegan Paul, London, 1960), pp. 180–2.

between the intention of the two plays is comprised in Eliot's Christian view of man. He wrote to me in the following year:[1]

I have always been most desirous to see ordinary plays *written by* Christians rather than plays of *overtly* Christian purpose. In the theatre, I feel that one wants a Christian mentality to permeate the theatre, to affect it and to influence audiences who might be obdurate to plays of directly religious appeal.

This last of his plays, like its predecessors in the post-war theatre, gives effect to that desire: and the shifts in emphasis from its Greek prototype are the natural outcome of Eliot's Christian thinking.

With the 'White Synopsis' is bound a sheet in which, for the first time, the characters are given names:

PERSONAGES

LORD CLAVERTON
ANGELA (his daughter)
CHARLES HEMINGTON (her fiancé)
FEDERIGO GOMEZ
MATRON-MANAGERESS of Badgley Court
MRS CAROLINE CARGHILL
MICHAEL CLAVERTON-FERRY Lord Claverton's son
MANNING, Lord Claverton's butler
A NURSE

Names always had a fascination for Eliot. In *The Naming of Cats*, Old Possum let himself go on the subject, asserting that the name had a mystical significance corresponding to the enigma of every cat's personality. A few years after *The Book of Practical Cats* was written, we acquired a female cat of very questionable lineage. My wife, who was at the time playing Hamlet's mother, christened her Gertrude. When Eliot next came to our flat and met her, he enquired her name. Gertrude would not do: a cat's name must have at least three syllables. Trying to save the cat from the confusion of a new name which would sound unfamiliar, I looked at her white 'shirt-front' and suggested Ermyntrude as a substitute; this was accepted.

In the later plays, the same importance is increasingly given to the names of humans. They must be as far as possible unique; they must have the right rhythm for the verse (which results in dactyllic names becoming more and more frequent); they must give the right indication of character. In this last play, changing one's name becomes

[1] 8 December 1959.

one of the most significant acts one can do. Gomez in the first Act suggests that both he and Claverton have in this way changed their natures, surrendering something of themselves, the consciousness of which, however, they must always retain. And in his confession, Claverton refers to the departed entities of himself and his youthful associates as

> my ghosts. They were people with good in them,
> People who might all have been very different

(*Collected Plays*, p. 343)

from those now before him and the audience. Changing one's name is like shedding one's skin.

Eliot altered only two of the names in this list. The Butler unobtrusively became Lambert. The Daughter's name caused more concern. 'Angela', clearly suggested by her guardianship of her father, was too like Lucasta Angel in *The Confidential Clerk* and so must be surrendered. A dactyllic alternative was demanded. 'Adela' was tried for a time; but she finally became 'Monica'.

This list of Personages must have been made after the first draft of 1956 (*ES*/1R), also in Hayward's bound volume, was written. I deduce this from the fact that the Male Intruder is in that typescript called Garcia. Against this name is written in the author's hand the alternative Gonzales, this again is scratched out and replaced by Gomez.

Already, however, the connection between one's name and oneself is fully developed. Gomez is the surname of Freddy Culverwell's wife, which he has adopted because it is 'a good deal more normal/ Where I live' than his own. Dick Ferry, his friend at Oxford, has done the same for reasons of social prestige: and finally on his ennoblement, the double-barrelled 'Claverton-Ferry' has given way to 'Lord Claverton'. Later in the scene, there is a manuscript note: 'Something about what names do to you.' It resulted in Gomez's description[1] of how he 'parted from myself with a sudden effort':

> It was jumping a gap—and you can't jump back again.

But Dick Ferry did it 'by easy stages' so that

> you weren't aware of becoming a different person.

Among the Personages, one has a first name which is never given

---

[1] *Collected Plays*, pp. 307–8.

to her in the script. Mrs Carghill is 'Caroline'. But when the character comes to life, so formal a name proves unsuitable for her: the first name she was humbly born with is the one she keeps on the stage— Maisie Batterson becomes the revue star Maisie Montjoy. And when she makes her safe and wealthy marriage to a manufacturer with a weak heart, she uses *his* first name and becomes Mrs John Carghill. The sequence perfectly reflects the metamorphosis of character as well as of situation.

Claverton's son also becomes involved in the business of name-changing. For him, it is the symbol of revolt against being just his father's son:

> A kind of prolongation of your existence;

and we are led to expect that he will carry out his threat to take a different name when he goes abroad with Gomez at the end of the play. But his sister will not let the brother she has known disappear entirely:

> Whoever you are then
> I shall always pretend that it is the same Michael.[1]

It may be pretence, but it will preserve something of his inalienable reality.

The first carbon'd rough, in Mrs Eliot's possession, is headed

THE REST CURE
or alternatively
THE MAN WHO CHANGED HIS NAME

Hayward's bound book of *The Rest Cure* (*ES*/1R) contains typescripts of Acts One and Two, marked in Eliot's hand 'First Rough. Sole Copy no Carbon', and the 'First Carbon'd Rough' of Act Two. Act One begins abruptly with the Statesman saying to his daughter:

> I have been studying my engagement book.

They are alone. Charles does not appear till page 6: and before that, Claverton's anticipation of a vacant future has been reinforced by the gloomy expectations of Badgley Court which his daughter expresses for them both:

> I think I know what it's going to be like:
> If you want it to be a convalescent home

[1] *Collected Plays*, pp. 331, 351.

You find it's a hotel. When you want a hotel
It's a convalescent home. While they think you should stay
You'll have to stay. When they think you ought to go
They'll turn you out. Why shouldn't they?
There's always a waiting list.

(ES/1R)

When Charles comes in, the Statesman soon goes to his study: but the talk between the young people is all of him, his hold upon his daughter and Charles's resentment of it. Charles leaves a moment after her father returns, and immediately the butler announces the arrival of 'a foreign person' and brings his note. The daughter takes herself out of the way. The scene with Culverwell/Gomez differs from later scripts mainly in discursiveness, and the final passage with the daughter remains almost unaltered.

The opening section of Act Two, designed to relax the tension built up at the end of Act One, differs only in detail from the final script. Two passages omitted from this are worth preserving. The first came after the lines[1] which are reminiscent of the late spring in Mary's *Family Reunion* speech:[2]

CLAVERTON But this early summer, that's hardly seasonable,
    Is so often a harbinger of frost on the fruit trees.
ANGELA Oh don't develop into one of those people
    Who are only satisfied when they can say
    'Nothing on earth could be worse than this!'
    And when things are going well, shiver with apprehension.
CLAVERTON I'm not so simple-minded as that;
    For in my experience it's always ill-omened
    To say 'nothing could be worse than this'.
    That's just an invitation to Destiny
    To produce something worse. Destiny always can.

(ES/1CR)

The wry humour of this prophecy is well in character; and it is matched by Angela's appreciative metaphor about her father in the second passage, which came after his speech about the 'self inside us'.[3] He ends:

This thought has only come to me within the last few days.
ANGELA I wondered what you had been brooding over lately.
    But perhaps what you're going through are merely the pangs
    Of the change from one kind of life to another.

---

[1] *Collected Plays*, p. 316. [2] *Ibid.*, p. 75. [3] *Ibid.*, p. 317.

You've lived for the nation, now you'll live for yourself.
You have been a silkworm chewing mulberry leaves
All your life, to provide silk for others.
Now it's time to leave off, burst out, become a butterfly!
My knowledge of silkworms, I admit, is very sketchy:
I don't even know whether the real silkworm
Is allowed to become a butterfly, or whether he perishes
In giving up his silk. No matter.
You see what I mean.

CLAVERTON   I see what you mean;
Though your *entomology* may be inaccurate.   (?information?)
Let's go on with it, however—my knowledge of silkworms
Being as vague as yours. I believe that the silkworm
Ends in hot water. That might happen to me—
Just at the moment when silk was superseded
By the newest form of nylon.

ANGELA   Let's drop the silkworm.
I'm sorry I introduced him. To return to where we started,
You admit that at the moment you find life pleasant,
That it really does seem quiet here and restful . . .

                                                          (*ES*/1R)

There is in these passages the hint of a livelier relationship between
father and daughter than is evident in the completed play, and of a
moral worth in Claverton's career.

The scene with Mrs Carghill stands here as in the published text,
with the exception of a few small cuts. Mrs Carghill and Mrs Piggott
do not meet. The son, Michael, has been brought into this Act as
Eliot hoped: but it ends quite abruptly with Claverton collapsing
after his daughter's return, Mrs Carghill bringing her bundle of
letters and Gomez approaching along the terrace. 'Do you know
him?' asks Mrs Carghill; and Claverton replies in the words of
Act One:[1]

It's a man I used to know

as Gomez enters and the curtain falls.

At this point in the play's growth, Eliot took a step which entirely
altered his life: on 10 January 1957 he married Valerie Fletcher. She
had been his secretary for seven years, and had cared both for him
and for his affairs during his various periods in hospital. She brought
him a happiness which he had never experienced and found almost

[1] *Collected Plays*, p. 315.

unbelievable; and it was a great joy to us to visit them, when we returned from New York, in a home which was a haven after his life of storm and loneliness. It was there that I first discussed with him the play which was now called *The Elder Statesman*.

His new-found happiness was already reflecting itself in the play. The relationship between Charles and Monica had hardly been defined; their only scene in *The Rest Cure* had concerned itself solely with Claverton. Now, they were to have a series of scenes in the first and last Acts, in which their love for each other was to be dramatised.

This proved a difficult task. Such a development was to the advantage of the play, since it rounded out the character of the daughter on whose compassion rested Claverton's achievement of final peace and provided a more vocal opposition to the Intruders. But it had not been envisaged in the original plan—there is no trace of it in the synopses. And Eliot himself was as yet an amateur in happiness. While there are occasional lines which distil the essence of fresh love in a fashion reminiscent of *The Tempest*, the scenes do not flow with professional ease. More re-writing and cutting went on here than in any other part of the play. It was an area of the writer's world in which this most exact and experienced of writers was quite inexperienced. And the fight to find words which Eliot had so persistently carried on all his life is, as he has Charles put it, part of the battle for love:

> It's strange that words are so inadequate.
> Yet, like the asthmatic struggling for breath,
> So the lover must struggle for words.

> *(Collected Plays, p. 355)*

The introduction of this element gave a new beginning to the play. Charles and his fiancée now enter together, and carry on a light banter until suddenly she finds herself saying the words of love:

> How did this come, Charles? It crept so softly
> On silent feet, and stood behind my back
> Quietly, a long time, a long long time
> Before I felt its presence. And I was unaware.
> Yet when I said 'I am in love with you'
> I was speaking the truth. But I didn't know it
> Until the words were spoken. Now I feel numb—
> Not at all as I should have expected to feel
> After saying to a man 'I am in love with you'.

I only know that the words I have spoken
Can never be retraced; they stand for something
That has left me, is lost to me, given up forever.
CHARLES I hear what you say as if they were my own words
Uttered inside my head, deceiving, pretending,
A voice inside me pretending to be your voice—
Is it you or I who speak? Your words seem to come
From very far away. Yet very near. You are changing me
And I am changing you.

(*ES*/2D. Cf. *Collected Plays*, p. 298; and cf. Harry in *The Family Reunion*, *ibid.*, p. 81)

The butler's entry with the tea-trolley turns the conversation towards Claverton. His daughter defends him to Charles:

I won't have you saying that my father is selfish.
I'm all the family he has to look after him.
You don't understand him. All of his life
He's put public duty ahead of private duty.
The reverse would have seemed to him a kind of self-indulgence.
He has sacrificed himself, always,
To his sense of public responsibility;
In sacrificing himself, he's had to sacrifice others.
And if he's identified himself with public causes
Isn't it natural enough, Charles,
After a lifetime, now that he's old
And tired and discouraged—he's fought for so much,
And so often alone—and so often in vain—
Isn't it natural that he should have come
In his personal relations—and there's noone but me—
To regard himself as a sort of public cause?

(*ES*/2D. Printed as originally drafted; the author has pencilled some cuts)

This speech, reduced, stood in the text until we were in rehearsal. It represents an attempt to win sympathy for the public image of Claverton. There is a page of manuscript (undated) which introduces his entrance with a shrewd and prophetic analysis by Charles, and then allows Claverton to present his own case. It begins abruptly:

ANGELA And what?
CHARLES   And knowing that it hasn't been worth it.
Or knowing that the man who's been successful
Isn't the real self—or that he has been striving
All these years, for success, to conceal from himself
Some deeper failure—or something he's ashamed of.
(*Enter* CLAVERTON)

The Elder Statesman

CLAVERTON I'm glad to see you, Charles. I hope you'll stay to tea.
ANGELA Oh yes, he'll stay to tea. That's part of the bargain.
CLAVERTON Bargain? What bargain? But I benefit by it.
　　He's doing me a kindness by staying to tea
　　And I'm sure A[ngela's] glad to have you with us.
　　She's seen enough of me. Too much, perhaps.
　　I've no doubt that Angela's explained to you
　　That I'm ordered to a sort of convalescent home
　　And Angela's insisted on coming with me.
　　It's going to be lonely for her there, I'm afraid.
　　We can't expect to find any young people there.
　　I feel some compunction at letting her come with me.
ANGELA Why, father, you'd never endure it by yourself—
　　You couldn't possibly manage without me.
　　And besides, what a splendid opportunity
　　To give up my job! It's been so thrilling
　　To be free all day! I've been dragging Charles about
　　To the shops, buying all sorts of things I needed
　　For going away—for a long holiday.
CLAVERTON She's only coming to look after me, Charles—
　　Wasting her life looking after her father,
　　And it's just like Angela to pretend it's a holiday.
　　When you get to my age, Charles,
　　If you should be a widower with an only daughter,
　　You'll understand how selfish one becomes.
ANGELA You're not selfish. You've given your life to public service.
　　It's only right I should give up a few months for you.
CLAVERTON You'll never guess what I've been doing,
　　Now that I've nothing to do. You see this?
CHARLES What's that, sir?
CLAVERTON 　　　　　　　My engagement book.[1]

In *ES*/1R, the climax of the engagement-book passage has a powerful image inserted in pencil:[2]

If only I had the energy to work myself to death,
How gladly would I face death! But waiting, merely waiting,
In a little bare cell, not even waiting to be executed.
Blankness of the walls mocks the blankness of the mind
With no desire to act, but a horror of inaction,
The fear of a vacuum, and no desire to fill it.
Six months of rest, they said. And after that, what?
To sit waiting, in an empty waiting room, waiting—
For no one. For nothing.

[1] Manuscript in Mrs Eliot's possession; cf. *Collected Plays*, p. 301.
[2] Lines 3 and 4 of the following quotation.

Against this, also in pencil, are the words 'develop image of waiting room'. This was done in the next draft, and the bare cell disappeared. This whole passage is typical in being worked over in careful detail; there are pencil notes in *ES*/1R which are again revised in pencil in the next draft.

The Gomez scene wants tightening, the author clearly feels, and would also benefit from interruptions. The whisky theme, which provides two entrances for the butler and some business for Gomez, is introduced in the first carbon'd rough. Cuts include several passages of deprecation, particularly by Gomez who comments 'that was a long speech' and 'that would only bore you'—suggestions which may too easily communicate themselves to the audience. The theme of Gomez's loneliness away from his native country is tried out in several different ways, of which this is from *ES*/1R:

> I tell you, Dick, the very word homesickness
> Sounds sickly sentimental, but what of the homesickness
> Of those who know that all they can do is to exchange
> The loneliness of home among foreign strange people
> For the loneliness of home which is only memories—
> And some of them very unpleasant memories—
> Of home among people to whom one has become foreign?
>
> (*ES*/1R)

This was replaced in the next draft by the passage printed on page 308 of *Collected Plays*.

The story of Dick Ferry running over the old man in the road and not stopping, which is Gomez's chief weapon against Claverton, was originally told in full including the lorry driver's part in it, in Act One:

GOMEZ Dick, do you remember the moonlight night
    We drove back to Oxford? *You* were driving.
CLAVERTON That happened several times.
GOMEZ   One time in particular.
    You know quite well to what occasion I'm referring:
                        the
    The night you ran over ~~an~~ old man in the road.
CLAVERTON You said I ran over an old man in the road.
                thought so too
GOMEZ You ~~knew what you had done~~. If you had been surprised
                     over somebody
    When I said 'You've run ~~someone down~~'

The Elder Statesman

Wouldn't you have shown it, just for a second?
You never lifted your foot from the accelerator.
CLAVERTON   We were in a hurry.
GOMEZ   More than in a hurry.
You didn't want it to be known where we had been;
You didn't want the girls who were with us
To be called to give evidence. You just refused to face it.
CLAVERTON   I remember the case very well indeed,
Though only because you called my attention to it.
An old man was lying in a road—a secondary road,
                        had taken
The same road, I agree, that I took
To cut the distance. He was run over
By a lorry driver, who stopped,
And his lawyer got him off. It was definitely shown
That the old man had died a natural death, in the road,
And had been run over after he was dead.
So, even if I *had* run over him
I should have been no more guilty than that driver.
GOMEZ   No one suggests that you were guilty of murder.
But *you didn't stop*—that is the point.
And incidentally, if you had stopped
We should have had to move him from the road
And the lorry wouldn't have run over him.
It wasn't very pleasant for the driver, was it,
(During the days) when he thought he had killed a man?
CLAVERTON   Having assumed that I had run over a man
And that I *knew* I had run over a man . . .
GOMEZ   I don't even know that you knew it—
But you didn't know for certain that you hadn't
And you *didn't stop* when I cried out.
If it hadn't happened that a lorry driver
Who was also in a hurry, took the same short cut
As you, it would have been a good deal more awkward
And you would have been a great deal more worried
By what we should have read in the paper.
But the lorry driver passed. And the lorry driver stopped.
He was superannuated, I dare say, many years ago—
It's you who ought to be paying him a pension!

                                    (*ES*/1R)

When shortening Gomez's very long scene, Eliot cut the lines which stressed the lorry driver's point of view and Claverton's measure of responsibility towards him. At Edinburgh, T. C. Worsley of the *New Statesman* suggested that it would be theatrically more telling to postpone revealing the lorry driver's part in the incident until Claverton's confession in Act Three, thus leaving the extent of his guilt in suspense. Eliot responded with the version printed on pages 312 and 343–4 of *Collected Plays*.

He also agreed with me that Claverton had altogether too passive a role in this scene. During the preparation for the first production he inserted all Claverton's speeches on page 314 to strengthen the part.

Act Two was subjected only to slight revision up to the exit of Mrs Carghill. The scene between her and Claverton is, I think, the most brilliant piece of comedy in any of the plays; and it came from Eliot's pen in a form which, except for slight cuts, remained unaltered.

On one of the manuscript sheets of synopsis for Act Three, Eliot made this note:

see ⌈ Make the Maisie episode later. C 30 M 18, shortly before his marriage.
Act ⟨ Just *in* Parliament. About to make an advantageous marriage. Maisie
II ⌊ only starts legal action on hearing of engagement announcement.

This revision was never carried out, though Maisie does give her age to Gomez in Act Three as 'just eighteen'.

We arranged to dovetail this scene in to the next by bringing Mrs Piggott on before Mrs Carghill could get off, and the encounter, leading to Maisie's going to do her breathing exercises, had some slight comic value.

The scene with Michael also underwent cutting. A passage eliminated from what stands on page 331 may be worth preserving for its account of the motives of father and son; and we note again the value Claverton attaches to his name:

MICHAEL   Oh, I want to go abroad.
CLAVERTON   You want to go abroad?
    Well, that's not a bad idea. A few years out of England
    In one of the Dominions, might set you on your feet.
    I have connections, or at least correspondents,
    Almost everywhere. Australia, no.
    The men I know there are all in the cities:
    An outdoor life would suit you better.
    What about sheep-farming, in New Zealand?
    Or how would you like to go to Western Canada?
    I think myself that what would be good for you

Would be a term of service in the Mounted Police—
An experience you'd be proud of later.
MICHAEL   The Mounted Police? Good Lord, no.
  That's not my idea. I want to make money.
  I want to be somebody on my own account.
  Do you really think I'd be willing to repeat,
  In New Zealand or Canada, the last two years,
  With some friend of yours—another Sir Alfred
  Whom you'd warn to keep a careful eye on me?
  He'd be sending you regular reports about me.
  Do you think I want to go back to school?
  Or work among people who'd all despise me
  Because they think I don't need to work,
  That I'm only there because I'm in disgrace at home,
  And that one day I'll go back and be a Lord in England?
  I want to go where nobody's ever heard the name of Claverton!
  I'm sick of this country. I've done my service;
  After that I was done out of Oxford;
  Now I've done two years in an office, to please you.
  I've been kicked around enough. I want a different life
  And a chance to make money.
CLAVERTON   Michael, Michael!
  This name of Claverton, of which you think so little,
  Don't you realise that I took the name
  That I might pass it on to you? If I had had no son
  Why should I have coveted a peerage?
  What would it have been worth to me? Things one wants for others
  Acquire absolute value, because of those for whom one wants them:
  Wanted for oneself alone, worthless.
  But in giving you an estate and a name
  I bequeath you also the responsibility
  Of that estate and name. You cannot surrender it.
MICHAEL   So because of the life that you have planned for me
  Because the planning of it gave you pleasure,
  I must look forward to serving a life sentence
  In the dullest of Victorian mansions—
  A miniature St Pancras Station!
  Imprisoned in the name of Claverton
  In the dullest of counties with the dullest of neighbours:
  People will say: 'Oh, that fellow Claverton—
  Ferry, his name is.' No thank you.
  The reasons why you want me in England
  Are the reasons why I want to leave it.
  I'm sick of the very name of Claverton.
  The people who dislike you won't like me any better,
  And the people who admire you will despise me

For not being the sort of man they think my father was.
The estate, and the name, and the responsibility—
I shall be very glad to turn my back on them all.
CLAVERTON But what do you want to do? Where do you want to go?...

(*ES*/1CR)

In *ES*/1CR, Michael had committed a serious offence. After having said 'no' to his father's questions about manslaughter and the young woman,[1] he goes on:

No, it's only
What you might call misapplication of funds.
CLAVERTON Then you've lied to me! When I asked you
Whether you'd taken any money from your firm
You said no, you'd gone to the money-lenders.
MICHAEL Well, I did go to the money-lenders—first.
CLAVERTON Does Sir Alfred know of this?
MICHAEL   No, he doesn't know—not yet.
But that's a good reason for my getting out at once
Before the auditors look into the accounts.
CLAVERTON Michael, you must do the right thing—
Stay and see it out. Go to Sir Alfred
And tell him the whole story. If I make the debt good
He may be able to prevent publicity.
MICHAEL Perhaps he can, if you foot the bill.
In any case, I prefer to be out of the country.
CLAVERTON It's a bitter humiliation to know
That my son should be both a thief and a coward.
MICHAEL Very well, a thief and a coward.

(*ES*/1CR)

Eliot soon decided that he did not want Michael to have committed a legal offence, any more than the young Richard Ferry. The last line of the above scene appears in *Collected Plays* without the word 'thief'. But Claverton there accuses his son of failure in another sense. Michael is

not a fugitive from justice—
Only a fugitive from reality.
Oh Michael! If you had some aim of high achievement,
Some dream of excellence, how gladly would I help you!
Even though it carried you away from me forever
To suffer the monotonous sun of the tropics
Or shiver in the northern night. Believe me, Michael,
Those who flee from their past will always lose the race.

(pp. 332-3)

[1] See *Collected Plays*, p. 332.

324

This is one of the very occasional passages where one feels that the language has spilled over from drama into rhetoric: it smacks more of the orator than of the father. Another is Monica's speech beginning at the bottom of the same page about 'love within a family'. In *ES*/1CR it extended to some matters afterwards treated elsewhere, and of much importance to the author:

Father, you know I would give my life for you.
Oh, how silly that phrase sounds!
But any words are silly between people like ourselves
Who've no vocabulary for love—but is there one
For love within a family? That love is most in silence,
For it's the love on which all else depends, the love
That stands between us and destruction, love that's lived in
But not looked at, love within the light of which
All else is seen, the love within which
All other human love finds speech—the speech of lovers
Whose speech is nonsense: but the love of father and daughter,
Father and son, brother and sister,
We do not look at that—it is the sight with which we look,
This love is silent, and the deeper is the love
The deeper is the silence. What can I say to either of you?
Except that love within a family should be indestructible?
We're of one blood. If those of one blood quarrel
Then blood is shed, the temple is destroyed,
Whatever Michael has done, Father,
Whatever Father has said, Michael,
You must forgive each other, you must love each other.

(*ES*/1CR)

The last section of the second Act, in which these speeches occur, was extensively rebuilt and strengthened in revisions. In *ES*/1R, as we have seen, the curtain fell within a minute of Michael's exit. I suggested that by using more of the characters here a big development was possible. It took place in two stages. The first draft of the extended Act is in some manuscript pages (*ES*/II MS), clearly of a fairly early date. They follow Claverton's line

It's a man I used to know.

(*Collected Plays*, p. 335)

MRS CARGHILL   He has a very good figure. And he's so good looking.
What an interesting face. He's quite exotic.   (romantic)
Is he a foreigner?
CLAVERTON   He's a citizen of some Spanish American republic.

325

MRS. CARGHILL   I do hope he's staying here?
CLAVERTON   I don't know.
    I'd no idea he was anywhere about.
MRS. CARGHILL   He's coming to speak to us, I do believe.
    You *must* introduce him.
GOMEZ   Good morning Dick.
CLAVERTON   Good morning, Fred.
GOMEZ   You weren't expecting me here, were you?
    But don't you remember that I told you
    That I was in need of a rest cure too?
    I knew you'd be here, and what better recommendation
    Could I want?
MRS. CARGHILL   Oh, so you two have met lately?
    Richard, I think you might introduce me.
CLAVERTON   Oh. This is—how do you want to be introduced?
GOMEZ   Why, as Federico Gomez of San Pedro.
    That's my name.
CLAVERTON   Then let me introduce you
    To Mrs—Mrs—
MRS. CARGHILL   Carghill, Richard.
GOMEZ   We seem a bit weak on surnames, Dick.
    Mrs. Carghill, I suppose you know Dick as Lord Claverton.
    To me, he's Dick Ferry.
MRS. CARGHILL   Now isn't that surprising.
    He's Richard Ferry to me, too. We're old friends.
    Are you an old friend too? But you can't have known him
    As long as I have.
GOMEZ   My dear Mrs. Carghill,
    You're not old enough to have known Dick Ferry
    As long as I have. We were friends at Oxford.
MRS. CARGHILL   Oh, at Oxford. Did you go to Oxford?
    Is that where you learned to speak such perfect English?
    For you do speak it perfectly. I'd never have known
    That you were anything but English. Except in your looks.
    I do like Spaniards, Dick. They look so high bred.
GOMEZ   Oh, we always spoke English in our family.
MRS. CARGHILL   I suppose you were at school in this country too?
GOMEZ   Yes, I was at an English school. It's a custom in my family.
MRS. CARGHILL   In your country, education's not so highly developed—
    No university?
GOMEZ   Yes, there is a university.
    But my father wanted me to go to Oxford.
MRS. CARGHILL   And I suppose you and Dick were in the same sporting set?
GOMEZ   Yes, Dick and I had many interests in common—
    Didn't we, Dick?—not strictly academic.
MRS. CARGHILL   I'm afraid you were both of you rather naughty boys.

You look it, Mr. Gomez. You led him astray,
Didn't you, Mr. Gomez. You might as well confess it.

GOMEZ   Oh, no, Mrs. Carghill, you're not going to get me to give Dick away.
Besides, Dick was always prudent—very prudent.

MRS. CARGHILL   Yes, I see you know Richard well, Mr. Gomez.
You know I'd lost sight of him for many years
Till we met here.

GOMEZ   The same with me.
How long is it since we met, Dick?

CLAVERTON   A great many years.

MRS. CARGHILL   It's strange that you and I never met, Mr. Gomez.
You were one of his intimate friends at Oxford
And Richard and I were great friends too,
Weren't we, Richard?

GOMEZ   I expect that was after I left England.

MRS. CARGHILL   Oh, of course, I suppose you went back to—where is it,
Your home?

GOMEZ   San Pedro.

MRS. CARGHILL   Went back to San Pedro.
Mr. Gomez, now you've come to Badgley Court,
I warn you—I'm going to cross-examine you.
I'm going to make you tell me all about Richard
In his Oxford days.

GOMEZ   On one condition—
That you tell me all about him when you knew him.
I suspect there's a great deal that you could tell me.
And about yourself too.

MRS. CARGHILL   Ah, that's a secret.

(ANGELA *has entered unobserved and is standing behind the three deck chairs*)

GOMEZ   This charming young lady is your daughter, I presume.
Miss Claverton-Ferry? Introduce us, Dick.

MRS. CARGHILL   Oh, Miss Claverton-Ferry, I'm happy to meet you.

GOMEZ   Mrs. Carghill and I are your father's oldest friends.

ANGELA   Will you introduce me, Father?

CLAVERTON   Yes, this is my daughter,
Mrs. Carghill. Señor Gomez.

ANGELA   How do you do? I've come to remind you
That it's time to lie down. You know that Dr. Selby
Was emphatic about your half-hour's rest
Before lunch and dinner.

CLAVERTON   That's true, that's true.
Will you excuse us?

MRS. CARGHILL   I'm afraid we've tired you.
Señor Gomez—it's thrilling to address you as Señor—
Won't you let me take you for a stroll round the garden
If you've nothing better to do until lunch-time?

GOMEZ I'd be delighted to explore a bit
    Under your guidance, Mrs. Carghill,
    While Dick is resting. Have a little snooze, Dick.
    I'm happy to have made your acquaintance, Miss Ferry—
    I beg your pardon—Miss Claverton-Ferry.
(*Exeunt*)
ANGELA Father, who are those awful people
    Who are so familiar with you? Are they really old friends?
CLAVERTON I knew them both long ago, at different times.
ANGELA

                         (*ES*/II MS)

Here the manuscript breaks off; but a snatch of synopsis gives the ending: 'Says she has seen G. and M[ichael] speak together. Reference to Charles. Exeunt.'

From this time on, until we went into rehearsal, Monica had the curtain, with an appeal to the absent Charles:

> Come, father, you must rest now. Don't think about these things
> Until you have rested. Oh, I wish that Charles would come.
> If Charles were only here! Oh Charles, come quickly!

                         (*ES*/Edin.)

The next stage is initiated by a page of notes from me which sets out a plan to keep all five protagonists on stage together. Instead of Michael having gone before Mrs Carghill comes in:

Mrs. C. to enter before Michael says a final goodbye, bringing her letters. She is introduced to Monica and Michael. Use existing dialogue anticipating Gomez' entrance, and his entrance. Introduce him all round.
    Five-handed scene . . . built up to the lines:
GOMEZ I suspect there's a good deal more you could tell me.
MRS C. Don't ask me to give away any secrets
or something with sufficient menace in it to cause Lord C. to appear to be about to collapse. Monica insists on rest.
    Mrs. C. takes Michael off, to walk him to the village pub.
    G. remains while C. is laid on the long chair; finally exit on a line with some threatening hint in it, and M(onica) calls on Charles as G goes off.

                         Curtain.

This, of course, provided the chance for the two Intruders to get their claws into Michael, and thus initiated a major development in the plot.

Two further advances were made at Edinburgh. The flirting between Gomez and 'Maisie'[1] added a lightness which followed

[1] *Collected Plays*, pp. 335–6.

naturally from her earlier scene with Claverton. But it seemed, after all the attacks which he had suffered in almost complete silence, absolutely necessary that the chief character should have the curtain. He also needed a springboard for his confession in the last Act. So, during rehearsals, Eliot wrote the speech about going to school with Michael: and Claverton leaves us with that vivid picture of father and son 'side by side at little desks' . . . if it is not too late.

The third Act was not begun until after Eliot's marriage. Mrs Eliot has, in manuscript, a series of three sheets of synopsis and the complete first draft of text (*ES*/III MS). None is dated, and it is not clear which of the synopses is the earlier. I will begin with one in which the first part of the Act is detailed:

SYNOPSIS III (a)

In the grounds further away from the house

Angela and Charles
Explanation of Charles' arrival
Angela's fears
Her appeal to Charles

Enter Lord C. Explication of his state of mind

Enter Gomez and Michael
Explanation of their plans.
Appeal by Lord C. to Michael
Angela and Charles join in
Enter Mrs. C. She supports Gomez and Michael
G, M. and Mrs. C. depart
Scene between Lord C., A. and Charles
  A. wants Lord C. to leave—where shall we go?

  Lord C. 'too late, no need to leave, you will soon be free'. Makes his confession, gives blessing to A. and Ch. Asks to be left alone.

The Voices in the Dusk

Michael	
Gomez	each remind him of some moment in the past (not hitherto mentioned) and taunt him
Mrs. C.	

Lord C. answers. He rises. It is now almost dark. He takes a few paces and collapses.

Enter A. and Charles. Love duet finale.

The second sheet is mainly concerned with alternative endings:

1. Angela and Charles	Arbour in remoter part
2. Enter Claverton	of Hotel grounds. Late
	afternoon.

3. Enter Michael ⎫
      Mrs. Carghill ⎬ in what order?
      Gomez ⎭ or together?

2.[1] Angela Charles Claverton on stage. Gomez, Carghill, Michael are seen together offstage. Claverton tells A. and Ch. of his relations with them.

3.[1] Enter trio. Gomez announces Michael coming to join his business in San Pedro. Marrying Mrs. C.[2]
    Exeunt

4. Claverton's final purgation. Stroke? Ask JH about St. JH.
    Cl. goes indoors (feeling unwell) leaving lovers together alone. Matron comes to announce his death. Is this too Family Reunion?

Alternatively let him send lovers away. Then you must have Matron in at the death.

Alternatively let him send lovers away and have M[ichael], Mrs C. and G. come in to hear his last words. In that case 3 above[3] wd. come here. Perhaps he dies quietly while last one is talking. *Twilight.*

Lastly, there is a sheet working out one particular idea: a plan (ultimately adopted) to have Mrs Carghill enter before the other two members of the 'trio':

SYNOPSIS III (c)

Mrs C. has met Michael while out for a walk, and has heard his version of his misfortune. She has enlisted the support of Gomez, who, sizing up the situation and taking advantage of it, has persuaded M. to return to San Pedro with him. Mrs. Carghill full of sympathy for Michael, and of reproach to Claverton for treating the son so badly, comes to report these plans to Claverton.

    Michael and Gomez arrive.
      A. and Ch. plead with Michael
      Michael deeply under G.'s influence.
      (Mrs. C. to visit S. Pedro?)
    The three leave.

The opening scene of this Act has been reduced, in the published version, to a third of its original length. It fell into two parts. The first was an exploration of the process of falling in love. I quote the text which was prepared for the Edinburgh production (*ES*/Edin.): this is a recension and slight expansion of *ES*/III MS.

---

[1] The sections marked 2 and 3 a second time are clearly expansions of the ones above them.

[2] This sentence is scored through.   [3] The second section numbered 3.

The Elder Statesman

(*Late afternoon.* MONICA *seated alone. Enter* CHARLES)

CHARLES Well, Monica, here I am. I hope you got my message?

MONICA O Charles, O Charles O Charles, I'm glad you've come.
    I'm so worried; and rather frightened.
    I was exasperated that they couldn't find me
    When you telephoned this morning. That Mrs Piggott
    Should have heard my belovèd's voice
    And I couldn't, just when I had been yearning
    For the sound of it, for the caress that is in it.
    Your little letters have been a comfort to me,
    But oh how I've longed to hear your voice.
    Oh Charles, how I've wanted you.

CHARLES   More than when we parted in London?
    When you told me that you'd come to love me, at last?

MONICA At last! You've no idea how long I've been in love with you:
    Nor have I, for the moment I knew I was in love with you . . .

CHARLES When I told you that I believed you were in love with me?

MONICA Oh, long before that! That was when I first *said* it,
    I mean, that was the first time I said it even to myself;
    But words are only the final way of knowing;
    I loved you, long before the words came;
    And when the words came, I knew that I'd loved you
    For a very long time. We only say 'love'
    When it reaches the surface and bubbles into consciousness,
    To love is to love a person more than you're aware of:
    While we've been apart, I've explored my love for you
    A little further, far enough to know
    That it's endless and fathomless, and has no beginning,
    For one's whole life has been the preparation for its advent.
    I expect it was I who fell in love first!

CHARLES That's ridiculous! There was such a long time
    During which you were very cold in your behaviour.

MONICA Oh Charles, you *are* stupid! You couldn't understand
    What the coldness meant. And neither did I.
    It's very frightening, falling in love:
    So frightening, that one refuses to recognise it,
    For to recognise it is to face the terror of it.
    And the terror aroused by the sight of the belovèd
    Freezes the blood.

CHARLES   I often felt very jealous;
    There were two men at least, whom you seemed to like better
    Than you liked me.

MONICA   Why, of course, Charles!
    I only *liked* them, so I wasn't afraid of them.
    But my feeling about you was accompanied with terror.
    And now all's reversed! Since we've come to Badgley Court

I've felt terrified and lost because of being parted from you.
I knew that I loved you—but not how much I *need* you.

(ES/Edin.)

This was the cue for Charles' second speech in the printed text.[1] In this, Charles has had a letter from Monica about her father. This dispenses with her explanation to him of what we already know. In all the drafts, she gave Charles an account of the happenings in Act Two. It contained a description of the change in her father—a change which affected also her own feelings towards him. This is made evident in acting, but I preserve the lines because they give the reader some additional insight.

ANGELA   A part of father's gone.
   He always used to seem so sure of himself.
   Now something has collapsed—perhaps it wasn't real:
   Perhaps it was only an artificial self
   That he willed himself to believe in. Perhaps
   What's left is the real man, if I could find it.
   Perhaps if I could find my way to what is left of him—
   It may be the real man whom he was born to be
   And I could love that man—but with a different love
   Than what I gave him—perhaps better.
   Perhaps I have been living in a world of make-believe
   With father. And the world of you and me, Charles,
   The world I share with you, that is my real world.   (ES/III MS)

Claverton's entrance into the scene, overhearing her concern for him, begins the confession which is the climax of the play. This, and his parting with Michael to his enemies, stand substantially unaltered. In the manuscript, there is a hint of remorse towards his wife:

                How open one's heart
   When one is sure of the wrong response?
   That was not her fault. I should have risked it
   Rather than live, as we lived, in silence . . .

and there is an illuminating word for the persecution by the two Intruders:

   There is a kind of persecution, Charles,
   Which doesn't come under the heading of blackmail.
   Let us call it teasing—a kind of teasing.
   All they want is to humiliate me,
   A long delayed revenge for the wrongs they think I did them.

(ES/III MS)

[1] *Collected Plays*, p. 339.

The Elder Statesman

There is a definite echo of the Orestes story in

> Though it is only now that the living persons
> Whose ghosts have always haunted me, have returned to hunt me.

It recalls that the titles of two of O'Neill's three plays in *Mourning Becomes Electra* are *The Hunted* and *The Haunted*.

Claverton's development, so long delayed, takes place in this Act. He speaks of the Intruders as

> agents for good, now, while they aim at doing evil.
> It is through this meeting that I at last escape them.
> It is here at Badgley, that I effect my expiation.
> Our meeting here was providentially directed.
> You don't understand yet, either of you,
> But you will understand at the end. (*ES*/III MS)

By the confession, which he has just made to his daughter and her Charles when he says this, he has not only purged his soul of what has troubled it all his life. He has also freed himself from the mask of flawless public rectitude that he has been wearing, and revealed both to them and to himself what he really is. But in the process, he has lost his son.

There is a prose synopsis of Claverton's summing up, after Michael has departed with Gomez and Mrs Carghill has followed to see them off:

> You think G. and Mrs C. have done me harm—they have kept me alive. I was waiting for this—I can now see clearly. When I worried over Michael—it was myself I worried about—my feeling at his several disasters was one of *humiliation* at his not playing the part I had assigned him. Now I have lost him I can love him. My compunction over Fred and Maisie was wounded vanity—I cared nothing for them. My feeling about Angela was merely that she supported my pose—the devoted daughter was a necessary justification of the noble father. Now I can begin to love—at least, can begin to understand what love is—and to understand it is to realise it. Humiliation has peeled off one artificial skin after another—when it is complete and can go no further then one is freed. Avowal of faults—sins—has separated me from the source of humiliation. No more humiliation, because no more pretence. Freed from my artificial self. Now I love you I can leave you.
> The elephant. (*ES*/III MS)

This outline leads one to expect a monologue. In the writing, it becomes a scene in which Monica and Charles have some part; and most of it comes after 'the elephant'.

This phrase refers to an attempt to allow Claverton a prophecy of his death, since it was to occur off-stage. In the manuscript, it is briefly introduced:

> Do you know the story of the dying elephant?
> No, you don't know what I mean. I'll explain it presently.

But he never does. In later versions it is developed, and by the time we got to rehearsals for Edinburgh it stood as follows:

> Do you know what is said about the dying elephant?
> Some natives in Africa believe it.
> The old elephant knows, as the time approaches,
> That he is going to die. They say he knows also,
> Or else he chooses, the spot on which to die—
> And nothing can deflect him from his destiny or purpose.
>
> (*ES*/Edin.)

This was cut, because it seemed better to give the desired hint of prophecy at Claverton's first entrance in connection with the old beech tree:

(CLAVERTON *has entered unobserved*)
MONICA   I never expected you from *that* direction, Father!
    I thought you were indoors. Where have you been?
CLAVERTON   Not far away. Standing under the great beech tree.
MONICA   Why under the beech tree?
CLAVERTON   I feel drawn to that spot.

(*Collected Plays*, pp. 339–40)

In *ES*/III MS, Charles and Angela make a second attempt to persuade Claverton to leave Badgley Court after Michael and the Intruders have departed. His reply contains some indications worth preserving:

CH   I agree with Angela. You should leave Badgley Court.
A   We must get away from Mrs Carghill.
CL   Mrs Carghill has come and gone.
    She has done, together with Fred Culverwell—
    Gomez, that is—what she never intended
    And could not understand. All my life
    Those two ghosts have haunted me,
    All my life humiliated me,
    And then, when they came together here
    Their presence here as human beings
    Banished the ghosts. They wished to torture me
    To make me undergo the last humiliation.

The Elder Statesman

They little knew that the torments they willed
Had been inflicted, all my life long,
And that the end of their tormenting
Would be to put an end to humiliation
By driving me over the humiliation line
Beyond which lies humility. For I've been freed
From the false, the specious self that pretends to be someone
And in becoming no one, I begin to live.
I am at last free. And I love you, my daughter,
The more, the more happily, for knowing
That you love and are loved. And if [I] love Michael
Now, as I never loved him, well, that is something.
What I tried to do for him before was nothing.

(ES/III MS)

The analysis of humiliation recalls Edward in *The Cocktail Party*, who says the same thing in a bitter vein to Lavinia.[1] After this speech, Claverton goes to 'take a little walk', to his death beneath the great beech tree. This is meant to have a mystical overtone which clearly derives from *Oedipus at Colonus*; and Eliot did not find it easy to carry out his intention within the frame of his naturalistic picture. He tried several different ways of doing it.

Looking back to the synopses, the 'White' one[2] has the suggestion of a thunderclap, which occurs in the Greek play. When we come to the fuller synopsis (a) of Act Three, the Greek convention has been abandoned and the death is to be on-stage. In the dusk, Claverton hears the voices of his accusers bringing up fresh moments from his past, and collapses under the impact. In synopsis (b), Eliot tries out various alternatives to this plan; but clearly he becomes convinced that none of these will work and reverts, in *ES*/III MS, to the off-stage death.

But how is it to be conveyed to the audience? In *ES*/III MS, Angela and Charles, after a lengthy declaration of their love for each other, feel impelled to search for her father, and she calls out:

Father! can you hear me?

VOICE OF CL   I hear you, my dear. I have been listening.
A   Father, come back to us.
VOICE   I shall not come back to you.
     I have gone too far for any returning.
A   Then we must come to you.

---

[1] *Collected Plays*, pp. 166–7.   [2] See above, p. 310.

VOICE   Not just yet.
     I have become no one. I have lost my name
     But I have at last found my love for you, my daughter
        The love that lay buried, in my life-time, in self-love.
     I am alone at last, yet always with you.
     I have found the place of my destiny and purpose
     To die in. Not far, among the beech trees.
     It is quiet and cold, and I am at peace here.
     Charles, you may come now.
CH   Stay here, Angela.
(*Exit* CHARLES. *Pause. Re-enter* CHARLES)
A   I know what has happened. You need not tell me.
     I can go to him now. It's only to-day,
     Why, just this afternoon, that he's been the father
     Whom I wanted, the father whom I really loved
     And longed for all these years. To-day he's come and gone.
     Oh, I'm so glad that I could speak to him,
     Recognise my father, look him in the face
     As the man he was, before he died.
     He's dead I know, yet now we're together
     As father and daughter, as we never were before,
     And I am happy. And oh, Charles,
     This end is the blessing of the dead upon the living.
     This morning, my beloved, when I heard that you were coming
     I was blissfully happy. If anyone had told me
     That I should love you more and more, I would have ridiculed them.
     I would have said, 'I love him already
     Completely, with my mind and soul and body
     I yearn and belong to him'. And yet
     Love that seems to the lover at every moment perfect,
     Complete, full grown, still goes on growing.
     Oh Charles, I love you, love you to the point of agony.
CH   And your love for me, as it unfolds itself,
     Discloses new depths, so reveals to me
     More and more, the depth of mine for you.
A   And more frightening intensity.
CH   So love given
     Responds to love received.
A   I feel utterly secure
     In you, as a part of you. Now lead me to my father.

                                                    (*ES*/III MS)

    The introduction of the Voice, although such a voice is reported
by the Messenger at Oedipus' death, seemed inconsistent with the
style of this play. Eliot next tried letting his daughter receive replies
from Claverton through extra-sensory perception:

MONICA   O Father Father!
    I could speak to you now. Charles! where has Father gone?
CHARLES   I will go and find him.
MONICA   No, Charles, not yet!
    I know what he meant. It's as if he was talking to me.
    Where are you, Father? He is very close at hand.
    Father, come back to us! He cannot come back.
    He has gone too far for any thought of returning.
    How far away? He is under the beech tree.
    Is it cold there? It is quiet and cold;
    But he is at peace there. He is free now;
    In becoming no one, he has become himself;
    He is only my father now, and Michael's.
    And I am happy . . .

(ES/Edin.)

This was played at Edinburgh, but was then rejected in favour of simple intuition; the text as published was performed in London.

I have quoted the ending which follows the hearing of the Voice in the manuscript, because it contains the first of a number of attempts at putting into words the climax of Charles's and Monica's experience in love. None of these were satisfactory: such analytical exploration of emotion cannot be dramatic, and in terms of the action it seems implausible at the moment when these two must urgently go to the body under the beech tree. In performance, the final passage was reduced even further than it has been in the printed text.

Henry Sherek, who had already taken a large part in shaping and cutting the script for rehearsal, had arranged once more for an Edinburgh Festival production. The steps towards this were by now familiar to all three of us.

Our most difficult problem was the casting of the title-role. Claverton should be a star part for an actor of the same age as the character—sixty—or even older. But of these there are not so many; and in certain respects the part is not attractive. After his opening scene, he has very little to say in the first two Acts; in all the big scenes he is on the defensive against one of the Intruders or against his son, each of whom pours out a stream of words to which he makes scant reply. This means that he reaches the last Act, where his change of heart and his death dominate the play, without having had the opportunity to establish himself as a fully known and fully convincing person. The actor must therefore to a large extent create Claverton's personality from within himself.

We settled for a younger actor whom we both knew and believed in. Paul Rogers had created Sir Claude Mulhammer for us at the age of thirty-six. Since then he had done a number of Shakespearian leads—Macbeth, Petruchio, Falstaff, Touchstone, Mercutio, Pandarus, culminating in King Lear, at the Old Vic. So although only forty-one, he could command the authority for the part, and we knew we were safe to get a fine performance. He achieved the necessary age through a crispness of manner covering an underlying weariness; and the appearance which matched this emerged uncannily like Harold Macmillan, who was prime minister at the time.

Monica also is not a fully rounded character. Eliot seems at first to have conceived her as resentful of her father's selfishness and as looking after him only out of duty. This would have given scope for a real change at the end of the play. But as written, she is so generously understanding of him from the first that his confession can make little difference. In the same way, after a page or two of light bickering with Charles, she is plunged into a discovery and declaration of her love for him; so that this relationship also has not much scope for development. We asked Anna Massey to play her and she did it very pleasantly, but since this was only her third part she had not the experience to add much of herself to the role. A few years afterwards, on television, Vanessa Redgrave was able to add a great deal, and show what Anna, who is the same age, could have done if the clock had been turned forward for her.

Much easier to make effective were the parts of the two Intruders. Gomez is a flashily successful rogue on the surface, a lonely and lost soul underneath; and once William Squire had the two sides of the character in proper balance he sustained the very long scene with great skill. Eileen Peel was really too young and too well-bred for Maisie Carghill, but the subtle ways in which she broadened herself to suit the part accorded with the delicacy of Eliot's wit, even though there may have been depths left unplumbed. Another striking performance came from Alec McCowen as Michael, providing the most electric moment in the play.

The atmosphere of the rehearsal period was different from any that had gone before. We were haunted by gossip writers: somehow, Eliot had become cosy news. The headlines were occupied by Anna's first stage kiss, by Eileen's lessons in cigar-smoking, above all by 'The Happy Eliots'. The advance information suggested that this would be 'Eliot's most human play'; and sure enough, *The Times* itself spread this description above the two columns of its first-night notice.

What seems a memory from Sophocles is used with characteristic elusiveness to let fall on a realistic psychological drama of self-revelation a gleam of extra-mundane meaning

says A. V. Cookman. He appreciates the author's intentions and his skill in fulfilling them:

Mr. Eliot plays his hand of guilty secrets very expertly, tabling them one by one with such effect that they assume the importance for us that they have for the man whom they imprison. The only way that Claverton can rid himself of the polite but insistently threatening Furies is the hard way. He can imagine no greater humiliation than that the daughter who idolises him and whose adoration he has needed so that he could believe in his pretences should learn that her paragon is a hollow man . . . what chiefly weighs with Claverton is the fear of losing his daughter's love.

His hesitations do not lack theatrical suspense; yet when he decides to submit himself to Monica's judgement we are conscious of some surprise that already his battle should have been won . . . It is part of Mr. Eliot's design that Monica should make things very easy for him. Her rather colourless lover shows a capacity for understanding sympathy.

The intention is that the shriving of Claverton should attest the charity of the shrivers and that the young people should be helped by the old man's purified moral vision to see into their own hearts. They must be fit to receive the illumination of love . . . Coming from the author of the *Four Quartets*, the language of the love scene is curiously conventional: even so, the gentle close makes the sought-for effect of a dry and beatific serenity . . .

(26 August 1958)

W. A. Darlington in the *Daily Telegraph* (26 August) acknowledged that the play had 'a fine theme' but was not sure that 'as an acting play it quite deserves to rank beside its two predecessors'. Later he points to the fact that

Mr. Eliot has not been kind to his actor here. He has allowed Claverton not one gleam of humour, or a suggestion of the charm which must have won such a man his worldly success.

(26 September 1958)

And Harold Hobson in the *Sunday Times*, though he receives 'the satisfaction of a play both peaceful and profound', is impelled to ask why it is so subtly and so insistently made clear that Claverton, not knowing any more than Oedipus what evil he has done, has never been a quite first-rate man?

(31 August 1958)

Whether or not, as Hobson suggests, there may be 'an implication about Oedipus himself', the effect of this treatment of the principal character is to lower the temperature of the play. Christopher Salmon, in 'Comment' on the BBC Third Programme, describes the theatrical lacuna which results:

If the real man is to bear with dramatic interest on the fake, they must first have remained in violent contradiction with each other and have been held apart within the one man under pressure. The contact, when they make it, should blind like light—the force should be explosive. In Mr. Eliot's play I found no single spark . . . From the first moment in the first act when he walks out of his library, Lord Claverton makes his entry as indubitably one of Mr. Eliot's hollow men. Even then he has almost no resistance left, and so no shining façade or front for the truth to knock down: he has eaten himself out already almost to the skin with his own misgivings. Life doesn't need to hit him then, but only to lean against him and he will collapse, and that is exactly what life does to Lord Claverton . . .

(Listener, 4 September 1958)

T. C. Worsley, who enjoyed the play and made a couple of good suggestions for its improvement,[1] characterises Eliot's 'chosen form of dramatic convention' as 'ironic melodrama'. He finds that the first two Acts are 'excellent' because, 'besides being profoundly interesting, they are alive with sardonic comedy' (*New Statesman*, 30 August 1958).

This word 'melodrama' works both ways. By those who like the first Act it is used as a compliment; but Christopher Small in the *Glasgow Herald* finds an Edwardian echo in Gomez:

Mr. Eliot lays his hand on the table: and behold they are the cards of Sir Arthur Wing Pinero.

(27 August 1958)

More than one writer remarks upon this old-fashioned quality. Kenneth Tynan, in the *Observer*, reveals its dangers:

Claverton . . . has learned patience and strength: the two lovers, left alone, celebrate their union in language more suggestive of Patience Strong.

It does not help to point out that Mr. Eliot has based his play on *Oedipus at*

---

[1] One of these is noted on p. 321 above.